Emerging Frameworks and Methods

Emerging Frameworks and Methods
CoLIS4

**Proceedings of the Fourth International Conference on Conceptions of
Library and Information Science
Seattle, WA, USA
July 21-25, 2002**

Organized by:
The Information School, University of Washington

In cooperation with:
Department of Information Studies, University of Tampere, Finland
Royal School of Library and Information Science, Denmark
American Society for Information Science and Technology

**Editors:
Harry Bruce, Raya Fidel, Peter Ingwersen, Pertti Vakkari**

2002
LIBRARIES UNLIMITED
A Division of Greenwood Publishing Group, Inc.
Greenwood Village, Colorado

LIBRARIES UNLIMITED
A Division of Greenwood Publishing Group, Inc.
7730 East Belleview Avenue, Suite A200
Greenwood Village, CO 80111
1-800-225-5800
www.lu.com

ISBN 1-59158-016-1

Contents

Abstracts of Posters

Preface

Library and Information Science is closely associated with a variety of other disciplines and its practice employs technologies that are changing rapidly. It is of utmost importance, therefore, to develop a solid base of conceptual frameworks and methods in this area. CoLIS4 provided a forum for presenting and discussing such existing and emerging frameworks and methods.

These proceedings are of the fourth in the series of international conferences whose general aim is to provide a broad forum for critically exploring and analyzing library and information science as a discipline and as a field of research from historical, theoretical, philosophical, and empirical perspectives. In previous CoLIS conferences, a variety of basic and applied problems have been addressed involving not only Library and Information Science but also related disciplines. CoLIS1 was held in 1991 at the University of Tampere, Finland. CoLIS2 was held at the Royal School of Library and Information Science, Copenhagen, Denmark. CoLIS3 was held at the Inter-University Centre, Dubrovnik (IUC), Croatia. CoLIS4 was held for the first time in the United States, at the University of Washington, Seattle.

The papers in this volume represent a wide variety of topics, from the theoretical to papers that focus on the interaction between conceptual and empirical approaches in Library and Information Science. The papers range from a re-examination of the core concepts in Library and Information Science research to empirical approaches for studying how people search the Web, databases and other information sources, to business intelligence and to the mapping of scientific fields. They include a reconsideration of principles for system evaluation, studying the context in which information seeking and retrieval takes place, and experiments in cross lingual information retrieval and term ranking in query expansion.

Presenters at the conference took a range of approaches to new and emerging frameworks and methods, but they were all focused on interactions—interactions between the old and the new, between theory and practice, and among intellectual areas that are seemingly far apart. This was carried out in many ways by: challenging existing and widely-used approaches and proposing new ways for employing them; pointing to new manners in which well established structures in information research can be used; conducting empirical research to create new models or expand on existing ones; turning to existing models and theories to guide empirical research both in natural settings and in laboratories; and employing theories, concepts, and constructs from other disciplines to both

ix

theoretical discussions and empirical research. Indeed, the diversity of topics and approaches reflected in these papers creates a comprehensive example of current conceptions in Library and Information Science.

This volume includes all the papers that were presented in the regular sessions during the conference and abstracts of the posters presented in the poster session. The papers are arranged in the order in which they were presented, and the posters are presented alphabetically by author.

The editors wish to thank the members of the Program Committee for their reviews of the papers and their constructive suggestions to the authors.

Raya Fidel, *Conference Chair*

Conference Committee

Conference Chair:
Raya Fidel
University of Washington

Program Chair:
Harry Bruce
University of Washington

Local Organization:
Lorraine Bruce
University of Washington
Danielle Miller
University of Washington

Regional Program Chairs:
Peter Ingwersen
Royal School of Library and Information Science
Pertti Vakkari
University of Tampere

Treasurer:
Matthew Saxton
University of Washington

Tutorial Chair:
David Levy
University of Washington

Publicity Chair:
Edie Rasmussen
University of Pittsburgh

Posters Chair:
Efthimis Efthimiadis
University of Washington

Sponsorship Chairs:
William Paul Jones
University of Washington
Karen Pettigrew
University of Washington

Workshops and Panels Chair:
Paul Solomon
University of North Carolina

Publication Chair:
Jens-Erik Mai
University of Washington

Information Architect:
Scott Schramke
University of Washington

Program Committee

Phil Agre
Tatjana Aparac
Ethel Auster
Marcia J. Bates
Clare Beghtol
Nicholas J. Belkin
Christine Borgman
Theo Bothma
Michael Buckland
Rafael Capurro
Ian Cornelius
Erica Cosijn

Mari Davis
Efthimis Efthimiadis
Birger Hjørland
Kimio Hosono
Joseph Janes
William Paul Jones
David Levy
Jens-Erik Mai
Gary Marchionini
Charles R. McClure
David Nicholas
Dennis N. Ocholla
Sam G. Oh

A. Mark Pejtersen
Karen Pettigrew
Edie Rasmussen
Catherine Ross
Tefko Saracevic
Reijo Savolainen
Dagobert Soergel
Paul Solomon
Sanna Talja
Helen R. Tibbo
Bob Usherwood
Irene Wormell

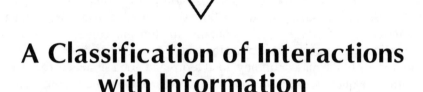

A Classification of Interactions with Information

Colleen Cool
Graduate School of Library
and Information Studies
Queens College, CUNY
65-30 Kissena Boulevard
Flushing, NY 11367, USA
ccool@qc.edunick

Nicholas J. Belkin
School of Communication,
Information and Library Studies
Rutgers University
4 Huntington Street
New Brunswick, NJ 08901-1071, USA
nick@belkin.rutgers.edu

ABSTRACT

A faceted classification of interactions with information is proposed, based on an empirical study of knowledge workers in their ordinary work environments. The purpose of the classification is to inform the design of information retrieval systems which can support, within a single framework, the whole variety of interactions with information that people engage in during the course of information seeking. The classification scheme has five major facets, by combination of which it is claimed that all those interactions of people with information which are related to information seeking can be described.

1

1. INTRODUCTION

1.1 The problem—why a classification at all?

Current systems for information retrieval (IR) are designed to support only one kind of information seeking behavior: specifying queries using terms to select documents from some database. But, IR is in fact accomplished by people in much more complex ways than just this method of query specification and selection. There is ample empirical evidence from a variety of research projects, as well as from everyday experience, of this variety of information seeking behaviors. These include such activities as browsing to find items whose characteristics one cannot specify, learning about the structure and content of the database with which one interacts, attempting to identify relevant databases from among a large variety of databases, finding good terms and good strategies for formulating effective queries, extending one's knowledge of the topic or domain in order better to formulate effective queries, exploring databases in order to find new ideas and to better understand one's problem, and so on. It is clear that no single IR technique can be appropriate for supporting all such interactions, and further, that the currently normal IR method of specified searching is singularly inappropriate for supporting most of them. It is also important to note that these different information seeking behaviors are not normally discrete and independent occurrences, but rather interact with one another during the course of information seeking episodes, which may well have retrieval of some particular information as their eventual goal. Furthermore, such information seeking behaviors seem also to interact with other interactions with information, in the course of information seeking, such as information evaluation, organization and interpretation (e.g., Belkin, 1998).

These observations have two strong implications, as far as improvement of IR is concerned. One is that merely making the current types of IR systems better at what they already do will not result in making better IR systems in the general sense. Indeed, the current state of the art in such systems is such that we can anticipate that following this course will result only in small, incremental improvements even within this single task (note the leveling-off of performance improvement between TREC3 and TREC4, for instance, as shown in Harman, 1996). The other is that focusing on interfaces or interaction structures which can support multiple information seeking behaviors, and multiple interactions with information, may lead to significant improvement in the performance of IR systems. It is the latter implication which motivates the research presented here, whose goal is to improve IR through designing IR systems which support more effective interaction of person with information.

It has been clear for some time that different kinds of IR techniques are required to optimally support different kinds of information seeking behaviors, such as specified search or browsing (e.g., Oddy, 1977; Bates, 1990; Ellis, 1989; Hancock-Beaulieu, 1990; Ingwersen, 1992). Different types of systems indeed exist which respond to a small number of such strategies, and there is an ever-increasing interest in this area (e.g., Hearst, et al., 1996). However, it is just as clear that people engage in multiple information seeking behaviors within the course of single information seeking episodes, or within the context of accomplishing a single task (e.g., Belkin, et al., 1990; Belkin, Marchetti and Cool, 1993; Lin and Belkin, 2000). Therefore, the strategy of constructing many different IR systems, each tailored to support a single type of information seeking behavior, is an inappropriate course. Rather, we should follow the strategy of incorporating within a single IR system framework the variety of IR techniques required to support, adaptively and interactively, the variety of information seeking behaviors. Furthermore, since many information seeking behaviors interact with other kinds of interactions with information, we should really follow the strategy of supporting the variety of interactions with information within a single system framework.

The problems that lie in the path of achieving such systems are three-fold:

- the lack of a robust, complete, and empirically founded classification of interactions with information, including, importantly, information seeking behaviors;
- the necessity to make explicit predictions about characteristics of systems which will respond optimally to different interactions with information;
- an implementation framework which will allow multiple support techniques to be instantiated within one system, which will allow change from one technique to another in real time, and which will structure such changes by predicting appropriate sequences of different support techniques in specific circumstances.

In this paper, we report on research aimed at addressing the first of these three problems, and comment upon its potential usefulness in addressing the second. To be quite clear, the goal of the research reported here is to devise a classification of people's interactions with information which will be useful for the design of IR systems. This research on classification of interactions with information was conducted in the course of a project designed to address all three problems mentioned above (Belkin and Perez Carballo, 1996).

1.2 Related work

Despite our statement that there is no empirically-founded classification of interactions with information, we recognize that there have been some notable attempts at describing and classifying information seeking behaviors. Wilson (1999) surveys a variety of this work, and presents his own proposal for understanding and characterizing people's interactions with information, primarily within the information seeking context. Wilson (1999) demonstrates that the studies he has reviewed have concentrated primarily on what he calls "information searching behavior," meaning the micro-level behaviors during the course of interaction within an IR system; and, to a lesser extent, "information seeking behaviors," meaning the entirety of a person's purposive seeking for information, whether in an IR system or elsewhere (Wilson, 2000, p.1). He goes on to suggest that it is appropriate to consider these two behaviors as nested one within the other (information searching within information seeking), and furthermore, that they should be considered as nested within "information behavior" in general, which he takes to include communication with others, for instance.

Ellis (1989) and Ellis, Cox, and Hall (1993), studying social scientists and engineers, identified eight different "features" associated with information seeking. These features are: starting (the search process); chaining (moving from one item to another); browsing; differentiating (to filter information); monitoring (to keep up to date); extracting (relevant material); verifying (checking accuracy); and ending. These appear to be a mix of Wilson's categories, since they include the possibility of communication with another (as in starting), and since they include both micro-level and more macro-level behaviors. These have all been identified through empirical study, but do not yet seem to have been evaluated in an implemented system.

One of the most notable classifications of information seeking strategies is that of Pejtersen (1989). On the basis of empirical studies of information seekers in libraries, she proposed three different high-level information seeking strategies: analytical search; search by analogy; and browsing. This classification was used to design an interactive library catalog system called BookHouse, which supported all three types of strategy, and which has not only been implemented, but also extensively evaluated.

Pettigrew, Fidel, and Bruce (2001) have recently surveyed work in developing conceptual frameworks of information behavior. From this review, it is clear that, although there has been significant work in how to understand people's interactions with information, there has been relatively little work done on the explicit and principled classification of such behaviors (as opposed to enumerating them).

1.3 Basis for our classification

Belkin, Marchetti, and Cool (1993) proposed an initial faceted classification of information seeking strategies. The goal of this classification, which was based on analysis of previous research and a cognitive task analysis of the information seeking problem in IR systems, was to identify and characterize the range of information seeking behaviors in which people engage in IR systems. This classification scheme had four facets with dichotomous values:

- Mode (recognition—specification)
- Method (scanning—searching)
- Goal (learning—selecting)
- Resource (information—meta-information)

Belkin, Marchetti, and Cool (1993) used this scheme to design an interface to a large operational IR system which could support both "browsing" and "querying" within a single integrated structure. Subsequently, Belkin, Cool, Stein, and Thiel (1995) used this same classification to design a complete prototype system which could support the variety of "information seeking strategies" allowed in the scheme. But even in this early work, it was recognized by the authors that the classification scheme was limited, in need of possible elaboration, and in need of empirical support. Although systems were built on this model, there was no strict evaluation of them. In particular, from the point of view of the work reported here, the scheme was quite strictly limited to only interactions with information aimed explicitly at information seeking.

Cool, et al. (1996) made an initial attempt at empirically identifying different information seeking strategies. This was done in two ways. The first was by asking subjects in an experiment how they would go about searching for information on a particular problem in a specific type of database. The second was by studying the behaviors of these people interacting with an experimental IR system which did not provide some common IR system functions (such as structured queries), and did provide some (at that time) entirely novel functions. This led to the identification of a number of different strategies, similar to, and extending those proposed by Bates (1979).

**Figure 1. Information retrieval as support for interaction
with information. (after Belkin, 1996)**

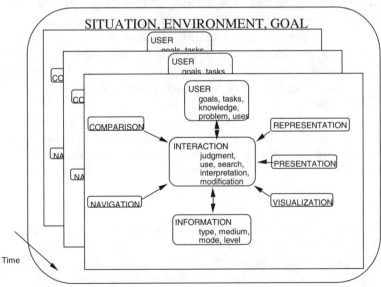

A model of IR as support for multiple interactions with information has been proposed by Belkin (1996) (Figure 1). In this model, the central process of IR is the user's interaction with information, and each of the traditional (and perhaps not so traditional) processes of IR are seen as means for supporting such interaction. In this model of IR, an information seeking episode is seen as a sequence of different interactions of the user with information, of different kinds, each specific interaction dependent upon the user's overall situation, current task, goals, intentions, the history of the episode, and the kind of information objects being interacted with. Of particular interest is that this model led quite naturally to extending the range of potential interactions with information beyond those implied by the previous four-facet classification, to include such interactions as evaluation and interpretation. But again, this model was based on a theoretical understanding of the information seeking process, and clearly required empirical support and elaboration.

The research and results reported in this paper are an explicit attempt to extend and elaborate empirically the classification scheme of Belkin, Marchetti, and Cool (1993), and to identify the types of interactions with information implied by Belkin's (1996) model of IR as interaction with information. We attempted to achieve these results through an investigation of people's interactions with information in the course of their everyday work activities.

2. METHOD

2.1 Goals

The original goal of our study was to identify, describe and classify a range of information seeking strategies in a group of knowledge-intensive workers. This goal was to be achieved in such a way that we would be able to establish relationships between the tasks and intentions of these workers, the information resources they interacted with, and their information seeking strategies. Furthermore, we required that we be able to predict what IR functionalities might be appropriate for supporting different information seeking strategies, and that we be able to identify patterns or sequences of information seeking strategies associated with different behaviors, intentions, resources and tasks, if such existed. As it turned out, the first of these goals was subsequently modified, on the basis of the evidence which we collected, to identify, describe and classify the range of interactions with information of these people.

2.2 Subjects

We began by identifying an appropriate group of subjects. By appropriate, we meant in particular that they be people whose everyday work requires substantial use of information, but who were not professional information workers themselves. Furthermore, we wanted to have a group with fairly wide representation of types of uses of information, and with varying degrees of urgency of information need. Finally, we needed to be able to observe, or otherwise collect data about these people in their ordinary working environments.

Constraints on selection of the subject group included problems of confidentiality; agreement of parent organization; numbers of subjects available; type of work in which subjects were involved; possibilities for observation of subjects. After investigating a variety of possibilities, we entered into an agreement with the Boeing Aircraft Company, Seattle, which was suggested and mediated by Michael Crandall, then External Systems Requirements Librarian at Boeing Technical Libraries. The terms of the agreement were that Crandall would recruit a set of potential subjects at Boeing, from which we would solicit volunteers to take part in the study. As a result of this arrangement, we were able to recruit a group of 14 engineers, managers and technical staff in various divisions of the Boeing Company in and around Seattle as our study group. Abbreviated position descriptions of this group are indicated in Table 1.

Table 1. Job titles of subjects in the study
(1 subject for each unless otherwise indicated)

System administration
Team Leader
    Web infrastructure
    Web standards and reuse
    Technology assessment and development
Web Infrastructure
Web Design
Technical writer
Strategy formulation
IS support manager (2)
Manager
    Enterprise architecture deployment
    Technical communication
    Technical library
Technology assessment

2.3 Data collection

Data collection for each subject proceeded as follows (Data collection instruments, including instructions to the investigator, are available at the following URL: http://www.scils.rutgers.edu/tipster3)

- On the day prior to the observation, each subject was contacted to confirm the appointment, and was asked at that time to bring a job description to the appointment the next morning.

- At the beginning of the subject's work day, an investigator met with the subject, to have the consent form signed, to explain the project and the nature of the subject's participation, and to give the subject the *Activity Notes* form which she/he was asked to complete during the day, with an explanation of what kind of data we expected them to enter on that form. The investigator collected the job description, and left.

- During the course of the day, each subject indicated on the Activity Notes form the specific activities, and reasons for or intentions behind those activities that she/he engaged in. During this period, the investigator who would be interviewing the subject later went over the job description in order better to structure the eventual interviews.

- Approximately two hours before the end of each subject's working day, one or more investigators would return to the subject's place of work, in order to administer the set of questionnaires and interviews.

- Each subject first completed a questionnaire about her/his general work experience and use of software, and about her/his use of, and satisfaction with a variety of information resources.

- While the subject was filling out the questionnaire, the interviewer(s) made a diagram of the subject's workplace including type and location of various information access devices and information resources (not all interviews were conducted in the actual workspace of the subject, however).

- On completion of the questionnaire, the investigator(s) initiated an interview about the tasks that the subject worked on that day, and about the activities in which they engaged. This interview, audio taped for subsequent transcription and analysis, asked questions about each activity entered on the Activity Notes form, focusing particularly on the communication and information behaviors in which the subject engaged.

- When all of the day's activities had been discussed, the interview then shifted to activities in which the subject might have engaged in support of the day's tasks, but did not during that day. The interview then shifted to discussion of the tasks which are part of the subject's work responsibility, but in which they did not engage during that day. For each task, the subject was asked to describe the activities and resources with which they normally engaged in order to accomplish that task.

- At the close of the interview, subjects were asked to comment upon their information activities in general, their satisfaction with the resources and systems available to them, and on what kinds of resources, functionalities and support systems they felt would be helpful to them.

2.4 Data analysis

The interviews with subjects ranged in length from one and one-fourth to two hours. The audiotapes of these interviews were transcribed. The transcripts were then subjected to detailed content analysis, to identify the tasks in which the subjects engaged, the resources and activities they used to support those tasks, the reasons for using those specific resources and activities, the information behaviors or information interactions in which they engaged within the resources or activities, and the intentions underlying the behaviors or interactions. The method by which the content-analytic scheme was developed, and through which the eventual categories were identified, was as follows:

- Eight different members of the research team each attempted a separate initial content analysis of a single transcript (that transcript being the same for all members), each using whatever codes and categories seemed best to that person. The encoding of the transcript was supported by the subject's job description and Activity Notes form.

- The results of the different encodings of the transcript were presented at group meetings of the research team, with explanations of how and why each code was applied. Differences between the different encodings were resolved through group consensus. This procedure was repeated for several weeks, until a relatively stable set of codes and rules was agreed upon.

- The research team was then split into four groups of two researchers each, and each group was assigned a different transcript to be analyzed. The instructions to each group were to attempt to code the transcripts according to the schema which had been developed, but to be careful not to force difficult cases into existing codes, rather trying to develop new ones.

- Over a series of group meetings, the results of each encoding of each transcript were discussed, as was done for the original single encoded transcript. This procedure resulted in a new schema for classifying information interactions and information behaviors, and the identification of a number of new category types for encoding the episodes.

- Each transcript was then reanalyzed according to the new schema, using each activity/resource episode within each transcript as the unit of analysis, and encoding each such episode according to all of the facets of the coding scheme.

3. THE CLASSIFICATION SCHEME

Based on our analysis of the interviews, we developed a faceted classification of interactions with information. In common with Wilson (1999), we identify two major classes of behaviors, Communication Behaviors, and Information Behaviors. By *Communication Behaviors*, we mean those behaviors that an individual or group engage in whose primary goals are communicative interaction with another person or persons. We assume that such behaviors often involve information exchange. By *Information Behaviors*, we mean those behaviors that an individual or group engage in whose primary goals have to do with engagement with information objects, or groups of information objects. In general, we expect that only some combinations of information behaviors and communication behaviors will ever arise, but feel that it is nevertheless necessary to maintain both types within the integrated scheme. The basic facets of the classification scheme are indicated in Figure 2.

Figure 2. Top level facets of a classification of interactions with information.

Communication Behaviors
        Medium, Mode, Mapping

Information Behaviors
        (By Type of Behavior)

Objects Interacted With
        Level, Medium, Quantity

Common Dimensions of Interaction
        Information Object, Systematicity, Degree

Interaction Criteria
        (By Type of Criterion)

Any particular interaction with information is classified through an appropriate combination of the isolates which occur in the detailed arrays within each facet. The facets themselves are mutually exclusive, and only one isolate from within a facet (or sub-facet) can be applied. Figures 3 through 7 indicate the detailed structure of each of the facets.

Communication Behaviors (Figure 3) are classified through combination of elements from each of the three sub-facets, Medium, Mode, and Mapping. For instance, an in-person meeting of several people could be indicated by *speech* as the Medium, *face-to-face* as the Mode, and *many-to-many* as the Mapping. Or, a spam email would be *text, mediated, one-to-many*.

Figure 3. The Communication Behaviors facet.

Communication Behaviors
        Medium
                        speech, text, video, …
        Mode
                        face-to-face, mediated, …
        Mapping
                        one-to-one, one-to-many, many-to-many

---

The Information Behaviors facet (Figure 4) is structured somewhat differently than the Communication Behaviors facet. Here are listed the different types of information behaviors, and within each type is a set of facets and related isolates relevant specifically to that type of behavior. By *type* we mean to indicate the mutually exclusive activities that people can engage in with respect to information (objects). In Figure 4 we indicate the detailed facets for only one type of information behavior, Access. Thus, for instance, the activity often called "browsing" could be classified as the Information Behavior: Access, and within access by *scanning* as the *Method* and *recognition* as the *Mode*. We leave specification of the facets other than Access to future work.

Figure 4. The Information Behaviors facet.

Information Behaviors
Create
Disseminate
Organize
Preserve
Access
Method
scanning….searching
Mode
recognition….specification
Evaluate
Comprehend (e.g., read, listen)
Modify
Use (e.g., interpret)

Any one of the Information Behaviors (or for that matter, the Communication Behaviors) can be combined with a combination of isolates from sub-facets of the Objects Interacted With facet (Figure 5). This facet specifies salient characteristics of the kind of information object being interacted with in any particular information interaction. This is accomplished by combining isolates from the three different sub-facets. Thus, when a person is judging a set of retrieved URLs, they will be interacting with (engaging in the Information Behavior: Evaluate) information objects characterized as *meta-information* as the *Level*, in *textual* form as the *Medium*, and with a *set of objects* as the *Quantity*.

Figure 5. The Object Interacted With facet.

Objects Interacted With
Level
information, meta-information
Medium
image, written text, speech,…
Quantity
one object, set of objects, database of objects

The facet Common Dimensions of Interaction (Figure 6) characterizes the nature of any specific interaction according to three sub-facets. Thus, when a person reads an instruction manual from front to back, that activity is characterized as the Information Behavior: Read, with the Object Interacted With being *information*, *text*, and *one object*, and with the Common Dimensions of *whole* as *Information Object*, *systematic* as *Systematicity*, and *exhaustive* as *Degree*. Flipping through the pages of one chapter of this book would be characterized by the Common Dimensions of *part* as the *Information Object*, *random* as *Systematicity*, and *selective* as *Degree*.

Figure 6. The Common Dimensions of Interaction facet.

Common Dimensions of Interaction
    Information Object
        part — whole
    Systematicity
        random — systematic
    Degree
        selective — exhaustive

The final facet in the classification scheme addresses the issue of the criteria used by the person to accomplish the particular interaction that is being engaged in. This facet consists of an empirically determined list of such criteria, of which we give some examples in Figure 7. Although this facet is not, strictly speaking, behaviorally determinable, we include it in our scheme since it is highly likely to affect what support mechanisms might be most appropriate in different circumstances. An example of its use is the decision by a person to search through one's email in order to find mail sent by one's immediate superior. This behavior would be classified as the Information Behavior: Access, *Method*: *scanning*, *Mode*: *specification*; the Object Interacted With being *Level*: *meta-information*, *Medium*: *text*, *Quantity*: *set of objects*; Common Dimensions the *Information Object*: *whole*; *Systematicity*: *systematic*; *Degree*: *selective*; and Interaction Criteria: *person*. Another example would be filing messages according to their sender's surname. This would be the Information Behavior: Organizing; Object Interacted With, *Level*: *information*, *Medium*: *text*, *Quantity*: *database of objects*; Common Dimensions, *Information Object*: *whole*; *Systematicity*: *systematic*; *Degree*: *exhaustive*; Interaction Criteria: *alphabet*.

Figure 7. The Interaction Criteria facet.

Interaction Criteria
    e.g., accuracy, alphabet, authority, date, importance, person,
    time, topic ...

4. DISCUSSION

The classification scheme outlined above provides us with a means for classifying interactions with information which analyzes the interactions according to a number of different observable facets of these behaviors, and through combination of those facets, synthesizes characterizations of a wide variety of different types of interactions. This method allows the concept of supporting different interactions with information with a limited number of techniques, each of which could be considered suitable for support of one facet of the observed behavior, but which in combination could support the entire behavior in a manner entirely specific to that synthesized combination. Thus, we hypothesize that when a person interacts with a set of objects, there could be some specific technique(s) which would best support this activity, regardless of the values on the other facets of the specific interaction with information.

Through our empirical observations of information behaviors, we identified four "prototypical" interactions with information, which all have to do with information seeking behaviors, but also go beyond the normal description of such behaviors. We call them prototypical because they have the characteristics of being quite different from one another on most of the facets of our classification scheme. These interactions are:

- Finding a (partially) known information object

- Recognizing useful information objects by scanning through an information resource

- Evaluating the usefulness of information objects

- Determining the content/structure of a set or collection of information objects

Each of these behaviors can be characterized explicitly according to our classification scheme, and by virtue of such characterization, can be related to one another. This allows us to attempt to identify common (or different) support techniques, and also to consider how to move gracefully from one combination of support techniques to the next.

5. CONCLUSION

Research in the area of information seeking behavior, and human interactions with information more generally, has progressed through multiple phases, as Wilson (1999) and Pettigrew, Fidel, and Bruce (2001) have pointed out. We believe that to further develop this area of research, it is necessary to develop empirically based models, taxonomies and classifications of interactions with information that cut across a variety of contexts of behavior. To this end, we have proposed a classification of interactions with information which we believe will be helpful in devising IR systems which will effectively support the variety of interactions necessary for effective information seeking and use.

Although the classification scheme we propose here is based on our study of only 14 subjects, we believe that it provides at least the basis for a general classification of knowledge workers' interactions with information, especially in information seeking and using contexts. Furthermore, this classification scheme seems both to support the concept of interaction with information being the core of IR, and to suggest how such interactions can be characterized and supported. Although there is still substantial detail left to be described in our scheme, its basic structure seems to us well founded, and a significant advance in the description and classification of human interactions with information.

6. ACKNOWLEDGEMENTS

This research was supported by Contract No. MDA904-96-C-1297 from the DARPA TIPSTER Phase 3 Program. We wish to thank Michael Crandall for invaluable help in arranging subject recruitment at the Boeing Company, our wonderful subjects themselves, and all of the members of our project research team: Shinjeng Lin, Jose Perez Carballo, Soyeon Park, Soo Young Rieh, Pamela Savage-Knepshield and Hong (Iris) Xie.

REFERENCES

Bates, M. J. (1979) Idea tactics. *Journal of the American Society for Information Science, 30*(5), 280–89.

Bates, M. J. (1990) Where should the person stop and the information search interface start? *Information Processing & Management, 26*(5), 575–91.

Belkin, N. J. (1996) Intelligent information retrieval: Whose intelligence In J. Krause, M. Herfurth, and J. Marx (eds.) *Herausforderungen an die Informationsvwirschaft. Informationsverdichtung, Informationsbewertung und Datenvisualiserung. Proceedings des 5. Internationalen Symposiums für Informationswissenschaft (ISI '96)* (25–31). Konstanz: Universitätsverlag Konstanz.

Belkin, N. J. (1998) An overview of results from Rutgers's investigation of interactive information retrieval In P. Cochrane (ed.). *Visualizing Subject Access for 21st Century Information Resources, Proceedings of the 34th Annual Clinic on Library Applications of Data Processing* (45–62). Champaign-Urbana: School of Library and Information Science.

Belkin, N. J., C. Cool, A. Stein, and U. Thiel. (1995) Cases, scripts and information seeking strategies: On the design of interactive information retrieval systems. *Expert Systems with Applications, 9*, 379–95.

Belkin, N. J., P. G. Marchetti, and C. Cool. (1993) BRAQUE: Design of an interface to support user interaction in information retrieval. *Information Processing and Management, 29*(3), 325–44.

Belkin, N. J., and J. Perez Carballo. (1996) Understanding and supporting multiple information seeking strategies. Proposal to the DARPA TIPSTER 3 Program. Retrieved April, 2002, from http://www.scils. rutgers.edu/tipster3/propose.html.

Belkin, N. J., S. Chang, T. Downs, T. Saracevic, and S. Zhao. (1990) Taking account of user tasks, goals and behavior for the design of online public access catalogs. In *Information in the year 2000: from research to applications. Proceedings of the 53rd Annual Meeting of the American Society for Information Science* (69–79). Medford, NJ: Learned Information.

Cool, C., S. Park, N. J. Belkin, J. Koenemann, and K. B. Ng. (1996) Information seeking behavior in new searching environment In P. Ingwersen, and N. O. Pors (eds.) *CoLIS 2, Proceedings of the Second International Conference on Conceptions of Library and Information Science: Integration in Perspective* (403–16). Copenhagen: Royal School of Librarianship.

Ellis, D. (1989) A behavioural approach to information retrieval design. *Journal of Documentation*, *45*(3), 171–212.

Ellis, D., D. Cox, and K. Hall. (1993) A comparison of the information seeking patterns of researchers in the physical and social sciences. *Journal of Documentation*, *49*(4), 356–69.

Hancock-Beaulieu, M. (1990) Evaluating the impact of an online library catalogue in subject searching behavior at the catalogue and at the shelves. *Journal of Documentation*, *46*(4), 318–38.

Harman, D. (1996) Overview of the fourth Text REtrieval Conference. In D. Harman (ed.) *The Fourth Text REtrieval Conference (TREC-4)* (1–24). Washington, DC: GPO.

Hearst, M., J. Pedersen, P. Pirolli, H. Schutze, G. Grefenstette, and D. Hull. (1996) Xerox site report. Four TREC-4 tracks. In D. Harman (ed.) *The Fourth Text REtrieval Conference (TREC-4)* (107–20). Washington, DC: GPO.

Ingwersen, P. (1992) *Information retrieval interaction*. London: Taylor Graham.

Lin, S. J., and N. J. Belkin. (2000) Modeling multiple information seeking episodes. In *Proceedings of the 63rd Annual Meeting of the American Society for Information Science* (25–38). Medford NJ: Information Today.

Oddy, R. N. (1977) Information retrieval through man-machine dialogue. *Journal of Documentation*, *33*(1), 1–14.

Pejtersen, A. M. (1989) The "BookHouse": An icon based database system for fiction retrieval in public libraries. In H. Clausen (ed.). *Information and innovation. Proceedings of the 7th Nordic Conference for Information and Documentation* (165–78). Aarhus: Aarhus University.

Pettigrew, K. E., R. Fidel, and H. Bruce. (2002) Conceptual frameworks in information behavior. *Annual Review of Information Science and Technology*, *35*, 43–78.

Wilson, T. D. (1999) Models in information behaviour research. *Journal of Documentation*, *55*(3), 249–70.

Wilson, T. D. (2000) Human information behavior. *Informing Science*, *3*(2), 49–55.

A Study of the Relationships Between Categories of Library Information As Typified by Young Children

Linda Cooper
School of Information and Library Science
Pratt Institute
200 Willoughby Avenue
Brooklyn, New York 11205
lcooper@suffolk.lib.ny.us

ABSTRACT

This paper presents a study of the manner in which children in Kindergarten—Grade 4 understand or *typify* relationships between broad categories of information in the library. Children's placement of information on a graphic representation of a bookshelf is examined for occurrence, type, pattern, and change of information clusters. These are compared within and across grade level to examine children's tendencies to construct personal vs. cultural types of information groupings, to discern possible movement towards a more cultural perspective of information clusters as grade level increases, and to consider the possibility of a culturally intersubjective perspective of information organization which might be shared by the user and the library.

1. INTRODUCTION

The way we categorize or *typify* information is reflective of our understanding of that information (Schutz and Luckmann, 1973; Zerubavel, 1991) and the manner in which we build those categories is based on our previous experience or *stock of knowledge* (Schutz and Luckmann, 1973). Since we each have a unique background, our personal typifications of information will vary. However, in order that we may communicate with each other, we have come to an agreement or *intersubjectivity* (Schutz and Luckmann, 1973) with our culture regarding the broader meanings of information. Within any culture there are also smaller groups of individuals or *thought communities* (Zerubavel, 1997) who share a common interest and perspective of information of special importance to that group. Each of those groups will also have its own understandings or typifications for that information. So, for example, my personal typifications regarding viruses based on my experience as a parent will be different from those of the broader community, as well as those of the thought communities of physicians or computer scientists.

The library is a thought community within our larger culture and has specific typifications by which information is categorized. In fact, if an individual wishes to find information in the library, she/he needs to move from their personal typifications of information to the library's typifications of information. One must know, for example, that while stories may be categorized as Fiction, the genre of Fairy Tales will be found (according to Dewey) in the Non-Fiction section of the library grouped with other subjects typified by Dewey as Social Sciences. If the information seeker is unable to make this transition, their search will be unsuccessful without the help of an intermediary. An understanding of this transition process is, therefore, of importance to the information science community.

While this transition process needs to take place for any information seeker to interact with the library, this study will focus on the process as it is experienced by very young children. This population has had less overall cultural experience than an adult population. Differences between their typifications of information and those of the library, as well as changes in their typifications, will be more observable.

Categories of library information can be thought of on several different levels. One level, for example, contains all the information in the library. The library does not contain every bit of information that exists. It contains certain information. Another level contains the various broad categories into which all library information is divided, for example, the Dewey categories. A more precise division of these broader categories reflects the contents of each individual Dewey area. This paper focuses on the information seeker's perception of that middle level of categories—the broader categories of information in the library and how they relate to each other.

2. RELATED LITERATURE

Schutz and Luckmann's (1973) observations regarding typification, stock of knowledge, and intersubjectivity have been cited above, as well as Zerubavel's (1997) work on thought communities and personal vs. social categories for information. Categories, their members, and their names are of interest not only for themselves but also for what they say about other things (Needham, 1979). Of particular interest to this study is Schwartz's (1981) investigation into vertical classification. "[T]he elements of any system are to be defined not by their intrinsic content but by their relations to other elements in the same system" (Schwartz, 1981, p. 25). "Vertical classification is metaphorical in that it involves a mapping of social reality into spatial units" (Schwartz, 1981, p. 36). "Across societies, vertical grading corresponds to social grading" and "operates in men's minds everywhere without their being aware of the fact" (Schwartz, 1981, p. 82).

Vygotsky's socio-cultural model of cognitive development proposes that children's cognitive development is shaped through their social interaction with other members of their culture (1978). They obtain knowledge through their culture, but in addition, they assimilate the manner of thinking about that knowledge through their culture (Vygotsky, 1978). Our understanding of information (i.e., the manner in which we categorize it), thus, becomes shaped by the culture to which we belong. The degree to which abstraction is employed is a function of the interests of social groups rather than the individual (Levi-Strauss, 1966). It is, therefore, to be expected that as school and community become increasingly important to children, their personal typifications will change to be reflective of the social group/community to which they belong. While personal typifications can be used to address many personal, everyday experiences, in order to operate effectively in the broader culture, as well as in various thought communities, the child must be able to typify in the manner used by each.

The classical view of categorization posits that categories have both fixed boundaries and members that share common properties (Lakoff, 1987, p. 16). This was first challenged by Wittgenstein (1953) and later elaborated upon by Rosch (Rosch, 1975; Rosch et al., 1976). Rosch proposed the idea of the basic level category—the first understood by children, first to enter the vocabulary of a language, most commonly used as a member label, and the level of categorization at which most of our knowledge is organized (Lakoff, 1987, p. 46). Lakoff further proposes that human categorization is based on both our experience and our capacity for imagination (Lakoff, 1987, p. 372). "Basic-level concepts are directly meaningful because they reflect the structure of our perceptual-motor experience and our capacity to form rich mental images. Kinesthetic image schemas are directly meaningful because they preconceptually structure our experience of functioning in space" (Lakoff, 1987, p. 372). These basic-level concepts and kinesthetic image schemas seem to relate to that vertical organization of which Schwartz (1981) speaks. Lakoff also speaks to the importance of metaphor in category construction (Lakoff, 1987, p. 372), again echoing Schwartz' (1981) comments regarding vertical classification as a metaphor for social reality.

2.1 Conceptual framework

Given that individuals tend to understand information through the construction of personal categories or typifications (Schutz and Luckmann, 1973) and that the thought community (Zerubavel, 1997) of the library categorizes information according to its own typifications, a gap is created between the manner in which information is perceived by these two groups. Since information is perceived or understood differently, it becomes difficult for the two groups to communicate effectively regarding an information need.

Being in different places, either physically or cognitively, will give people different perspectives of the same information landscape. Certainly, three-dimensional perspectives of information have been examined (see, for example, Wiss and Carr, 1998). If one can envision the clusters of information contained in a library as having three-dimensional locations in relation to each other, if one then moves to different points within this three-dimensional landscape, the relationships between the various clusters of information will change when viewed from each different perspective. While the project described on the following pages does not involve participants in a three-dimensional interaction with information, it is the concept of different cognitive perspectives impacting on the manner in which clusters of information are perceived that is important to this study.

Both the individual user's and the library's understanding of information clusters are more prescribed; they are narrower than that of the larger culture to which they both belong. Recall that the larger culture has adopted certain cultural typifications in order to maintain/approach a state of intersubjectivity so that its members might communicate with some confidence. The user's typification of information and the library's typification of information may be thought of as two differing narrow perspectives with the commonality of a broader socio-cultural perspective betwixt them. If a mode of typification held by the broader culture, can be identified which can be understood by both the individual and by the library, this may serve as a bridge of communication between the two. Bates (1998) has recognized the importance of "starting general" (p. 1193) in the reference interview. Since both the library and the individual user operate in a mutual socio-cultural setting, it is likely that there may be some mutually typified understanding regarding the relationships between broad categories of information.

We are already familiar with the formalized ways in which the thought community of the library relates information clusters to each other. For example, the Dewey Decimal Classification System, commonly used in public and school libraries, is one method of organizing the information in a library. In this system of classification, there are ten main classes of information. Each of these is divided into ten divisions and each of these divisions is further divided into ten sections. Each section is divided again as many times as needed. Classes are constructed based on academic discipline rather than subject (Chan, 1994). That the thought community of the library chooses to cluster or classify according to Dewey may make the best sense from the perspective of the library, but it is a perspective from which few users might tend to view their personal information problem. In order to investigate the possibility of a broader, culturally intersubjective perspective of category clusters shared by the user and the thought community of the library, an examination of the manner in which users tend to view clusters of information is in order.

3. RESEARCH GOALS

The purpose of this study is to:

1. explore the relationships young children discern between broad categories of library information;

2. note whether these typifications change between Kindergarten and Grade 4;

3. note whether these typifications move towards a more socialized understanding of information categories and/or one that is more specific to the thought community of the library;

4. investigate the possibility of intersubjective typifications for category clusters that may serve to facilitate communication between the user and the thought community of the library.

4. RESEARCH DESIGN

4.1 Background

This study included 518 children in primary (grades K–2) and intermediate (grades 3–4) schools. Male/female ratio of students in both schools was approximately equal, ethnic diversity was limited, the majority of children were Caucasian and economic background somewhat diverse. While the primary school does not serve children in special education classes, the intermediate school does and ten fourth graders from a special education class participated in this study as part of their regular inclusion library class. Each session of the project was conducted as part of the participants' normal library curriculum. As such, it was not an unusual situation for the children. An effort was made to keep things normal so that children's responses would not be contrived. Students in first, second, third, and fourth grades did the same exercises. Kindergarten exercises differed, as described below, since many of these children could not yet read. The researcher was the school library media specialist (slms).

4.2 Procedure

Participants in this study had been working on a project in knowledge organization in their school library media center (Cooper, 2000). Each grade level had indicated by brainstorming and then voting what they felt was the most important information to include in a library. The most often cited information terms by each grade were given to that grade to sort into groups representative of books on library shelves. Children in grades 1–4 worked in self-selected groups of four to sort the "books" into shelf categories which they felt belonged together and that would facilitate easy access. Kindergarten children worked as a whole class with the slms/researcher. When the shelf categories were complete, the children gave each shelf category a name representative of its contents.

This paper focuses on the session that followed those briefly described above and addresses the manner in which participants perceived the relationships between those shelf categories of information which they constructed. Children in grades 1–4 rejoined their work groups from the previous session. Each group was given the sheet on which they had recorded the categories they constructed and the labels given them in the previous session. They were also given a graphic representation of a wall of empty shelves (Figure 1). The bookshelf metaphor has been used successfully by Borgman et al. (1995) and Pejtersen (1989). In this study, children were instructed to copy each shelf label on to a small piece of paper, thus constructing a sign. When all category signs were written, children were instructed to place each sign on a shelf in the graphic where they felt it best belonged and then paste it into place.

Each Kindergarten class worked as one group led by the slms/researcher. The Kindergarten's shelf graphic was drawn on a large board in front of the children and adjacent to an actual bookshelf. A direct comparison was made between the actual bookshelf and the drawn bookshelf to ascertain that the children understood the meaning of the drawn bookshelf. Reduced reproductions of all book covers from each category they had previously constructed plus a verbal reminder of the label they had given each category provided a non-alphabetic method of shelving the Kindergarten's categories on the drawn book shelf.

The resulting bookshelves gave a physical indication of where each group thought a category of books should be placed in relation to all other categories they constructed. Data were examined within and across grade level to discern types, patterns, and changes in clusters and their placement. Discerned clusters were considered indicative that children felt that the information categories were related in some manner. Changes in placement of categories in relation to each other were considered indicative of changes in the children's perspective of how categories of library information are related to each other. Placement of category labels based on an articulated personal experience (for example, "I can reach that shelf more easily") or in a manner that was not recognizable by the slms/researcher (an experienced member of the child's community) as one relating to a cultural typification was considered a personal typification. Placement of category labels in a manner that was recognized as one relating to organizational methods employed by the library specifically or by the culture in general (i.e., alphabetical order) was considered a cultural typification and a move towards intersubjectivity. Placement of category labels in a manner that was recognized as a cultural typification (i.e., a cluster of science related labels) was also considered a move towards intersubjectivity.

**Figure 1. Graphic representation of shelves with
the category labels placed by one group of children.**

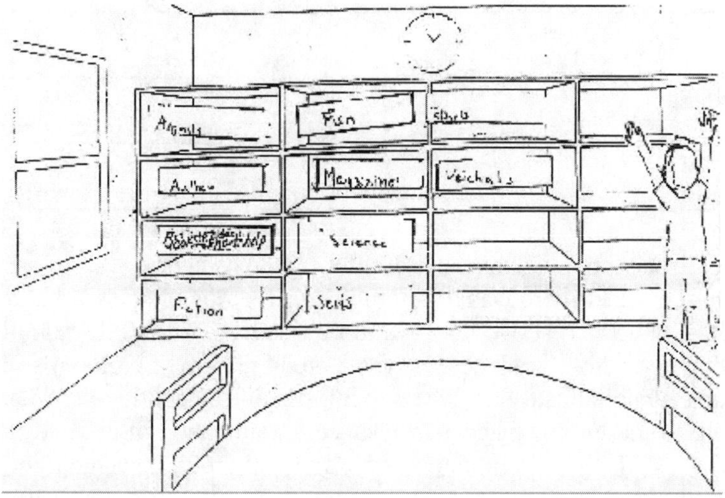

5. RESULTS

Children's placement of information categories on the graphic representation of shelves was examined by grade level in order to ascertain whether there was a pattern in or across grade shelf placement of:

1. particular categories (for example, frequently named or "popular" categories, such as Animals);

2. types of categories (for example, categories that appear to be library related);

3. number of categories on a shelf;

4. number of categories in a shelf area.

Table 1. Comparison of shelf label clusters across grade levels
(# type cluster/total # cluster=%that type of total)

	Kindergarten 6 groups 14 clusters	Grade 1 41 groups 48 clusters	Grade 2 36 groups 38 clusters	Grade 3 14 groups 16 clusters	Grade 4 18 groups 18 clusters
Cultural	11 79%	39 81%	20 53%	12 75%	8 44%
Alphabetical	0	0	5 13%	3 19%	6 33%
Library	3 21%	9 19%	13 34%	1 6%	4 22%
Hierarchical	0	12 25%	2 5%	1 6%	0
Horizontal	na	1 2%	4 11%	4 25%	4 22%

Each work group's placement of information categories was also examined to ascertain whether there was a pattern in construction of shelving indicative of the points enumerated above but on a more minute level. While examination of data within and across grade level gives a broad picture of children's placement choices, it cannot indicate exactly which information categories were placed adjacent to each other in any particular instance. Examination of each work group's placement reveals this. Examination of individual group placement indicates:

1. categories which are placed in close proximity to each other

2. categories which appear in a hierarchical configuration

A comparison of cluster types discerned across grade level is presented in Table 1. Since the number of children participating on each grade level differed, comparisons between grade levels were made by setting up ratios. Five types of label clusters or overall organization of shelf labels were identified. These include:

1. culturally typified labels clusters (i.e., Boats, Science, Animals, and Electricity may be considered a cluster of science related labels);

2. alphabetically organized shelves;

3. library related label clusters (i.e., Author, Fantasy, and Series are all library related labels);

4. Hierarchical/totem clusters (i.e., Animals, Dogs, Clifford is hierarchical because the label at the top of the totem includes all the labels beneath it);

5. Horizontal clusters are noted separately because the vast majority of clusters are vertically oriented making a horizontal cluster exceptional.

Table 2. Comparison of types of cultural clusters across grade levels

	Kindergarten (10 cultural)	Grade 1 (39)	Grade 2 (20)	Grade 3 (13)	Grade 4 (8)
movement	10%	-	-	-	-
people/social	30%	13%	10%	-	-
information	10%	3%	20%	-	-
animals	50%	15%	5%	-	13%
magic	-	-	5%	-	-
amusement	-	41%	60%	23%	36%
sports	-	3%	-	23%	-
imagination	-	10%	-	-	-
reptiles	-	3%	-	-	-
science	-	8%	-	-	13%
stories	-	3%	-	-	-
areas of study	-	-	-	15%	-
formats	-	-	-	8%	-
music	-	-	-	8%	-
media	-	-	-	15%	-
history	-	-	-	8%	-
technology	-	-	-	-	25%
modes expression	-	-	-	-	13%

Table 2 compares the change in the nature of the cultural clusters discerned across grade level.

Examination of shelf label placement of the Kindergarten as a whole did not indicate any particular overall pattern of label placement within this grade. Most labels appeared on any particular shelf only one time. In general, there was a slight tendency for shelves on the bottom or on the far right to be left empty. More labels tended to be placed on shelves toward the upper left side of the configuration. Children of this age are beginning school and are encouraged to begin written work at the upper left corner of their page. In our culture, in general, we read from left to right and from top to bottom. There did not appear, from examination of the individual group configurations, to be any strong overall pattern of placement of information type.

While an examination of cluster types (see Table 1) indicates both cultural and library types of clusters were discerned, the reasons articulated by the Kindergarten for label placement were of an egocentric nature reflective of personal typification. They did not exhibit a clear understanding regarding the placement of category labels that could be called intersubjective either with general cultural classification or classification specific to the thought community of the library. For example, at one point, the shelf spaces on the large bookshelf graphic were numbered so that the children could identify from a distance the shelf on which they wished to place a label. However, when asked why a label was placed on a particular shelf the child might respond that the label was placed (for example) on Shelf 5 because she/he was 5 years old. Label clusters that did occur were either of people or animal labels (see Table 2). It is noted that there were a large number of instances of horizontal clustering as opposed to vertical clustering, possibly because the shelves were numbered horizontally. For this reason, a comparison of horizontal clusters constructed by the Kindergarten was not included in Table 1.

Overall label placement in Grade 1 showed a definite movement from left to right and top to bottom. The number of labels placed on shelves decreased in a progression from top to bottom shelf rows and from left to right shelf columns. If number of labels placed on a shelf bears any relation to importance of placement, the top row of shelves appears to hold the position of greatest importance to Grade 1. An examination of the placement of the most frequently named ("popular") categories from a previous session indicates that Sports and Animals, named more often than any other labels (Cooper, 2000), tend to occupy positions of 'importance' in the upper left portion of the shelf configuration. These left to right, top to bottom placements are in keeping with the mode of reading taught to these children in school and indicate a move towards cultural intersubjectivity regarding the communication of information in our culture. The possible significance of a top to bottom hierarchy of importance is in keeping with cross-cultural studies indicating a vertical classification system or totem that places members of importance towards the top of the totem (Schwartz, 1981).

Examination of label placement by individual groups in Grade 1 (see Table 1) showed approximately the same percentage of children in this grade place together what would be considered similar according to broad cultural standards and even according to particular library placement as did the Kindergarten. This placement usually took a vertical configuration. Twenty-five percent of clusters were of hierarchical arrangement. For example, in one group column one was composed of all animal labels and, in fact, the label at the top of the totem was Animals. Another column contained Sports, Baseball, Pokemon, and Magic. This cluster can be considered one reflective of what might be culturally typed as amusements (see Table 2).

Examination of Grade 2 shelf configuration indicates overall placement in a manner similar to that of Grade 1. More labels were placed towards the top and left portions of the configuration and less towards the bottom right. Those labels that were named most often tend to appear more often toward the top left. Examination of shelving constructed by individual groups also shows tendencies similar to those in Grade 1. For example, Cartoons and Dr. Seuss appeared in a vertical configuration, as did Singing groups, TV shows, and Sports.

Several groups in Grade 2 appeared, at least in part of their label placement, to be attempting an alphabetical order of labels (see Table 1). This may indicate a movement towards intersubjectivity with the thought community of the library (and the wider culture in general) since much of the order in a library (the Fiction section, indexes, dictionaries, encyclopedias) is alphabetical. This use of alphabetical order was not found in Grade 1 configurations. While alphabetical order is taught in Grade 1, its use as a tool to find information becomes more comfortable for the children in Grade 2. Adjacent placement of labels such as Singing groups, TV shows, and Sports may be considered a cluster pertaining to amusement or entertainment which is in keeping with cultural typifications of those concepts (see Table 2).

Four instances of horizontal placement in Grade 2 were noted. For example, one group placed Authors, Chris Van Allsburg, Medal (they meant Caldecott), and Fiction books in a horizontal configuration. This is a cluster that is strictly library related. Other examples of library related clusters (these vertical) included Dr. Seuss and Easy to Read; Fiction books and Authors; Authors, Fiction, Poems; Picture books, Series, Caldecott; Fairy tales, Information, Chapter books. These clusters do not always make sense in any other manner than that they are library related terms. It is the children's recognition of the cluster members having the shared quality of library-ness that indicates a move toward library thought.

Overall label placement on shelves in Grade 3 was in keeping with previous grades in that it followed a left to right and top to bottom priority of placement. The top row of shelves was again the row that was used the most and the most often used shelf was Shelf 1 in the upper left corner. Sports and Animals, the two most often named category labels, were placed most often on this shelf, an indication of its importance in the configuration. There was an increase in the use of alphabetical order in the placement of shelf labels. There were also label clusters that reflected an understanding of cultural groupings, such as placement of Records adjacent to History, Biography adjacent to History or Sports adjacent to Teams.

Overall placement of category labels on shelves by Grade 4 was the same as in previous grades regarding left to right and top to bottom placement of labels. Animals and Sports, the most often named labels, were placed most often on the upper left shelf. There was also placement of label clusters indicative of cultural associations. For example, Information was placed next to Science; Electricity was placed next to Videos; Boats, Science, Animals, and Electricity were clustered. One of the only library related clusters was Series, Fiction, Biography in horizontal placement and adjacent to Junior Fiction and Magazines. There was a further increase in the use of alphabetization to order shelf labels.

6. DISCUSSION

Data did not evidence a very strong tendency in participating children to construct discernible clusters of information categories. Table 3 compares the relative number of clusters discerned on each grade level in order to see if the tendency to create information clusters differs between grades. Given sixteen shelf slots in which to place category labels, the average group of children on all grade levels constructed 1.3 discernible shelf clusters. The Kindergarten constructed more but it is recalled that the slms/researcher led them in their exercise and her verbal encouragement and questioning may have influenced the outcome of the exercise.

On all grade levels, the placement of information categories on the shelf representation was similar in that the upper left shelves were used the most and the lower right shelves were used the least. This follows the direction in which children participating in the study are being taught to read. In primary grades, great emphasis is put on the ability to track alphabetic symbols in this manner. It is a necessary prerequisite in the reading process in our culture. The most often named category labels were placed in the upper left hand corner. Beginning in Grade 2, children increasingly organized their categories alphabetically. Since this method of organization is emphasized in children's library education, its adoption by children in their typification indicates a movement toward intersubjectivity with the thought community of the library.

Table 3. Comparison of average number of shelf label clusters constructed per group across grade levels (#clusters/#groups) and average number of labels per cluster.

	Average # clusters constructed	Average # labels per cluster
Kindergarten (14 clusters/6 groups)	2.3	2.2
Grade 1 (48 clusters/41 groups)	1.2	2.9
Grade 2 (38 clusters/36 groups)	1.1	2.6
Grade 3 (16 clusters/14 groups)	1.1	2.5
Grade 4 (18 clusters/18 groups)	1.0	2.5

Certainly any results are largely affected by the choices made by children in previous sessions since these were the choices sorted on to shelves in this session. However, types of clusters discerned may indicate an aspect on which children tend to associate and thus typify broader information categories. Table 2 indicates that clusters built by children in Kindergarten, Grade 1 and Grade 2 focus on animals and people. This is reflective of children's typifications of both the material that belongs in a library and the cognitive categories which children construct for this material (Cooper, 2000). Children in Grades 1–3 constructed clusters reflective of a concern with amusement and also of a broader stock of knowledge in general. Children in Grades 3 and 4 show a continued growth in stock of knowledge and interests in keeping with a culturally traditional library. This indicates a movement toward intersubjectivity with the thought community of the library which generally strives to encompass a corpus of information representative of many aspects of a culture's collective knowledge.

In a traditional library, the shelving arrangement moves first in a horizontal (across a shelf), then vertical (down to the next shelf), then horizontal direction (to the next bookshelf). Overwhelming construction across all grade levels of vertical clusters of information categories (shelf labels) as opposed to horizontal (see Table 1) supports studies by Schwartz (1981) indicative of the importance of vertical classification. The vertical relationships of information constructed by children in this study were usually not hierarchical in the traditional sense. In fact, hierarchies were not immediately discerned in the examination of data because the mode of thought employed in the examination was typical of the thought community of the library. The initial search for hierarchies focused on the particular hierarchy type used in libraries (for example, Animals, Mammals, Felines, Domestic Cats, Siamese Cats). However, when this library mode of thinking was overcome, a type of non-classical hierarchy became apparent. It was a *folk hierarchy*—not to be confused with *folk classification* which is used by different cultures to classify their plants and animals (Bates, 1998, p.1190)—of popularity reminiscent of Schwartz's (1981) comments regarding vertical classification as a metaphorical "mapping of social reality into spatial units" (p. 36). Animals and Sports, the most frequently named categories from previous sessions (Cooper, 2000) were most often placed on the top of the bookshelf. The concept of an information hierarchy based on popularity also supports Vygotsky's (1978) observations regarding socio-cultural influence on people's understandings because popularity is a socio-cultural phenomenon. Children's hierarchies in this study are most likely more reflective of their typifications than are the hierarchies of information used in libraries. "*Folk access*" is a term used by Bates (1998) to refer to "identifiable patterns in what people expect of information systems." While the above may not exactly be what people expect of present information systems, there is an identifiable pattern in the results. Given that participants configured their broad information clusters in this way, these configurations may be indicative of a manner in which they would prefer or tend to look for those clusters of information in the library if given that opportunity.

7. CONCLUSION/FUTURE RESEARCH

Children's placement of shelf labels for categories of books on a graphic bookshelf indicate that:

- frequency of shelf use tends to move from left to right and top to bottom;
- "popular" categories (Animals or Sports) were usually the most frequently placed categories across the top shelves. On other shelves, placement of particular labels was not definitive;
- number and placement of clusters did not follow any particular pattern across grade level.

A move towards a more socialized typification of category relationship is indicated by:

- an increase in the construction of category cluster types reflective of a concern with a broader scope of cultural knowledge as opposed to a narrow, more personal scope;

- an increase in the placement of information categories in alphabetical order reflective of an important method of information organization in traditional libraries.

Issues regarding data collection in a non-contrived, 'normal' setting need to be worked out. For example, the Kindergarten children were too young to work on their own and needed the assistance of the slms/researcher to get through the project. This assistance may have affected their responses. While Table 1 indicates that the Kindergarten constructed both cultural and library clusters of information, their verbal articulations at the time of data collection did not support this. This could be because they were not actually clustering terms based on any cultural influence and that the discerned cultural clusters were coincidental. It could also be that their typifications were, indeed, culturally based but they were not verbally experienced or socially aware enough to recognize and articulate this. While the work sheets from Grades 1–4 give concrete evidence of category placement, they do not give reasons for the placement. In addition, participation of an inclusion class in Grade 4 may have affected outcome, as well. However, given the school venue of data collection, children could hardly be excluded for the purpose of constructing an ideal research situation. Given these problems, it would be helpful to rerun the study taking these issues into account.

Results of this study suggest interesting possibilities regarding people's use of folk hierarchies in their typifications of information and one thread of future research might investigate the importance of these. Participants in this study constructed a kinesthetically related visual representation reflective of their mental image of the relationships between broad categories of information in the library. Their constructions support observations by Lakoff (1987) regarding the importance of both imagination (i.e., imagery) and kinesthetic experience in category construction. They also support observations by Schwartz (1981) regarding the importance of vertical classification in people's typifications, as well as Vygotsky's (1978) observations regarding culture's effect on people's understandings. Results from this study suggest that a folk hierarchy, for example, may be closer to people's understandings of information organization than a more classical hierarchy. Presentation of information ranked by popularity is already a method of knowledge organization used in some search engines on the Web. Further research is recommended. An enhanced understanding of the information seeker's typifications of relationships between broad categories of information may lend insight into the development of systems more supportive of their search efforts.

REFERENCES

Bates, M. (1998) Indexing and access for digital libraries and the internet: Human, database, and domain factors. *Journal of the American Society for Information Science, 49,* 1185–1205.

Borgman, C., S. Hirsh, V. Walter, and A. Gallagher. (1995) Children's searching behavior on browsing and keyword online catalogs: The Science Library Catalog Project. *Journal of the American Society for Information Science, 46,* 663–84.

Chan, L. (1994) *Cataloging and classification: An introduction.* 2d ed. New York: Mc-Graw Hill.

Cooper, L. (2000) The socialization of information behavior: A study of the move from personal typification towards intersubjectivity in children's understanding of library information. *Dissertation Abstracts International* (University Microfilms No. AAT 9991871).

Lakoff, G. (1987) *Women, Fire, and Dangerous Things: What categories reveal about the mind.* Chicago: University of Chicago Press.

Levi-Strauss, C. (1966) *The savage mind.* Chicago: The University of Chicago Press.

Needham, R. (1979) *Symbolic Classification.* Santa Monica, CA: The Goodyear Publishing Company.

Pejtersen, A. (1989) *The Book House: Modeling searcher's needs and search strategies as a basis for system design.* Denmark: Riso National Laboratory.

Rosch, E. (1975) Cognitive representations of semantic categories. *Journal of Experimental Psychology: General, 104,* 192–233.

Rosch, E., C. Mervis, W. Gray, D. Johnson, and P. Boyes-Braem. (1976) Basic objects in natural categories. *Cognitive Psychology, 8,* 382–489.

Schutz, A., and T. Luckmann. (1973) *Structures of the life-world.* Evanston: Northwestern University Press.

Schwartz, B. (1981) *Vertical classification: A study in structuralism and the sociology of knowledge.* Chicago: University of Chicago Press.

Vygotsky, L. (1978) *Mind in society: The development of higher psychological processes.* Cambridge, MA: Harvard University Press.

Wiss, U., and D. Carr. (1998) *A cognitive classification framework for 3-dimensional information visualization* (Technical Report No. 1998-04). Lulea University of Technology, Sweden: Department of Computer Science and Electrical Engineering, Division of Software Engineering. [online] available: http://epubl.luth.se/1402-1536/1998/04/LTU-TR-9804-SE.pdf.

Wittgenstein, L. (1953) *Philosophical investigations.* New York: Macmillan.

Zerubavel, E. (1991) *The fine line: Making distinctions in everyday life.* Chicago: University of Chicago Press.

Zerubavel, E. (1997) *Social mindscapes: An invitation to cognitive sociology.* Boston: Harvard University Press.

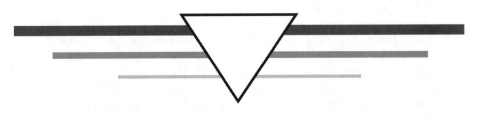

Students' Cognition and Information Searching While Preparing a Research Proposal

Mikko Pennanen and Pertti Vakkari
Department of Information Studies
University of Tampere
33014 Tampere, Finland

ABSTRACT

The paper focuses on analysing students' information needs in terms of conceptual understanding of the topic they propose to study and its consequences for the search process and outcome. The research subjects were 22 undergraduates of psychology attending a seminar for preparing a research proposal for a small empirical study. They were asked to perform a search in the PsychINFO database for their task at the beginning and end of the seminar. A pre- and post search interview was conducted in both sessions. The students were asked to think aloud in the sessions. This was recorded as were the transaction logs. The results show that during the preparation of research proposals different features of the students' conceptual structure were connected to the search success, and that process variables did not commonly intermediate between the search outcome and conceptual structure.

1. INTRODUCTION

In this paper we will focus on analysing students' information needs in terms of conceptual understanding of the topic they propose to study and its consequences for the search process and outcome.

It is evident that users' ability to articulate information needs conceptually and express them as queries affects the search success. It is known that people who have ample knowledge about a subject have a comprehensive and structured conception concerning it (Robertson, 2001). Their knowledge structure consists of several specific and interrelated concepts. (Heit, 1997; Patel and Ramoni, 1997). We may suppose that the more structured and richer users' conceptual structure representing the information need is, the more exhaustively they can articulate the aspects of the query and the more specific concepts they will use in query formulation. The exhaustivity and specificity of a query, in turn, enhance search success by increasing precision (Harter, 1986; Sormunen, 2000).

Although connections between users' conceptual structure, query formulation and search outcome seem plausible, we have not been able to identify studies covering the whole process, only parts of it. There are studies concerning users' conceptual structure and its connection to text representations. These studies are attempts to empirically represent users' anomalous states of knowledge (ASK) (Belkin et al., 1982; Brooks et al., 1985; Oddy et al., 1986, Oddy et al., 1992). Studies on the connections of users' problem stages or subject knowledge to search process or outcome (Allen, 1991; Hsieh-Yee, 1993; Shute and Smith, 1993; Spink et al., 1998; Vakkari, 2000a,b; Vakkari and Hakala, 2000; Wildemuth et al., 1995) indirectly provide information about the relations between conceptual structure and searching. It is supposed that the level of subject knowledge or the stage of problem solving is associated with the extent and specificity of conceptual structure in some indefinite way.

2. EARLIER EMPIRICAL RESULTS

A major supposition of the ASK hypotheses is that a user's inadequate state of knowledge is the fundamental element in the IR situation. In this situation the users are unable to specify precisely what is needed to resolve the anomaly. (Belkin et al., 1982; Oddy et al., 1986) It is supposed that from the representations of ASK it is possible to infer ideas for improving text representations or other elements of a retrieval system for more successful searching. This assumption led to empirical analyses of users' ASKs.

ASK was represented by analysing users' problem statements. Belkin et al., (1982) asked users, students and faculty members, to discuss the problems which led them to approach an information system. The ASKs were represented as association maps between concepts elicited from these problem statements. A categorization of ASK types was created based on how specific or well-defined the problem and the topic were.

Brooks et al. (1985) focused on user-intermediary interaction in the IR situation in order to identify user models and problem descriptions. Oddy et al. (1986) analysed users'—mainly postgraduate students'—problem statements to reveal their ASK structures concerning the topic. The structure was based on word associations. Using partially the same data Oddy et al. (1992) analysed discourse level structural components of abstracts of empirical research papers and users' problem statements. In the abstracts the authors could identify a well-defined discourse-level structure, but not in the oral problem statements.

In sum, the empirical work with ASK hypotheses succeeded in constructing conceptual maps of knowledge structures, but left the question about the relations between knowledge structures, search process and outcome unanswered.

Hancock-Beaulieu et al. (1991) studied the relationship between the expressed topic as articulated in the questionnaire by the users and the search terms used to formulate a query in accessing an OPAC. They found that in most cases the search articulation closely matched the search formulation. If not, the users tend to formulate broader rather than narrower queries compared to topic articulation.

Next we will present the results from studies on relations between subject knowledge or stage of task performance and searching, supposing that users' subject knowledge or stage of task performance in some undetermined way reflects their conceptual structure concerning a topic or task. Studies on problem solving support this conclusion. The more the individuals have subject knowledge, the more structured their understanding of the topic is (Robertson, 2001).

Kuhlthau (1993) has shown that people search for and use information differently depending on the stage of their information search process. In the beginning of the process when they select and explore the topic they look for general background information. When people have construed a focus they search more for more specific information. Vakkari (2000b) confirmed and elaborated Kuhlthau's findings in a longitudinal study showing that while preparing research proposals for masters' theses, students searched first for general and theoretical information, and later for specific and methodological information. Vakkari (2000a) also showed that as the students progressed in the process, they began to use more facets, more and increasingly specific search terms, more varied operators and more tactics, which enhanced search success. Wang (1997) has also shown that when subjects progress in their research process, they use more and more specific terms. The students' relevance judgements in Vakkari's study (Vakkari and Hakala, 2000) became more selective in terms of the number of references accepted in the process. Results by Tang and Solomon (1998) also refer to this. Spink et al. (1998) found that at the beginning of their task the more students knew about their problem, the more items they judged as relevant.

Allen (1991) found that undergraduates with extensive knowledge of a topic used more search expressions than low-knowledge students. Shute and Smith (1993) compared 24 Chemical abstract searchers by two intermediaries. They showed that the searcher with more domain knowledge used more terms, especially parallel terms, in searches. Hsieh-Yee (1993) compared the search tactics of librarians and educational administration students when they searched their own or others' subject domain. She found that subject knowledge became a factor only after searchers had a certain amount of search experience. Regardless of the subject knowledge the experienced searchers used more parallel terms and OR operators, but used as many terms as the novices. Contrary to these findings Wildemuth et al., (1995) found no strong relationship between medical students' domain knowledge and search results.

These findings suggest that as users' conceptual constructs concerning the topic becomes more structured and rich (i.e., when their level of knowledge of a topic or task increases), the more and more specific search terms they use, the more tactics they apply, and the more selective they become in their relevance judgements. However, it seems that search experience is required of users for them to be able to use parallel terms and OR operators in their searches.

3. RESEARCH DESIGN

The aim of the study is to analyse how students' conceptual structure of their subject is connected to the use of search tactics and terms and utility judgements in preparing a research proposal for a small empirical study. The study subjects were 22 undergraduate students of psychology who attended a seminar on preparing a research proposal. The seminar meetings continued for three months during the autumn term 2000. At the beginning the students selected a topic and were expected to come up with a proposal. The seminar continued in the spring term 2001, at which time the students were expected to realize their proposals.

In their searches the students used the www version of PsychINFO, which is a Boolean system. This is the major bibliographic database in psychology. The students' responses to our questionnaire showed that none of them was familiar with it. Out of the 22 students 18 attended a training session for PsychINFO lasting one hour. The rudiments of the system were explained including the use of Boolean operators, field restrictions, thesaurus, index and search formulation support. The analysis showed that the searching behavior of those who participated in the instruction differed from that of those who did not in only one respect: only the former used the NOT operator.

3.1. Research questions

The aim of the study is to analyse connections between students' conceptual structure concerning their topic, search process and outcome while writing a research proposal. The specific research questions are as follows: In the two successive searches 1) How is the conceptual structure related to the choice of search tactics and terms and the number of useful references found, and how do these factors interact?; 2) do the interrelations between the conceptual structure, search process and outcome vary according to the students' stage in Kuhlthau's (1993) model (i.e., at the beginning and end of the seminar)?

3.2. Data

Data for describing the students' understanding of the topic, their problem stages, search tactics and terms, and utility judgements of the references found were collected in several ways. The students were asked to make two searches for their proposal: at the beginning and also at the end of the seminar when they were finishing the proposal. The aim was to collect data in the students' pre-focus and post-focus stages according to Kuhlthau's (1993) model. A pre- and post-search interview was conducted in both cases. The pre-search interview consisted of Kuhlthau's (1993) process survey questionnaire (p. 97–98). The questionnaire measured the students' feelings, thoughts and actions in the respective problem stages. It also included a request to describe the topic in a few sentences and draw a conceptual map of the central factors and their relationships. A semi-structured interview was conducted measuring students' search goals and intended actions. After the interview they each performed a search in PsychINFO. They were asked to think aloud during the search session, which was recorded. The transaction logs were also recorded. In the post-session interview data was collected using a questionnaire on the students' assessments of the usefulness of the references found. In the first session the students searched on average 30–60 minutes, and in the second one 30–45 minutes.

3.3. Concepts and operationalisations

Kuhlthau's (1993) model was used for structuring the students' progress in their proposal writing. Kuhlthau (1993) has shown that learning tasks by students and library users consist of several stages. Her theory holds that people search for and use information differently depending on the stage of the process.

Kuhlthau (1993) differentiates the learning task process into six phases. At *initiation,* people become aware of their lack of knowledge and understanding. Thoughts centre on understanding the task and relating the problem to prior knowledge. During *selection*, the task is to identify and select a topic to be investigated. In *exploration*, subjects investigate information on the general topic in order to extend personal understanding. In *formulation*, a focused perspective on the topic is formed. This is a crucial phase in the task completion process because it helps a person to focus on relevant information. *Collection* is the stage of the process when the interaction between the user and the information system functions most efficiently. The user with a clear sense of direction can specify the need for pertinent, focused information to systems (Kuhlthau, 1993). In the *presentation* stage, the task is to complete the search and use the findings.

Kuhlthau (1993) has shown that individuals exhibit thoughts, actions and feelings that are typical of each particular stage of the longitudinal search process. The process survey questionnaire (Kuhlthau, 1993, p. 97–98) is designed to measure these three dimensions. In our study the students' stages in the process were operationalised as answers to questions in Kuhlthau's (1993) process survey questionnaire (97–98). The answers were coded and the students placed at the stages of the model according to the coding scheme received from Kuhlthau jointly by the three researchers in the team. The stages were scored in an ascending order from initiation to presentation where initiation = 1 and presentation = 6.

3.3.1. Conceptual structure

The students' knowledge of their subject was measured by asking them to describe their topics in a few sentences in the questionnaire and draw a conceptual map in both sessions. In the topic descriptions the main concepts and their sub-concepts were identified by the three members of the research team. Main concepts were upper-level concepts, which typically had either a causal or comparative relationship with each other. The sub-concepts typically specified the main concepts or acted as their attributes. Sub-concepts were either hierarchically narrower concepts or had an associative relation to the main concept. A few differences in identifying the concepts were solved by discussions in the team.

The following measures were formed: 1) the number of concepts used by a student indicates the extent of the conceptual structure; 2) the portion of sub-concepts of all concepts indicates the specificity of the conceptual structure. The more sub-concepts in relation to all those used, the more specific the construct is; 3) the portion of concepts expressed in query terms indicates the students' ability to express the conceptual construct in the query language. The more exhaustively the concepts are expressed in the query language, the more comprehensive the translation is. This variable is called coverage in query language.

Each of the three members of the research team compared the concepts and query terms. The thesaurus of PsychINFO was utilized for clarifying the meanings and relations of concepts and terms. A concept was expressed by a query term if they were synonyms or conceptually similar. A sub-concept expressed by a query term was coded only as an instance of the sub-concept, not as the main concept. The differences in coding was discussed and resolved in the research team.

In this study the term "conceptual structure" refers to these operationalisations. The term "knowledge structure" is used in parallel with "conceptual structure."

3.3.2. Knowledge level

Kuhlthau's (1993) process model implies that as individuals proceed through the model's stages, they learn about their topic. Moving from confusion to clarity in the understanding of a learning task and an ability to formulate a focus for it are signs of learning and growth of knowledge. Thus, progressing in the model implies a growth in an individual's knowledge level.

Studies in cognitive psychology and problem solving show that the more individuals know about a subject—the more expertise they have—the more extensive, specific and structured their knowledge structures are (Gavin, 1998; Robertson, 2001) Thus, this evidence suggests that there is a systematic connection between individuals' degree of knowledge of a subject and their conceptual structure concerning the subject.

By combining this evidence we may infer that progressing along the stages in Kuhlthau's model implies learning and growth of knowledge of a topic, which is associated with the growth and specificity of individuals' conceptual structure.

We measured students' knowledge level of their topics by asking them to rate to what extent they were familiar with their topic in a four point scale from not at all (=1) to a great degree (=4).

3.3.3. Query facets and terms

Terms and facets were identified from the search logs by the three members of the research team. They were classified first by each member. The differences in coding were discussed, solved and accepted jointly in our group.

The terms added in the second session were classified into four categories, which were adopted from Wang (1997). A synonym (ST) is a term that is interchangeable with another term. A broader term (BT) refers to a term that is broader in hierarchy. A narrower term (NT) refers to a term narrower in hierarchy. A related term (RT) is a term that is associated with another term.

3.3.4. Search tactics

The students used several tactics in their searches. The three most frequent tactics were Intersect, Vary and Limit (Table 1). Compared with the two main query formulation tactics—Intersect and Vary—other tactics were seldom used, each by a maximum of five students per session. The two former were used by 21 and 14 searchers respectively. Therefore we focused on the main query formulation tactics. The complete distribution of the tactics can be found in Vakkari et al. (2002).

Limit means the use of field restrictions provided by the system. It is an operational tactic, which does not change the conceptual content of a query (Fidel, 1991). Limit was excluded from the analysis, because this study focuses on conceptual relations between students' knowledge structure and searching. A check of the data also showed that using the Limit tactic did not correlate with the main variables of this study.

The major search tactics used are presented in Table 1. They were identified from the search logs by two members of the research team. The differences in coding were discussed and resolved in the research team.

A query is a representation of a user's information need, which consists of search terms and of possible operators connecting them. A facet is an exclusive aspect of a query, which may contain one or more search terms. The terms within a facet are combined by OR-operators (Sormunen, 2000).

A move in a search is the basic unit of analysis. A move is an identifiable thought or action that is a part of information searching (Bates, 1990) for improving search results (Fidel, 1991). In our study a move was a change made in a query in order to achieve the goals of the search. A move was operationalised as a change in the query statement to improve the search. Tactics consist of a set of moves.

Table 1. Definitions and operationalisations of search tactics.

Definitions*	Operationalisations§
Search formulation tactics	
Intersect: Add conjunction representing another query facet	Terms added to the query using an AND operator
Vary: Replace one existing query term with another	At least one new term was substituted for one of the terms in the preceding move so that the number of terms remained the same
* Definitions of tactics are based on Bates (1990), Fidel (1991), Sormunen (2000). § Operationalisations are based on Sormunen (2000).	

3.3.5. Utility assessment of the references

During the search the students marked the references they thought would be useful in their respective tasks. We asked them to select references they assessed as useful for their proposal writing. Thus, we were interested in the situational relevance of the references (Cosijn and Ingwersen, 2000), i.e., in those references that might contribute to the students' proposal writing. After the search the students evaluated the references marked for their task on a four-point scale: totally—partially—potentially—not useful. In the analysis we only take into account references that were useful at least to a certain degree.

3.3.6. Statistical tests

The statistical test used was Wilcoxon's test and the test for Pearson's correlation coefficient. When the data consists of a small number of test subjects like ours, using statistical tests is not simple. Statistical testing is only one means of distinguishing differences caused by change from systematic differences. Information about the consistency of the differences in subgroups is also important as well as how reasonable and compatible the results are with earlier findings. In our study we utilise statistical tests to reveal the volume of the differences, not with a view to accepting or rejecting the results in a straightforward way.

4. RESULTS

We will first present the mean values of the main variables of the study in the two search sessions to reveal the change in trends. After that we analyse the connections between the variables by using correlation coefficients.

4.1. Trends between the search sessions

The statistically significant changes were students' progress in Kuhlthau's (1993) model and their self-reported familiarity with their topics (Table 2). At the beginning of the seminar the students were typically exploring the topic, and towards the end they were commonly collecting material for the proposal according to the focus formed. The students reported that their familiarity with the subject increased from a little to some degree of familiarity. Their conceptual structure measured by the number of concepts became only slightly richer, whereas its specificity decreased a little. The structure of the construct was quite undifferentiated during the seminar in terms of the proportion of the sub-concepts used. This finding is not in line with the students' progress in Kuhlthau's model, which predicts that subjects' conception of the topic becomes more focused and clear. However, a closer analysis of students' topic descriptions revealed that the concepts used became somewhat more specific between the sessions.

The coverage of the conceptual structure in query language did not change much. The students were able to translate into query terms only slightly more than half of the concepts they used for describing the topic. Thus, it seems that the students' ability to articulate their request in query language was rather poor. A closer look at the students' problem statements suggests that in the second session especially they described their topics in more general concepts than they used in query formulation. This may partially explain the low coverage of the concepts used in the queries. The phenomenon also refers to the label effect (Ingwersen, 1992).

Among the search process variables the number of terms and the total number of tactics used increased somewhat between the sessions. The number of facets, Intersect and Vary tactics used remained unchanged in subsequent sessions. However, in the second session the students accepted fewer references as useful than in the first session. This may be a sign of the students' increased selectivity when their knowledge of the topic was improved (cf. Tang and Solomon, 1998; Vakkari and Hakala, 2000).

Table 2. Mean values of main variables per student in sessions I and II.

Variable	I session (n=22)	II session (n=22)	p.
Stage in Kuhlthau's model	2.9	4.8	0.001
Familiarity with the topic	2.2	2.9	0.004
Number of concepts	5.9	6.4	0.37
Proportion of sub-concepts (%)	39	35	0.50
Coverage in query language (%)	51	55	0.86
Number of facets	3.5	3.6	0.65
Number of terms	5.4	6.2	0.19
Total number of tactics	6.7	8.4	0.24
Number of Intersect tactics	1.9	2.0	0.84
Number of Vary tactics	1.3	1.8	0.92
Number of useful references	6.8	4.4	0.10

4.2. Conceptual structure, the process and outcome of searches in the first session

The aim of this analysis is to find out how the conceptual structure of the students is connected to the search process and outcome variables. We are interested to see if the features of the conceptual construct have consequences for the search outcome, and if they have, which search process variables link the students' knowledge structure to search outcome.

The search outcome correlated significantly ($r > .36$; $p < .05$; $n = 22$) with only one variable reflecting students' conceptual structure (Table 3). The correlation between the portion of concepts articulated in query terms and the number of useful references found was .43. Thus, the more able the students were to express their knowledge structure in query terms, the more useful references they found. The other features of knowledge structure were not connected to the search success.

Table 3. Correlations of knowledge structure, search process and outcome variables in the first session.

Variable type	ISP	Conc	Sub-conc	Cover	Facet	Term	Tact	Inters	Vary
Conceptual structure									
# of Concepts	.10								
% of Sub-concepts	.04	**.63**							
Coverage	.19	-.04	-.06						
Search process									
# of Facets	.23	**.57**	.28	.10					
# of Terms	**.40**	**.54**	**.57**	.28	**.78**				
# of Tactics	**.54**	.15	.15	.14	**.57**	**.73**			
# of Intersect	**.41**	**.39**	.18	.04	**.64**	**.60**	**.76**		
# of Vary	.27	-.01	.19	-.13	.20	**.38**	**.67**	**.59**	
Outcome									
# of References	.32	.16	-.02	**.43**	.06	.05	.10	.07	.34

Legend: n=22: r>36, p<.05 (indicated as bold); ISP= students' stage in Kuhlthau's model

The only search process variable that correlated to a certain degree ($r = .34$) with the number of useful references found was the number of Vary tactics used. When its correlation with the portion of concepts covered by the query terms is as low as -.13, the use of Vary does not depend on the coverage of query terms. Thus, the use of Vary tactics was not the mediating link between that dimension of the knowledge structure and the search outcome.

It seems, however, that the number of concepts and the proportion of sub-concepts in the problem statement were linked to students' search outcome via the number of search terms used and replaced. The correlation between the number of terms, and the number of concepts and the portion of sub-concepts were .54 and .57, respectively. Moreover, the correlation between the number of terms and Vary tactics (replacing terms) was .38. Thus, the more concepts and relatively more sub-concepts in the students' constructs, the more search terms they used; and the more terms they had, the more they replaced them (Vary tactics) leading to a greater number of useful references found.

A closer analysis of students' search logs and verbal protocols revealed that Vary tactics were used either for increasing the size of a retrieved set or for conceptually mapping the search topic. In the previous case vary was used as a clumsy substitute of parallel tactics (the use of OR operator). In the latter, students systematically divided the search topic into conceptually smaller fields for inspecting the references retrieved.

In all, although the search success depended on the students' ability to express their problem statement in query terms, the search process variables used did not mediate this feature of knowledge structure to the search outcome. It led to search success as such. On the other hand, it seems that a greater number of concepts and sub-concepts in the students' construct facilitated a greater replacing of search terms in Vary tactics leading to a greater number of useful references found. Thus, there were two mechanisms that led to search success. Students were either better able to cover their concepts by search terms resulting in a successful search independent of the structure of the search process, or they had to use a lot of terms and frequently replace them in queries exploiting their more extensive knowledge structure, which led them to found more useful references.

Students' self-reported familiarity with the topic had a low correlation with the coverage of query terms ($r = .13$). Thus, students' own perception of their knowledge level does not explain their ability to articulate the problem statement in query terms. Nor was it related to the number of useful references found ($r = .06$). *Mutatis mutandis* this holds also for the relation between the students' stages in Kuhlthau's (1993) model, conceptual coverage and search outcome. Thus, it is mainly the students' ability to express the problem statement in query terms which contributes to the search success.

It is interesting to note that the students' capacity to express their conceptual structure in query terms did not depend on the number of concepts ($r=.04$) or the proportion of sub-concepts ($r=-.06$) it consisted of. In a situation when students were not familiar with their topic, the extent or specificity of their knowledge structure did not help them to articulate search terms.

The students' conceptual construct had connections with the process variables although these did not have an impact on search success. The number of facets ($r=.57$) and terms ($r=.54$) in the queries were associated with the number of concepts in the students' problem statements and also with the portion of sub-concepts in the statements ($r=28$; $r=57$ respectively). Thus, the extent and specificity of the knowledge structure affects the number of search facets and terms used. Apart from that, the portion of concepts covered by the query terms was not connected with the number of facets and only slightly with the number of query terms used. We may conclude that it is not the quantity but the pertinence of the expressions used to articulate the conceptual construct by query terms, which matters.

In the first session the only feature in the students' knowledge structure which directly affected search success was their ability to articulate it in query terms. The more comprehensive the articulation, the more useful references the students found. The ability to infer query terms from the conceptual structure seemed to affect the search success directly without the mediation of the number of search facets and terms or the search tactics used. Neither the number of concepts nor the portion of the sub-concepts of all concepts used by the students affected their ability to express them in query terms. However, they facilitated the students to use more search terms and replace them more frequently, which in turn was reflected in a search outcome with more useful references.

4.3. Conceptual structure, the process and outcome of searches in the second session

In the second session we also take into account the type of new terms introduced by the students as process variables.

The students' conceptual structure was differently related to the search success than in the beginning of the process (Table 4). The number of main concepts in the construct correlated to a certain extent (r=-.32) with search success. The fewer main concepts in the construct, the more useful references retrieved by the students. Thus, a sparse conceptual construct was associated with finding useful references. In this latter part of the process the search outcomes were not associated with the other features of the conceptual structure or with the search process variables.

Table 4. The correlation of knowledge structure, search process and outcome variables in the second session.

Variable type	ISP	Conc	Main conc	Sub-conc	Cover	Facet	Term	ST	NT	BT	Tact	Inters	Vary
Conceptual structure													
# of Concepts	.29												
# of Main conc	.22	.06											
% of Sub-conc	-.01	**-.66**	**-.64**										
Coverage	-.11	**-.47**	-.07	**-..39**									
Search process													
# of Facets	-.15	-.02	-.15	.10	.29								
# of Terms	-.04	-.05	-..21	.07	**..37**	**.75**							
# of ST	-.05	-.06	-.26	.16	.09	.12	**.47**						
# of NT	.03	.06	-.17	.18	.21	**.48**	**.46**	-.19					
# of BT	-.16	-.01	-.09	.10	-.16	-.13	-.25	-.20	-.03				
# of Tactics	-.04	.03	-.19	.15	.12	**.86**	**.83**	.30	**.57**	-.27			
# of Intersect	-.15	-.11	-.08	.03	.05	**.37**	**.31**	.13	.08	**.45**	**..33**		
# of Vary	-.24	-.14	-.09	.04	**.43**	**.76**	**.70**	-.07	**.76**	-.19	**.73**	.14	
Outcome													
# of References	**-.50**	-.06	-**.32**	.21	-.04	.16	.12	.26	.02	-.05	.11	.04	.10

Legend: n=22: r>36, p<.05 (indicaed as bold); ISP= students' stage in Kuhlthau's model

The students' advancement in Kuhlthau's (1993) model and their self-reported familiarity with the subject correlated significantly with their search success (r=-.50; r =-.41, respectively) and slightly with the number of main concepts (r=.22; r=.23). Those more advanced in the proposal preparation expressed the most main concepts, but they retrieved significantly fewer useful references. The correlation between students' perceived familiarity with the subject and their stage in Kuhlthau's model was .58. Thus, it is evident that those knowing most about their topic were also most critical in assessing the usefulness of the references leading to the acceptance of only few of them (cf. Spink et al., 1998; Vakkari and Hakala, 2000). The partial correlation between the number of main concepts and search success decreased when the stage in Kuhlthau's model is controlled ($r_{xy,z}$=-.24) Thus, it was mainly the students' relatively modest knowledge about their topic reflected in their sparse conceptual construct compared to that of their fellow students, which led to the identification of useful references.

5. DISCUSSION AND CONCLUSIONS

This study extends our knowledge about the relation between users' knowledge structure and search process and outcome in task performance. Linking users' cognition to search process and outcome has been practically *terra incognita*. The results show that during the preparation of research proposals a few features of the students' conceptual structure were connected to the search success, and that process variables did not commonly mediate between the search outcome and conceptual structure.

5.1. Conceptual structure and search success

At the beginning of the proposal preparation process, two mechanisms were found to connect students' conceptual construct to search outcome. Firstly, the proportion of concepts the students were able to articulate in query terms was correlated statistically significantly with search success. The more concepts were expressed in query terms, the more useful references were found. The search outcome and the proportion of articulated concepts were not linked by the search process variables. The search success depended solely on the students' capacity to cover the concepts with query terms, not on the number of facets, terms or tactics used. Their ability to achieve this articulation did not depend on the number of concepts or the portion of sub-concepts in the knowledge structure. Thus, the extent and specificity of the students' conceptual structure did not help them to express the query more exhaustively. This implies that at least when the users' knowledge of the topic is meagre, as among the students of this study in the beginning of their process, it is not the subject knowledge as such which matters, but the ability to translate the concepts into query terms.

Secondly, there was an indirect connection between the number of concepts and sub-concepts in students' construct and search outcomes bridged by the number of terms used and replaced in queries. The more concepts and sub-concepts representing the students' constructs, the more the students tended to use terms in their queries and the more they replaced them, which led to a search outcome with more useful references.

In the end stages of the process the features of students' conceptual constructs or their search efforts were not connected to the number of useful references found. However, those students who were less familiar with their subject tended to find more useful references than their more knowledgeable fellow students independent of their search patterns. This reflects the tendency of those less familiar with the subject not to be able to differentiate sharply between relevant and non-relevant information (Isenberg, 1986; Patel and Ramoni, 1997), which leads to acceptance of more references as relevant (Spink et al., 1998; Vakkari and Hakala, 2000).

5.2. Conceptual structure and process variables

In the beginning of the seminar the most process variables—the number of facets, terms and Intersect tactics—were associated with the extent and specificity of the students' conceptual structure. This is in line with the findings based on the studies on relations between subject knowledge or the stage of task performance, which suggests that the more developed knowledge structure in terms of the number and specificity of the concepts the users have, the more facets and terms and search tactics they use (Allen, 1991; Shute and Smith, 1993; Vakkari, 2000a). However, at the end of the seminar, the conceptual structure and the use of terms, facets and tactics by the students seemed to differentiate. There were fewer associations between them. A closer analysis of the data revealed that the query terms were expressed more specifically than the concepts in the constructs by the students. Contrary to this finding Hancock-Beaulieu et al. (1991) found that the expressed topic as articulated in the questionnaire by the users and the search terms used to formulate a query matched closely in most cases.

The inter-correlation between process variables were strong in both sessions. In general, the search outcome seemed to be fairly unconnected with the process variables, especially in the second session. A more detailed analysis of these connections can be found in Vakkari et al. (2002).

5.3. Conceptual construct, process variables and search outcome

Search outcome was associated in the beginning of the process with certain factors of students' conceptual construct, but not at the end of the process. The lack of connections in the second session may be partly due to a possible discrepancy between the search goals and problem descriptions by the students. It may be that the problem statements reflect more closely their state of knowledge of the subject than their specific search goals. In the second session the students seemed to express their subject in more general terms than those they used in query formulations.

Although some search process variables linked certain features of students' conceptual constructs to their search outcome, in most cases search outcomes were associated neither with students' search efforts nor conceptual constructs. A plausible explanation for this lack of connection is the students' restricted search skills in PsychINFO, which is a Boolean system. Their answers to the questionnaire and their minimal use of some features of the system—like OR and NOT operators—revealed that they were novices in using a Boolean system. Searchers have to master the system to a certain extent in order to be able to benefit from their subject knowledge (Hsieh-Yee, 1993; Vakkari et al., 2002). Their restricted search skills explain the lack of associations between search process variables and the search outcome. It explains also why there were few links between the students' conceptual structure and search outcome, although the features of conceptual structure co-varied with many search process variables in the first search session.

It seems that some features of students' knowledge structure contribute, on one hand, to the retrieval process by helping to articulate pertinent search terms and replace terms, and on the other hand, by contributing to the identification of useful items from the result set. The results of this study are tentative. Work remains to be done to uncover searchers' conceptual understanding of the topic, and its connections with search process and outcome.

REFERENCES

Allen, B. (1991) Topic knowledge and online catalog search formulation. *Library Quarterly, 61*, 188–213.

Bates, M. (1990) Where should the person stop and information interface start? *Information Processing & Management, 26*, 575–91.

Belkin, N. J., R. N. Oddy, and H. M. Brooks. (1982) ASK for information retrieval I & II. *Journal of Documentation, 38*, 61–71, 145–64.

Brooks, H., P. Daniels, and N. J. Belkin. (1985) Problem descriptions and user models. In *Informatics 8* (pp. 191–214). London: Aslib.

Cosijn., E., and P. Ingwersen. (2000) Dimensions of relevance. *Information Processing and Management, 26*, 533–50.

Fidel, R. (1991) Searchers' selection of search keys: I. The selection routine. *Journal of the American Society for Information Science, 42*, 490–500.

Gavin, H. (1998) *The Essence of Cognitive Psychology*. London: Prentice Hall Europe.

Hancock-Beaulieu, M., S. Robertson, and C. Neilson. (1991) Evaluation of online catalogues: Eliciting information from the user. *Information Processing & Management, 27*, 523–32.

Harter, S. (1986) *Online information retrieval*. Orlando: Academic Press.

Heit, E. (1997) Knowledge and concept learning. In K. Lamberts, and D. Shanks (eds.). *Knowledge, Concepts and Categories* (pp. 7–41). Hove: Psychology Press.

Hsieh-Yee, I. (1993) Effects of search experience and subject knowledge on the search tactics of novice and experienced searchers. *Journal of the American Society for Information Science, 44*, 161–74.

Ingwersen, P. (1992) *Information retrieval interaction.* London: Taylor Graham.

Isenberg, D. (1986) Thinking and managing: a verbal protocol analysis of managerial problem solving. *Academy of Management Journal, 20*, 775–88.

Kuhlthau, C. (1993) *Seeking Meaning.* Norwood, NJ: Ablex.

Oddy, R., R. Palmquist, and M. Crawford. (1986) Representation of anomalous states of knowledge in information retrieval. In *ASIS '86: Proceedings of the 49th ASIS Annual Meeting* (pp. 248–54). Medford, NJ: Learned Information.

Oddy, R., E. D. Liddy, B. Balakrishnan, A. Bishop, J. Elewononi, and E. Martin. (1992) Towards the use of situational information in information retrieval. *Journal of Documentation, 48*, 123–71.

Patel, V., and M. Ramoni. (1997) Cognitive models of directional inference in expert medical reasoning. In P. Feltovich, K. Ford, and R. Hoffman (eds.). *Expertise in context: human and machine* (pp. 67–99). Menlo Park, CA: AAAI Press.

Robertson, S. (2001) *Problem solving.* Hove: Psychology Press.

Shute, S., and P. Smith. (1993) Knowledge-based search tactics. *Information Processing & Management, 29*, 29–45.

Sormunen, E. (2000) *A method of measuring wide range performance of Boolean queries in full-text databases.* Acta Universitatis Tamperensis 748. Doctoral Dissertation. Tampere: Tampere University Press.

Spink, A., R. Greisdorf, and J. Bateman. (1998) From highly relevant to non-relevant: examining different regions of relevance. *Information Processing & Management, 34*, 599–622.

Tang, R., and P. Solomon. (1998) Toward an understanding of the dynamics of relevance judgment: an analysis of one person's search behavior. *Information Processing and Management, 34,* 237–56.

Vakkari, P. (2000a) Cognition and changes of search terms and tactics during task performance: a longitudinal study. *Proceedings of the RIAO 2000 Conference* (pp. 894–907). Paris: C.I.D. Also available: http://www.info.uta.fi/informaatio/vakkari/Vakkari_Tactics_RIAO2000.html

Vakkari, P. (2000b) Relevance and contributory information types of searched documents in task performance. *Proceedings of SIGIR2000 Conference, Athens 2000* (pp. 2–9). New York: ACM.

Vakkari, P., and N. Hakala. (2000) Changes in relevance criteria and problem stages in task performance. *Journal of Documentation, 56*, 540–62.

Vakkari, P., M. Pennanen, and S. Serola. (2002) Changes of search terms and tactics while writing a research proposal. Accepted for publication.

Wang, P. (1997) User's information needs at different stages of a research project: a cognitive view. In P. Vakkari, R. Savolainen, and B. Dervin (eds.). *Information Seeking in Context* (pp. 307–18). London & Los Angeles: Taylor.

Wildemuth, B., R. de Blieck, C. Friedman, and D. File. (1995) Medical students' personal knowledge, searching proficiency, and database use in problem solving. *Journal of the American Society for Information Science, 46*, 590–607.

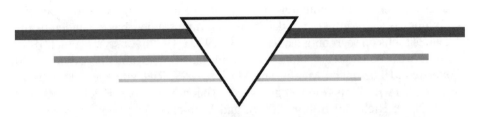

An Integrated Framework for Web Searching Research: Learning, Problem Solving, and Search Tasks

Rong Tang
School of Information Science and Policy
University at Albany, SUNY
113 Draper Hall, 135 Western Avenue
Albany, NY 12222, USA
tangr@albany.edu

ABSTRACT

The Web searching process consists of multiple cognitive operations such as learning and problem solving. Whether a search segment is acquisition-oriented or problem-based depends on the nature of the task and characteristics of the user. Current empirical work has focused on analyzing Web query patterns based on search logs, or observing actual searching sessions to model users' cognitive strategies. The differences in the area of investigation and research design reveal one-sided conceptualizations on Web searching. Through an example study, it is suggested that a comprehensive investigation is accomplished by incorporating participants' original search topics, taking into account both learning and problem-solving scenarios, and conducting multi-dimensional, integrated data analyses for the purpose of deriving a broad and in-depth understanding of Web search interactions.

1. INTRODUCTION

The Web presents users with a simpler and easier mode of searching as compared to commercial database systems. However, effective and efficient retrieval remains challenging for users (Fidel, et al., 1999). Research on Web searching, as a continuation of database searching studies, has expanded from a previous focus on searching tactics (Bates, 1979a, 1979b) or styles (Fidel, 1985) to issues of Web query patterns (e.g., Jansen, Spink, and Saracevic, 2000; Silverstein, Henzingger, Marais, and Moricz, 1999, Rieh and Xie, 2001), users' interactions with Web search engines (e.g., Hsieh-Yee, 1998; Fidel, et al., 1999; Bilel, 2000; Rieh and Belkin, 2000), and Web-specific cognitive moves and learning strategies (e.g., Hill and Hannafin, 1997; Ford, et al., 2001; Rogers, 2001). Multiple empirical approaches have been undertaken, including content analysis, survey or interview, search simulation experiment, and field observation. These studies yield a rich set of results, many of which carry great importance to the design of Web search engines. It is now time to formalize a conceptual framework of Web search interactions. Such a framework will enable us to identify an effective research methodology, recognize gaps in the current research and help us progressing forward.

This paper begins with presenting a model on Web searching that integrates the perspectives of learning, search interaction, and problem solving. Next, a review on the current research is provided and aspects of cognitive processes are highlighted. Following that, some preliminary results of a study on public library users' Web searching behaviors are reported and those results form the evidence for the interlinking between types of search tasks and users' learning or problem solving strategies. The paper concludes with a call for future studies that focus on a combination of problem-solving and learning activities on the Web.

2. WEB SEARCHING AS LEARNING AND PROBLEM SOLVING

Information seeking has been considered by scholars a multidimensional activity associated with human judgments, sense-making, cognitive state, and individual personality (Dervin and Nilan, 1986; Kuhlthau, 1993; Wilson, 1999). Information seeking in an electronic environment, as pointed out by Marchionini (1995), is "a fundamental human process closely related to learning and problem solving" (p. 8). Marchionini suggests that learning and problem solving are instantiated through two primary forms of online processing strategies: analytical and browsing. While most analytical strategies are utilized during the retrieval process, browsing takes place mainly in the context of information gathering and document selection. The author further claims that as analytical strategies are activated during query formulation, they require high concentration, "careful planning, the recall of query terms, and iterative query reformulations and examinations of results" (p. 8). Browsing strategies, on the other hand, demand less cognitive and attentional load, and are "heuristic and opportunistic and depend on recognizing relevant information" (p. 8). Marchionini states that although these cognitive operations are at times distinct, "information seeking is often part of learning and problem solving" (p. 8).

2.1. Learning

Definitions on learning are varied based on the perspective. From an experiential point of view, learning is described as "the literal retention of knowledge often achieved through repetition and recitation," or "an interpretative process aimed at understanding reality" (Schmeck, 1988, p. 3). From a behavioral perspective, learning is characterized as "a relatively permanent change in behavior potential that occurs as a result of experience" (Davis and Palladino, 1995, p. 194). Researchers, represented by Anderson and Bower (1973) and Corno and Mandinach (1983), have outlined two information-processing steps for learning: acquisition and transformation. While the acquisition process involves activities such as *alertness* and *monitoring*, the transformation process is specified by *selection, connecting,* and *planning.*

Corno and Mandinach (1983) further identified four forms of cognitive engagements: *self-regulated learning, task focus, resource management* and *recipient.* Self-regulated students concentrate highly on both acquisition and transformation. Task focus learners emphasize on transformation and underrate the acquisition process, while resource management learners act the opposite. In a classroom setting, resource management takes place with students who "deliberately avoid the extra mental effort of carrying out information transformation on their own," whereas students who are highly task focused are functional for "tasks requiring quick analytic responses and little self-checking or use of external cues" (p. 96). Recipient learning exercises at a low level of both acquisition and transformation activities, and "represents a true learning short-cut or relative passivity, with little mental investment by the student" (p. 96).

2.2. Problem solving

In the field of cognitive psychology, problem solving is defined as "cognitive processing directed at transforming a given situation into a goal situation when no obvious solution is available to the problem solver" (Myer, 1990, p. 184). In a problem space, in order to establish the path from the initial state to the goal state, problem solvers apply specific techniques including operators, facts, algorithms, subroutines, or heuristics (Newell and Simon, 1972; Myer, 1983). Myer (1990) indicates that a problem solving process involves steps of *representing, planning, executing,* and *monitoring.* Representing is to translate a given problem into a mental representation. Planning deals with constructing a set of sub-goals for solving the problem. The execution step involves performing a series of actions according to the plan, and, finally, monitoring is to analyze the progress and evaluate actions.

Learning and problem solving are cognitive processes often embedded within each other. The difference between the two is that problem solving is more task-oriented and goal-driven. While the objective of problem solving is to establish the solution path, the goal of learning is to improve one's knowledge state. Problem solving sometimes is a one-shot process and has a definite end point, whereas learning is often continuous, cumulative and the outcome of which is not evenly assessable. In the Web searching environment, an observable learning activity is gathering information about a broad topic. A problem-solving scenario is searching on a question and formulating the best possible queries in attempt to retrieve items containing the answer. Here a Web query statement is considered an operator or algorithm that leads to problem resolutions. Learning and problem solving activities are frequently applied together in performing a Web search task. Whether a particular segment of the Web search interaction is oriented towards learning or problem solving partially depends on users' search needs.

2.3. Information searching tasks

Multiple taxonomies of information need (IN) or search types were produced prior to the WWW era (e.g., Lipetz, 1972; Hawkins and Wagers, 1982; Frants and Brush, 1986; Ingwersen, 1992). For instance, Meadow (1992) identifies two kinds of information needs: specific IN and general IN. A specific IN can be represented by concrete attributes or values, for example, the question of "On what date was President Kennedy assassinated?" An example of a general topic is to collect information on "the status of a company being considered for acquisition." For such a need, "there is no one way to describe the subject," and "it is essential to probe to find out what information may be available and even what attributes and values should be used . . . " (p. 243).

Meadow (1992) further outlines four types of database searching: *the known-item search, the specific-information search, the general-information search, and a search to explore the database.* For a specific-information search, the user knows what the final answer or set of information should look like, although not necessarily how to find it. A general-information search is characterized as the user knowing the overall topic but not exactly what he or she is looking for. In a known-item and specific information search, the user has a well-defined problem and a clear goal state, and the search may easily lead to a problem-solving approach. The general-information and database exploration search, on the other hand, leaves better room for information acquisition or learning. In the Web environment, a known-item is when users search for a web document already known to them. An exploratory search is to learn about the functionality of a Web search tool in relation to a task. All four types of searching are applicable to the Web searching environment, and are incorporated into an integrated model as detailed below.

3. WEB SEARCH INTERACTIONS: AN INTEGRATED MODEL

Compared to many well-established procedural-driven information behavior models (e.g., Ellis, 1989; Kuhlthau, 1993; Marchionini, 1995; Hill, 1999), the model illustrated in Figure 1 is not a sequential stage model on Web searching. The purpose is to reveal interconnections among the nature of search topics, search interaction paths, and associated cognitive processes. The user starts with one of the two categories of information needs: specific and known-item or general and exploratory. The first group of INs has a tendency (as expressed through dotted line in the graph) of using the problem-solving approach, while the second one may be learning-oriented. However, there are also possibilities for a general search progressing towards problem solving, and a specific search turning into a learning process. Which approach the user takes depends essentially on the interaction environment and the user's personal characteristics.

A Web search interaction takes place as the user starts to convert the information need into a query statement and enters it to a search engine. During the search process, the user may sequentially or simultaneously go through a learning and problem-solving phase, or they may quickly move to the cognitive operation that they deem to be most productive in helping them to accomplish their tasks. In general, learning appears to occur when users browse through their search results, while problem solving is actualized through query reformulation. Both learning and problem solving may take place several times in a search loop until the improvement of knowledge state is realized or the problem solution is found.

Figure 1. An integrated model of Web search interactions.

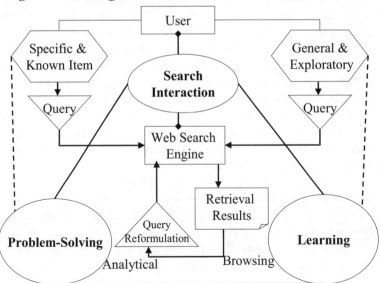

The model (Figure 1) presents several unique features. Firstly, the connection between cognitive processes and the nature of search tasks, as revealed in the model, has not been addressed in previous information seeking models. Secondly, the model as a whole illustrates a network of cognitive processes featuring learning, interaction and problem solving. All these operations are linked together through the user with a search task. Therefore, placing focus on any single process would have the potential danger of being incomplete in uncovering the whole process. In the following section, a review of recent Web searching literature maps areas of investigations into corresponding components of the model.

4. WEB SEARCHING RESEARCH: AREAS OF INVESTIGATION AND APPROACHES

Three predominate topical threads emerge from the current research on Web searching. One thread centers on analyzing query patterns from log data provided by specific search engine companies such as excite.com or altavista.com. The second involves investigations into users' actual Web search processes, focusing on searching behaviors and navigation strategies. The third group draws from educational theories investigating learning approaches on the Internet. Each set of these studies reveals a part of the Web search interaction by end-users.

4.1. Web query log studies: a problem-solving perspective

Representative studies that center on query log are the "Excite" study and the "AltaVista" study. The former has been conducted by Spink and her colleagues (Jansen, Spink, and Saracevic, 2000; Jansen, Spink, and Pfaff, 2000; Spink, Milchack, Sollenberger, and Hurson, 2000; Spink, Wolfram, Jansen, and Saracevic, 2001), and the latter was performed by Silverstein and his team (Silverstein, Henzingger, Marais, and Moricz, 1999). The focus of these studies was to define the specific nature of Web querying transactions as revealed through the amount of queries used in a search session, linguistic patterns, and the subject content of the query. Most of the Excite and AltaVista users were found to use few queries per session and view only 1–2 pages of search results. They were also found to frequently avoid advanced search syntax and to favor some forms of natural language in constructing query statements. Jansen, Spink and Pfaff (2000) point out that "users do not apply the normal rules of English syntax in any coherent or consistent manner. . . . Users rely on a variety of lexical patterns to 'explain' to the 'computer' the information need, item or topic they are trying to locate" (p. 172). For a detailed comparison between Web searching and searching on traditional IR systems and Online Public Access Catalog (OPAC), see Jansen and Pooch (2001).

A study by Rieh and Xie (2001) addressed the question of query reformulation in Web searching. By examining 183 randomly selected Excite log queries, the authors identified six major patterns of query reformulation: specified reformulation, parallel reformulation, generalized reformulation, dynamic reformulation, format reformulation and alternative reformulation. With a deep-level mapping on the movement of query modification, the study links Web searching research to previously established database searching theories and findings, which in turn addressed the issue of multiple search styles (Fidel, 1985) and a berry-picking pattern of query formulation process (Bates, 1989).

Web query log studies typically adopt a content-analysis methodology. Multiple coding schemes were developed to categorize topical content and linguistic features of Web queries and patterns of query reformulations (Spink, et al., 2000; Jansen, et al., 2000; Rieh and Xie, 2001). Conceptually, these studies address the aspect of problem solving in Web searching. Many important findings were produced, yet some aspects of the actual Web search interaction were missing. These aspects include the background information on users' information needs, the exact searching and interaction conditions, and users' satisfaction with retrieved hits. In addition, these studies are unable to describe the problem-solving process in full, since they run short of investigating the initial and goal states of the problem-solver, i.e., the user.

4.2. Web searching behavior: a search interaction perspective

Many of the users studies recorded real-time Web search interactions with the presence of the researcher (Schacter, Chung, and Dorr, 1998; Fidel, et al., 1999; Lazonder, Biemans, and Wopereis, 2000; Bilal, 2000; Rieh and Belkin, 2000; Ford, et al., 2001; Bilal and Kirby, 2001). Examples are Dania Bilal's (1998, 1999, 2000, 2001) research on children's Web searching and Fidel, et al.'s (1999) paper on Web searching by high school students. Bilal (2000) observed 22 seventh-grade students searching fact-based questions on Yahooligans and investigated their search strategies, browsing patterns, cognitive, and physical behaviors. It was found that children had preferences for keyword searching over browsing, yet, as indicated by the author, this may be the result of children's problem-solving style, the search interface, or the fact-driven query type. In Fidel, et al.'s (1999) case study, eight high school students participated in Web searching on homework assignments. The team observed a total of 21 search sessions, and they found that for assignment type tasks, students conducted very focused searches and went through the results swiftly without much tolerance for long lists.

In a search simulation study, Hsieh-Yee (1998) compared the Web search tactics used for different types of searches. Although there were no statistically significant differences found between searching for text and for graphics, nor between searching for known-items and topical searches, the author was able to identify some unique Web search tactics such as START, MORE, and NONE.

Note that this project is not an observation study, and data were collected via a special designed study instrument.

Overall, these studies provide rich insights into Web search behaviors and strategies. Many of the projects applied a combination of qualitative and quantitative methods (Hiseh-Yee, 1998; Bilal, 2000), which are exemplary for successful Web searching research. However, the shortcoming of this and the next group of studies is that search topics were controlled. By making participants searching on prescribed topics, the search process being investigated is missing the potential connection between the nature of information needs and consequent cognitive processes. What's more, even though researchers have touched upon cognitive behaviors (e.g., Bilal, 2000), most of the studies stayed at the search interaction level without pursuing the depth of users' problem-solving and learning mentality.

4.3. Web searching and navigating: a learning perspective

A number of observational studies deal explicitly with users' Web learning behaviors. For example, Hill and Hannafin (1997) carried out a very detailed research plan to explore four adult learners' cognitive strategies as they searched the Web. It was found that participants' prior knowledge base (both system and subject) and levels of self-efficacy are related to the degree of disorientation in searching and the ultimate success of a search task. The authors also pointed out that in contrast with a conventional learning environment, the Web encourages individual control, divergent thinking, multiple perspectives, and independent thinking. They suggest that "efforts to foster divergent thinking and multiple perspective building, as well as critical thinking and problem solving are needed to assist learners in adapting to these environments" (p. 62).

Ford, et al. (2001) also discovered that low self-efficacy was associated with poor retrieval performance. In addition, retrieval effectiveness was related to low cognitive complexity, imager cognitive style, and male gender. The authors applied Pask's (1988) and Entwistle's (1990) scheme on learning styles, and investigated 69 MLS and MSIS students' Web searching on a predefined topic. With a focus on the relationship between individual differences and searching performance, the research aimed mainly at associating the outcome with the cognitive and experiential profile of the searcher.

In examining the applicability of Corno and Mandinach's self-regulated learning model in the Web environment, Rogers (2001) observed 80 undergraduate students searching on a task selected from a list of general topics. Out of 8,000 search behaviors, *selecting* and *connecting* are the two most frequently used cognitive strategies. Additionally, the author identified search strategies for different learner groups. For instance, *task-focus* learners were found to frequently use Boolean keyword and phrase entries and make relevance assessments, while *recipient* learners tend to choose links in a serial order without much consideration of relevance. Evidently, *task-focus* learners share a good resemblance with problem solvers in attending to query formulation.

Studies on Web learning styles and cognitive strategies have presented well-designed research procedures featuring comprehensive data collection, coding, observation, and think-aloud approaches. Findings concerning users' learning and cognitive movements are valuable. Note that except Hill and Hannafin's (1997) study that allowed all four participants to search their own topics, the rest used prescribed search topics. Interestingly, most of the pre-selected topics used by this group of researchers were general subject topics, whereas the ones used by the previous group on search interactions were fact-based. More systematic investigations are needed to explore the relationship between Web searching and learning. Currently, given the learning focus of this group of studies, the report on query reformulation process, i.e., the problem-solving perspective, is relatively insufficient.

4.4. Research gaps

Research gaps are present, as the focus of recent empirical work has been limited to a particular cognitive operation in Web searching, without linking to other aspects nor to users' search topics. Among the studies reviewed above, a split in conceptualization is seen as they all orient toward separate segments of Web search interactions. Another notable research gap is that most of the observational studies of Web searching have targeted two groups of people: children/young adults (Schacter, et al., 1998; Bilal, 1998, 1999; Fidel, et al., 1999; Lazonder, et al., 2000) or academic users (Rieh and Belkin, 2000; Ford, et al., 2001; Swan, et al., 1998/99; Reinking, 1998; Roger, 2001). The general public or common adults, as an influential user group of over 544 million worldwide netizens, have not been examined as frequently. It is reported that over 75 percent of Internet users are public library patrons, while over 60 percent of public library goers also use the Internet (Jorgensen, D'Elia, Woelfel, and Rodger, 2001). Empirical research on the general public Web searching behaviors is lacking.

In the sections below, a study on public library users' Web search interactions is briefly described. Some preliminary results are introduced to support the integrated model. It should be noted that not all the results of the study are included here. Formal content analyses on users' learning strategies and reading patterns are currently in progress.

5. WEB SEARCHING BY THE GENERAL PUBLIC

The study was conducted in the spring and summer of 2001. Patrons from Albany Public Library (APL) and Guilderland Public Library (GPL) in the state of New York were invited to participate the Web searching project. Lotus ScreenCam was installed in one of the Internet workstations at the library. Both libraries host distinct clienteles, with APL serving patrons from all walks of life and GPL featuring a relatively balanced and well-educated community. These two libraries were chosen based on the intent to include a diverse range of public library settings.

Project announcements were distributed in the libraries, interested patrons signed up at the reference desk and were subsequently contacted for an on-site individual observation. Each was compensated for his/her time with $20 in cash. The sessions at APL were conducted from March to June, and GPL from July to August. The total number of participants is 41, and 21 were from APL and 20 from GPL. There were 21 females and 20 males.

Each session consisted of three parts: *Pre-Search Interview, Search Process*, and *Post-Search Interview*. The length of an observational session varied from 50 to 90 minutes. Participants were asked about their Internet search experience, library use experience, and the details about their search topics during the pre-search interview. The interview was semi-structured and audio-recorded. As they proceeded to search, participants were asked to talk aloud. The search process was both audio-recorded and screen-captured by ScreenCam™ software. Immediately following the search, a post-search interview required participants to articulate their levels of satisfaction with the results, their reactions and evaluation of the search process and search engine performance. Finally, their expectations of an ideal search engine were solicited. Appendix A includes pre-and post-search interview questions.

5.1. Participants' background

Fifty-nine percent of the participants indicated that they owned a computer at home. About 12 percent of the participants reported using the Web for less than two years. More than half of the participants said that they use the Web daily, and most people use the Internet for *email, research,* and *searching information.* Over 40 percent of the people picked Yahoo! as their favorite search tool and many of them indicated that a successful retrieval is the best measure of a good search engine. In actual search sessions, close to half of the participants used Google, and over half of the participants used multiple search engines. About seven percent of the participants used the "Advanced Search" or "Power Search" feature.

5.2. Search topics

The total number of topics searched is 58, with an average of 1.41 topics per session. Participants' topics cover a wide spectrum of themes, ranging from *gun control*, to *tennis instruction*, and *musical tuning systems*. In analyzing the subject content of participants' topics, the 14 Yahoo! top-level categories were used, and each coding was confirmed by searching the original topics on Yahoo! and backtracking results to their top-level headings. The most popular topics were related to "Society and Culture," the next popular topical groups were "Recreation and Sports," "Business and Economy," and "Social Science." The "Arts and Humanities," "News and Media," and "Education" topics were not sought by the participants.

At the task level, participants' search topics were grouped into four types as described by Meadow (1992): *known-item, specific, general,* and *exploratory.* The coding of topic types was performed by the author at three different times in a two-month period to ensure the consistency. No exploratory type of search was found. An example for a known-item is a search on a Jewish Rabbi whose Web site was previously known to the participant. Cases for specific topical needs include the ferry schedules to Monhegan Island, ME, or apartments for rent in Albany. Examples for the general search are "archaeology," "stem cells," or "anti-Semitism." The distribution of kinds of topics is shown in Table 1. Note that half of the topics were general ones.

Table 1. Search topics.

Type	Known-Item	Specific	General	Exploratory
No. of Topics	4	25	29	0
Proportion (N=58)	7%	43%	50%	-

5.3. Query patterns and search behaviors

A total of 200 queries were entered, and 167 were unique. The average number of queries per person was 4.9, which is higher than AltaVista's 2.02 (Silverstein, et al., 1999) or Excite's 2.8 (Jansen, et al., 2000). The average query length is 3.17 terms, which is higher than Excite's 2.02, and AltaVista's 2.35. This may imply that as users become comfortable and more proficient in searching the Web, the length of their queries increases accordingly. Figure 2 displays proportions of queries in forms of 1 term, 2 terms, etc.

Figure 2. Query length.

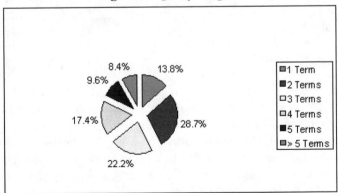

About 8 percent of the participants used Boolean operators, although not in all cases were those operators applied consciously. This proportion is slightly higher than Spink, et al.'s (2001) data, but lower than the 29 percent as by Xu (1999) and the 44 percent by Ford, et al. (2001). Seven percent of the people used

"+" in their search statements, and about 16 percent included punctuations. Typical punctuation usage was double quotes for phrase or exact wording (e.g., "room for rent") and commas for regional location (e.g., Albany, NY). Hyphens or commas were also used as a means of signaling the breakdown of multiple themes, for example, *CNN news—Supreme Court—gun control* and *multiple sclerosis, exercise, balance.*

Eighteen percent of the queries were in natural language format. Examples are "map of New Jersey," "Chondroitin sulphate in dogs," and "fun things to do in Paris." A relatively high percentage of the people were comfortable with keying in multiple keywords for searching, and some of them even invented their own ways of expression, as in the previous example with the hyphen or comma usage. This may suggest that an average public library user has the confidence in performing non-natural language forms of Web searching, regardless whether the correct search syntax was applied.

Query reformulation patterns were investigated using the combination of Fidel's (1985) and Rieh and Xie's (2001) classifications. Specifically, little change in a query statement throughout a search session was marked as "operationalist move" for the fact that participants relied heavily on reading what the system retrieved rather than changing the query. Other patterns were categorized according to Rieh and Xie's model along the dimensions of content, format and resource. Table 2 shows the statistics of participants' search moves as classified at the content level.

Table 2. Query reformulation patterns.

Search Moves (by person)	Counts	Proportion (N=41)
Content: Specification	14	34.1%
Content: Parallel Move	10	24.4%
Operationalist Move	9	22.0%
Content: Replacement With Synonym	6	14.6%
Content: Generalization	2	4.9%

An example of specified reformulation is a move from *CNN news—gun control* to *CNN news—Supreme Court—gun control.* An example of "Content: Generalization" is: *"brain injury"* + *coma* + *'rousal* → *"brain injury."* The most popular query reformulation pattern was specification, while 12 fewer people employed the "generalization reformulation" approach. The highest format-related move was "operator usage" (20 percent), and the only resource-related strategy used was "Resource: Site URL."

Participants also demonstrated several specialized search strategies. While searching, participants were found to purposefully take advantage of their knowledge of individual search engines and conducted effective comparative searches. While doing business research on *full-color printing* and *silk-screening shirts*, one participant brought up search screens of MSN, Yahoo!, Excite and Lycos, entered the same query to all four engines, and subsequently compared the results. This particular move is called the "split screen" technique in Rogers' (2001) study. Another interesting move was URL guessing. During the search on Monhegan Island, the participant typed monheganisland.com and monheganisland.org in the URL box without knowing whether the sites existed. Table 3 presents some special moves made by the participants.

Table 3. Specialized search strategies.

Special Moves	No of People	Frequency (N=41)
Comparative use of multiple search engines	6	15%
URL guessing	4	10%
Aware of and benefit from the distinctions among search engines	4	10%
Seeking clues to evaluate Web document quality	2	5%

5.4. Interaction types: resource-oriented or query-oriented

Participants may be categorized into two groups according to their interaction strategies. The first is labeled "resource-oriented" searching. Typically people in this group made no change or only minor changes to the initial query statement. They focused on eliciting information from the retrieved hits, and relied heavily on reading through retrieval screens and exploring Web sites. There are two sub-modes of searching in this group. People who entered a search statement into multiple search engines and examined the results simultaneously and comparatively, were distinguished from people who sequentially followed the links provided by the search engine and browsed though a large number of Web pages diligently. One participant, when searching on *military tactics,* looked at 16 screens of MSN search results and read texts from 23 Web pages.

In contrast, "query-oriented" searchers placed their attention on query reformulation and modification, and treated the searching as a process of problem solving. An example of this is seven rounds of query modification as follows: *Saratoga racetrack handicapping → Saratoga racetrack statistics → Saratoga racetrack trackprofile → Saratoga racetrack track profile → Saratoga handicapping statistics → Saratoga statistics → Saratoga racetrack track bias.* The operational definition for a query-based search is that a query has been modified (excluding typographical corrections) more than twice. Table 4 displays the distribution of types of interactions, and Table 5 contrasts topic types with interaction types.

Table 4. Interaction types.

	Resource-oriented	Query-oriented
No. of Topics	34	24
Proportion (N=58)	59%	41%

Table 5. Interaction types versus topic types.

	Query-oriented		Resource-oriented	
Known-Item (N=4)	1	25	3	75%
Specific (N=25)	19	76%	6	24%
General (N=29)	4	14%	25	86%

The chi-square test between the topic variable (Known-item versus Specific versus General) and the interaction variable (Resource versus Query) shows that that the relationship between the two variables is statistically significant (df=2, χ^2 = 21.89, p<0.01). Even though the small number of known-item topics forbids further speculation on this particular type of topics, the connections were evident between specific topics and the query-orientation (i.e., the problem-solving approach), and between general topics and the resource-orientation (i.e., the learning approach). Recall the integrated model depicts this kind of tendency. Data also show that a particular type of topic is not linked exclusively to one type of cognitive process. Users are the determining factor for which route to take in finding needed information.

5.5. Satisfaction and expectations

During the post-search interview, a majority of the people (81 percent) expressed satisfaction with results. Participants' major complaint was that current search engines present too many non-pertinent links and that the retrieved information is largely unstructured. A quarter of the participants suggested the implementation of an interactive help feature to assist users to conduct query reformulation. Table 6 shows participants' answers (one missing data) when asked to provide recommendations for search engine performance and design. Only suggestions made by more than one participant are listed. Note that 18 percent of the people were completely satisfied with the search engine performance, while others suggested clustering results and differentiating types of searches, etc.

Table 6. Recommendations to search engine design.

Ideal Search Engine Features	No. of Responses	Proportion (N=40)
Interactive help feature (to assist topic refinement and query interpretation)	10	25.0%
No improvement/recommendations	7	17.5%
Results Categorization	5	12.5%
Differentiate specialized search with subject search	4	10.0%
Exclude inaccessible sites	3	7.5%
Provide direct answer with more visuals	3	7.5%
No commercials	2	5.0%
Sort feature customized to users' needs	2	5.0%
Successful retrieval with extended summary on hits	2	5.0%
Up to date	2	5.0%

Shared conclusions from Fidel, et al.'s (1999) and Bilal's (2001) studies are that 1) more training on searching skills is needed for the targeted group, and 2) search engine designers should improve the system for better and more user-friendly retrieval. The results of this study suggest that although training is important, another key to a successful retrieval is users' practical knowledge gained from their own search experience. Some of the skills and tactics are not learned from workshops on advanced search syntax, but from personal practice and individual interaction with search engines. Many people in this study applied their knowledge of a particular search engine to derive a good problem-solving path and to implement engine-specific search strategies. With regard to the search engine design, a noteworthy recommendation from users of this study is to automatically predict and/or anticipate what a query input means. A good start is Google's "did you mean . . . " prompt that allows typographical correction. If a search engine can be programmed to interactively interpret users' information needs, assist users' query modification, identify inactive websites, and categorize retrieved hits based on users' interest, the search engine would be much more appreciated and widely used by the general public.

6. SUMMARY

This paper explored the relationship between cognitive operations in Web searching and types of information needs. Following a presentation of a conceptual framework that interconnects learning and problem solving with search interaction and search tasks, an intensive review on Web user studies reveals inadequate, segmented conceptualizations in current research of Web searching. Preliminary results from a public library users' Web searching project were used to augment the integrated model. A promising direction for Web searching research is to center on the linkage between the execution of cognitive processes and search tasks. An effective empirical approach, as exemplified by many previous studies, is to incorporate a suite of procedures that permit rich and stage-wise data collection, i.e., pre, post, and during search. Researchers need to implement multiple methods such as interview, survey, naturalistic inquiry, think-aloud protocol, content analysis, and other viable techniques in their research design in order to conduct a full investigation to users' Web search interactions.

ACKNOWLEDGEMENT

The author is grateful to Harry Bruce and two referees for their comments and suggestions on the earlier version of the paper. Special thanks to the directors and librarians at Albany Public Library and Guilderland Public Library for their assistance in conducting the project. Christina Chang contributed to a part of the data collection and Kaela Wallman assisted in the editing of the final version of the paper.

REFERENCES

Andersen, J. R., and G. H. Bower. (1973) *Human associative memory.* Washington, DC: V. H. Winston.

Bates, M. J. (1979a) Idea tactics. *Journal of the American Society for Information Science, 30*(5), 280–89.

Bates, M. J. (1979b) Information search tactics. *Journal of the American Society for Information Science, 30*(4), 205–14.

Bates, M. J. (1989) The design of browsing and berrypicking techniques for the online search interface. *Online Review, 13*(5), 407–24.

Bilal, D. (1998) Children's search processes in using World Wide Web search engines: An exploratory study. *Proceedings of the 61st Annual Meeting the American Society for Information Science, 35,* 45–53.

Bilal, D. (1999) Web search engines for children: A comparative study and performance evaluation of Yahooligans!, Ask Jeeves for Kids, and Super Snooper. *Proceedings of the 62nd Annual Meeting the American Society for Information Science, 37,* 70–82.

Bilal, D. (2000) Children's use of the Yahooligans! Web search engine: I. Cognitive, physical and affective behaviors on fact-based tasks. *Journal of the American Society for Information Science, 51*(7), 646–65.

Bilal, D., and J. Kirby. (2001) Factors influencing children's and adults' information seeking on the Web: Results of two studies. *Proceedings of the 64th Annual Meeting of the American Society for Information Science and Technology, 38,* 126–40.

Corno, L., and E. Mandinach. (1983) The role of cognitive engagement in classroom learning and motivation. *Educational Psychology, 19*(2), 88–108.

Davis, S. F., and J. J. Palladino. (1995) *Psychology.* Englewood Cliffs, NJ: Prentice Hall.

Dervin, B., and M. Nilan. (1986) Information needs and uses. *Annual review of information science and technology, 21,* 3–33.

Ellis, D. (1989) A behavioral approach to information retrieval system design. *Journal of Documentation, 45*(3), 171–212.

Entwistle, N. (1990) Learning styles. In M. Eysenck (ed.). *The Blackwell dictionary of cognitive psychology,* pp. 208–13. Cambridge, MA: Blackwell.

Fidel, R. (1985) Moves in online searching. *Online Review, 9,* 61–74.

Fidel, R., R. K. Davies, M. H. Douglass, J. K. Holder, C. J. Hopkings, E. J. Kushner, B. K. Miyagishima, and C. D. Toney. (1999) A visit to the information mall: Web searching behavior of high school students. *Journal of the American Society for Information Science, 50*(1), 24–37.

Ford, N., D. Miller, and N. Moss. (2001) The role of individual differences in Internet searching: An empirical study. *Journal of the American Society for Information Science and Technology, 52*(12), 1049–66.

Frants, V. I., and C. B. Brush. (1988) The need for information and some aspects of information retrieval systems construction. *Journal of the American Society for Information Science, 39*(2), 86–91.

Hawkins, D. T., and R. Wagers. (1982) Online bibliographic search strategy development. *Online, 6,* 12–19.

Hill, J. R. (1999) A conceptual framework for understanding information seeking in open-ended information systems. *Educational Technology Research and Development, 47*(1), 5–27.

Hill, J. R., and M. J. Hannafin. (1997) Cognitive strategies and learning from the World Wide Web. *Educational Technology Research and Development, 45*(4), 37–64.

Hsieh-Yee, I. (1998) Search tactics of Web users in searching for texts, graphics, known items and subjects: A search simulation study. *Reference Librarian, 60,* 61–85.

Ingwersen, P. (1992) *Information retrieval interaction.* Los Angeles, CA: Taylor Graham.

Jansen, B. J., and U. Pooch. (2001) A review of Web searching studies and a framework for future research. *Journal of the American Society for Information Science, 52*(3), 235–46.

Jansen, B. J., A. Spink, and M. A. Pfaff. (2000) Linguistic aspects of Web queries. *Proceedings of the 63th Annual Meeting the American Society for Information Science and Technology, 37,* 169–76.

Jansen, B. J., A. Spink, and T. Saracevic. (2000) Real life, real users, and real needs: A study and Analysis of user queries on the Web. *Information Processing and Management, 36,* 207–77.

Jorgensen, C., G. D'Elia, J. Woelfel, and E. Rodger. (2001) The impact of the Internet on public library use: Current status and trends for the future. *Proceedings of the 64th Annual Meeting of the American Society for Information Science and Technology, 38,* 171–55.

Kuhlthau, C. C. (1993) *Seeking meaning: A process approach to library and information services.* Norwood, NJ: Ablex Publishing.

Lawrence, S., and C. L. Giles. (1998) Searching the World Wide Web. *Science, 280*(5360), 98–100.

Lazonder, A. W., H. Biemans, and I. Wopereis. (2000) Differences between novice and experienced users in searching information on the World Wide Web. *Journal of the American Society for Information Science, 51*(6), 576–81.

Lipetz, B. A. (1970) *User requirements in identifying desired works in a large library.* New Haven, CT: Yale University Library.

Marchionini, G. (1995) *Information seeking in electronic environments.* London: Cambridge University Press.

Meadow, C. T. (1992) *Text information retrieval systems.* San Diego: Academic Press.

Myer, R. E. (1983) *Thinking, problem solving, cognition.* New York: Freeman.

Myer, R. E. (1990) Problem solving. In M. Eysenck (ed.). *The Blackwell dictionary of cognitive psychology,* pp. 284–88. Cambridge, MA: Blackwell.

Newell, A., and H. A. Simon. (1972) *Human problem solving.* Englewood Cliffs, NJ: Prentice-Hall.

Pask, G. (1988) Learning strategies, teaching strategies and conceptual or learning style. In R. R. Schmeck (ed.), *Learning strategies and learning styles* (pp. 83–99). New York: Plenum Press.

Reinking, D. (1988) Computer-mediated text and comprehension differences: The role of reading time, reader preference, and estimation of learning, *Reading Research Quarterly, 23,* 484–98.

Rieh, S. Y., H. Xie. (2001) Patterns and sequences of multiple query reformulations in Web searching: A preliminary study. *Proceedings of the 64th Annual Meeting of the American Society for Information Science and Technology, 38,* 246–55.

Rogers, D. M. (2001) *An investigation of components in Corno and Mandinach's self-regulated learning model applied to Internet navigation.* Doctoral Dissertation, University at Albany.

Schacter, J., G. Chung, A. Dorr. (1998) Children's Internet searching on complex problems: Performance and process analyses. *Journal of the American Society for Information Science, 49*(9), 840–49.

Schmeck, R. R. (1988) *Learning strategies and learning styles.* New York: Plenum Press.

Silverstein, C. M., M. Henzinger, H. Marais, and M. Moricz. (1999) Analysis of a very large Web search engine query log. *ACM SIGIR Forum, 33*(1), 6–12.

Spink, A., S. Milchak, M. Sollenberger, and A. Hurson. (2000) In A. Agah, J. Callan, and E. Rundensteiner (eds.). *Proceedings of the Ninth International Conference on Information Knowledge Management,* November 6-11, McLean, VA, pp. 134–40.

Spink, A., D. Wolfram, M. B. Jansen, and T. Saraceivic. (2001) Searching the Web: The public and their queries. *Journal of the American Society for Information Science, 52*(3), 226–34.

Swan, K., J. Bowman, J. Vargas, S. Schweig, and A. Holmes. (1998/1999) Reading the WWW: Making sense on the information superhighway. *Journal of Educational Technology Systems, 27*(2), 95–104.

Wilson, T. D. (1999) Models in Information Behaviour Research. *Journal of Documentation, 55*(3), 249–70.

Xu, J. L. (1999) Internet search engines: Real world IR issues and challenges. Paper presented at the Conference on Information and Knowledge Management, Kansas City, MO.

APPENDIX A: INTERVIEW QUESTIONS

1. Pre-Search Interview

1) Do you own a computer at home? If yes, do you have Internet access at home? If no, where do you access the Internet?
2) How long have you been using the Internet?
3) How often do you access the Internet a week?
4) What is the primary purpose that you use the Internet for? (e.g., Email, Searching, Social fun, Education, Shop, etc.)
5) Which search engine do you usually use for searching information?
6) What is/are your favorite search engine(s)?
7) What are the reasons you prefer that particular search engine?
8) Which topic(s) are you going to search today? What keywords will you use for the topic(s)?
9) How much information do you expect to get?
10) How often do you visit this library? For what purpose?
11) How often do you use reference service here? For what purpose?

2. Post-Search Interview

1) Are you satisfied with the information you retrieved?
2) What was the thing you liked the most about on search engine regarding the information you searched?
3) What specific feature supported by search engine that you found helpful in your search?
4) What are the characteristics of an ideal Web search engine in your mind?
5) What would you recommend to improve the Web search engine design and search performance?

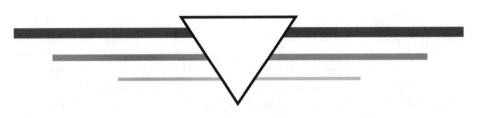

An Analysis of Collaboration in Three Film Archives: A Case for Collaboratories

Morten Hertzum, Annelise Mark Pejtersen,
Bryan Cleal, and Hanne Albrechtsen
Centre for Human-Machine Interaction
Risø National Laboratory
4000 Roskilde, Denmark
{morten.hertzum, amp, bryan.richard.cleal, hanne.albrechtsen}@risoe.dk

ABSTRACT

Collaboratories are based on communication technologies such as the Internet and are intended to foster increased collaboration and sharing of resources within and among organisations. This study analyses three European film archives to assess the potential of designing a collaboratory that supports, enables, and enhances the work in the archives. The analysis shows that collaboration—the focal point of collaboratories—is an intrinsic element of this work. Though all three archives have preservation, analysis, indexing, and retrieval of films as core activities there are important differences in how these activities are perceived and performed. A work analysis such as the one in this study may facilitate the archives in identifying a common ground on which to base a collaboratory, and in acknowledging the distinctiveness of each archive. The development of a firmer common ground seems a prerequisite for exploiting a collaboratory that goes beyond sharing of data. Coupling of work, readiness for collaboration, and readiness for collaboration technologies are also discussed as conditions for effective use of collaboratories.

1. INTRODUCTION

Since silent, black-and-white films began to appear in the early twentieth century, films have crossed national borders to be shown abroad. However, even neighbouring countries sometimes have quite different perceptions of what may and may not be shown, said, and implied in films. These differences, manifested in national censorship regulations, have led to countless country-specific cuts and changes to films, and to many films appearing in different versions in different film archives. This makes film research a truly international affair and it also makes films a valuable source of input for research on cultural and societal issues. Unfortunately, access problems severely impede the exploitation of the comprehensive collections held in film archives. This study analyses three European film archives to understand the work that goes on in the archives and assess the potential of designing a collaboratory that supports, enables, and enhances this work.

The film archives analysed in this study are Deutsche Film Institut (DIF), Filmarchiv Austria (FAA), and Národní Filmovy Archive (NFA). These three film archives—from Germany, Austria, and the Czech Republic—participate in the Collate project, the context in which this study is performed. The field data from the archives have been collected and analysed according to the principles of cognitive work analysis (Rasmussen, Pejtersen, and Goodstein, 1994). Following these principles work within the archives has been categorised into goals, tasks, and other discrete units, achieved through a means-ends analysis of the empirical data. By conducting such an analysis this study aims at illustrating how cognitive work analysis offers a conceptual framework for structuring and guiding the analysis of a complex, dynamic work domain.

The purpose of the work analysis is to clarify the needs for and prospects of a film collaboratory—a distributed multimedia repository where archivists are provided with the means for collaborating and sharing resources. A first step in devising such a collaboratory could be to provide online access to digitised versions of the original materials, such as film footage, film posters, and censorship documents, as well as to more dynamic information such as reviews, previous requests from users, and the replies to these requests. Shared access to data is, however, a limited and superficial way of supporting complex activities such as preservation, analysis, and indexing of film materials. Hence, at a general level a film collaboratory should:

1. Provide access to materials and resources.

2. Enable national and international collaboration among archivists and other users of the stored materials.

3. Enhance archivists' possibilities for analysing, indexing, annotating, and otherwise working with film materials.

Section 2 briefly introduces cognitive work analysis, the methodology we used in conducting and analysing the field studies. Section 3 provides an introduction to the concept of collaboratories. Section 4 documents the collaborative nature of the work in the archives and, thereby, provides a basis for contemplating the application of a collaboratory. The work analysis is completed, in Section 5, with a discussion of the extent to which the archives satisfy four general conditions for making effective use of collaboratories.

2. METHODOLOGY: COGNITIVE WORK ANALYSIS

Cognitive work analysis (Rasmussen, et al., 1994) is an approach to the analysis of complex, dynamic work domains, such as archives. These domains are characterised by a rich set of interactions between, on the one hand, the goals and constraints of the work domain and, on the other hand, the actors' skills and performance criteria. In such domains stable, proceduralised work tasks are not the norm. Consequently, the unit of analysis cannot be restricted to the task. To understand the activities of the involved actors it is necessary to analyse not only what the actors are doing but also how and why this course of activities was chosen. This involves analysis of the array of actions available to the actors as well as of the constraints they operate within. In support of such analyses cognitive work analysis proposes to study work domains in terms of means-ends relations (see Figure 1). The means-ends relations form an abstraction hierarchy where reasons propagate downward from goals toward specific work processes and physical objects whereas causes propagate upward from work processes and physical objects toward goals. If we focus on *what* goes on at a certain abstraction level then the level above provides the reasons *why* it is going on and the level below describes *how* it is carried out.

Figure 1. The abstraction hierarchy.

Level of abstraction	Means-ends relations			Examples (from the film archives)
Goals and constraints	Why			Active cultural mediation of films and film history
Priority measures	Why	What		Visibility and uniqueness of services and collections
Tasks	Why	What	How	Collect new materials; transfer nitrate films to safety stock
Work processes		What	How	Screening meetings; enter information into databases
Physical objects			How	Film footage; scripts; posters; restoration equipment; databases

An analysis in terms of the means-ends relations of a work domain provides a structured view of the general work contents. The means-ends structure relates goals and constraints to a variety of functional resources but says nothing about *who* is doing what or *with whom* they do it. The first step toward recognising how the individual actors' skills and performance criteria impact on the work that is being done—and thereby on the work domain as such—is to extend the means-ends analysis with a breakdown of the involved actors into stakeholder groups. This way the goals, constraints, tasks, and other elements of the means-ends analysis become specific to distinct stakeholder groups (see Section 5.1 for an example). A very important part of the analysis is to ensure inclusion of all the groups that have a stake in the work, including managers, the people who perform the tasks, and those who use the results of the work. Different stakeholders may hold different and even conflicting goals, which are balanced against each other by a variety of criteria. In dynamic domains the relative weight of these criteria will frequently change. Such changes are, for example, likely to occur when cognitive work analysis is used in systems design as a precursor to the introduction of a new or modified system.

Figure 2. The multiple perspectives involved in cognitive work analysis (the thick grey arrow indicates the main focus of the analysis in this paper).

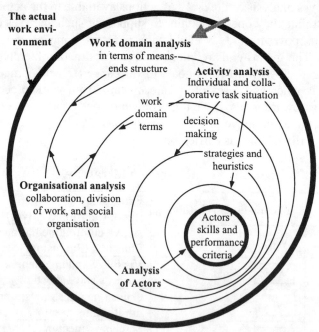

In addition to the means-ends analysis of the involved stakeholder groups, cognitive work analysis comprises analyses where the focus is shifted from the domain to progressively narrower objects of analysis (see Figure 2). This includes analyses of selected task situations, decisions, and strategies. Common to this progression is a move from a disembodied means-ends description of the domain toward analyses of individual actors' behaviour, skills, and performance criteria. Analysis of the collaborative element of the actors' work is currently less developed. A supplementary aim of this study is to work with the analysis of collaboration and, thereby, provide input to the ongoing elaboration of cognitive work analysis.

The present work analysis consists mainly of a means-ends analysis at the work-domain level (as indicated by the thick grey arrow in Figure 2) but the multiple analytic perspectives involved in cognitive work analysis are highly interrelated. Thus, while the abstraction hierarchy is the main thread in the present work analysis it will, due to the interrelatedness of real-world affairs, also contain elements of the other analytic perspectives.

The levels of the abstraction hierarchy are reflected in the overall research questions for the analysis of the film archives. This way the research questions open up for an analysis that uses the concrete activities performed in the three archives as starting points in an effort to uncover the goals that are being pursued and the manifold resources employed in pursuing them. Concretely, the research questions also provided the agenda for a focus group meeting in each film archive, and they were worded with this purpose in mind. In abbreviated form the research questions were:

1. What are the strategies and organisational structure of the archives? (i.e., goals and constraints)

2. What are the services of the archives? (i.e., tasks)

3. What kinds of collaboration take place within the archives and with outside parties? (i.e., work processes)

4. What tools do the archives apply in providing their services? (i.e., physical objects)

5. What do the archivists envision in terms of future developments?

These research questions were addressed through field studies at the archives. The three field studies, which lasted 2–5 days each, started with a focus group meeting and then continued with interviews and more informal interactions. Across the three archives we conducted 14 interviews and collected a total of 23–25 hours of focus group and interview data. These data have subsequently been transcribed and analysed, followed by discussion with the informants about assumptions and preliminary results. The data analyses have consisted of means-ends analyses combined with analyses of collaboration.

3. COLLABORATORIES: SUPPORTING COLLABORATION IN RESEARCH

When Wulf (1989) coined the term collaboratory—a fusion of collaboration and laboratory—collaboratories were seen as one of the potential tools that could be obtained from the anticipated growth in information and communication technologies. Collaboratories were seen as providing solutions, in the future, to problems relating to the increasing specialisation in the knowledge of individual scientists and the concomitant growth in the necessity of collaboration.

The aim of developing systems to support scientific practice is what distinguishes collaboratories from other cooperative work systems. Yet while any individual collaboratory will be designed after the requirements of the work domain it is supposed to support, it is still possible to identify elements in these systems that have been present regardless of the specific support that is being provided. Such generic functions include teleoperation, data sharing and annotation tools, audio and video conferencing facilities, and tools to enable real-time distribution of data and control to remotely located collaborators (Finholt and Olson, 1997). Clearly none of these are unique to collaboratories and it is more in the way that they have been combined and put to work that the unique characteristics of collaboratories can be seen. The respective importance of these different functions has shifted over time. When the concept was first coined teleoperation was seen as the most potentially promising tool to facilitate scientific collaboration. The hope here was that it would be possible to enable the remote operation of experimentation equipment, thereby allowing both intellectual and financial resources to be pooled. Progress on this front has, however, been superseded by advances, driven by the Internet industry, in technology supporting collaborative storage, exchange, and annotation of data and, to a lesser extent, audio and video conferencing.

Looking to extant examples of collaboratories (e.g., Bly, 1998) it is possible to identify systems that include all of the generic functions noted above. For example, the Upper Atmosphere Research Collaboratory has, in addition to providing resources for data sharing, allowed researchers from across the world to remotely operate various scientific instruments located in Greenland. For the most part, though, the remote operation of technical equipment remains problematic, partly due to limitations in the technology and partly due to the difficulty of designing interfaces that enable scientists to obtain the requisite level of remote control. Acknowledging these limitations in certain areas, it is also the case that not all scientific activity involves expensive equipment in scarce supply. In such areas of research it will be the tools provided for the management and sharing of data that will be most important. With these areas of research, provision of a level of technical support beyond that found in digital libraries and Internet-based communication tools can only be achieved when the specification of the system is determined in accordance with the specific requirements of the research activity.

4. THE COLLABORATIVE NATURE OF ARCHIVE WORK

It is a common characteristic of the three archives that collaboration is an intrinsic element of the work that is being done (Pejtersen, Albrechtsen, Cleal, Hansen, and Hertzum, 2001). Hence, it would be misconceived to introduce tools that treat the activities involved in the preservation and research of films as activities performed by single individuals. An example from each of the three archives may serve to illustrate the intrinsically collaborative nature of activities such as information seeking (FAA), analysis and indexing (NFA), and research and development (DIF):

Collaborative information seeking. FAA's library service has gradually changed into the use of a collaborative information-seeking method, where a team of archivists work together on satisfying the requester's information need. The collaboration is informal and initiated on an ad-hoc basis according to the content of the request and the other activities competing for the archivists' time. There is consensus among the archivists that they share the archive's users and that this gives the best service because the archivists' different backgrounds and interests complement each other. The collaborative information seeking also helps the archivists maintain a current awareness of what is going on in the archive and share their knowledge with their colleagues as well as their users. If an online facility for handling user requests disregards the collaborative nature of the archivists' work with the user requests it will only support a relatively minor part of this work. The collaborative nature of information seeking has also been analysed in several recent studies (e.g., Ehrlich and Cash, 1994; Fidel, et al., 2000; Karamuftuoglu, 1998).

Collaborative analysis and indexing. Watching films is vital work and this is precisely why NFA attaches so much importance to its weekly screening meetings. These meetings provide a forum where the filmographers and database manager of NFA meet regularly with national film specialists from other institutions. During the meetings, these specialists watch films and contribute information about accurate titles, film studios, locations, directors, literary model, and so forth. The participants also complement the films with information from secondary sources such as censorship cards and dialogue lists. After a screening meeting the filmographers enter a first version of the indexing of the screened film into the filmography database. Subsequently, this version is revised and refined through further communication, mostly by phone. Online screening meetings could potentially be a valuable collaboratory facility enabling people from distributed geographical locations to share evolving film descriptions and exchange contributions to the analysis and indexing of films. Collaborative aspects of classification and indexing have also been studied by, for example, Albrechtsen, Pejtersen, and Cleal (2002) and Bowker and Star (1999).

Research and development (R&D). At DIF most R&D work is done in externally funded projects. In these projects DIF provides input to the projects in terms of materials and the archivists' knowledge and gains new knowledge, materials, and tools to improve the collections of DIF. The R&D activities include 1) development of common tools such as archive information systems in general and databases containing specific filmographic data, 2) knowledge sharing by visiting other archives and gaining insight in their methods and services, and 3) work on archival development and standards. Collaboration with other archives and organisations is inherent in these activities. Indeed, common tools, visits, and standards can only be accomplished through collaboration across organisational boundaries. However, some R&D activities are performed through collaboration internal to the archive. One example is the work on the acquisition and daily administration of technology. This work is performed by an informally organised group, which meets and discusses. Everybody has his or her own functions, but the group members do the technology work together. The information flows in R&D organisations have been studied extensively by, for example, Allen (1977).

Figure 3. The connections between archived materials and user requests are established by means of databases and, most importantly, the archivists' knowledge and expertise.

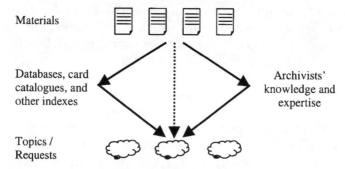

In the three archives collaboration becomes necessary because, normally, no single resource contains all information of relevance to a topic or request. Rather, the connections between requests and materials are established by means of several databases and the archivists' knowledge and expertise (see Figure 3). The archived materials are themselves not enough to answer the users' requests because the materials as such are not searchable in any other way than by browsing the shelves. Even if all the materials were digitised it would still not be possible to match user requests directly with the relevant films, censorship cards, and other materials. This is partly due to current limitations in multimedia retrieval (e.g., Forsyth, 1999). Another basic complication is, however, that many of the archived films exist in several and often incomplete versions. Some of these versions are simply foreign language replicates of the original film, others are brought about by censorship decisions that banned different scenes at different times or in different countries, and still others are complete remakes by a different director. In many situations it is no simple matter to determine whether two films should be considered independent films or versions of the same film. Further, considerable amounts of footage are missing or in bad condition due to old age. It may be a genuine research task to determine whether individual scenes from different pieces of footage were included in a film or cut out. Consequently, a seemingly simple—known-item—request for a film on the basis of its title, director, and production year may turn out to be anything but trivial.

Further, the existing indexes of the archived materials are not enough to answer the users' requests because only part of the materials have been indexed and different parts have been indexed for different purposes. This could be considered a temporary phenomenon, but it is more likely to remain a permanent condition. DIF alone has a collection of more than 11,000 films and estimates that it takes them an average of about one day to index a film according to their current criteria. All three archives have developed a number of databases to classify, index, and provide access to parts of their collections. These databases have been developed individually to suit the needs of different projects. For example, FAA has digitised seven of the 50 years of the Wochenschau newsreels and made them searchable on a CD-ROM. This was done for the Wochenschau's 50th anniversary. The Wochenschau database is, however, not integrated with the other local databases in terms of, for example, a common format or a single point of access. This illustrates the situation in all three archives. The archivists often find themselves in situations where they have to search several databases—and card catalogues—to answer user requests. Knowing where to search and knowing the format, scope, and limitations of the individual databases require detailed knowledge of the different databases. This knowledge cannot be acquired from documents as it has seldom been written down (see also Hertzum, 1999). It is usually held by only a few archivists who have been involved in the creation of the database.

Finally, one archivist is often not enough to answer a user request. Staff at the archives are, however, adept at using each other as information sources. So while it might not always be straightforward for one person to establish exactly what a user requires someone else, with a different area of expertise, can be called upon to assist in this process. Colleagues are a source of expertise in two ways. Firstly in relation to the knowledge they have of the film domain, and secondly through their knowledge of the archive's information content and the ways in which this can be accessed. In the first instance it is often self-evident who the most appropriate person to work with would be as they are the responsible party for the relevant materials. Furthermore, most archivists are aware of areas where their colleagues are interested and well informed. In general, the archivists' personal interests outstrip the areas for which they are responsible. An exception is in relation to knowledge of the databases where those most closely associated with the database are most likely to be consulted. The archivists' reliance on their colleagues' expertise, as opposed to information held in databases, was repeatedly emphasised by the archivists. As one of the archivists expressed it, "the best database is the brain of our colleagues."

5. DISCUSSION

The conditions for effective, non-collocated collaboration have been analysed by, among others, Dix (1997) and Olson and Olson (2000). These analyses caution that high hopes about what technology has to offer have seldom been attained in actual applications. Olson and Olson (2000) formulate four key concepts for successful introduction and use of collaboratories: common ground, coupling of work, collaboration readiness, and collaboration technology readiness. They conclude that non-collocated groups have a chance at succeeding with collaboratories if they have a firm common ground, loosely coupled work, and readiness for both collaboration and collaboration technologies.

5.1 Common ground

At a basic level, it is possible to identify common goals for the three archives. They all embrace the role as protector and mediator of cultural heritage. Also, the archives have a common interest in increasing the visibility of their services and collections to the public domain, for instance through increasing participation in international collaboration. However, a more in-depth analysis reveals that this goal of visibility and service to the public domain is perceived differently in the three archives.

FAA's commitment to the public domain is seen in the commitment to and realisation of user services. More than simply providing users with good resources for accessing FAA's collection, the goal at FAA is to anticipate user interests and develop the archive's collection accordingly. This philosophy is based partly on a particular vision of archives as information centres. However, it is also based in the belief that users are a potential source of expertise that can both assist archivists in understanding their collection more fully and contribute directly to the available knowledge about specific films or personalities.

NFA has a clear commitment to the public domain in their role as a national institution. They emphasise their role as custodians of unique material that has both national and socio-historical importance. It is against this background that NFA's emphasis on preservation and acquiring new material should be understood. In the services they provide users they supply information about the archive and its information content, primarily through expertise of the staff. This expertise is perceived as NFA's primary resource whereas users are seen as more passive receivers of information.

At DIF it is possible to identify a commitment to the public domain that reflects aspects found in the other two archives. There is, for example, a similar commitment to user service as seen in FAA. For DIF this is, however, primarily about improving the organisation of and access to its collection and less about seeking inspiration directly from users. At the same time DIF also strives to provide services that inform the public about the archive's collection and the activities with which it is engaged. One strategy in this respect is to conduct research that will contribute to the public understanding of filmmaking and film history.

Figure 4. Abstraction level and stakeholder domain matrix, FAA

Domain Level	Archivists	Researchers	Technicians
Goals and constraints	Manage archive collection	Produce new knowledge	Restore/preserve film material
Priority measures	Provide quality user service	Reveal archive resources	Historical authenticity
Tasks	Seek/retrieve information	Study archive; write articles	Care for film; support archive
Work processes	Serve users; work databases	Seek/produce information	Seek information; treat/edit film
Physical objects	Film; literature; databases	Archive; other academic tools	Film; editing desks; film literature

Thus, while major activities, such as preservation and indexing of films, are common to DIF, FAA, and NFA there are important differences in how these activities are perceived and organised. Further, it must be born in mind that each of the archives is in itself a heterogeneous entity consisting of staff groups with different backgrounds and responsibilities. Figure 4 shows three of the staff groups at FAA and hints at the differences in their goals, tasks, and so forth. The figure also illustrates how abstraction levels and stakeholder domains provide a way of breaking the concept of common ground into a number of its constituent elements. Specifically, an analysis may find that the common ground of two organisations is restricted to some levels of abstraction (for example, the level of goals only) and/or a subset of the staff groups.

In terms of organisational structure DIF is undergoing a transition from a hierarchical to a project-based organisation, FAA consists of self-organising groups that arrange their work according to the overall framework provided by management, and NFA has a hierarchical structure where the management and the heads of departments coordinate the work. These different kinds of organisational structure permeate the archivists' perception and performance of their work and, for example, influence how they communicate about activities. Organising a collaboratory according to any one of the work organisations found in the archives—project-based, self-organising, or hierarchical—is likely to alienate the two other archives from the collaboratory. It is by no means easy to devise an organisation of the collaboratory that fosters collaboration and sharing among the archives and, at the same time, acknowledges their individual identities, ways of working, and organisational cultures. In this respect the introduction of a collaboratory shares many of the properties of an organisational merger, including that the benefits are most likely to show up gradually and concomitantly with the creation of a firm common ground.

5.2 Coupling of work

The archivists in the three archives complement each other's knowledge and collectively possess a detailed and extensive knowledge of the film domain and intersecting disciplines such as history. The spread of knowledge and skills across the archivists also evidences that high-quality results can often only be accomplished through extensive sharing of information and expertise. One task that often leads archivists to seek assistance from other staff groups and other institutions is the processing of user requests. This kind of collaboration is ad hoc and loosely coupled. Other tasks, such as preservation at NFA, are accomplished through a formal division of labour involving several staff groups. Hence, the coupling of work varies considerably from task to task. The amounts of film material held in the archives combined with the limited resources available to the archives mean, however, that the coupling across tasks has not been sufficiently tight to foster a gradual development of an integrated and consistent indexing of the materials. NFA is responsible for the continued development of a national filmography of Czech films and DIF is in the process of creating a complete filmography of German films, but the archives have the resources for only very few projects of this scope. Consequently, the filmography databases are not integrated with the databases covering books, newsreels, posters, and photos. Rather, each database is a standalone system targeted at the needs of an individual project. Extra resources have not been available for maintaining a common format or creating links among the databases. In relation to coupling of work across archive boundaries, the situation is compounded by the differences among the archives and a general lack of international standards for the classification of film materials. Though a complete and consistent classification of all the materials in the three archives is an intriguing thought it would probably be counterproductive to base a collaboratory on it. To acknowledge the conditions of the archivists' work and enable loose couplings across archive boundaries a collaboratory could, instead, provide support for evolving classifications, which can be created and revised gradually as new portions of the archived materials are being analysed.

5.3 Collaboration readiness

All three archives are involved in a number of national and international collaborations. These collaborations are necessary for the archives to fulfil their mandate, and they are initiated through the personal initiative of staff and through the archives' participation in the International Federation of Film Archives. For example, censorship material is important to the work of all three archives but NFA does not have its own collection of censorship material. DIF and FAA have such collections but need to develop tools and procedures for working with this material. As a result the three archives have, through their involvement in the Collate project, initiated collaboration on the further development of a selected area of the archives' research. This collaboration unfolds around the design and implementation of a prototype version of a collaboratory for working with censorship material. Due to its central role in film analysis, censorship material is a good candidate for an area that can both provide an initial focus of a collaboratory and point toward opportunities for the gradual inclusion of a range of activities and materials central to the archives. Thus, the archives are ready for and already involved in collaboration with other film institutions. Parenthetically, it can be noted that the archives hold different views on some aspects of what collaboration entails, such as the extent to which they can benefit from a more permeable boundary between film specialists and laypersons.

5.4 Collaboration technology readiness

Due to the tight coupling between the institutional context and investments in information technology, the archives have each developed their particular configuration of information resources. For local databases, NFA's information resources are much more developed and sophisticated than those at DIF and FAA. In contrast, access to global communication channels such as email and the Web is most restricted at NFA. DIF and FAA have created intranets that serve as internal notice boards, and web sites that serve to increase the visibility of the archives and their activities. However, these facilities are neither used for internal debate among the archivists, nor for communication with lay users and collaborating institutions (except for providing contact email information). The differences in the archives' current information resources may instigate different expectations as to the facilities and technical sophistication of a collaboratory and different intimidation barriers for engaging in the use of a collaboratory. Though the criterion of collaboration technology readiness may seem to be of a more mundane nature than the three other criteria for effective use of collaboratories, Star and Ruhleder (1996) show that it may mask subtle issues and be crucial to the success of collaboratories.

6. CONCLUSION

Collaboratories are based on communication technologies such as the Internet and intended to foster increased collaboration and sharing of resources among organisations in a domain. The film heritage domain seems suited to the application of collaboratories because films and film-related materials are scattered across institutional as well as national borders. The three film archives analysed in this paper all have preservation, analysis, indexing, and retrieval of films as core activities but there are important differences in how these activities are perceived and performed. The analysis documents that collaboration—the focal point of collaboratories—is indeed an intrinsic element of the work of the archives. It is, however, an important theme how and to what extent the archivists can transfer their knowledge, skills, and collaborative practices to a collaboratory. While the present work analysis calls for modest claims about the short-term benefits of a film collaboratory it also points to the, allegedly, most important area on which to focus in the effort to make effective use of such a collaboratory. This area is the identification of a common ground that cuts through incidental differences between the three archives but at the same time acknowledges and accommodates the essential differences. This puts careful work analysis at the heart of the design and application of collaboratories.

Cognitive work analysis provides a conceptual framework for conducting such analysis of complex, dynamic work domains. Specifically, the analysis of means-ends relations for the various stakeholder groups was an effective means of identifying commonalities and differences among the archives as well as among groups within the individual archives. Such analyses seem suited for the identification of the common ground on which to base collaboratories and, hence, highly relevant to the design of collaboratories. At present, the focus of cognitive work analysis is mainly on decomposing work into its constituent elements. This supports the analyst in seeing beyond the current organisation of work but it also means that analysis of how collaboration is accomplished is currently less developed within the framework of cognitive work analysis. Our ongoing and future work is directed at providing analytic means of describing how actors, in their day-to-day performance of their tasks, bring the various elements of their work together in dynamically determined courses of events. That is, we seek to elaborate on the analysis of collaboration.

ACKNOWLEDGEMENTS

This study was supported by the Danish National Research Foundation through its funding of the Centre for Human-Machine Interaction and by the European Commission's Information Society Technologies Programme through its funding of the Collate project on collaboratories for annotation, indexing, and retrieval of digitised historical archive material (IST-1999-20882). We thank Camilla Buhr Hansen and our informants at Deutsche Film Institut, Filmarchiv Austria, and Národní Filmovy Archive.

REFERENCES

Albrechtsen, H., A. M. Pejtersen, and B. R. Cleal. (2002) Empirical work analysis of collaborative film indexing. In H. Bruce, R. Fidel, P. Ingwersen, and P. Vakkari (eds.). *Emerging Frameworks and Methods: Proceedings of the Fourth International Conference on Conceptions of Library and Information Science*. Greenwood Village, CO: Libraries Unlimited.

Allen, T. J. (1977) *Managing the flow of technology: Technology transfer and the dissemination of technological information within the R&D organization.* Cambridge, MA: MIT Press.

Bly, S. (ed.). (1998) Collaboratories [Special section]. *ACM Interactions, 5*(3), 31–72.

Bowker, G. C., and S. L. Star. (1999) *Sorting things out: Classification and its consequences.* Cambridge, MA: MIT Press.

Dix, A. (1997) Challenges for cooperative work on the Web: An analytical approach. *Computer Supported Cooperative Work (CSCW), 6*(2&3), 135–56.

Ehrlich, K., and D. Cash. (1994) Turning information into knowledge: Information finding as a collaborative activity. In J. L. Schnase, J. J. Leggett, R. K. Furuta, and J. Metcalfe (eds.). *Proceedings of Digital Libraries '94* (119–25). College Station, TX: Texas A&M University.

Fidel, R., H. Bruce, A. M. Pejtersen, S. Dumais, J. Grudin, and S. Poltrock. (2000) Collaborative information retrieval (CIR). *The New Review of Information Behaviour Research, 1*, 235–47.

Finholt, T. A., and G. M. Olson. (1997) From laboratories to collaboratories: A new organizational form for scientific collaboration. *Psychological Science, 8*(1), 28–36.

Forsyth, D. A. (1999) Computer vision tools for finding images and video sequences. *Library Trends, 48*(2), 326–55.

Hertzum, M. (1999) Six roles of documents in professionals' work. In S. Bødker, M. Kyng, and K. Schmidt (eds.). *ECSCW'99: Proceedings of the Sixth European Conference on Computer Supported Cooperative Work* (41–60). Dordrecht: Kluwer.

Karamuftuoglu, M. (1998) Collaborative information retrieval: Toward a social informatics view of IR interaction. *Journal of the American Society for Information Science, 49*(12), 1070–80.

Olson, G. M., and J. S. Olson. (2000) Distance matters. *Human-Computer Interaction, 15*(2&3), 139–78.

Pejtersen, A. M., H. Albrechtsen, B. Cleal, C. B. Hansen, and M. Hertzum. (2001) *A Web-based—multimedia—collaboratory: Empirical work studies in film archives.* Risø Report No. Risø-R-1284(EN). Roskilde, Denmark: Risø National Laboratory. Available at http://www.risoe.dk/rispubl/SYS/ris-r-1284.htm.

Rasmussen, J., A. M. Pejtersen, and L. P. Goodstein. (1994) *Cognitive systems engineering.* New York: Wiley.

Star, S. L., and K. Ruhleder. (1996) Steps toward an ecology of infrastructure: Design and access for large information spaces. *Information Systems Research, 7*(1), 111–34.

Wulf, W. A. (1989) The national collaboratory—a white paper. In J. Lederberg, and K. Uncaphar (eds.). *Towards a National Collaboratory: Report of an Invitational Workshop at the Rockefeller University* (Appendix A). Washington, DC: National Science Foundation.

Empirical Work Analysis of Collaborative Film Indexing

Hanne Albrechtsen, Annelise Mark Pejtersen, and Bryan Cleal
Centre for Human-Machine Interaction
Risø National Laboratory
P.O. Box 49
4000 Roskilde, Denmark
hanne.albrechtsen@risoe,dk
annelise.m.pejtersen@risoe.dk
bryan.richard.cleal@risoe.dk

ABSTRACT

The present study explores document indexing as a collaborative work activity in the case of the creation of a filmography at a national film archive. The study, which was conducted according to the framework for cognitive analysis, identified two prototypical collaborative task situations in collaborative film indexing at the archive: screening meetings, where the subjects of films are analyzed in a collective, synchronous work arrangement, and ongoing consultation among filmography staff on entering information in a filmography database. The focus of the study is on how the current common conceptual tools like databases and cataloging rules supported or failed to support the collaborating actors in contributing to the archive's overall priorities of mediating research to a diversity of user communities. A means-ends model for mapping the diverse perspectives is introduced. The paper contributes with ideas for the development of future common conceptual tools, based on the new means-ends model. Such common conceptual tools would provide a stable interpretive environment for collaborative film indexing, retaining the diversity of interpretive perspectives of films.

1. INTRODUCTION

The purpose of indexing is to facilitate subject access to documents in information retrieval systems through the creation of subject representations. Indexing is usually described in the library and information science (LIS) literature as an individual work activity which relies primarily on the indexers' experience and discretionary choices (e.g., Lancaster, 1991; Foskett, 1982). The indexing activity is explained as a stable procedure, comprising a number of steps, or task decisions: 1. interpretation or subject analysis of the object of work, the document; 2. translation of the interpretation to a linguistic statement or draft subject expression; 3. translation of the draft subject expression to subject expressions, using conceptual tools like a classification scheme or a thesaurus. However, recent contributions to indexing theory (notably, Hjørland, 1997; Pejtersen, 1994; Albrechtsen, 1993; Soergel, 1985) have argued that the first decision task of subject analysis is not necessarily dependent on stable procedures or on the indexer's cognitive structures or individual preferences. Rather it is argued that subject analysis and the subsequent steps of translating a subject analysis to a subject representation of a document are dependent on broader socio-cognitive factors. Such factors include, for instance, the indexers' knowledge of the socio-historical production context for a document and its relation to other documents (intertextuality), as well as the possible information needs of target groups that the document may serve.

The present study explores indexing as a collaborative work activity where socio-cognitive factors are continually articulated, discussed and negotiated in a professional work context. The study is based on empirical work analysis of collaborative film indexing at the national film archive, Národni Filmovy Archive (NFA), of the Czech Republic. The empirical work analysis of collaborative film indexing was carried out within current research on collaborative work contexts and activities in three European film archives (Pejtersen, Albrechtsen, Cleal, Buur, Hansen, and Hertzum, 2001). The overall aim of these work place studies is to contribute to the development of a future web-based research collaboratory for European film archives (Hertzum, Pejtersen, Cleal, and Albrechtsen, 2002). The empirical work-studies of collaboration within and between the archives and their collaborating partners (individuals and institutions) have been conducted according to the framework for cognitive work analysis (Rasmussen, Pejtersen, and Goodstein, 1994). The central emphasis of the present study is to contribute to a preliminary understanding of film indexing as a collaborative work activity, through an empirical analysis of its common workspace and activities, based on the framework of cognitive work analysis.

Section 2 introduces the methodology of cognitive work analysis, which is applied by the present study for empirical analysis of collaborative film indexing at a national film archive. Section 3 addresses the archive's current practice of collaborative film indexing in terms of the common work domain and its means and ends. Section 4 explores the collaborative indexing task situations of screening meetings and film description at the archive. Section 5 identifies the common resources applied by the archive for collaborative film indexing, with special emphasis on its common conceptual tools of database formats, cataloging rules and lists of indexing terms. The constraints of the current common conceptual tools applied by the archive are discussed in Section 6. In Section 7, a means-ends model of collaborative film indexing is introduced. The intent of this model is to provide a foundation for designing new common conceptual tools that can support continual joint access to film interpretations that are shared among collaborating indexers. Section 8 discusses the findings of the study in the light of recent contributions to indexing theory and makes some suggestions for application of the new means-ends model for constructing new conceptual tools for collaborative film indexing. Section 9 is the conclusion.

2. METHODOLOGY

The framework for cognitive work analysis is part of the Cognitive Systems Engineering (CSE) methodology for work-centered evaluation and design of information systems which was developed at Risø National Laboratory (Pejtersen, Sonnenwald, Buur, Govindaraj, and Vicente, 1997; Rasmussen, Pejtersen, and Goodstein, 1994). Figure 1 (the Onion Model) illustrates the overall units of analysis that are addressed in empirical work analysis, using the framework of cognitive work analysis. Following this model, *work domain analysis* identifies the overall *means and ends structure* of the work domain. This activity results in a means-ends representation of the work domain. According to the Onion Model (Figure 1), collaborative work is analyzed in terms of the *collaboration, division of labor and social organization.* In this paper, the emphasis is not on a general analysis of collaborative work activities at the national film archive, but on analysis of the specific activity of collaborative film indexing. Consequently, this paper addresses collaboration primarily through *activity analysis* of collaborative task situations, in terms of collaborative work arrangements and collaborative task decisions in film indexing. In addition to analysis of decision-making activities in a work domain, the Onion Model addresses the actors' local competence to tackle situational work problems. Such competence can be found in the *strategies and heuristics* that the actors apply for coping with the work problems at hand. In collaborative work, the actors' strategies and heuristics are developed not only through individual work experience and formal professional background, but are also a function of collective factors, such as shared work problems and ongoing sharing of interpretations of work. In other words, the actors' competence to cope with situational work problems is also built up more informally through their choices of particular collaboration forms or work arrangements.

At the present stage, the empirical work analysis of collaborative film indexing at a national film archive primarily considers the following units of analysis:

1. The common work domain content in terms of means and ends;

2. Collaborative task situations, in terms of work arrangements and decision-making activities undertaken by the actors (situational dynamics);

3. The information resources and tools required for the actors' coping with situational dynamics

Figure 1. The Onion Model.

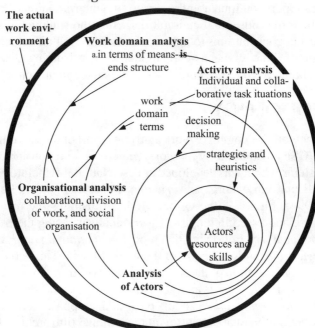

1.1 Addressing the common work domain

The present empirical analysis of collaborative film indexing builds on field studies at the Národni Filmovy Archive (NFA) (Pejtersen, Albrechtsen, Cleal, Buur, Hansen, and Hertzum, 2001). The field studies employed focus group interviews to gain knowledge about the common work domain and tasks of NFA, and the archivists' understandings of the means and ends of the common work domain. The study also draws on participant observation of work activity and interviews with archivists on collaborative indexing, with particular emphasis on the creation of a national filmography. The overall common work task, in which NFA is engaged, is research in Czech film history, based on a documentary research approach of collecting, storing, preserving and restoring national films. The research involves ongoing mediation of research results in the shape of a national filmography and through information services to and cooperation with other national research institutions. The work activity of collaborative film indexing at NFA is an important contribution to the creation of the national Czech filmography, and hence to NFA's ongoing film research activities.

The generic means ends model applied by the present study to analyze the common work domain of collaborative film indexing has five levels. The lowest level represents the resources and physical configurations that are involved in work. The next level describes the work processes in which the various resources and configurations are involved. Work functions are represented by more general concepts without reference to the work processes or resources that constitute a function. The fourth level presents the priorities that are used to coordinate resource allocation to the various general work functions. The highest level of abstraction contains the goals and constraints. In addition, the means-ends model of collaborative work domains in concurrent engineering (Pejtersen, Sonnenwald, Buur, Govindaraj, and Vicente, 1997) has inspired the present study's analysis of the common work domain of collaborative film indexing. The means-ends model developed for concurrent engineering captures and represents the interpretive perspectives from different work domains that needs to be available for actors to cope with their knowledge and information exploration in engineering design decisions.

1.2 Addressing collaborative task situations

According to for instance Schmidt (1994), the purpose of collaborative work among actors in work domains is:

a. augmenting of individual actors' capacity;

b. providing for a differentiation and combination of specialties, through involving actors with different skills and knowledge; and/or

c. opening up to mutual critical assessment or confrontation and combination of perspectives, where actors share multiple strategies and heuristics to solve a work problem or task decision.

In complex and dynamic work domains, such as film archives, stable work procedures are not the norm. Work objects, like film materials, in such domains are amenable to multiple interpretations and applications. For instance, preservation of film materials requires assessment and description of their physical states. Information retrieval of films necessitates input of information in a film database, for instance addressing interpretations and descriptive attributes of films. Actors' collaborative work procedures vary, then, according to the work problem at hand, from preservation to information retrieval of films. Regardless of such situational dynamism, the general work problems addressed in a work domain can be contextualized within the stability of a means-ends representation of work, following the framework for cognitive work analysis (see for instance

Figure 2: means-ends representation of NFA). As a further contribution to analyzing stable patterns of collaborative work contexts, the framework for cognitive work analysis considers recurrent patterns of situational dynamics in terms of the following prototypical collaborative work arrangements (Rasmussen, Pejtersen, and Goodstein, 1994):

i) *Collective work in groups*. This work arrangement is formed ad hoc to address a particular work problem or task decision. This work arrangement quickly dissolves into individual work.

ii) *Collaboration in teams*. This work arrangement is formed in the long term and may address one or several work problems or task situations in collaborative work.

iii) *Consulting colleagues in individual work*. This work arrangement is formed informally at a day-to-day basis among the actors. The criteria for choice of collaborating actor is either particular expertise or technical/domain knowledge or the closest colleague with respect to common experience with related work problems.

Analysis of decision tasks serves to determine the interpretive dynamics occurring during an individual or collaborative work task. Decision-making is more manageable when decomposed into possible subroutines shared among collaborating actors. For analysis of collaborative film indexing, the decision tasks identified may involve different interpretations of films among the actors and ongoing negotiation of interpretations of work. In addition, the actors' access to common work resources such as conceptual tools may constrain the decision-making activities in collaborative work.

1.3 Addressing common information resources and tools

Finally, cognitive work analysis considers the information resources and tools that the actors apply or develop for coping with work tasks in collaborative as well as individual task situations. Resources like human domain expertise on the one hand, and conceptual tools like cataloging rules and database formats on the other hand, may shape as well as constrain the outcome of collaborative work, for instance the outcome of collaborative film indexing at NFA: the filmography. An important feature of work domains considered by cognitive work analysis is how such resources and tools support or fail to support the actors in coping with the work problems at hand, while simultaneously supporting the actors in meeting overall priorities of the domain. Hence, the purpose of the present study on collaborative film indexing at a national film archive is not only to analyze indexing as a collaborative activity, but also to explore how current resources and tools support collaborative film indexing so as to contribute to the archive's priority of documentary film research. Consequently, the study also investigates how new models or conceptual tools may support a higher degree of accordance between the goals of the overall work task of film research, and the outcome or product of the function related to this goal, collaborative indexing. The product of collaborative indexing is in the present case a national filmography. In order to explore new models and conceptual tools for collaborative film indexing, the present study applies the interpretive model for the related domain of fiction mediation developed by Pejtersen (1994; 1986). This latter model captures the stable semantic structure of the information required by actors to cope with their decision-making activities during indexing and information retrieval of fiction.

3. THE COMMON WORK DOMAIN OF COLLABORATIVE FILM INDEXING

The overall work problem addressed by NFA is film research. This overall work problem is reflected in the goals and priorities of the archive. The means-ends representation in figure 2 shows the five work domain dimensions (1–5) of NFA in terms of its (1) goals and constraints, (2) priorities, (3) functions, (4) work processes and (5) physical resources and configurations. An important overall goal (1) of NFA is to collect, archive, and preserve and restore all film-related materials relevant for the Czech republic. This goal implies the priority of documentary research in terms of (2) collection building, documentation, preservation and publication activities. The production of a national filmography in Czech and English language is an important publication activity. This activity documents the archive's research activities and in addition contributes to the development of international awareness of Czech film culture, as reflected in NFA's overall goals (1). A number of functions (3) contribute to this priority, for instance indexing and description of films and film-related materials, acquisition of new material, participation in international activities in film indexing and description, and development and implementation of IT resources, such as databases. The work processes (4) of film indexing involve for instance weekly screening meetings and input of information in a filmography database. The physical resources (5) applied for the work processes involved in collaborative film indexing comprise full-length feature or short films, a screening room, computers, a database, a local IT-network environment and conceptual tools, such as a database format, cataloging rules and lists of indexing terms. The common work domain for collaborative film indexing, then, consists of the above-mentioned elements in the goals, priorities, and functions, processes and physical resources of the overall means-ends representation of NFA (Figure 2).

The objectives of the Czech national filmography (Opela, 1998) are to document research results by NFA and its collaborating national partners (universities, historical archives, film distributors, schools) on Czech film history. Thus, the production of the filmography is founded on a historical, documentary interest. Additional objectives include cultural mediation and dissemination of Czech film production at a national as well as international level. The primary target groups for the filmography are researchers, film students and film archivists. Important secondary target groups include film distributors, educators and other cultural mediators. The primary sources used to produce the filmography are the surviving film copies and negatives. Secondary sources comprise censorship documents, screenplays, advertisement materials and film periodicals. The information about primary sources (the films) is primarily obtained from discussions

Figure 2. Means-ends representation of NFA; Bold refers to what is discussed in the text.

Goals	Collect, archive, preserve and restore all film-related materials relevant for the Czech Republic. Ensure commercial viability, via exploitation of materials owned by NFA. National and international collaboration with archives and other professional institutions in and out of film domain. **Develop international awareness of Czech film culture.**
Constraints	Obliged to hold all films released in Czech Republic. **International code of practice for cataloging.** All income beyond 28% provided by state must be generated by NFA itself. Ownership of rights restricts commercial exploitation of archive information content. Annual audit by Ministry of Culture. Acquisition criteria.
Priorities	Dedication to collection building, documentation, preservation and publication of research results. Preservation and restoration of disappearing knowledge. Broaden appreciation for singularity of NFA collection.
Functions	Index and describe all materials of collection. Acquire new materials based on archive's own agenda. Publishing activities: **production of annual Czech filmography**, Iluminace (quarterly) and Film Review (monthly), film books. Collect material from amateur filmmakers, organize retrospectives nationally and internationally, and participate in international film festivals. **Participate in international standardization activities in film indexing**, restoration and mediation. **Develop and implement new IT resources.**
Processes	**Two groups meet weekly to watch and analyze films. Input information in filmography database.** Communication with three sites (buildings) via face-to-face contact, telephone, fax, and email. Cut, edit, and restore film material, restore and scan posters, identify and label new material.
Resources and physical configurations	**Full length feature and short films**, masters, print and negatives, videocassettes, books, journals, magazines, film scripts, digital laboratory, scanner and color printer, restoration equipment, workbenches and special chemicals, editing equipment. Cinema. **Screening room. Computers, databases, local IT-network environment. Conceptual tools: database format, cataloging rules, list of indexing terms. Human resources: staff, colleagues outside the institution**

among NFA filmography staff and national film experts at weekly film screening meetings. The screening meetings constitute one of two prototypical work situations of collaborative film indexing, explored by the present study: (1) screening meetings, and (2) film description.

4. COLLABORATIVE INDEXING TASK SITUATIONS

The overall justification for collaborative film indexing in NFA is to ensure that the production of the national filmography is carried out in compliance with the evolving body of knowledge and interests in Czech film production and mediation. Likewise, an important aim is to ensure that the film descriptions in the filmography represent a balanced reconciliation and representation of such knowledge and interests. In the terminology of document indexing, the production of the filmography involves (i) capturing knowledge of the socio-historical production context for a film and its relation to other documents (secondary sources and other primary sources—"film intertextuality"), and (ii) addressing the possible information needs of target groups that the film may serve. Currently, collaborative film indexing at NFA consists of two prototypical collaborative task situations:

(a) *Screening of film and collaborative subject analysis*: Weekly meetings at NFA where a film is screened, discussed and analyzed in a collective, synchronous work arrangement. A group of actors discuss and assess themes and socio-historical and -cultural contexts of the film.

(b) *Collaborative film description:* Entry of subject data and descriptive data by NFA's filmography staff, and carried out as distributed collaborative work. Each staff member functions as consultant for colleagues involved in the joint workspace.

4.1 Screening meetings and collaborative subject analysis

The prototypical task situation of film screening and collaborative subject analysis of films takes place at a screening room at NFA. This is an important event for collaborative film indexing, where national film experts outside NFA are invited as regular participants together with NFA's filmographers and database manager. The common workspace is the screening room, a film and an agenda for the meeting. The common work activity is to watch the film itself, participate in discussions, following a meeting agenda, and contribute with subject analyses of a film. There is a weekly screening meeting at NFA, and each screening meeting addresses one film only. The main purpose is to decide on the subjects of a film, through inviting contributions from all participants on the *overall theme(s)* as well as *interpretive contexts* of a film. Interpretive contexts addressed are the socio-cultural, -historical and technical backgrounds for the production of the film as well as subsequent reinterpretations and new versions of the film. Collaborative subject analysis of films is thus dependent on the collaborating actors' contributions on the contexts of a film across time, cultures, technologies and disciplinary paradigms and assessments of its potential for knowledge discovery, cultural mediation and contribution to new aesthetic forms. Further constraints for this work arrangement are the time schedule (one-day) and the reliability of experts involved. By the experts' reliability is meant: their ability to contribute to decisions on subject analyses and draft subject expressions that are balanced and robust enough to meet the diverse information needs of the filmography's target audiences.

The corresponding collaborative task decisions are: 1. Subject analysis of a film 2. Formulating draft subject expressions.

4.2 Collaborative film description

Following the screening meeting the staff communicate, mostly by phone, with the national film experts that participated in the screening meeting for further clarification of understandings, concepts, attributes and names of the film that was screened and discussed. The filmographers also coordinate data entry for the film with their colleagues within NFA. For this prototypical task situation, the common workspace involves the filmography, the archive's collections, a database structure, a list of indexing terms and the cataloging rules of the International Federation of Film Archives (FIAF). Although the primary work object of this collaborative task situation is still the film itself, the attention focus of the staff shifts to the creation of filmography entries. In addition, there is a shift in the division of labor, in the sense that the decision tasks of film description are carried out by the staff only. Conversely, during the screening meetings, the decision tasks involve not only the staff, but also the invited participants in the meetings.

Corresponding collaborative task decisions are: 1. Analysis of the draft subject expressions, formulated at the screening meeting, 2. Translation of this analysis into subject representations, 3. Planning filmographic entries, that is, decisions about what attributes of the database format to apply for describing a film, 4. Entering filmographic data and 5. Evaluating, reformulating and finishing the filmographic record.

5. COMMON RESOURCES APPLIED

The common resources that are applied in collaborative film indexing at NFA comprise full-length feature and short films, screening room, computers, databases and local IT-network environment. In addition, the common resources comprise a set of conceptual tools for indexing: an *alphabetical list of indexing terms*, a *database format* and the *FIAF cataloging rules for films* (Harrison, 1991). Furthermore, human expertise (staff, experts invited to screening meetings) constitutes an important common information resource in collaborative film indexing (see for example Figure 2, means-ends representation of NFA, level 5: Resources and physical configurations).

Figure 3. Database format for NFA's filmography.

Descriptive levels (field segments):	Attributes (field names):
1. Subjects of a film	Abstract Indexing terms Literary model Cast
2. Communication of film formats	Types of film materials Censorship documentation Sound systems Sources
3. Descriptive attributes, identifying the film as a unique work	Titles Names Location Year of production
4. Provenance and mediation	Name of first distributor Production and film studies Premieres Awards

NFA's filmography staff has created a *list of indexing terms*, using a bottom-up approach of ongoing indexing and cataloging of films. Management and development of the alphabetical list of indexing terms are negotiated between the database administrator and the filmographers to ensure uniformity and consistency of assigned subject representations. In addition to this list, NFA has compiled an overall list of 12 genres of films, reflecting NFA's overall typology of target groups. Presently, the semantic relationships between the indexing terms are not made explicit through, for instance a linking to the list of genre terms. Nor are they linked through the structure of, for instance, a thesaurus or a clustering of semantically related terms.

Figure 3 shows the *database format* that is currently applied in task decisions for collaborative film description by the archive. This database format has been created to comply with the *FIAF cataloging rules* (Harrison, 1991). The FIAF cataloging rules provide much guidance on how to describe a film as a unique work, through its detailed examples for each possible descriptive aspect of a film. However, the FIAF cataloging rules provide very little guidance on how to represent the *subjects* of a film. According to these rules, the decision task of creating subject representations is recommended to follow the structure and contents of universal classification schemes, in particular the Dewey Decimal Classification System, DDC (Miksa, 1998). Universal classification schemes, such as the DDC, are usually structured according to a fundamental division of scientific disciplines. Each discipline is subdivided in compliance with an assumed consensus of particular educational or disciplinary basic concepts or categories (Hjørland, and Albrechtsen, 1999; Bliss, 1929). Presently, there are few standard classification schemes for the film domain (see for instance, Rasmussen, 1997; Turner, 1994; O'Conner, 1985). The classificatory structures of these schemes reflect similar divisions of knowledge, into basic concepts and categories of a particular scholarly consensus on division of film labor. Such classifications may fruitfully represent possible knowledge interests in films, from a scholarly or educational point of view (see e.g., Hjørland, 1997; Pejtersen, 1985). However, the films' potentials for cultural or emotional experience and understanding of particular socio-cultural and -historical periods and contexts are rarely made explicit in the classifications through the presence of pertinent basic concepts. NFA's list of film indexing terms has been built to compensate for the current lack of standard conceptual tools like international classification schemes for films to support the decision task of subject representation of emotional, socio-cultural and -historical themes in films.

6. CONSTRAINTS OF CURRENT CONCEPTUAL TOOLS

NFA has been a major contributor to the development of the international FIAF cataloging rules applied for film description, through its contributions to their creation and ongoing revision. Hence, the filmography staff at NFA is committed to particular work practices that can only be learned and developed within their particular field of work. The database format for the filmography has been designed to comply with the film attributes listed in the FIAF cataloging rules. As standardized conceptual tools for filmography work, the film cataloging rules and the filmography database format applied by NFA could be said to reify particular professional practices and expertise developed within this field of work. Contrary to the stability and standardization of work practices and their reification in tools, the size of NFA's collections has grown rapidly over the last decade. Furthermore, NFA's services to their users are evolving from an almost exclusive focus on compilation and restoration of films and on-demand search requests from users, toward strategic research in the socio-cultural history of films and proactive collaborations that are targeted towards a diversity of professional user communities, at a national as well as international scale.

NFA's database format does not readily support subject representation of the diversity of film interpretations, brought forward by the participants at film screening meetings. By use of this conceptual tool for film description and information input, all interpretive contexts are currently merged into two database fields: a. indexing terms and b. abstract (Figure 3). It should be mentioned that a merging of subject representations in database fields does not in general imply that interpretive context would be lost. Using an indexing approach of pre-coordinated or syntactic indexing, information about interpretive contexts can be expressed through the sequence of indexing terms or through the assignment of roles or links between the terms (Foskett, 1982). Alternatively, such contextual information can to some degree be made explicit through arrangement of indexing terms in term networks such as thesauri or clusters of associated terms. Presently, NFA applies a post-coordinate approach to indexing, which means that terms are combined in the search phase. This in turn means that information retrieval in the filmography database is currently constrained by the lack of explicit representations of the film interpretations brought forward and discussed during collaborative subject analysis at screening meetings. The current conceptual tools (database format, cataloging rules, list of indexing terms) applied by NFA for input of information in the filmography database could be said to constitute a rather narrow conceptual cage for the rapidly growing and changing body of film knowledge. This makes it difficult to address the diversity of information needs among users searching the database.

The constraints of current conceptual tools applied for collaborative film indexing may be an important cause for a semantic drift observed in NFA's translation of subject analyses and draft subject expressions of films into subject representations of films. Semantic drift of interpretations of work is a major challenge in any collaborative work arrangement, involving actors with different skills and knowledge. In particular in loosely coupled work domains where work objects are often characterized by high degree of interpretive flexibility or ambiguity (Pinch, and Bijker, 1987). Examples in point are the design and implementation of large-scale computer-systems (Robinson, and Bannon, 1991) and case handling (Gerson, and Star, 1986). By semantic drift in the present case of collaborative film indexing is meant a shift in meaning, with respect to the extent to which subject representations (indexing terms) reflect or do not reflect particular interpretations of a film. Semantic drift in translating interpretations and subject analyses of documents to representations can be a consequence of a change in place of the object of interpretation, or work object (a film) and the interpretation itself (the subject analysis of a film). For instance a shift from the screening room at NFA to a filmographer's individual work place (e.g., Robinson, and Bannon, 1991; Gerson, and Star, 1986). Likewise, a semantic drift can be due to a change of attention focus, in the present case, from a focus on a film as the work object to a filmography entry as the work object, or it can be due to a change in the division of labor (Schmidt, 1994). However, as will be discussed in the following, the semantic drift in the present case of collaborative film indexing is in particular due to the lack of affordances in existing applied conceptual tools to express an overall conceptual view of recurrent interpretive perspectives of a film.

7. A MEANS-ENDS MODEL FOR COLLABORATIVE FILM INDEXING

Following the framework of cognitive work analysis, the common resources applied by the actors involved in collaborative work may constrain the actors' coping with a situational work problem. Conceptual tools like cataloging rules, database formats and classification schemes are a particular type of common resources, as symbolic artifacts (Schmidt, 1994) that provide collaborating actors with stable representations of shared work objects as well as shared interpretations of these objects. In the case of collaborative film indexing at NFA, the films and their interpretive contexts are the primary work objects for filmography production. Figure 4 illustrates the means-ends perspectives of collaborative film indexing (subject analysis and description), from original goals and values of a film (level 1) to archive attributes (level 5). The means-ends perspectives of collaborative film indexing (figure 4) are introduced here as a model that can be applied as a basis for design of new conceptual tools for collaborative film indexing. A means-ends model that was previously created for the related common work domain of fiction mediation inspired the model. (Pejtersen, 1994; 1986). The compliance and difference in means-ends perspectives of subject analysis and description of films between NFA's current model, as implemented in NFA's database format for the filmography, and the means-ends perspectives of collaborative film indexing are also illustrated in figure 4. In this figure, the field attributes of NFA's database format are mapped towards the means-ends perspectives of the new suggested model for film indexing.

7.1 Decision tasks in collaborative subject analysis with reference to the means-ends model for film indexing

The collaborative decision tasks of film analysis during discussions at screening meetings at NFA currently address all levels of film knowledge, as represented in the means-ends model for film indexing (Figure 4). The participating actors are experts representing a diversity of knowledge interests in film research and mediation. The collective and synchronous task situation of a screening meeting is intended to bring forward knowledge from all actors on overall theme(s) of a film as well as its interpretive contexts. While the actors at the screening meetings contribute with information on original titles, locations and production and film studios, a main emphasis is on exploring the overall theme of a film and the film's interpretive contexts over time. These perspectives or attributes of a film are in particular addressed in dimensions 1 and 2 of the means-ends model for film indexing (Figure 4): 1. Goals and values of film, and 2. General and specific content in a film. Corresponding collaborative task decisions are (i) subject analysis and (ii) translation of subject analysis to draft subject expression.

7.2 Decision tasks in collaborative film description with reference to the means-ends model of collaborative film indexing

An important general hypothesis of the means-ends approach to conceptualization of work domains is that the objects and concepts of the work domain are ontologically distinct. The structure of knowledge is modeled in a stratified hierarchy, ranging from resources and physical configurations to high-level purposes that can be met by several resources and physical arrangements (Rasmussen, Pejtersen, and Goodstein, 1994). The objects or concepts in one stratum are

Figure 4. Means-ends model for collaborative film indexing; Italic/bold = attribute expression, applied in the NFA filmography.

1. Goals and values of film	
Why?	*(1)Intentions and goals:* Communication of information; education; promotion and stimulation of ideas and emotional, socio-cultural and aesthetic experience; ***Literary model (novel, novella, short story, theatre play)*** *Constraints*: **censorship,** production means
Why?	*(2) Originators' affiliation and attitude:* Professional paradigms (narrative/aesthetic style, form, etc.) and their socio-historical context, political and cultural movements, or other value criteria
2. General and specific content in film	
When?	*(3) General frame/time content:*Time, year, historical period
Where?	*(4) General frame/place content:* Place and setting, geographical, historical, socio-cultural contexts of the topic
What?	*(5) Subject matter content:*Specific topic and plots; psychological and social phenomena; ending of film; ***Contents (abstract of film), keywords (indexing terms)***
Who?	*(6) Living beings, institutions and artifacts:* Main characters, persons, animals, plants, institutions that are involved in the topic ***Cast (names)***
3. Communication and presentation of film format	
How?	*(7) Film types and formats* ***Types of film materials***
How?	*(8) Accessibility level:* ***Censorship documentation cards, contemporary documentation, sources, bibliography (reviews etc.), indexes***
How?	*(9) Physical characteristics:* ***Sound systems,*** etc.
4. Filmography attributes	
Who?	*(10) Filmographic data and identification numbers:* ***Film titles, names of director, assistant director, story, screenplay, director of photography, set designer, art director, costume designer, editor, sound, introductory title designer, production manager, music and songs (composers, titles)***
Where?	***Locations***
When?	***Year of production***, version
What?	Type of material
How?	Size and format
5. Archive attributes	
Why?	*(11) Archive goals and policies* *(12) Local archival conditions:*Shelving, storage
When?	Preservation, restoration, sales and lending of films and videos
6. Distribution, provenance, mediation	
Why?	*(13) Distributors', donators' etc. goals and policies:* ***Name of first distributor***
Where?	(14) ***Production and film studios***
When?	(15) ***Premieres (dates), awards***

what can be applied as means to generate the end of a higher stratum. Such linkages can be identified in the means-ends model for collaborative film indexing. For instance, the physical characteristics of sound systems used in a film (level 3) can be regarded as means to give voice to the dialog among the characters of a film (level 4). Conversely, the promotion of particular ideas through the medium of a film (level 1) can be realized through the choice of a particular time frame, subject matter content (plot), main characters and cast (level 2).

This quality of the means-ends model is applicable for the actors' decision tasks in collaborative film indexing of formulating subject representations and evaluation of a filmographic entry. For instance, an entry for the filmography database can be evaluated at any stage in the work process, through circumscribing a filmographic description to a linguistic statement. A means-ends representation of Gustav Machatý's film "Ecstasy" (English title), 1932, is provided in Figures 5a–5b.

Linguistic circumscriptions of means-ends film representations can iterate throughout the task decisions of collaborative film indexing. Thus, it can be assumed that a conceptual tool, based on the means-ends model for film collaborative indexing, can facilitate the work task, regardless of whether collaborative film indexing is carried out in a sequential or concurrent manner. The following example illustrates a linguistic circumscription of the means-ends representation of Gustav Machatý's film "Ecstasy" (English title), 1932 (see Figures 4 and 5a–b):

> This film received its premiere on 20 January 1933, was produced at Vinohrady Studios and external locations of Prague etc., and is distributed by Slavia-film (level 6). Produced in 1932, its original title is "Extase" (cz.), director is Gustav Machatý, assistant director is Alexander Hackenschmied, etc. (level 4). The general and specific content

Figure 5a. Means ends representation of "Ecstacy" by Gustav Machatý.

1. Goals and values of film	
Why?	*(1) Intentions and goals:* Women's sexual emancipation as a path to social and cultural liberation; personal freedom linked to gender equality in society; rebellion against previous models of relations between women and men; passion as original individual life force; the human being in a natural, instinctual state ***Literary model:*** drama ***Censored***: 1933 (grounds: nudity, violation of traditional values of marriage and women's sexuality)
Why?	*(2) Originators' affiliation and attitude:* Cultural movement: Czech modernism; Socio-cultural background: youth rebellion; distancing from pre-nazi movement in Germany
2. General and specific content in film	
When?	*(3) General frame/time content:* Time: 1930s
Where	*(4) General frame/place content:* Prague; bourgeois environment; country side; estate
What?	*(5) Subject matter content:* Women's emotions; marriage between young woman and elderly man; pedantry; divorce; young lover; passion; sex; nudity; husband's suicide; child birth ***Contents: see figure 5 b.***
Who?	*(6) Living beings, institutions and artifacts:* Young woman; old man; father; young lover ***Cast/stars:*** Hedy Kieslerová (Eva); Zvonimir Rogoz (Emil Jerman); Aribert Mog (Adam)
3. Communication and presentation of film format	
How?	***Types of film materials***: [omitted]
How?	*(8) Accessibility level,* ***Sources:*** [omitted]; ***Bibliography:*** [omitted]
How?	*(9) Physical characteristics:* ***Sound systems:*** n/a
4. Filmography attributes	
Who?	*(10) Filmographic data and identification numbers:* ***Film title***: Exstase (cz.); ***Director:*** Gustav Machatý; ***Assistant director:*** Alexander Hackenschmied; ***Original source:*** Gustav Machatý, ***Screenplay:*** Gustav Machatý; Frantisek Horký; ***Camera:*** Jan Stallich; ***Art director:*** Bohumil Hes; ***Editor:*** Antonín Zelenka, ***Sound supervisor:*** Josef Zora; ***Commentary written by:*** František Halas; ***Production supervisor:*** Frantísek Horký; ***Music composer:*** Guiseppe Becce
Where	***Locations:*** n/a
When?	***Year of production***: 1932; ***Version:*** Gustav Machaty, Elekta
What?	Type of material: n/a
How?	Size and format: n/a
5. Archive attributes	
Why?	*(11) Archive goals and policies* *(12) Local archival conditions* Shelving, storage (n/a)
When?	Preservation, restoration, sales and lending of films and videos (n/a)
6. Distribution, provenance, mediation	
Why?	*(13) :* ***Name of first distributor:*** Slavia-film
Where?	*(14)* ***Production and film studios; studios:*** Vinohrady ***External locations:*** Podkarpatská Rus; Prague; Brrandov; Slovensko
When?	*(15)* ***Premiere:*** 20 January 1933; ***Awards:*** n/a

Figure 5b. Content description of "Ecstacy" by Gustav Machatý
(From Opela, 1888, pp. 88-89)

Re: Means-ends level 2, General and specific content of film
Contents: Eva, the daughter of a landowner, marries the well off but many years older Emil Jerman. Upon returning from the marriage ceremony to their luxurious Prague apartment she realizes her mistake: her husband shows no interest in her as a woman. The sensitive girl suffers from his cold and bachelor's meticulousness so much that she returns to her father's estate and requests a divorce on grounds of insuperable revulsion. While bathing in the pond Eva meets Adam, a young civil engineer working close by on a highway construction site. The man is the exact opposite of her husband: though he looks robust, he acts gently. During a nighttime storm Eva goes after him to his house and becomes his lover. Only now she knows the passion of love. Her husband receives a court dispatch and sets off after Eva and beseeches her, to no avail, to return. On the way back he comes across Adam and realizes who he is. Both men are staying in a village inn where Eva comes to visit Adam. The husband commits suicide in his room. His death comes between the lovers. Adam returns to his work, Eva gives birth to a child.

of the film is the 1930s of bourgeois environment in Prague in conflict with the environments of an estate and a village on the countryside. The main characters are a young woman, elderly man, father, young lover (cast: Hedy Kieslerova, Zonomir Rogoz and Aribert Mog). The plot involves the topics of women's emotions, marriage between a young woman and an elderly man, pedantry, divorce, young lover, passion, sex, nudity, husband's suicide, child birth (level 2). The overall intentional value of the film is, through its genre as a drama, and coming from the director's affiliation with Czech modernism and sympathy with the youth rebellion, to promote the idea of women's sexual emancipation as a path to general social and cultural liberation. To show how personal freedom is linked to gender equality in society, to offer an alternative to previous models of relations between men and women, such as marriage, to show how passion is the original individual life force and to show the human being in its natural, instinctual state. These intentional values were the major motivations for the censorship of the film in 1933 (level 1).

In comparison, the corresponding entry for the film in the filmography (Opela, 1998, pp. 88–89) primarily addresses film content and attributes that are related to the levels 2–6 of the means-ends model (Figures 4 and 5a–5b). For level 2 of the means-ends model (General and specific content in film), NFA's filmography entry neither addresses the general frame/time content, nor the general frame/place content. As a result it could be claimed that the socio-cultural and -historical contexts of the film's intentions and goals, which in the present case constitutes the overall theme of the film, are only marginally available as subject representations in the present filmography entry (Opela, 1998, pp. 88–89).

8. DISCUSSION

The high degree of task uncertainty in subject analysis during the indexing activity in general has been discussed in the library and information science (LIS) literature by in particular Hjørland (1997), Albrechtsen (1993) and Frohmann (1990). These contributions to indexing theory consider the socio-cognitive factors like production context of documents (for example, scientific paradigms, discourse communities and disciplines) and the use of documents by particular disciplines or discourse communities as fundamental interpretive constraints and opportunities for the indexers' decision task of subject analysis. However, the decision task of translating a subject analysis to a subject representation will equally constrain or facilitate subject access. This latter problem has rarely been addressed in the LIS literature, except as generic recommendations (e.g., Lancaster, 1991; Foskett, 1982). Recently, Mai (2001) has reintroduced the theme of translating a subject analysis and draft subject expression to a subject representation as a fundamental interpretive constraint for users' subject access to documents in information retrieval systems. Traditionally, the decision task of translating draft subject expressions to subject representations like indexing terms is considered an individual cognitive process of mapping between terms in linguistic draft subject expressions towards the conceptual tools of indexing languages like classification schemes, thesauri or alphabetical lists of indexing terms. According to Mai (2001), however, all decision tasks that are involved in document indexing, including the assignment of indexing terms, are primarily dependent on socio-cognitive factors such as the indexer's knowledge of a document's possible interpretive contexts. In other words, it is argued that interpretive contexts of a document may constitute a stable conceptual environment throughout all steps or decision tasks of document indexing. This contribution by Mai implies that regardless of an indexer's shift of attention focus, from a document during subject analysis, to application of indexing terms from indexing languages to represent the subject of a document, the *work object—the document and the indexer's interpretation of the document*—remains as primary. In collaborative indexing, then, interpretive stability of indexing is not only driven by conceptual tools such as classification schemes or database formats, nor solely a function of consensus building among actors, but is equally determined by the indexers' access to a diversity of interpretations shared among collaborating actors.

The present study has addressed the theme of translating a subject analysis to indexing terms through an empirical analysis of collaborative film indexing activities at a national film archive. Using the framework for cognitive work analysis, the study identified two recurrent collaborative task situations: (a) screening of film and subject analysis, and (b) film description and information input. During the collaborative task situation of film screening, the film and its possible interpretations were a primary attention focus for the participants' joint subject analysis. During the subsequent collaborative task situation of film description, the actors' attention focus was found to shift to the filmographic entry. The actors' ongoing communication with colleagues inside and outside the archive during this latter task situation could, in the terminology of cognitive work analysis, be viewed as a recurrent strategy to retain the stability of a film analysis. Furthermore, because the task situation of film description involves clarification of analyses brought forward by participants at the meeting, it can be assumed that it may give rise to new possible interpretations of a film. The current practice of collaborative film analysis at the workplace studied was found to have the advantage of eliciting a diversity of interpretations of films. However, it was found that a semantic drift, or a shift in meaning, occurred when subject analyses and draft subject expressions were translated into subject representations. Such semantic drift may be due to the actors' ongoing reinterpretations of the film itself during their consultations with colleagues following a screening meeting. The present study has argued, however, that a primary constraint for sustaining interpretive stability in the empirical case of collaborative film indexing was the common conceptual tools currently applied for film description: the database format, the standard code of cataloging practice and the list of indexing terms.

The study introduced a means-ends model for collaborative film indexing (Figure 4). The intent of this model was to provide a foundation for designing new common conceptual tools for continuous support of collaborative film analysis and description. The current common conceptual tools for film indexing applied by the archive studied, in particular the database format and cataloging rules, function as codes of practice for input of information in the archive's filmography database. Due to their lack of attributes to support the articulation of interpretive contexts of a film, these conceptual tools are not readily applicable for film analysis, for instance during discussions at film screening meetings. In other words, the affordances of current conceptual tools applied by the archive are not completely in alignment with the overall ambition of the archive's approach to documentary research, addressing a diversity of user needs. Alternatively, a new conceptual tool for collaborative film indexing, based on the means-ends model (Figure 4), may function not only to support the work processes of film interpretation and analysis as well as film description. A conceptual tool, based on the means-ends model, may also align the work processes of collaborative indexing with the archive's overall priority, or implicit indexing policy of addressing heterogeneous user needs. Possible applications and opportunities of the means-ends model include:

- Making visible the state of work in collaborative indexing activities, ranging from film screening to production of filmographies. The conceptual tool can be introduced at screening meetings as a schema for taking notes on decisions made, and be used for iterations and evaluations of decisions if applied for minutes from the meeting. If the conceptual tool is made available for task decisions involved in collaborative film indexing, it can be applied for continuous backtracking and reassessment of filmographic entries.

- Concurrent collaborative film indexing, where all actors participating in a screening meeting on a film have access to annotate filmographic entries with comments as the entries are developed locally in a filmography database, provided that the state of work is made visible to all actors throughout the production process.

- Design of a classification scheme or a thesaurus, through using the perspectives of the means-ends model as a fundamental division of lists of indexing terms.

9. CONCLUSION

The empirical work analysis of collaborative film indexing has focused on the means and ends of the common work domain, the collaborative task situations, the conceptual tools applied and the decision activities of collaborative film indexing at a national film archive. Traditionally, indexing is considered an individual activity, relying on stable procedures and the indexer's preferences. Based on the framework for cognitive work analysis, the study addressed the indexing activity as a common work problem, shared by several actors within one work domain, engaged in the production of a national filmography. Several common points of reference and work practices were found to guide the actors' decisions. These common factors included the common work overall problem of national film research and mediation through the creation of a national filmography and the common resources applied. The study in particular focused on how the current common conceptual tools supported or failed to support the actors in coping with work problems at hand so as to contribute to the archive's overall priorities of addressing a diversity of user communities. An important aim of the empirical work analysis of collaborative film indexing was not only to understand the current work practice of the archive, but also to contribute with new ideas for the development of common conceptual tools that may articulate a stable interpretive environment for collaborative film indexing. It was argued that such conceptual tools could be developed on the basis of a means-ends model of the interpretive perspectives of film mediation. Future work on development of conceptual tools for collaborative film indexing will focus on empirical evaluation of prototypes of conceptual tools, based on means-ends analysis of film mediation. This will look, in particular, at how annotations to filmographic data entries created locally at several film archives may involve collaborating actors across and outside archive sites and contribute to the creation of an open-ended and interactive film research collaboratory for European film archives.

ACKNOWLEDGEMENTS

This study was supported by the Danish National Research Foundation through its funding of the Centre for Human-Machine Interaction and by the European Commission's Information Society Technologies Programme through its funding of the Collate project on collaboratories for annotation, indexing, and retrieval of digitized historical archive material (IST-1999-20882). We thank our informants at Národni Filmový Archive, Prague, Czech Republic.

REFERENCES

Albrechtsen, H. (1993) Subject analysis and indexing: from automated indexing to domain analysis. *The Indexer, 18*, 217–24.

Bliss, H. (1929) *The organization of knowledge and the system of the sciences.* New York: Holt.

Foskett, A. C. (1982) *The subject approach to information.* London: Clive Bingley.

Frohmann, B. (1990) Rules of indexing: a critique of mentalism in information retrieval theory. *Journal of Documentation, 46*, 81–101.

Gerson, E., and S. L. Star. (1986) Analyzing due process in the work place. *ACM Transactions on Office Information Systems, 4*, 257–70.

Harrison, H. (1991) *The FIAF cataloging rules for film archives.* New York: K. G. Saur. (Papers and reference tools for film archivists dealing with audiovisual material, vol. 1).

Lancaster, F. W. (1991) *Indexing and abstracting in theory and practice.* London: The Library Association.

Hertzum, M., A. M. Pejtsersen, B. Cleal, and H. Albrechtsen. (2002) An analysis of collaboration in three film archives: A case for collaboratories. In H. Bruce, R. Fidel, P. Ingwersen, and P. Vakkari (eds.). *Emerging Frameworks and Methiods Proceedings of the Fourth International Conceptions of Library and Information Science.* Greenwood Village, CO: Libraries Unlimited.

Hjørland, B., and H. Albrechtsen. (1999) An analysis of some trends in classification research. *Knowledge Organization, 26*, 131–39.

Hjørland, B. (1997) *Information seeking and subject representation. An activity-theoretical approach to information science.* London: Greenwood Press.

Mai, J. E. (2001) Semiotics and indexing: an analysis of the subject indexing process. *Journal of Documentation, 57*, 591–622.

Miksa, F. (1998) *The DDC, the universe of knowledge, and the post-modern library.* New York: Forest Press.

O'Conner, B. (1985) Access to moving image documents: background concepts and proposals for surrogates for film and video works. *Journal of Documentation, 4,* 209–20.

Opela, V., ed. (1998) *Czech feature film II, 1930–1945.* Prague: National Film Archive.

Pejtersen, A. M., H. Albrechtsen, B. Cleal, C. B. Hansen, and M. Hertzum. (2001) *A web-based multimedia collaboratory. Empirical work studies in film archives.* Roskilde: Risø National Laboratory (Risø-R-1284 (EN)—CHMI-02-01).

Pejtersen, A. M., D. Sonnenwald, J. Buur, T. Govinderaj, and K. Vicente. (1997) The design explorer project: using a cognitive framework to support knowledge exploration. *Journal of Engineering Design, 8,* pp. 289–301.

Pejtersen, A. M. (1994) A framework for indexing and representation of information based on work domain analysis. H. Albrechtsen, and S. Ornager (eds.). *Knowledge Organization and Quality Management: Proceedings of the International ISKO Conference, 3, held 20–24 June 1994, Copenhagen, Denmark* (252–62). Frankfurt: Indeks Verlag.

Pejtersen, A. M. (1986) Implications of users' value perception for the design of a bibliographic retrieval system. J. C. Agrawal, and P. Zunde (eds.). *Empirical Foundations of Information and Software Science* (23–39). New York and London: Plenum Press.

Pinch, T. J., and W. Bijker. (1987) The social construction of facts and artifacts: or how the Sociology of Science and the Sociology of Technology might benefit each other." In W. E. Bijker, T. P. Hughes, and T. J. Pinch (eds.). *The Social Construction of Technological Systems. New Directions in the Sociology and History of Technology.* Cambridge (London): The MIT Press, 1987, 17–50.

Rasmussen, E. (1997) Indexing images. *Annual Review of Information Science and Technology (ARIST), 32,* 169–96.

Rasmussen, J., A. M. Pejtersen, and L. P. Goodstein. (1994) *Cognitive Systems Engineering.* New York: John Wiley.

Robinson, M., and L. Bannon. (1991) Questioning representations. *Proceedings of 2nd European Conference on Computer-Supported Cooperative Work, ECSCW 91, held Amsterdam, September 1991* (219–33). Amsterdam: Kluwer.

Schmidt, K. (1994) *Modes and mechanisms of interaction in cooperative work.* Roskilde: Risø National Laboratory (Risø-R-666-EN).

Turner, J. (1994) *Determining the subject content of still and moving image documents for storage and retrieval: an experimental investigation.* Toronto: University of Toronto (PhD thesis).

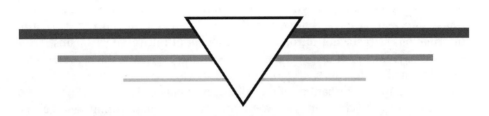

Principia Informatica:
Foundational Theory of Information
and Principles of Information Services

Birger Hjørland
Royal School of Library and Information Science
6 Birketinget, 2300 Copenhagen S, Denmark
bh@db.dk

ABSTRACT

Library and information science (LIS) may alternatively be labeled library, information and documentation studies (LID) or just information science (IS). In taking IS serious as a research field, this paper presents an understanding of one of its core concepts (information) and outlines its fundamental principles. It is shown that there exist hierarchies of information processing mechanisms in nature and culture and that IS is concerned with only the highest forms of such mechanisms, which consist of libraries, electronic databases and related information services. Theories about such high-level information systems are closely related to theoretical views of knowledge, language, documents, cognition, science and communication. Information scientists are not the only experts involved in the handling of information, and a view of our special role is presented. The aspiration of this article is to provide a synopsis of the fundamentals of IS: Principia Informatica.

1. INTRODUCTION: INFORMATION DEFINED

The complex etymological, transdisciplinary and theoretical status of the information concept has been surveyed by Capurro and Hjørland (2002). In this paper one theoretical view will be presented based on Karpatschof's interpretation of information and activity theory, or AT. (2000, p. 128ff.) In order to define information, Karpatschof introduces the concept of release mechanisms, being systems having at their disposal a store of potential energy, with the systems being "designed" to let this energy out in specific ways whenever trigged by a signal fulfilling the specifications of the release mechanism. The signal that triggers a certain release mechanism is a low energy phenomenon fulfilling some release specifications. The signal is thus the *indirect cause*, and the process of the release mechanism *the direct cause* of the resulting reaction, which is a high-energy reaction compared to the energy in the signal. *Information* is thus defined as a quality by a given signal relative to a certain mechanism. The release mechanism has a double function: (1) it reinforces the weak signal and (2) it directs the reaction by defining the functional value of a signal in the pre-designed system of the release mechanism. There has been a tendency to consider information to be an obscure category in addition to the classical categories of physics. Information is indeed a new category, but it cannot be placed, eclectically, beside the prior physical categories. Information is a category, not *beside*, but indeed *above* the classical categories of physics. Therefore, information is neither directly reducible to these classical categories, nor is it a radically different category of another nature than mass and energy. Information is, in fact, the causal result of existing physical components and processes. Moreover, it is an *emergent* result of such physical entities. This is revealed in the systemic definition of information. It is a relational concept that includes the *source*, the *signal*, the *release mechanism* and the *reaction* as its relatants. The release mechanism is a signal processing system and an information processing system.

2. THE BIOLOGICAL DEVELOPMENT OF INFORMATION PROCESSING MECHANISMS

Living organisms can be seen as material systems that are genetically programmed to maintain and replicate themselves by engaging their worlds in goal-directed ways. This is, according to Bogdan (1994), "the trick of life" (p. 1). Living organisms have goals that must be satisfied, and for that, organisms must locate and identify their goals. Organisms must guide themselves to their goals. In order to do so organisms need behaviourally relevant information about their environment. Such information can be processed by the organism, data can be stored, problems solved and behaviour modified. In short: organisms perform cognitive tasks, and in the course of evolution, they develop cognitive mechanisms (perception, memory, thinking, etc.) in order to adapt themselves to their environments. This is the point of view of evolutionary biology and psychology.

Information is not in itself the basic motivation or the goal for "the informa-tion processing organism." Food, sex partners or a safe place to reside could be the goal. Information is just something that helps guide the organism to a goal. The same object may inform one organism about some kind of possible actions and another organism about other possible actions. The informativeness of an object is thus subjective in its dependence on the perceiving organism, its goals, cognitive apparatus, pre-existing knowledge and its current state. The same ob-ject (and the same physical signals from that object) can mean "enemy" and "danger" to one organism while meaning "food" or "pleasure" to another.

The Russian psychologist A. N. Leontyev (1981) described the develop-ment of psychological functions as a set of functions developed by higher ani-mals in order to improve their adaptation to the changing conditions of life. He distinguishes five stages or levels from primitive organisms to Homo sapiens:

1. *The stage of irritability* is characteristic of the absorption of food par-ticles through the surface of the body of one-celled animals. Leontyev does not see such behaviour as evidence of something psychical. (It is a pre-form of psychological behaviour.)

2. *The stage of sensory psyche* can be exemplified by insects, birds and fish. It is characterised by the ability of the organism to sense influ-ences, but the animal cannot integrate different influences into a whole. Animals at this stage of development show stiff or rigid pat-terns of reactions, i.e., instinctive forms of behaviour. Leontyev sees this stage as psychical in its most primitive form.

3. *The stage of perceptual psyche* is first and foremost characterised by the perception of objects. The organism is now not just limited to sensing and responding to sound, light, simple forms, etc., but per-ceives specific objects (e.g., flies). This allows much more flexible forms of behaviour directed towards that object.

4. *The stage of intellect* is associated with actions which presuppose the use of tools. The organism is no longer solely dependent on its own body. This stage is found in man and chimpanzees.

5. *The stage of consciousness* is specifically human. According to the the-ory of Leontyev it is associated with language and societal production.

What is described here can be interpreted as a theory of the development of biological stages of information utilisation behaviour from more primitive, spe-cific and passive forms of sensing information towards more advanced, com-plex, flexible and active forms of information utilisation.

The theory is materialistic in the sense that its stages are motivated by the view of the psychical as being something secondary compared to its environ-ment. The subjective, consciousness, concepts, psychological processes and states are all seen as phenomena developed from the material world in order to

improve higher animals' adaptation to their environment. Psychological phenomena cannot be understood without considering the environment and the
challenges that face the organism. Subject and object are two interwoven parts,
which can be understood as a historically developed relationship. From
Leontyev's perspective psychical and subjective phenomena are naturalistic;
they developed with birds, fish and insects, and further through evolution. Although dominant theories in cognitive science may also be termed materialistic,
they are reductive and eliminative in a sense disapproved by activity theory. Although not recognized as part of the foundation of *biosemiotics* by, for example,
Hoffmeyer (1998), activity theory is in fact a *semiotic* theory (a social semiotic
theory). Organisms are seen as reacting to informative objects as signs. For
Charles Sanders Peirce a sign is a triadic unity of *something* (the sign vehicle,
e.g., a footprint) which stands to somebody (the interpretant) for *something else*
(the object, e.g., that a person has passed by). Information is not a thing or sub-
stance but a sign.

Anything can thus be informative for somebody about something. It is always possible to construct some release mechanism that reacts to some specific
signal or difference. Buckland (1991) writes that the concept of information can
be used about things, about processes and about knowledge: According to Buckland things can be informative. A stump of a tree contains information about its
age as well as about the climate during the lifetime of the tree. In similar ways,
anything might in some imaginable circumstances be informative: "We conclude that *we are unable to say confidently of anything that it could not be information*" (Buckland, 1991, p. 50. Italics in original). Just as *any* thing
could/might be symbolic, Buckland maintains that any thing could be informative and thus information.

3. THE CULTURAL DEVELOPMENT OF INFORMATION PROCESSING MECHANISMS

Compared to other species human beings are far less depending on their biological cognitive systems and much more depending on their cultural heritage.
This is something strongly neglected by mainstream behavioral and cognitive
theories from the 20th century. A person's capacity to process and store information is not just depending on her biological make-up, but also on the language
and symbolic systems that the person masters. This is empirically shown by cultural anthropologists like Goody (1987) and theoretically mostly developed in
activity theory. Recently cognitive scientists like Lock and Peters (1999) have
begun to study *Human Symbolic Evolution*. Jack Goody is probably the most important researcher on the cognitive implications of writing, literacy, and the alphabet. His research has immense relevance for cognitive science and LID.

The line of theory developed by Vygotsky . . . maintains that when an individual comes to master writing, the basic system underlying the nature of his mental processes is changed fundamentally as the external symbol system comes to mediate the organization of all his basic intellectual operations. Thus, for example, knowledge of a writing system would alter the very structure of memory, classification and problem-solving by altering the way in which these elementary processes are organized to include an external (written) symbol system. (Goody, 1987, p. 205)

Important cultural developments include the development of oral languages, the development of written languages, the development of mathematical symbols, music scores and other symbolic systems. Also the development of institutions of learning, of different media and genres, different kinds of quality management (including peer reviewed scientific journals, historical criticism or source criticism and research methodologies such as experimental methods) are important. All such kinds of developments alter the ways in which information is being processed both in an individual and in a social perspective.

How, for example, our concepts are formed by our languages is shown in the figure below. It shows that there is no one-to one relation between meanings in different languages. Languages affect the way we conceptualize the world. According to Hjelmslev (1943) each language put *arbitrary* borders on reality, while AT finds that our symbolic systems tend to capture functional aspects or affordances in the things we perceive (cf. Albrechtsen, et al., 2001).

Figure 1. Cultural relativity in word meanings.

English	*German	*Danish	*French	Italian	Spanish
Tree	Baum	Træ	arbre	albero	Árbol
Wood	Holz		bois	legno	Leña
		skov			Madera
Woods	Wald			bosco	Bosque
Forest			forêt	foresta	Selva

*Originally presented by the Danish structural linguist Louis Hjelmslev, 1943.
Extended by information from Buckley (2001).

For human informative activities, the proper perspective of the meaning of "meaning" is very important. This is a difficult concept of which activity theory provides a fruitful understanding. The production of books, texts and other documents is a special development in literate cultures. Documents are tools having specific kinds of functional values in those cultures. The view of *social semiotic* theories is that meanings, signs and documents are developed to function in relation to *standardized practices in communities*. We use, for example, the Bible and the Hymn Book in our standardized religious practices. We use textbooks in our standardized teaching practices, law books in standardized legal practices, etc. Concepts and documents have more or less stable functional values in relation to such standardized practices. There are of course always different views of whether such standardized practices should be changed or remain unchanged, and there are always different kinds of possible changes of those practices. Often scientific and technological development changes standardized practices in a rather uncontroversial way. In other cases, however, changes in practices are related to different political interests, to different theories or "paradigms." Different paradigms tend to influence given practices in different ways, and by doing so they also tend to change our symbolic systems as well as our production of documents and the form, content and use of those documents. The proper study of symbols and documents is thus based on the study of the functions and interests those documents are serving.

Any given tool (including a sign, concept, theory, finding or document) has *given* potentialities in relation to new social practices and paradigms. Users of libraries may discover that hitherto neglected documents may be very useful to develop a new social practice or to defend an existing practice. Or they may find that well-known documents may be re-interpreted and used in new ways. Especially the kinds of documents known as "classics" have such abilities to be re-used and re-interpreted by each generation. But even the most humble documents may turn out to be of value. "The dust of one age is the gold of another" (Hesselager, 1980). This does not, of course, imply relativism regarding the relevance of documents: mostly tools quickly become obsolete and "only of historical interest." There may of course also be a discrepancy between the potential value of some documents and the cost of storing, organizing and using them.

The meaning of any sign is its potential quality of referring to some objects or states of affairs (Karpatschof, 2000, p. 197). A tool is something that has a functional value for some human (sub)culture. Languages (and sublanguages) are also tools with functional values. In languages, there are terms for tools. The meaning of a word for a certain kind of tool is the functional value of referring to a certain functional value, defining the quality of the tool. (Karpatschof, 2000, p. 197) A hammer may, for example, be termed "hammer" (denotation) or "murder-weapon" (connotation). The word we use about a tool facilitates one or another use of it. Words may be more or less appropriately used for a specific object in relation to a given task, activity or discourse. In other words: To use words is a kind of act (verbal acts) often used to accomplish something extra-verbal. The meanings of the words we use may be more or less suitable for our purpose, and in that case we try to develop new words or change the meaning of some old words. Such changes in meanings are visible in the study of different fields, traditions and paradigms.

It is very naive and reductionistic to disregard such kinds of cultural inter-mediating factors in people's relationship with information. The dominant traditions in both information science and in behavioral and cognitive sciences have, however, neglected such cultural aspects and just tried to study generalized persons' relation to something termed "information." This dominant approach may broadly be termed "behavioral" in spite of different attitudes to versions of behaviorism. In this tradition people are expected to react to something in a specific, mechanical way without considering the culturally determined meanings and without considering the different goals and values in the meanings and in the documents. This has, in my opinion, brought about a situation in which we have inherited very little useful knowledge from these areas on which to advance our field and practice. That view is also expressed by Beaugrande (1997) in linguistics. "I would certainly be happier if my findings had turned out to be less sobering or disturbing; but I can only report what I have in fact found" (p. 89).

4. INFORMATION PROCESSING AND THE SOCIAL DIVISION OF LABOR

The official definition of information science given by *American Society for Information Science and Technology* states that:

> Information science is concerned with the generation, collection, organization, interpretation, storage, retrieval, dissemination, transformation and use of information, with particular emphasis on the applications of modern technologies in these areas. (Borko, 1968; Griffith, 1980)

This definition does not discuss how other professions than information scientists are concerned with "the generation, collection, organization, interpretation, storage, retrieval, dissemination, transformation and use of information." Just a little thinking tells us that many professions can claim to be equally concerned. By neglecting this issue, the definition in fact fails to define information science because a definition of IS should specify the *special role* of information professionals in studying or handling information.

Astronomers, for example, can be seen as experts who identify, process and interpret information from the universe. Astronomers "read" both nature and books, but nature is mostly considered the key information in the sciences. As products of their activities they may publish their empirical and theoretical findings. The library, documentation and information profession although interested in all kind of documents, has a core interest and expertise connected to communication of published documents. Information scientists are *not* experts in interpreting the information from the stars, but at the most experts in information documented by, for example, astronomers (by indexing and retrieving astronomical documents, etc.). In this example information has been defined in a broader sense than usually implied in information science. A closer discussion about this dilemma in the definition of information is provided by Capurro and Hjørland, 2002.

Just as astronomers can be said to handle information professionally, all other professions can be said so as well. Publishers, researchers, historians, lawyers, teachers and anybody else can be said to be professionals in handling information in some way or another. The role of information specialists may be relatively clear when the target group is, for example, astronomers: Information specialists are experts on forms of publications, databases, reference tools, etc. In the case of, for example, historians and lawyers, the borders are much more unclear because the key information that these professions are seeking, interpreting and using is itself contained in publications and other documents. The historian, not the librarian or information specialist, is the expert in seeking, organizing, interpreting and utilizing the documents (mostly unpublished) needed in his or her professional work. Still, an information professional is more professional regarding some specific problems such as databases, cataloging, etc. A basic difference in knowledge about information sources is typically that the subject specialist starts from a narrow point and is working bottom-up to more general information sources, while the information specialist starts from a broad overview and is working top-down. In this way their competencies are supplementary.

The domain-analytic paradigm is a theoretical approach to information science, stating that the best way to understand information in IS is to study the knowledge-domains as "discourse communities," which are parts of the society's division of labor. Knowledge organization, -structure, cooperation patterns, language and communication forms, information systems and relevance criteria are reflections of the objects of the work of these communities and of their role in society. The individual person's psychology, knowledge, information needs and subjective relevance criteria should be seen in this perspective. Each domain develops its own terminology and kinds of documents, such as astronomic atlases, law books or musical scores.

Within a discourse community, there can be more or less consensus. There will always be different views regarding theoretical issues, the best way to proceed, the best policy, the most adequate "paradigm" *and consequently what information is most relevant* (e.g., Hjørland, 2002). Such communities are not static, but are more or less dynamic. The most important thing is, however, that different groups in society process information according to criteria that are specific to the dominant views in that community. Different communities may be interested in the same object (such as a stone in the field) but may interpret it differently (from an archeological or geological point of view, for example). What is informative (and thus information) depends on the point of view of the specific community. Criteria for information are neither universal nor individual but linked to specific roles in society.

Bazerman (1985) has made an empirical investigation of how physicists read physics. One could say that he investigated their information processing patterns. The reader is not an isolated mind, devoid of experience and community. Texts are read against a continuing disciplinary activity in the world and judgements about how that activity might be most successfully continued. The scanning process of the physicist shows that the schemas they use are deeply impressed in the subconscious. They scan so rapidly over tables of contents that they cannot give conscious thought to each title. Rather certain words seem to trigger the attention. The reading is also specific in relation to sub-specializing within physics. Theoreticians, for example, may go right to the results of experimental articles to see what kind of date is obtained and must be accounted for by their theory. They are likely to skip over methodological sections as uninteresting and the theoretical sections as familiar. Even problem formulations and conclusions may not contain much that is helpful to them. This example demonstrates how the information processing mechanisms of physicists are socially and historically shaped.

The question is if such information processing by individuals in disciplines or discourses can be generalized? Hjørland (2002) demonstrated that paradigms imply general patterns of information seeking. The background assumptions that form the different approaches to a field represent generalized criteria of information processing. The most general (cross-disciplinary) schemata that people use in seeking information are provided by their epistemological attitudes:

Figure 2. Simplified relevance criteria in four epistemological schools. (From Hjørland, 2002)

Empiricism	Rationalism	Historicism	Pragmatism
Relevant: Observations, sense-data. Induction from collections of observational data. Intersubjectively controlled data.	*Relevant*: Pure thinking, logic, mathematical models, computer modeling, systems of axioms, definitions and theorems.	*Relevant*: Background knowledge about pre-understanding, theories, conceptions, contexts , historical developments and evolutionary perspectives.	*Relevant*: Information about goals and values and consequences both involving the researcher and the object of research (subject and object).
Non-relevant: Speculations, knowledge transmitted from authorities. "Book knowledge" ("reading nature, not books") . Data about the observers' assumptions and pre-understanding.	*Low priority* is given to empirical data because such data must be organized in accordance with principles which cannot come from experience.	*Low priority* is given to decontextualized data of which the meanings cannot be interpreted. Intersubjectively controlled data are often seen as trivia.	*Low priority* (or outright suspicion) is given to claimed value-free or neutral information. For example, feminist epistemology is suspicious about the neutrality of information produced in a male dominated society.

5. A FEW BASIC PRINCIPLES OF INFORMATION SCIENCE

If we accept information retrieval as a core issue in information science, some important consequences may be drawn from the above. Information retrieval is the searching for documents (or parts of documents) in bibliographical databases or in full text databases. The first thing to consider is, in my view, that a collection or database is a *merger* of many different texts and "voices," influencing the retrieval task in a fundamental way by introducing a greater or smaller amount of semantic ambiguity and unclarity. The fundamental problem posed by polysemy for IR is that particular words can take on an almost indefinite number of subtle meaning variations. The lexicon is not fixed; word use is flexible and generative. This runs counter to the largest part of controlled vocabulary systems, which require every descriptor to be specified in advance and all potentially relevant sense distinctions to be permanently encoded. As more sophisticated IR becomes necessary the effectiveness of a fixed lexicon design quickly diminishes.

When a user poses a question to a database, the user always does so from some perspective or paradigm. The concepts used may be more or less ambiguous and may unconsciously be more related to some specific views and interests about the underlying problem than to other views. The database on the other hand may be more a less a merger of different journals and other sources using different conceptions. By the merging, implicit information about different discourse communities and views may be eliminated. For example, journal names are mostly not utilized in IR why implicit information regarding the specific views and qualities of different journals is usually lost during IR. All this implies that the terms used in the question/query may correspond more or less adequately to different subsections of the database.

An example: We have a user asking a question about a medical problem to a merged database containing both medical science and alternative medicine. If the user puts a question to such a database using concepts from alternative medicine, then relevant documents from established medical science are not likely to be identified during the search. The user may believe he has obtained the answer and may evaluate the system positively. In reality, however, he may just have got a (possibly false) confirmation that his search terms and their underlying conceptions were adequate.

Any kind of algorithm or search profile identifies some information and relatively hides other information. What is identified or hidden is not just a question of neutral efficiency. Of course some kinds of hits are obviously wrong (such as false drops or dead links). Also algorithms may identify specific attributes in specific languages and hereby improve retrieval (e.g., Pirkola, and Jarvelin, 1996). In such cases a neutral technology can improve IR by eliminating non-relevant items or by making implicit information retrievable. The nature of language and concepts implies however, that such examples might be the exception from the rule: that search mechanisms are not neutral but tend to favor one kind of view or need at the expense of other kinds of views or needs.

Discourses are based on social conventions, e.g., to cite new methods in references and to name new products in titles or abstracts or descriptors. An algorithm that applies citation indexes may be superior at identifying chemical methods while another algorithm utilizing descriptors performs better on identifying chemical substances. *No algorithm can be superior to any kind of question in any domain or paradigm.* Basically an algorithm must always select information based on some paradigms rather than other (i.e., reflecting some values at the expense of other values). *An algorithm cannot be neutral, but will have some kind of bias that favors some views or needs at the expense of others.* One research goal should be to uncover such biases and to provide a selection of algorithms for users to choose from (but it should not be our only goal to develop algorithms).

The implications for IS are that one should give up the search for one ideal language for knowledge representation, for one ideal algorithm and for one universal law or model of information seeking behavior. Information science should study the rich manifold of discourses, domains and documents. IS should investigate the informative potentials of all possible kinds of subject access points (Hjørland, and Kyllesbech Nielsen, 2001). The informative potential of a given access point is shown to be relative to different domains and conventions.

Subject analysis and systems for knowledge organization are thus not just neutral, technological processes, but kinds of action aimed at promoting the policy goals of information systems. Such goals may be "enlightenment" (in, for example, public libraries), supporting scientific education and knowledge (in research libraries) or a narrow strategy to achieve a specific goal such as a cure for an illness (a pharmacological firm). Such goals should determine what is considered information and thus how documents are selected and organized. An essential difference between IS and computer science (CS) should be that IS should be more open to alternative views, more reflective and meta-oriented and present users for gaps and uncertainties in knowledge. This is very different from making, for example, an expert system that performs optimally by utilizing mainstream tendencies in the view of knowledge.

REFERENCES

Albrechtsen, H., H. H. K. Andersen, S. Bødker, and A. M. Pejtersen. (2001) *Affordances in activity theory and cognitive systems engineering.* Denmark: Risø.

Bazerman, C. (1985) Physicists Reading Physics: Schema-Laden Purposes and Purpose-Laden Schema. *Written Communication, 2*(1), 3–23. Reprinted in: Shaping Written Knowledge. The Genre and Activity of the Experimental Article in Science. (1988).

Beaugrande, R. de (1997) On history and historicity in modern linguistics. Formalism versus functionalism revisited. *Functions of Language, 4*(2), 169–213. http://www.beaugrande.com/

Bogdan, R. J. (1994) *Grounds for cognition. How goal-guided behavior shapes the mind.* Hillsdale, NJ: Lawrence Earlbaum Associates.

Borko, H. (1968) Information science: What is it? *American Documentation, 19*(1), 3–5.

Buckland, M. (1991) *Information and information systems.* New York: Greenwood Press.

Buckley, G. (2001). *Semantics.* http://www.ling.upenn.edu/courses/Spring_2001/ling001/semantics.html [visited 2002-03-10]

Capurro, R., and B. Hjørland. (2002) The Concept of Information. *Annual Review of Information Science and Technology, 37.* In press.

Goody, J. (1987) *The Interface Between the Written and the Oral.* Cambridge: Cambridge University Press.

Griffith, B. C., ed. (1980) *Key Papers in Information Science.* New York: Knowledge Industry Publications.

Hesselager, L. (1980) The Dust of one age is the gold of another. Om pligtafleveringsbestemmelserne [On Deposit Law]. *Nordisk tidsskrift för bok- och biblioteksväsen, 67,* 33–55.

Hjelmslev, L. (1943) *Omkring sprogteoriens grundlæggelse.* København: B. Lunos bogtrykkeri a/s. (Many later editions and translations, e.g., *Prolegomena to a theory of language.* translated by Francis J. Whitfield. Baltimore: Waverly Press, 1953.)

Hjørland, B. (1992) The concept of "subject" in Information Science. *Journal of Documentation, 48*(2), 172–200.

Hjørland, B. (1997) *Information Seeking and Subject Representation. An Activity-Theoretical approach to Information Science.* Westport and London: Greenwood Press.

Hjørland, B. (1998) Information retrieval, text composition, and semantics. *Knowledge Organization, 25*(1/2), 16–31.

Hjørland, B. (2001) Information Seeking Behavior. What should a general theory look like? *The New Review of Information behaviour research: Studies of information seeking in context, 1,* 19–33.

Hjørland, B. (2002) Epistemology and the Socio-Cognitive Perspective in Information Science. *Journal of the American Society for Information Science and Technology, 53*(4), 257–70.

Hjørland, B., and L. Kyllesbech Nielsen. (2001) Subject Access Points in Electronic Retrieval. *Annual Review of Information Science and technology, vol. 35,* 3–51.

Hoffmeyer, J. (1998) Biosemiotics. In P. Bouissac, (ed.). *Encyclopedia of Semiotics* (pp. 82–85). New York and Oxford: Oxford University Press.

Karpatschof, B. (2000) *Human activity. Contributions to the Anthropological Sciences from a Perspective of Activity Theory.* Copenhagen: Dansk Psykologisk Forlag. ISBN 87 7706 311 2.

Leontyev, A. N. (1981) *Problems of the Development of the Mind*. Translated from Russian. Moscow: Progress.

Lock, A., and C. R. Peters, eds. (1999). *Handbook of Human Symbolic Evolution*. Oxford, UK: Blackwell.

Pirkola, A., and K. Jarvelin. (1996) The Effect of Anaphor and Ellipsis Resolution on Proximity in a Text Database. *Information Processing & Management, 32(2)*, 199–216.

Structure-Based Interpretation of Scholarly Book Reviews: A New Research Technique

Jeppe Nicolaisen
Royal School of Library and Information Science
Birketinget 6
2300 Copenhagen S, Denmark
jni@db.dk

ABSTRACT

Scholarly book reviews contain evaluative parts, which, if decoded properly, hold great potential value for scholars, scientists, librarians, collection developers, information seekers, and LIS-researchers who are depending on access to valuated information and test collections. This paper introduces a new structure-based research technique for the interpretation of opinions reflected by authors of scholarly book reviews. The structure-based technique combines the strengths of two prevalent content analytical approaches, while additionally utilizing the typical rhetorical organization of book reviews as an enriched point of analytic departure. The validity of this research technique is established by statistically correlating results derived from the structure-based interpretation of 60 LIS book reviews, results of a quantitative content analysis of the same sample, and results obtained from questioning the actual reviewers about their genuine opinions of the books under study.

123

1. INTRODUCTION

Indexed documents are only occasionally explicitly evaluated in databases. Sociological Abstracts did, however, provide simple ratings in book review (BR) records. These ratings were generally provided for reviews published in the core literature (e.g., journals with the word sociology in the title or published by a department or school of sociology). The indexers would read the reviews and assess the reviewers' general opinions of the books under review on a 5-point rating scale. The potential utilizations of such summarized information in both information retrieval and informetrics appear to be many. But unfortunately, Sociological Abstracts ceased providing this service in 1998.

It has been pointed out by various commentators (e.g., Snizek, and Fuhrman, 1979; Ingram, and Mills, 1989) that BRs, despite the eternal growth and dissemination of recorded knowledge, make it possible for scholars and scientists to keep up with the latest developments in their fields and disciplines. According to Lincoln (1983), custom decrees that in BRs reviewers put their names publicly to evaluations of the works of others, and Schubert, et al. (1984) have consequently characterized signed BRs as *the visible tip of the peer review iceberg*. The scientific merits of such published peer reviews have yet been questioned. Some have branded BRs as *the second-class citizens of scientific literature* (Riley, and Spreitzer, 1970), while others have maintained that BRs merely reflect individual opinions, which disqualify them entirely as scholarly contributions (Sabosik, 1988). These allegations, however, are not supported by empirical investigations. A study based on an actual survey of scholars' conception of the utility and importance of book reviews (Spink, Robins, and Schamber, 1998) concludes, on the contrary, that scholars synthesize and critically evaluate the work of peers into book reviews, which contribute to the development of new ideas, theories, and research hypotheses. The authors consequently finish their study by proposing an extension to Garvey and Griffith's (1971) traditional model of scholarly communication to include book reviews.

The scientific merit of BRs is, consequently, beyond dispute yet only two recent studies (Motta-Roth, 1998; Hyland, 2000) have sought to explore some of the special characteristics of this genre and knowledge on how the evaluative content of BRs are organized, interpreted and summarized is therefore sparse. In order to exploit the latent potential contained in scholarly BRs on a scientific basis, we need to advance the knowledge of the genre and its unique qualities. This paper will consequently explore the organization of scholarly BRs in the field of LIS, and propose a new research technique for the interpretation of BRs. We will start out by outlining and discussing two prevalent methods for the interpretation of opinions reflected by authors of scholarly BRs, the quantitative and the qualitative approaches, and the inherent shortcomings of these. Next, we will propose a new structure-based technique for interpretation, which utilizes the distinct strengths of the prevalent approaches, and subsequently, we will test the new technique by applying it to a sample of 60 LIS BRs. By statistically comparing the results derived from the structure-based technique with results of a quantitative content analysis of the same sample, and the results obtained from questioning the actual reviewers about their genuine opinions of the books under study, we will finally demonstrate that application of the structure-based technique enables the researcher to make more valid interpretations of scholarly BRs than previously.

2. CONTENT ANALYTICAL APPROACHES

Broadly speaking, there exist two types of content analysis: quantitative and qualitative (North, et al., 1963). The former attempts to assess the number of times some words, phrases, or similar entities appear in the document under study; the latter seeks to uncover the meanings and symbolism behind the text being analyzed. Both types of content analysis have been applied in previous studies dealing with the interpretation of evaluative contents in scholarly BRs.

2.1. Quantitative content analysis

The technique of quantitative content analysis has been described in-depth elsewhere (e.g., Berelson, 1952; North, et al., 1963; Krippendorff, 1980), and is based on the premise that the many words, phrases, sentences, paragraphs or the like inherent in written communications can be reduced to categories in which entities share the same meaning or connotation. The procedure employed to accomplish this reduction must naturally be consistent so that anyone, with proper training, would get the same results. Therefore a quantitative content analysis consists of the following parts:

- *Selection of a sample* (quantitative content analysis can be applied to a group of input materials that constitute a coherent population).

- *Establishment of clearly defined categories* (the categories chosen should be exhaustive, mutually exclusive, clearly defined, and conceptually valid in relation to the research question).

- *Establishment of a unit of analysis* (some decision has to be made regarding the basic unit for consideration; whether it is to be each word, each line, each sentence, each paragraph, each column, or each page).

- *Coding and collection of sample data* (the coding can be done through the use of a checklist or a computer-based equivalent).

- *Calculation of frequency counts and percentages* (conclusions are later drawn from the results of these statistical procedures).

A number of studies have addressed the problems associated with the interpretation of content in scholarly BRs by utilizing quantitative content analysis as a tool for decoding reviewers' opinions of reviewed books. These previous studies, however, all differ in regard to selected samples, defined categories, and units of analysis. Snizek and Fuhrman (1979) deduced the favorableness of 150 BRs appearing in three scholarly journals in the field of Sociology by constructing a ratio of the number of positive to the number of negative sentences in each review. A number of distributed categories have been defined and implemented in other studies. Bilhartz (1984), for instance, probed 560 American History BRs for comments, both pro and con, about some two dozen evaluative categories. Schubert, et al. (1984) and Meho and Sonnenwald (2000) respectively investigated the favorableness of BRs in such diverse fields as Chemistry and Kurdish Studies using seven broad categories and evaluative comments as the unit of analysis. Taylor (1967) chose the paragraph as the recording unit of his analysis concerning the favorableness of 369 BRs from three sociological journals, but limited himself to the use of just two categories (paragraphs dealing with either the author of the reviewed book or the book itself). All of these analyses are, however, concluded by calculations of the overall or total score for each review under study and thereby with the collapse of several distributed categories into one single all-embracing one.

The obvious strength of quantitative content analysis is the high degree of inter-coder reliability that one can attain by implementation of clearly defined categories and through the use of checklists. Calculations of inter-coder reliability in the aforementioned studies all show highly significant agreement between the coders. However, the validity of this research technique is, on the other hand, not touched upon, and one may therefore rightfully question if the method of quantitative content analysis is really measuring what it is supposed to, i.e., the reviewers' opinions of the reviewed books. Hyland (2000) distinguishes the referential foci of evaluative comments in BRs by categorizing these comments as being either general or specific. General evaluations concern the book as a whole (i.e., overall discussion: e.g., coverage, approach, interest, currency, quality) contrary to specific evaluations, which concern fractions of a book (e.g., style, text, author, publishing). In his empirical study, Hyland found that while 80 percent of the positive commentary on content addressed general aspects of the book, critical observations tended to be more specific, with 60 percent referring to particular content issues. By calculating ratios of positive and negative comments in BRs one neglects the fact that most reviewers apparently provide some focused criticism throughout their texts despite the fact that they frequently conclude their examinations by praising the *books* under review.

2.2. Qualitative content analysis

Qualitative content analysis bears a faint resemblance to the practice of literary interpretation, and is to be regarded as a highly subjective or, as indicated, qualitative research technique. A number of studies have previously utilized this approach when interpreting opinions reflected by BR authors (e.g., Champion, and Morris, 1973; Carlo, and Natowitz, 1996; Jordy, McGrath, and Rutledge, 1999). The method is straightforward: examine every BR in a given sample by *reading*, and assess the overall opinion of a particular reviewer by subjectively determining the tone of the review under study.

The major shortcoming of this approach is, from an empirical research methodological point of view, that the inter-coder reliability of these studies normally is reported to be quite low. The strength of the qualitative content analysis is, on the other hand, that coders are allowed to make independent interpretations of reviewers' opinions without rigorously limiting themselves to schemes, categories, and units of analysis, which probably, as illustrated above, result in deduction of invalid or even false conclusions.

2.3. Structure-based Interpretation

In order to maximize both the reliability and the validity of interpretations concerning scholarly BRs, there seems to be a need for a third research technique, which combines the respective strengths of the two content analytical approaches. We have developed such a technique and named it 'Structure-based Interpretation' (SBI) since it exploits the typical *structural* organization of book reviews as an enriched point of analytic departure.

Attempts on classifying communications into categories, or genres, with similar form, topic or purpose dates back to Aristotle. Rhetoricians, however, are still debating on the correct description of the concept of genre (e.g., Harrell, and Linkugel, 1978; Miller, 1984; Tonkin, 1992; Berkenkotter, and Huckin, 1995), but the definition of Swales (1990) seems to capture the essence of these. According to Swales, a genre is a class of communicative events with some shared set of communicative purposes, as defined by a discourse community, and which share some restraints on allowable content, positioning, and form. Academic document and genre studies have traditionally been undertaken by researchers in the field of linguistics and allied disciplines (e.g., composition studies), who have focused their attention on a variety of written genres (for a comprehensive overview of studies see Swales [1990] and Hoffmann [1998]). The obvious relevance of this kind of study for the strengthening of full text information retrieval theories has previously been outlined by Hjørland (1998) and Hjørland, and Kyllesbech Nielsen (2001). Moreover, the emergence of full text databases and hypertext media has also spurred a certain amount of interest on genre analysis among researchers in LIS (e.g., Walker Vaughan, and Dillon [1998]; Crowston, and Williams [2000]; Dillon, and Gushrowski [2000]).

BRs are centrally evaluative, and consequently more interactively complex than other academic genres as they do not simply respond to a general body of more or less impersonal literature. Motta-Roth (1998) conducted a genre-analytical study of 60 academic BRs, divided evenly among three disciplines—Linguistics, Chemistry, and Economics. The results of her study demonstrate that BRs in all disciplines have a consistent pattern of information organization corresponding to four rhetorical moves, comprised of one or a number of sub-functions, which allow writers and readers to recognize different reviews as being exemplars of the same genre. The moves are identified in terms of the functions they play in the genre and are often visually signaled by paragraph shifts so that alternations between them co-occur with paragraph boundaries. Figure 1 illustrates the four rhetorical moves and their specific sub-functions. It mirrors a similar illustration (Motta-Roth, 1998, p. 35), supplemented by two additional sub-functions (12 and 13), which we recently discovered through the examination of 60 LIS BRs.

FIGURE 1.   **RHETORICAL MOVES IN SCHOLARLY BOOK REVIEWS**

MOVE 1.   INTRODUCING THE BOOK

Sub-function 1.   Defining the general topic of the book
Sub-function 2.   Informing about potential readership
Sub-function 3.   Informing about the author
Sub-function 4.   Making topic generalizations
Sub-function 5.   Inserting the book in the field

MOVE 2.   OUTLINING THE BOOK

Sub-function 6.   Providing general view of the organization of the book
Sub-function 7.   Stating the topic of each chapter
Sub-function 8.   Citing extra-text material

MOVE 3.   HIGHLIGHTING PARTS OF THE BOOK

Sub-function 9.   Providing specific evaluation

MOVE 4.   PROVIDING GENERAL EVALUATION OF THE BOOK

Sub-function 10.   Definitely recommending the book
Sub-function 11.   Recommending the book despite indicated shortcomings
Sub-function 12.   Neither recommending nor disqualifying the book
Sub-function 13.   Disqualifying the book despite indicated positive aspects
Sub-function 14.   Definitely disqualifying the book

The quotations below (Smith, 2000) demonstrate the four rhetorical moves and a few selected sub-functions in action:

1. *Introducing the book:* [sub-function 1] "*Information Seeking in the Online Age* is a textbook about retrieval from electronic databases, [sub-function 5] and is the successor to the same authors' *Online Searching: Principles and Practice* published in 1990."

2. *Outlining the book:* [sub-function 7] "The book starts with an overview of the searching process, and a review of the literature of information seeking behavior."

3. *Highlighting parts of the book:* [sub-function 9] "Given the title, it is a pity that the important area of search strategy and tactics is dealt with in only seven pages, and does not, for instance, draw on Marcia Bates' contributions."

4. *Providing general evaluation of the book:* [sub-function 11] "However, these are relatively small criticisms, and overall *Information Seeking in the Online Age* deserves a place on the bookshelf of every information searcher, and should be a strong contender as a resource for courses in information searching."

Since most reviewers commonly provide their general opinions of the books under review in the concluding paragraphs of their BRs, it seems particularly logical to confine all textual investigations of reviewers' opinions to such passages of the majority of BRs. The closing move is usually explicitly signaled at the beginning of the last paragraph by a metadiscoursive marker such as *in sum, altogether, in summary/conclusion, finally*, etc. (Motta-Roth, 1998), and are as such relatively easy to locate within most BRs. In the few instances where no closing moves can be found, one should instead direct the attention to the introductory part of the review (move 1), which likely then contains the general evaluation of the reviewer.

The final interpretation of the reviewers' opinions of the books is completed by establishing the nature of the general evaluation provided in each case, i.e., which of the sub-functions (10–14) that is reflected in the BRs under study. By correlating these sub-functions to the categories on the ordinal scale shown in Figure 2, the coder finally assesses the reviewers' general opinions of the books under review on the 5-point rating scale.

FIGURE 2.	ORDINAL SCALE AND CORRELATING SUB-FUNCTIONS
ORDINAL SCALE	SUB-FUNCTIONS
Very Favorable	10. Definitely recommending the book
Favorable	11. Recommending the book despite indicated shortcomings
Neutral	12. Neither recommending nor disqualifying the book
Unfavorable	13. Disqualifying the book despite indicated positive aspects
Very Unfavorable	14. Definitely disqualifying the book

The assignment of a particular BR to one of the five rating categories on the ordinal scale is thus dependant solely on whether the reviewer makes reservations during the concluding part of the review or if the reviewer unconditionally recommends or disqualifies the book. From our previous example of the four rhetorical moves in action, we can consequently infer that Smith's (2000) review is 'favorable,' since he ends up recommending the book despite of the indicated shortcomings.

The structure-based technique of interpretation consequently draws on the strengths of the two content analytical approaches. By implementation of clearly defined categories, units of analysis, and schemes, it maintains the high degree of inter-rater reliability from the quantitative approach. Simultaneously, as the qualitative approach, it leaves the final interpretation to the individual coder, instead of inferring it from invalidated word-counts and adjective-frequencies.

3. THE VALIDITY OF STRUCTURE-BASED INTERPRETATION

In order of testing the validity of the structure-based interpretation technique, we have analyzed 60 LIS BRs and compared the results obtained by SBI with the results of a quantitative content analysis (QCA), and the results of a simple one-question survey e-mailed to the authors of the sampled reviews (1).

3.1. Methodology

We drew a proportionate stratified sample consisting of 60 BRs published in 2000 in the LIS-core journals. The core journals of the discipline were determined from a previous list (White, and McCain, 1998) and extended with the inclusion of one journal, *Knowledge Organization,* that represents an LIS-domain, which, it could be argued, was inadequately embodied in the original list. Core journals publishing at least four BRs in 2000 were finally selected for sampling (cf. Table 1).

TABLE 1.   LIST OF SELECTED LIS CORE JOURNALS

Information Processing & Management
Information Technology and Libraries
Journal of Documentation
Journal of the American Society for Information Science
Knowledge Organization
Library & Information Science Research
Library Resources & Technical Services
Program – Electronic Library and Information Systems
Electronic Library

The 60 BRs were analyzed using the technique of structure-based interpretation. All reviews were coded for moves according to Figure 1, analyzed for paragraphs reflecting the general opinions of the reviewers, interpreted by identification of the types of sub-functions found in these concluding paragraphs, and placed in one of the five ordinal rating-categories of Figure 2.

Secondly, the same BRs were quantitatively content-analyzed. The number of evaluative sentences of each review were counted, and the total score (T) was established by calculation of the ratio $[T = s_+ - s_- / s_a]$ where s_+ equals the number of positive sentences, s_- the number of negative sentences, and s_a the number of all positive, negative and ambivalent (±) sentences. An ordinal score of each review's degree of favorableness/unfavorableness was finally constructed from this total score.

When the coding of BRs was completed, questionnaires were e-mailed to all reviewers whose e-mail addresses were traceable in either the BRs themselves, in the affiliation of journal articles, or by searching the Internet. Using this procedure, we were able to track at least one valid e-mail address in 56 of the 60 cases. Each of the 56 reviewers were then asked to indicate his or her opinion of the book, which he or she previously had reviewed, on a five point rating scale.

Finally, we were able to measure the validity of the structure-based technique by correlating its derived results with the results obtained from the e-mail questionnaire, and, simultaneously, we were able to test whether SBI performs better than the prevalent quantitative approach. We calculated the correlations between the variables by measuring both the *Pearson's product-moment correlation coefficient* and the *Kendall's tau-b correlation coefficient*. The first measure usually assumes an interval scale of ratings, while the second is designed for measuring the association between ordinal variables. By implementing both measures, we sought to explore the *common assertion* (Snizek, and Fuhrman, 1979) that these procedures produce resembling results.

3.2. Results

The distribution of moves in the sample is presented in Table 2. The absence of the last move was evident in only seven BRs. In six of these instances, the general opinions of the reviewers were instead located in the introductory paragraphs. The seventh review did not reflect any general opinion at all, and was consequently counted as "neutral."

TABLE 2.	DISTRIBUTION OF SAMPLE MOVES	
Move 1	59 BRs	98,33 percent
Move 2	48 BRs	80,00 percent
Move 3	54 BRs	90,00 percent
Move 4	53 BRs	88,33 percent

Thirty-eight of the 41 reviewers, who kindly replied to the e-mail questionnaire (response rate=71,9%), indicated a valid answer. Two reviewers replied that they were not able to rate the book under study on a five-point rating scale, and one reviewer provided the answer using none of the prescribed ratings. Table 3. illustrates the distribution of BRs on the five-point rating scale inferred by the three approaches. The results of the quantitative content analytical approach are far more varied than the results of the structure-based technique. It is for instance striking that while the reviewers did not indicate a very unfavorable opinion in any case, the SBI technique assigns a few BRs to this category, but, on the other hand, not quite as many as the quantitative content analytical approach.

TABLE 3.	DISTRIBUTION OF BRs ON A FIVE-POINT RATING SCALE (%)		
	SURVEY	SBI	QCA
VERY FAVORABLE	26,3	31,6	34,2
FAVORABLE	28,9	23,7	13,2
NEUTRAL	23,7	26,3	18,4
UNFAVORABLE	21,1	15,8	21,1
VERY UNFAVORABLE	0	2,6	13,2

The correlation between the results obtained from the survey and the results derived from the SBI technique was shown to be respectively r=0,814 and τ=0,767 (p<0,01), which indicates a conclusively strong relationship between the variables. While the correlation between the results of the survey and the QCA technique was shown to be r=0,566 and τ=0,459, indicating a much weaker but nonetheless significant (p < 0,01) relationship. Although the two measures of relationship are found to produce quite resembling results, we find that *Kendall's tau-b* in both cases generates slightly more conservative outcomes.

Interpretation of opinions reflected by authors of scholarly BRs is an essential issue in practice and consequently an important methodological challenge. Findings of the present study show that LIS BRs, like BRs in other disciplines, share a regular structure, concerning the organization of content, separated by four rhetorical moves. Additionally, the study demonstrates that general evaluations, which concern the reviewers' concluding judgments of the reviewed books, most often are located in the closing paragraphs of BRs. These novel insights into the typical organization of scholarly BRs enable researchers to make more valid interpretations than previously.

The structure-based interpretation technique is easily applied. A researcher starts the interpretation of a particular BR by locating the section containing the reviewer's general evaluation of the book (usually the closing paragraph). Next, he or she focuses on this paragraph and infers which sub-function is used (cf. Figure 1). Finally, the researcher correlates the inferred sub-function to an ordinal scale of ratings (cf. Figure 2), and thereby concludes the interpretation of the favorableness of the review under study. The structure-based technique has distinct advantages over previous content analytical approaches. By implementation of clearly defined categories, units of analysis, and schemes, it maintains a

high degree of inter-rater reliability, and simultaneously, leaves the final interpretation to the individual researcher, consequently retaining a superior level of
validity in preference to the quantitative content analytical approach. The application of both the structure-based technique and a quantitative content analysis
to a sample of 60 LIS BRs confirms this superiority. The correlation of the results derived from the structure-based technique and the results obtained from
questioning the actual reviewers about their genuine opinions of the books under
study was found to be very strong, contrary to the correlation between the quantitative content analysis and the genuine opinions of the actual reviewers, which
was found to be significantly weaker.

Although more studies, including studies with larger sample sizes and BRs
from other disciplines, are needed to further verify the generalizability of these
results, at present we should at least feel more confident about the relative success of the structure-based procedure as an applicable research technique for the
interpretation of general opinions reflected by authors of scholarly BRs. Academic genres are constantly transforming. We consequently need to monitor the
enduring alternation of scholarly BRs in order to adjust the SBI technique to the
ever-changing conditions. It is therefore hoped that this study will be replicated
repeatedly to reach a better understanding of scholarly BRs, their unique characteristics, and further research potentials.

NOTES

(1) Data are on file. Inquiries may be addressed to the author.

REFERENCES

Berelson, B. (1952) *Content analysis in communication research.* New York: Free
Press.

Berkenkotter, C., and T. N. Huckin. (1995) *Genre knowledge in disciplinary communication: Cognition/culture/power.* Hillsdale, NJ: Lawrence Erlbaum.

Bilhartz, T. D. (1984) In 500 words or less: Academic book reviewing in American
History. *The History Teacher, 17*(4), 525–36.

Carlo, P. W., and A. Natowitz. (1996) The appearance of praise in Choice reviews
of outstanding and favorably assessed books in American History, Geography, and Area Studies. *Collection Management, 20*(3/4), 97–116.

Champion, D. J., and M. F. Morris. (1973) A content analysis of book reviews in
the AJS, ASR, and Social Forces. *American Journal of Sociology, 78*(5),
1256–65.

Crowston, K., and M. Williams. (2000) Reproduced and emergent genres of communication on the World Wide Web. *The Information Society, 16,* 201–15.

Dillon, A., and B. A. Gushrowski. (2000) Genres and the Web: Is the personal
home page the first uniquely digital genre? *Journal of the American Society
for Information Science, 51*(2), 202–5.

Garvey, W. D., and B. C. Griffith. (1971) Scientific communication: Its role in the conduct of research and the creation of knowledge. *American Psychologist, 26*, 349–62.

Harrell, J., and W. A. Linkugel. (1978) On rhetorical genre: An organizing perspective. *Philosophy and Rhetoric, 11*, 262–81.

Hjørland, B. (1998) Information retrieval, text composition, and semantics. *Knowledge Organization, 25*(1/2), 16–31.

Hjørland, B., and L. Kyllesbech Nielsen. (2001) Subject access points in electronic retrieval. *Annual Review of Information Science and Technology, 35*, 249–98.

Hoffmann, L., ed. (1998) *Fachsprachen: Ein internationales Handbuch zur Fachsprachenforschung und Terminologiewissenschaft.* Berlin: de Gruyter.

Hyland, K. (2000) *Disciplinary discourses: Social interactions in academic writing.* Harlow: Longman.

Ingram, H. M., and P. B. Mills. (1989) Reviewing the book reviews. *PS: Political Science and Politics, 22*(3), 627–34.

Jordy, M. L., E. L. McGrath, and J. B. Rutledge. (1999) Book reviews as a tool for assessing publisher reputation. *College & Research Libraries, 60*(2), 132–42.

Krippendorff, K. (1980) *Content analysis: An introduction to its methodology.* Beverly Hills, CA: Sage.

Lincoln, T. (1983) The book review business. *Nature, 302*, 757.

Meho, L. I., and D. H. Sonnenwald. (2000) Citation ranking versus peer evaluation of senior faculty research performance: A case study of Kurdish scholarship. *Journal of the American Society for Information Science, 51*(2), 123–38.

Miller, C. R. (1984) Genre as social action. *Quarterly Journal of Speech, 70*, 151–67.

Motta-Roth, D. (1998) Discourse analysis and academic book reviews: a study of text and disciplinary cultures. In I. Fortanet (ed.). *Genre studies in English for academic purposes* (pp. 29–58). Castelló de la Plana: Universitat Jaume.

North, R. C., O. R. Holsti, M. G. Zaninovich, and D. A. Zinnes. (1963) *Content analysis.* Chicago: Northwestern University Press.

Riley, L. E., and E. A. Spreitzer. (1970) Book reviewing in the social sciences. *The American Sociologist, 5*, 358–63.

Sabosik, P. E. (1988) Scholarly reviewing and the role of Choice in the postpublication review process. *Book Research Quarterly, Summer,* 10–18.

Schubert, A., S. Zsindely, A. Telcs, and T. Braun. (1984) Quantitative analysis of a visible Tip of the peer review iceberg: Book reviews in chemistry. *Scientometrics, 6*(6), 433–43.

Smith, A. (2000) Information seeking in the online age: Principles and practice [Book review]. *The Electronic Library, 18*(4), 296–97.

Snizek, W. E., and E. R. Fuhrman. (1979) The evaluative content of book reviews in the American Journal of Sociology, Contemporary Sociology, and Social Forces. *Contemporary Sociology, 8*(3), 339–40.

Spink, A., D. Robins, and L. Schamber. (1998) Use of scholarly book reviews: Implications for electronic publishing and scholarly communication. *Journal of the American Society for Information Science, 49*(4), 364–74.

Swales, J. M. (1990) *Genre analysis: English in academic and research settings.* New York: Cambridge University Press.

Taylor, W. R. (1967) *The influence of professional status differences upon book reviewing in Sociology.* PhD dissertation, Purdue University.

Tonkin, E. (1992) *Narrating our pasts: The social construction of oral history.* Cambridge, England: Cambridge University Press.

Walker Vaughan, M., and A. Dillon. (1998) The role of genre in shaping our understanding of digital documents. *Proceedings of the Annual Meeting of the American Society for Information Science, 35,* 559–66.

White, H. D., and K. W. McCain. (1998) Visualizing a discipline. An author co-citation analysis of information science, 1972–1995. *Journal of the American Society for Information Science, 49*(4), 327–55.

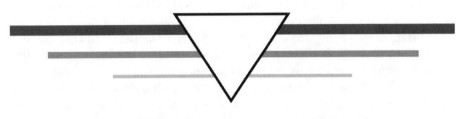

Speculations on Browsing, Directed Searching, and Linking in Relation to the Bradford Distribution

Marcia J. Bates
Department of Information Studies
Graduate School of Education and Information Studies
University of California, Los Angeles
Los Angeles, CA 90095-1520, USA
mjbates@ucla.edu

ABSTRACT

Extensive literatures exist on information searching theory and techniques, as well as on the Bradford Distribution. This distribution, also known as "Bradford's Law of Scattering," tells us that information on a subject is dispersed in a characteristic and robust pattern that appears consistently across many different environments. This pattern may be expected to have important implications for information searching theory and techniques. Yet these two research literatures are rarely considered in relation to each other. It is the purpose of this article to distinguish three Bradford regions and speculate on the optimum searching techniques for each region. In the process, browsing, directed searching in databases, and the pursuit of various forms of links will all be considered. Implications of growth in size of a literature for optimal information organization and searching will also be addressed.

1. INTRODUCTION

Extensive research literatures exist on information search techniques and on the Bradford Distribution—but rarely are the two considered in relation to each other. (A search produced a handful of references linking the two—Lancaster, et al., 1991; Leimkuhler, 1977; White, 1981—but none of these items address the questions being considered in this paper.) The Bradford Distribution, or, Bradford's Law of Scattering, describes how information on a subject is distributed among the resources where such information may be expected to be found. The distribution will be described in more detail shortly, but the key point is that the distribution tells us that information is neither randomly scattered, nor handily concentrated in a single location. Instead, information scatters in a characteristic pattern, a pattern that should have obvious implications for how that information can most successfully and efficiently be sought.

It is the object of this paper to link the Bradford Distribution with searching techniques, and to consider what techniques might work the best for which regions of the Bradford distribution. In the process, I will also speculate on a variety of other possible implications of the connections between Bradford's Law and searching.

2. THE BRADFORD DISTRIBUTION

Samuel Bradford originally developed his data on the basis of studying the distribution of articles in journals in two areas, applied geophysics and lubrication. He studied the rates at which articles relevant to each subject area appeared in journals in those areas. He identified all journals that published more than a certain number of articles in the test areas per year, as well as in other ranges of descending frequency. He wrote:

> [I]f scientific journals are arranged in order of decreasing productivity of articles on a given subject, they may be divided into a nucleus of periodicals more particularly devoted to the subject and several groups or zones containing the same number of articles as the nucleus, when the numbers of periodicals in the nucleus and succeeding zones will be as $1:n:n^2$ . . . (Bradford, 1948, p. 116).

In principle, there could be any number of zones, with the number of articles in each zone being the total number of articles divided by the number of zones. In his empirical data, however, Bradford identified just three zones, and three will be used here for simplicity's sake. Bradford found in his empirical data that the value of "n" was roughly 5. Suppose, then, that someone doing an in-depth search on a topic finds that four journals constitute the core, and contain fully one-third of all the relevant articles found. ("Relevant" is used here strictly in the sense of topical relevance.) If the value for n is 5, then 4 X 5 = 20 journals will, among them, contain another third of all the relevant articles found. Finally, the last third will be the most scattered of all, being spread out over $4 \times 5^2 = 100$ journals. See Figure 1.

Figure 1. The Bradford regions. Each search region contains one-third of the articles on the subject. Each ring is five times the area of the next smaller one.

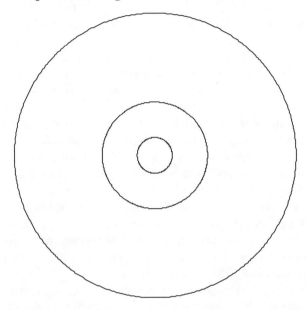

The distribution indicates that one could find a great many relevant articles on a topic nicely concentrated in a few core journals. But finding the rest of the relevant articles involves an increasingly more extensive search, as the average yield of articles per additional journal examined becomes smaller and smaller the farther out, i.e., the more remotely from the core journals, one goes. The Bradford data thus tell us that desired material is neither perfectly concentrated in one place, as we might hope, nor is it completely randomly distributed either, as we might fear.

There has been considerable debate about the exact formulation of the distribution. However, for our purposes, the general formulation given by Bradford himself (above) is sufficient. Many types of recorded information have been found to follow the Bradford Distribution. See reviews in Chen, and Leimkuhler (1986), Fedorowicz (1982), and Wilson (1999). Recently, Hood, and Wilson (2001) found the same pattern operating regarding the number of databases to search to find the literature on 14 test queries. (For simplicity's sake, the discussion in this paper is restricted to materials on a subject, though other kinds of searches, such as for materials by authors, materials coming out of research institutes or government agencies, etc., probably also follow a Bradfordian pattern.) In sum, it seems reasonable to assume, in the absence of any contrary information, that recorded information of all types on a subject, and in many different physical forms, is distributed in this same Bradfordian manner.

3. SEARCHING THE BRADFORD REGIONS

Assuming then that information on a subject is distributed in the Bradfordian pattern, what are the implications for search strategy? The proposed relationship between the Bradford Distribution and searching techniques will first be described below in a general way, then more specific details will be developed.

From the searcher's perspective, the innermost core of the distribution—let us call it Region 1—is the richest in materials on one's subject of interest. One might therefore expect it to be the easiest to search, because there is so much wheat, so little chaff. Perhaps one might even be able to find items in Region 1 without any conventional formal search techniques at all—one may simply browse.

In the next ring, Region 2, there are still a good number of items on one's subject to be found, but they are now scattered more widely, and many non-relevant items (that is, many items not on the desired subject) are interspersed among the (topically) relevant items. In this region, it is no longer adequately efficient to search by browsing, though one can, of course, always browse if one wants. But for any reasonably efficient search effort, some kind of formal information organization of the material is needed, coupled with search techniques specifically designed to take advantage of that organization. Region 2 is where indexing and database searching come into their own. This approach is here called "directed searching." More precisely, directed searching is done in situations where some form(s) of information organization, description, and/or indexing of the information exists, thus enabling explicit query development and search of that query.

In Region 3, the outermost area, a substantial number of relevant items are still to be found, but they are so widely dispersed that finding the occasional relevant item is rather like the proverbial problem of "finding a needle in a haystack." Here, following citation or other links from articles closer to the core may prove to be the most efficient sort of searching. Of course, links may lead to articles in any part of the distribution, from the core out to the periphery.

However, in the far edges of the distribution linking may be especially useful as a search technique. In conventional database searching terms, as one moves outward from the center, the precision gets worse and worse—one must review more and more irrelevant items to find any one relevant item, and the recall climbs more and more slowly. Here, conventional indexing/retrieval may be seen to break down. Searching through vast resources becomes inefficient, and the number of "false drops" is so high that it becomes ever harder to detect the occasional desired item. Here, in Region 3, the best solution may be to create links, or to take advantage of pre-existing links, such as article notes/citations or Web links.

Thus, at the most generalized level, we may see the core region of the Bradford distribution as the ideal location for browsing, the middle region as the ideal location for searching in the mode of indexing/retrieval, and the outer region as the ideal location for pursuing links.

Having conjectured this pattern for ideal searching, however, it will be demonstrated shortly that all three generic search techniques are currently used throughout the Bradford regions. Should they be?

4. GENERIC SEARCH TECHNIQUES

We will want to examine the Bradford regions in more detail shortly, but in the meantime, it will reward us to examine these three general search techniques in more detail—browsing, directed searching, and linking.

4.1. Browsing

The first generic search technique is *browsing*, which involves successive acts of glimpsing, fixing on a target to examine visually or manually more closely, examining, then moving on to start the cycle over again. This definition is strongly based on Kwasnik's (1992) conceptualization of browsing. (See also discussion in Chang, and Rice, 1993.)

We can see browsing as having several functions in information searching. First, with respect to the Bradfordian distribution of literature, *one purpose of browsing is to find the core.* Browsing, in its nature, ignores the file structure or other formal organization of information. For example, when we browse in library stacks or in a bookstore, our glimpsing of the materials on the shelves does not follow the call number or alphabetical order of the materials. In other words, we generally do not scan in a strict left to right order along the shelf. Our glance is not systematic—though we do take advantage, in a larger sense, of any relatedness in the arrangement of the materials on the shelves. Browsing is therefore a quick technique, but also a chancy one. When one does not know where the heart of a subject area is to be found, however, this rapid technique may enable one to zoom in quickly on the richest area to be searched.

A second purpose of browsing is to search the core. As the core is densely populated with relevant material, it is generally not necessary to create or negotiate one's way through additional formal information organization structures. The population of relevant items is large enough that one can simply browse the area and reliably locate a good number of desirable materials in a short time.

Two techniques described in Bates (1989) represent specific forms of this generic browsing technique. ***Journal run*** consists of reviewing contents pages of core journals in an area.

[This] technique, by definition, guarantees complete recall within that journal, and, if the journal is central enough to the searcher's interests, this technique also has tolerably good precision. (p. 412)

Journal run is a clear case of browsing in the Bradford core (Region 1) of a subject. The materials are collocated in the journal because editorial decisions have brought them together, not because anyone indexed them and collocated them in an information system.

The second specific browsing technique described in Bates (1989) is *area scanning*. This technique consists of browsing the materials that are physically collocated with materials located earlier in a search. The classic example of area scanning is browsing through the classified arrangement of books on library shelves. So, in effect, area scanning is a kind of browsing that is used in the second Bradford region, where directed searching normally takes place.

Another common type of browsing is *Web-browsing*, that is, moving around via links between and within documents on the World Wide Web. Materials from all three Bradford regions may be found on the Web. However, finding Region 3 items may be particularly successful, given the nature and structure of the Web.

Thus, some form of browsing has been used in all three regions of the Bradford Distribution. In general, the strengths of browsing are its intuitiveness (building on age-old foraging behavior of our hunter-gatherer forbears—Sandstrom, 1994) and its directness—what you see is what you get. The downside of browsing is that it is limited; we can do it only for so long and in a relatively narrow area, before we are overcome by our modern need to move on to the next task.

4.2. Directed searching

The second generic searching technique is what is here being called *Directed searching,* to distinguish it from "searching" in general. Directed searching is done (and can only be done) where some sort of previous indexing, cataloging, or classification has been done on the materials being searched. To put it differently, the information is deliberately structured in order that subsets of the information can be selectively targeted for retrieval. The deliberate structuring may be as simple as the automatic coding of all individual words in a database so that they can be individually searched ("free-text" searching), or as intellectually complex as deep and detailed human indexing and cataloging.

In either case, a descriptive or metadata structure is created by human beings in front of or in addition to the original target information. The searcher then may utilize whatever searching capabilities are provided to exploit this representational structure, in order to find desired information from among a much larger set of resources.

In Bates' 1989 article, two of the techniques described there are classic directed searching techniques: *subject searches in bibliographies and abstracting and indexing (A & I) services*, and *author searching* (p. 412). Directed searching has been a primary focus of information science research and discussion over the last thirty years. Most of the 29 searching tactics described by Bates (1979) are moves that the searcher can make to promote an effective search in the context of these elaborate indexing structures and retrieval capabilities.

Directed searching has been used on all three Bradford regions. The browsable core generally is automatically included in any good search formulation, so that items located in both Regions 1 and 2 are retrieved. Region 3 items have long been found in online searching through use of extensive search formulations containing many OR'd terms ("hedges"), as well as by searching several databases representing peripheral subject areas. The strength of directed searching is its thoroughness and extensive reach. Its weaknesses are that it lacks the directness of browsing and the targeted precision of the citation link.

The advent of the more-effective Google search engine, which is based on linkage patterns as well as conventional search engine retrieval mechanisms, suggests that heavy utilization of links in *really* large information environments, especially in the outer limits of Region 3, may be the best way to go when the Bradford territory has grown very large. On the other hand, because of the recency of the Internet, we may simply have not yet found the best forms of directed searching for it.

Incidentally, Jaime Pontigo-Martinez' dissertation work (1984) tested whether scientific experts, unaware of which Bradford ring specialist articles in their field came from, would judge the articles from all rings as being of equal value. The null hypothesis, that there would be no difference in assessed value between the rings, was supported. This result suggests that, despite the difficulties in searching for articles in outer rings, it is still valuable to locate them, if possible.

4.3. Linking

Linking long pre-dates the Internet, but has come into its own in recent years with the advent of sophisticated networking technology (Kleinberg, 1999; Lempel, and Moran, 2001). *Links* are deliberate connections created by people or automatically by software between parts of a document or between documents. Linking has been utilized to connect texts with relevant related references (footnotes) for centuries. Linking may include the references from index entries to page numbers in books, the "see" and "see also" references between catalog entries, the links within and between documents on the World Wide Web, and the citation links in citation indexes, among other things.

Strictly speaking, we should distinguish between the *creation* of links by authors or Web-page designers, and the *pursuit or following* of links by searchers. It is the latter sense that is being used in association with the discussion of searching techniques in this paper.

In their nature, links may be made between records in any Bradford ring to any other ring. Thus, in principle, searching via links may move anywhere in the Bradford space. Links, while very targeted and precise, may also be capricious and incomplete. Following links, the searcher may range widely, but incompletely, across the relevant materials.

Two of these kinds of links are mentioned among the search techniques described in Bates' 1989 article, *footnote chasing*, and *citation searching*. (p. 412). Footnote chasing, also called "backward chaining" (Ellis, 1989), "involves following up footnotes found in books and articles of interest, and therefore moving backward in successive leaps through reference lists" (Bates, 1989, p. 412). Each such leap, of course, takes one farther back in time.

To utilize citation searching, or "forward chaining," there must be in existence citation indexes that have already located in a single index the relationships of a large number of citing and cited works. Major citation indexes are the three produced by the Institute for Scientific Information, the *Science Citation Index,* the *Social Sciences Citation Index,* and the *Arts & Humanities Citation Index.* One searches in a citation index by looking up an earlier article or book of interest and discovering who has cited it since its publication, thus coming forward in time.

Linking has exploded with the advent of the World Wide Web; indeed the Web, even in its name, can be seen as the primary and best place to manifest links between every imaginable form of information, so long as it can be resident in a computer.

5. IMPACT OF DOMAIN SIZE

We have been skirting an important issue, which now needs to be addressed. If we think about real-world searching, the size of the domain has a very important impact on searching; specifically, different search techniques are appropriate for differently-sized bodies of information, regardless of ring. It turns out that there is a nice illustrative analogy that can be used here. It has been long recognized in the field of geography (Wilson, and Bennett, 1985, p. 84) that towns and cities grow in patterns that look very much like our circular model of the Bradford Distribution. Indeed, such distributions are universal statistical phenomena. Bradford did not so much as invent his distribution, but rather applied this general phenomenon to information science.

When communities grow, they follow a certain characteristic pattern. This pattern was well illustrated in the settling of the American West. A new area opening up would draw farmers, ranchers, or miners. Then a merchant would set up a general store to serve the needs of these groups. As the community grew, the filling in of the community would follow the pattern of Figure 1, with denser settlement in the heart of town, and characteristic scattering toward the edges of town. Thus the distributional pattern remains the same throughout the time of growth, from village to metropolis.

Nonetheless, cities do not look like villages. With the growth in size and increased density at that core, more and more kinds of activities became sustainable. Saloons, livery stables, and assay offices appeared next, followed later by the sheriff, schools, and churches. Continued growth eventually supported concert halls, libraries, operas, and many other less common institutions.

A town of regional importance can sustain more rarefied types of institutions than smaller towns in the area. So in the growth of towns, we can see that size matters a lot. Though the Bradford-style distribution characterizes the scattering of settlement from the time of the tiny beginning outpost to the large city, the kinds of institutions that these settlements will support varies tremendously with size.

The same pattern can be seen with information resources. That is, the Bradford pattern operates throughout, from the time of a tiny beginning literature known to only a handful of people to the development of a vast literature of interest to millions of people. On the other hand, the kinds of searching, the kinds of access that make sense for selecting information from this literature will vary with the size of the total domain.

Derek de Solla Price illustrated this pattern in his discussion of the early days of science. He noted that in the seventeenth century, scientists initially developed journals in order to lighten the load of reading books, personal correspondence, and other sources of information on the ever-growing scientific enterprise. Initially, the journals "had the stated function of digesting the books and doings of the learned all over Europe" (Price, 1963, p. 63). After a while, the journals themselves became important publication venues for new discoveries. Eventually, however, it became difficult to follow all the journals being published, and abstracting indexes were developed (Price, 1961, pp. 96ff). Indeed, it may well be that every major technological and intellectual development in information access in succeeding centuries has arisen out of the pressures of literature growth.

Let us now look more closely at what a Bradford-distributed literature would look like as it grows in size. When a small group of originators begins producing small numbers of documents, the absolute size of the domain is so small that while Bradford regions might be present in an incipient form, they are not yet very evident. One individual or one paper may be more important than others, and form the Region 1 focus of social and documentary networks. However, the total number of resources and connections among them are few, and interested individuals can generally find all they want by browsing and following citations. In very small towns one does not need a map, because everything is visible on one street; likewise, one needs little or no assistance once one has come upon the "small town" of a starter literature on a subject.

With the growth in the literature, however, just as with the growth of the town, auxiliary devices are necessary to enable one to find desired locations—maps and directories for geographical locations, classifications and indexing for bibliographical regions. As the literature grows, one access method after another is shed, as more sophisticated techniques and technologies must be developed to maintain effective access to the literature.

With very small literatures, one may need only one or two distinct types of search method to do effective searching over the whole subject matter domain. In a very mature, highly developed literature, there may be half a dozen discernible Bradford regions, each, perhaps, requiring different search techniques to maximize search effectiveness.

Until the late nineteenth century, library collections, and topical literatures on given subjects were still comparatively small. As Price, Senders, and others have demonstrated, the numbers of book and journal titles have been growing exponentially since the scientific journal (seventeenth century) and the modern printed book (fifteenth century) began. In practical terms, exponential growth means that the number of titles doubles every so many years—for journals, every fifteen years (Price, 1961, p. 100), and books every 22 years (Senders, 1963, p. 1068). Such growth does not make much difference in the early days—1,000 book titles doubling to 2,000 book titles in 22 years is not particularly conspicuous—but book titles doubling from 20 million to 40 million in 22 years is *very* conspicuous! Thus the publishing and library collecting of documentary forms of various types was quite stable for centuries, with relatively glacial change. The need for innovation became particularly acute in the nineteenth century, however, as the absolute numbers of new titles quickly outdistanced every new innovation introduced.

It is probably not accidental that the modern profession of librarianship emerged at that same time. The days of the interested amateur librarian ended when the need for attention to ever-newer techniques and ever-larger buildings made library work a full-time focus of whoever took the job.

It may even be the case that the growth of collections and of materials within any given subject area reached the point in the nineteenth century that sophisticated Region 2 devices had to be introduced for the first time. Before then, catalogs were barely more than inventories of collections. With growth, however, anyone who was not a dedicated scholar in a narrow subject field needed the selectivity offered by more advanced techniques of cataloging, indexing, and classification, in order to maneuver among the growing collections.

In the speculative spirit of this paper, I would suggest that as literatures grew over the last century and a half, each major new intellectual and physical technology for information access represented another "institution," in the geographical analogy, in the growing turf that was information. Just as larger cities can sustain orchestras and concert halls, so also can larger literatures sustain databases, bibliographies, and sophisticated indexing and online system design.

In the meantime, more sophisticated forms of browsing and linking have been introduced recently as well. Online browsing is becoming better supported through subtler and more user-centered system design. The introduction of the citation indexes in the 1960s and 1970s enabled forward chaining as a linking method, and, of course, the Internet created an explosion of linking possibilities for the searcher.

6. FINAL SPECULATIONS: BEST SEARCHING TECHNIQUES?

We have seen in the prior discussion that on the one hand, browsing, directed searching, and linking, respectively, might best be matched with Bradfordian Regions 1, 2, and 3. On the other hand, we have seen that all three generic techniques have been used with all three regions, indeed, have generally been used in the absence of thinking about the Bradford Distribution altogether.

A profusion of technologies continues to develop, which supports improvements in all three generic searching techniques. How should we move forward on the question of the relationship between the Bradford Distribution and searching techniques?

In teaching undergraduates, I have observed that it is common for them to expect to find resources or Websites that provide all the relevant information for their paper in a single location, exactly matching the topic of their paper. In other words, the naive assumption is that chunks of information are perfectly self-contained and complete. At the same time, I have found that beginners often have no idea how to start finding information, and, appear to believe that their one perfect chunk of information may be literally anywhere, that there is no rational way to find it.

Both of these assumptions are inaccurate. Having a generalized understanding of the Bradfordian distribution of all information may provide the basic grounding for a realistic search. As librarians rarely understand this distribution either, we are not always in the best position to help.

What has long been an article of faith among librarians is that all information is findable through the mechanisms of indexing, cataloging, and classification, and that the good searcher invariably utilizes these carefully developed intermediary bibliographic resources. Information literacy instruction for non-librarians is almost always centered around bringing the user into fluency with these sorts of resources.

The experienced humanities scholar constitutes an interesting contrast to the college student and the librarian. The scholar does not have librarian training, but is nonetheless familiar with a number of library research techniques, learned in the course of acquiring the Ph.D. The information seeking research indicates that these scholars rely heavily on browsing and on following citation links (footnote chasing). They rarely, if ever use periodical index databases, and tend to use catalogs only for searches for known items (Stone, 1982; Watson-Boone, 1994; Wiberley, 1989).

The naive user, say, the beginning college student, thus has two models to follow: the librarians, who encourage use of every intermediary access device, from catalogs to online databases, and their professors, who rely most heavily on browsing and footnote chasing.

Another historical metaphor may be suitable at this point. We may view the primary use of browsing and citation linking as an "artisan" approach to searching, that is, a method that dates from the age of skilled craftsmanship. Scholarly research methods have been passed down from mentors to protégés for centuries. By keeping their scholarly focus narrow and deep, humanities researchers have been able to continue that artisan tradition. By searching in a narrow area, the scope of the intellectual territory is kept small enough to allow the continuation of such individualized techniques.

The nineteenth century explosion of new methods of access through classifications, subject indexes, and card catalogs, constituted the beginning of the "industrialization" of searching. With the aid of such devices, one may search vastly more resources in a given period of time (the advantage of "mass production"), but without the personalization made possible by the countless individual search move decisions made in a browsing/footnote-chasing searching technique.

Librarians professionalized in the nineteenth century, at a time when new (Region 2) cataloging and classification techniques were flourishing. Perhaps for that reason, the field created a fused identity with Region 2 devices. Librarians have thus operated on the assumption that all regions of the Bradford distribution of a subject area are best accessed by Region 2 devices, such as catalogs and indexes. In the meantime, scholars and general users tended to muddle along with browsing and footnote chasing as their primary retrieval mechanisms.

Finally, in the late twentieth century, we arrived at the beginning of the Networked Age. When the Web came along, scholars expanded their searching to following Web links, because this technique had a lot of similarities with the footnote chasing they were already familiar with. There have been impressive developments in the potential of networked retrieval to date, but we are still very early in the development of information searching design through networking.

In the end, I believe we should have all three broad types of searching available to us. Work by craftsmen was not abandoned with the advent of the Industrial Revolution, and mass production has not been given up in the Networked Age. We will use them all, with ever more powerful technologies, and ever greater flexibility and effectiveness in our searching. Further, by designing systems to facilitate all three information access methods, effective searching can be supported for all literature sizes and regions.

At the same time, having an understanding of the dynamics of literature distributions may enable us as searchers to make better and more sophisticated decisions about how we want to search and where. It may also prove valuable to test the general conjecture made here, that areas with high numbers of topically relevant materials (relative to all materials in the area) are best searched by browsing, areas with middling numbers of topically relevant items are best searched by directed searching on information-organizational structures, and areas with very sparse ("needle in a haystack") numbers of relevant items are best searched by using links.

REFERENCES

Bates, M. J. (1979) Information search tactics. *Journal of the American Society for Information Science, 30,* 205–14.

Bates, M. J. (1989) Design of browsing and berrypicking techniques for the online search interface. *Online Review, 13,* 407–24.

Bradford, S. C. (1948) *Documentation.* London: Crosby Lockwood.

Chang, S.-J., and R. E. Rice. (1993) Browsing: A multidimensional framework. In M. E. Williams (ed.). *Annual Review of Information Science and Technology* (Vol. 28, pp. 231–76). Medford, NJ: Learned Information.

Chen, Y. S., and F. F. Leimkuhler. (1986) A relationship between Lotka's Law, Bradford's Law, and Zipf's Law. *Journal of the American Society for Information Science, 37,* 304–14.

Ellis, D. (1989) A Behavioural approach to information retrieval system design. *Journal of Documentation, 45,* 171–212.

Fedorowicz, J. (1982) The Theoretical foundation of Zipf's Law and its application to the bibliographic database environment. *Journal of the American Society for Information Science, 33,* 285–93.

Hood, W. W., and C. S. Wilson. (2001) The scatter of documents over databases in different subject domains: How many databases are needed? *Journal of the American Society for Information Science and Technology, 52,* 1242–54.

Kleinberg, J. M. (1999) Hubs, authorities, and communities. *ACM Computing Surveys, 31,* (supp. 4), U21–U23.

Kwasnik, B. H. (1992) Descriptive study of the functional components of browsing. Paper presented at the Proceedings of the IFIP TC2\WG2.7 Working Conference on Engineering for Human-Computer Interaction, Elivuoi, Finland, August 10–14, 1992.

Lancaster, F. W., V. Gondek, S. McCowan, and C. Reese. (1991) The relationship between literature scatter and journal accessibility in an academic special library. *Collection Building, 11,* 19–22.

Leimkuhler, F. F. (1977) Operational analysis of library systems. *Information Processing & Management, 13,* 79–93.

Lempel, R., and S. Moran. (2001) SALSA: The stochastic approach for link-structure analysis. *ACM Transactions on Information Systems, 19,* 131–60.

Pontigo-Martinez, J. (1984) Qualitative attributes and the Bradford Distribution. Unpublished Ph.D. Dissertation, University of Illinois–Champaign-Urbana, Champaign-Urbana, Illinois.

Price, D. J. d. S. (1963) *Little Science, Big Science.* New York: Columbia University Press.

Price, D. J. d. S. (1961) *Science Since Babylon.* New Haven, CT: Yale University Press.

Sandstrom, P. E. (1994) An optimal foraging approach to information seeking and use. *Library Quarterly, 64,* 414–49.

Senders, J. W. (1963) Information storage requirements for the contents of the world's libraries. *Science, 141,* 1067–68.

Stone, S. (1982) Progress in documentation: Humanities scholars: Information needs and uses. *Journal of Documentation, 38,* 292–312.

Watson-Boone, R. (1994) Information needs of humanities scholars. *RQ, 34,* 203–16.

White, H. D. (1981) 'Bradfordizing' search output: How it would help online users. *Online Review, 5,* 47–54.

Wiberley, S. E., Jr., and W. G. Jones. (1989) Patterns of information seeking in the humanities. *College & Research Libraries, 50,* 638–45.

Wilson, A. G., and R. J. Bennett. (1985) *Mathematical Methods in Human Geography and Planning.* New York: Wiley.

Wilson, C. S. (1999) Informetrics. In M. E. Williams (ed.). *Annual Review of Information Science and Technology* (Vol. 34, pp. 107–247). Medford, NJ: Information Today.

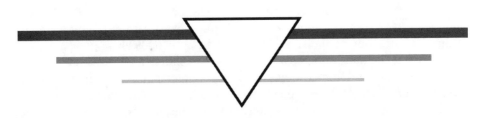

Preliminary Study of the Potentiality of Bibliometric Methods for the Construction of Thesauri

Jesper W. Schneider and Pia Borlund
Royal School of Library and Information Science
Langagervej 4
9220 Aalborg East, Denmark
jws@db.dk; pb@db.dk

ABSTRACT

The paper presents the overall idea of how bibliometric methods may be applied to thesaurus construction as a supplement to intellectual and manual construction and maintenance processes. The paper reports on the initial experiment of the bibliometric based creation of a text corpus from which candidate thesaurus terms can be extracted and relationships uncovered. The results are promising as to the possibility of creating a valid sample of overlapping documents by use of the data set isolation method.

1. INTRODUCTION

The aim of the present paper is to describe and report on the preliminary experiment of (semi)automatic thesaurus construction by use of bibliometric methods, that is, the bibliometric based creation of a text corpus from which candidate

151

thesaurus terms can be extracted and relationships uncovered. The reported research project investigates the applicability of bibliometric methods (e.g., Kessler, 1963; Small, 1973; White, and McCain, 1989) as a supplement to the intellectual manual based thesaurus construction process (e.g., Soergel, 1974; Aitchison, Gilchrist, and Bawden, 2000; Lykke Nielsen, 2001). The research project is to be seen as a continuation of former investigations of automatic thesaurus construction methods, since bibliometric methods also utilise automatic clustering techniques (e.g., Sparck Jones, 1971; Salton, and McGill, 1983). The idea of applying bibliometric methods as a supplement to construction of thesauri is supported by Rees-Potter (1987; 1989; 1991) who takes a similar approach. The approach taken is inspired partly by the theory of polyrepresentation put forward by Ingwersen (e.g., 1992; 1996), and partly by the work of Noyons and van Raan (1998).

As for the theory of polyrepresentation we expand the theory (e.g., Ingwersen, 1992; 1996) to comprise construction of indexing languages, too. Hitherto, the polyrepresentation theory has focused on information retrieval (IR). The fundamental idea is that different methods, that is, bibliometric as well as intellectual manual thesaurus construction methods in combination will enrich the final indexing language with a variety of different aspects, and thereby improving IR. The objective of the project is to investigate to what degree bibliometric methods in a polyreprensentative way may be an alternative and thus supplementing already existing construction methods. In the paper we apply the polyrepresentation theory to the construction of the basis candidate term corpus. The corpus is generated as a result of overlapping document sets from different databases—turning the inconsistencies of individual databases to an advantage by merging and exploiting the inconsistencies (Ingwersen, and Christensen, 1997).

Noyons and van Raan (1998) investigate bibliometric mapping techniques and their possible use for visualising the structure of scientific fields. They identify sub-domains within a research field by clustering topics, which are considered core topics for the field. Potential topics are identified by frequency analysis of noun phrases in titles and abstracts. The most frequent noun phrases are subjected to a co-word analysis, creating a matrix, which is then subjected to a clustering analysis. These clusters are assumed to be sub-domains within the field. Consequently, publications are assigned to a sub-domain on the basis of the noun phrases from the titles or abstracts. This approach creates a field structure similar to Research Fronts (Garfield, 1994). White and McCain (1998) take a different approach. They employ author co-citation analysis, assuming that co-cited authors represent the intellectual base of the citing research, for visualising the field structure.

In the present paper the work by Noyons and van Raan (1998) primarily serves as a source of inspiration. We plan for future experiments to follow the method outlined by Noyons and Van Raan (1998) much closer in our attempt to visualise term relationships.

The paper is structured as follows: Section 2 outlines partly the characteristics of a thesaurus, and partly the conditions required for thesaurus construction in general. This is followed by reviews of research on automatic thesaurus construction approaches and bibliometric methods. Section 3 describes the hypothesis, purpose and focus of the research project. Section 4 outlines the initial part of the experiment and presents the empirical findings. The concluding section, Section 5, discusses the experimental and empirical results and outlines directions of future work.

2. AUTOMATIC THESAURUS CONSTRUCTION: RELATED RESEARCH

2.1. Characteristics of thesauri

A thesaurus is a controlled indexing vocabulary formally displaying a priori relationships between concepts (Aitchison, Gilchrist, and Bawden, 2000). Traditionally, a thesaurus functions as an indexing and retrieval tool, helping with the selection of terms. Thesauri might differ in detail but they share a basic principle, in that they record a set of terms (word or phrases) covering some knowledge domain, and three types of relationships—equivalence, hierarchical and associative relationships (Miller, 1997).

Thesaurus construction requires collecting a set of terms (preferable nouns and noun phrases), and subsequently terminological and semantic treatment plus relational structuring of the collected term classes (Aitchison, Gilchrist, and Bawden, 2000). The classes cover restricted topics of specific scope, and collectively they cover the complete subject area in question. Thus, thesauri are fundamentally linguistic in nature (Miller, 1997). Structural, semantic and terminological problems are ever present (Aitchison, Gilchrist, and Bawden, 2000). This leads to a general understanding that manual intellectual construction work is necessary when dealing with these inherent problems. This is usually done by a group of experts who review the subject matter, suggest potential terms and propose reasonable class arrangements (Lancaster, 1998). A major disadvantage inherent to the use of any thesaurus, due to the dynamic nature of language, is the necessity to maintain the thesaurus. Thus, manual construction and maintenance of a thesaurus is a resource demanding and costly process, which motivates to the research on automatic or semi-automatic methods, that is, less resource demanding methods for thesaurus construction and maintenance (Aitchison, Gilchrist, and Bawden, 2000).

2.2. Automatic thesaurus construction

Historically, the research on automatic thesaurus construction approaches is illustrated by the work of Styles (1961), Sparck Jones (1971), Salton, and McGill (1983) and Van Rijsbergen, Harper, and Porter (1981). Styles (1961) uses term association methods to improve IR performance. Sparck Jones (1971) works on term classification, Salton, and McGill (1983) include query expansion techniques, and van Rijsbergen, Harper, and Porter (1981) work on term co-occurrence to automatic thesaurus construction. Numerous approaches to automatic thesaurus construction are based on statistical co-occurrence of word types in text corpora (e.g., Salton, and McGill, 1983; Crouch, 1990; Chen, et al., 1995; Schütze, and Pedersen, 1997). Basically, the co-occurrence approach uses the collection of documents as a source for thesaurus construction according to a three-step procedure: 1) automatic identification of concepts within a given domain; 2) extraction of word types from the text; and 3) cluster analysis to form possible thesaurus classes (Salton, and McGill, 1983).

Using a collection of documents as a source for thesaurus construction entails that a representative body of text is available for application of statistical procedures to identify important terms as well as their significant relationships (Srinivasan, 1992). The assumption behind statistical methods is that contextually related co-occurring words (i.e., often appearing in the same sentence, paragraph, or document) are semantically related and hence should be classified together in the same thesaurus class (Srinivasan, 1992).

The traditional approach to automatic construction of thesauri is expressed in Salton's vector space model and term discrimination theory (Salton, and McGill, 1983). Based on cluster analysis of terms in documents, the model has been extended from automatic indexing to automatic thesaurus construction. Usually, the first step of cluster analysis is to convert raw data (e.g., weights such as tf-idf) into a matrix of inter-individual similarity measures. This means transposing the term-by-document matrix in order to calculate similarity measures on terms rather than documents (similarity between documents is processed when searching). Similarity coefficients, such as cosine, Jaccard, or Dice are often obtained between pairs of terms, based on coincidences of the terms in the text corpus (Srinivasan, 1992). When pair-wise similarities are available between all term pairs, a clustering algorithm can distribute all terms with sufficient large pair-wise similarities into common classes (Sparck Jones, 1971). The most typical used clustering method is single-link hierarchical clustering (Rasmussen, 1992). This is considered an agglomerative technique because each term must have a similarity exceeding a stated threshold value with at least one term in the same class (Rasmussen, 1992). The problem with this approach is the inherent dimensionality problem, which makes it computer intensive, and applicable only to smaller collections. In addition, problems exist as to the difficulty in identifying synonyms within the same documents, and the ever-present semantic problems caused by automatic indexing (Schütze, and Pedersen, 1997; Lancaster, 1998).

Later research elaborates on Salton's basic work (e.g., Salton, and McGill, 1983; Crouch, 1990; Jing, and Croft, 1994; Schütze, and Pedersen, 1997). Crouch (1990) carries out automatic thesaurus construction by use of the term discrimination value and complete-link clustering. Here each term in the class is associated with all other terms in the class above a given threshold. The basic problem is defining the threshold value determining the actual classification.

Peat and Willett (1991) argue against the utility of co-occurrence information in thesaurus construction. They observe that synonyms often do not occur together in the same context, and consequently the co-occurrence based approach may have difficulty identifying synonym relations. Although synonyms frequently do not co-occur, they do share neighbours that occur with both.

Jing and Croft (1994), and Schütze and Pedersen (1997) investigate lexical co-occurrence for determining word similarity rather than document occurrence. Two terms lexically co-occur if they appear in text within some distance of each other. Both research teams use vector space and similarity measures, but here word synonyms are defined to be its nearest neighbours with respect to similarity measures.

The purpose of automatically constructed thesauri, apart from making the construction and maintenance processes less resource demanding, is to improve retrieval performance by substituting the appropriate cluster of terms for one of its members. The classes formed by statistical procedures will tend to contain relatively more semantically different terms than those of a conventional thesaurus (Lancaster, 1998). According to Lancaster (1998, p. 263), the 'purity' of the class is not always the main issue. It is important whether the class is potentially useful in IR. The heterogeneous nature of the clusters makes it more likely that recall rather than precision will be enhanced. Tests have shown improved retrieval performance up to 15 percent (Crouch, 1990; Chen, et al., 1995).

Statistical based thesaurus construction may yield acceptable results when constructed from a large corpus of text with a specialized vocabulary, but the technique is questionable with heterogeneous text corpora (Salton, and McGill, 1983; Jing, and Croft, 1994). Moreover, the technique simply detects terms and possible relationships (e.g., synonyms and near-synonyms, broader and narrower terms). Detecting the specific semantic nature of these terms, and their relationships, is usually beyond their scope. Automatic thesaurus construction methods cannot function alone, if an elaborate structure and semantic term validity is desired (Lancaster, 1998).

2.3. Bibliometric indexing tools

Bibliometrics is the study of documents and their bibliographic reference and citation structures (Egghe, and Rousseau, 1990). Bibliometrics encompasses a number of empirical methods, such as bibliographic coupling and co-citation analysis (Kessler, 1963; Small, 1973). The methods have been successfully applied to examine the intellectual structure of many disciplines (Borgman, 1990; White, and McCain, 1998).

Bibliometric methods are substantially different from traditional term co-occurrence approaches. The analyses and clustering are not depended on the frequency distribution of index terms, but on the frequency distribution of citations and bibliographic references in the documents. Term class construction based on citations and references has a major advantage over classes created from conventional co-word analysis. Obviously, the construction of term classes based on citations and references is independent of language and changing terminology (Leydesdorff, 1997). The independency increases the features available for cluster generation. A mutual understanding exists that bibliometric methods may point to common topical characteristics of the documents and their authors, and may be used to uncover otherwise hidden knowledge structures about a discipline and its users (e.g., Borgman, 1990). Thus, these indications ought to be used advantageously in connection to thesaurus construction (Hjørland, 2002a).

The use of bibliometric methods to the construction of knowledge organisational systems is not new, KeyWords Plus® and Research Fronts® (Garfield, 1990; 1994) by the Institute of Scientific Information® (ISI®) are examples of this. These products have relied fully on bibliometric computation and automatic indexing. However none of the products deal with either the inherent problems of indexing languages such as terminological and semantic issues, or the possible relationship types between indexing terms in the language (Lancaster, 1998). In order to acknowledge the problems a combination of bibliometrics and intellectual manual construction methods is recommendable (e.g., Hjørland, 2002b). Rees-Potter's research on thesauri maintenance is a fine example (1987; 1989; 1991). However, in contrast to Rees-Potter who uses citation, co-citation analysis and citation context analysis, we plan to use the data set isolation method (Ingwersen, and Christensen, 1997), bibliographic coupling and semantic maps for the verification and extraction of candidate thesaurus terms.

3. PURPOSE AND FOCUS OF RESEARCH PROJECT

The underlying hypothesis of the research project is that bibliometric methods can be used as a supplement to the established methods of thesaurus construction, since the bibliometric methods may uncover conditions, patterns and relationships between documents and their concepts. With Noyons and van Raan's work as inspiration, a variety of possibilities exits, such as creating document clusters through co-citation analysis or bibliographic coupling from cited works or author names. In addition, maps may be created by use of multi-dimensional scaling (MDS), consisting of document clusters of cited articles (White, and McCain, 1998). Subjects may be identified by frequency analysis of noun phrases in titles and abstracts of the publications, and they may be the basis for candidate thesaurus terms. Hence, the aim of the research project is to apply bibliometric methods to generate different clusters and semantic maps potentially to be used as supplement for manual intellectual thesaurus construction.

Three major research areas constitutes the kernel and focus in the investigation of the applicability of bibliometric methods as supplement for thesaurus construction, these are: 1) the construction and maintenance of a thesaurus vocabulary and structure; 2) the extent to which clusters can create synonyms and uncover relations between terms; and 3) the use of bibliometrics for maintenance of a thesaurus in a given domain over a given time.

4. EXPERIMENTAL METHOD AND EMPIRICAL FINDINGS

In this section we report on the initial part of the empirical investigation. The empirical investigation aims at identifying suitable methods for generating a text corpus from which candidate thesaurus terms can be extracted and relationships uncovered. The proposed method consists of five sub-steps of which step one and two are described in the present paper. Step one concerns the creation of document sets from an initial search strategy. At step two document clusters are generated based on the documents sets by use of bibliometric methods. Subsequently, follows a third, fourth and fifth step, not reported in this paper, dealing with term extraction, manual thesaurus construction, and evaluation of the quality of the extracted terms.

4.1. Step one: the creation of overlapping document sets

A search strategy is created with the purpose of establishing overlapping document sets at various points in time. This is done by use of the *data set isolation method* outlined by Ingwersen and Christensen (1997). The main idea behind the data set isolation method is to constructively exploit the inconsistent indexing inherent in databases by the merger of document representations from different databases, thus resulting in overlapping documents sets which are consider 'enhanced' due to the theory of polyrepresentation.

The overlapping sets of documents are created through the merger of document representations from different domain dependent as well as ISI® databases. The domain dependent databases are preferred due to their thorough document descriptions, especially the indexing terms. The ISI® databases are used with respect to the bibliographic references and citations.

The subject area for investigation is periodontics, a sub-domain to dentistry. The exact databases are: MEDLINE® and Science Citation Index® (SCI®). The well-established indexing language in MEDLINE®, Medical Subject Headings® (MeSH®), will be used for two purposes. Partly as a measure for agreement of descriptor distributions between overlapping document sets and the population, and partly as a baseline for the quality of the vocabulary created by use of bibliometric methods.

4.1.2. Application of the data set isolation method

The data set isolation method (Ingwersen, and Christensen, 1997) is processed according to three steps:

1. Initial search (including a search strategy, cross-file search and tuning of the data set),

2. Duplicate removal and reversed duplicate removal procedures, and

3. Isolation of the overlapping documents.

The formulation of the search strategy includes a cross-file searching. This entails a restriction due to the different search parameters in various databases to be cross-searched. The rationale behind the search string is as follows, the first parenthesis cover the subject area in MEDLINE® by use of an explode search mode in the MeSH® hierarchy, and a corresponding free text subject search in SCI®. To be able to investigate possible changes in the domain language, the aspect of time is incorporated through publication year, respectively 1989, 1993 and 1997. The search is narrowed to English language documents due to a need for English language terms, and a fine-tuning of the documents is done by use of document types (also a transparent field code)—resulting in the following search string:

(periodontics! or periodont?) and py=1989 and la=english and dt=(article or journal article or review).

The search string is processed simultaneously in both MEDLINE® and SCI® through the database host Dialog® by use of DialogLink®. Three searches are undertaken, one for each of the chosen years.

We acknowledge that the use of periodontics as a search term may limit, and possible bias, the range of documents initially retrieved, due to the possible dependency of the term being explicit represented in the documents. However, the use of co-citation analysis at the initially retrieved document sets may uncover links to documents external to the sets dealing with the subject matter—though this will never fully rectify the imbalance. Further, we need to explore if this has serious consequences for the method presented, or whether an exhaustive document set is required at all.

According to step two of the data set isolation method duplicate documents are removed. In this respect, it is of importance from which database to remove the duplicates, and in which file to keep the duplicates (Ingwersen, and Christensen, 1997, p. 208). This is called the sequential order, that is, the file order in the cluster, and a subsequent analysis will therefore depend on the file structure and contents of this file. The Reversed Duplicate Removal (RDR) technique provides the analyst with different data sets containing the same items. A set containing the files A and B in that sequence will place the duplicates in file A, when RDR is effectuated. If the sequence is reversed, the overlapping items will be placed in file B. Consequently, one can switch back and forth between the files to carry out different analyses depending on purpose and focus of the research.

4.1.3. Results of the data set isolation method

The three searches, one for each year, result in three overlapping document sets (samples), containing the same documents in either MEDLINE® or SCI®, depending on the file order, see Table 1. It is essential that the samples have a similar distribution of MeSH® like the population from where they are extracted.

As a similar distribution indicates a variety in the representation of subjects, and then the MeSH® can be used for evaluation of extracted potential candidate thesaurus terms (for example, a skewed distribution could yield a foul result due to a one side subject representation). Since the aim of the research project is to investigate possible construction methods and not an entire construction of a thesaurus, the need for the complete text corpora is not vital. The overlapping document sets (samples) cover 25 percent, 33 percent, and 41 percent of the population (MEDLINE®), respectively (see Table 1).

Table 1. Number of documents in sample and population distributed according to year.

Document sets	1989	1993	1997
Number of overlapping documents (sample)	322	595	752
Number of documents in MEDLINE (population)	1274	1793	1822
Percentage of overlap of population	25%	33%	41%

The MeSH® terms can be used beneficially in the evaluation of the extracted terms, thus the search results from MEDLINE®, including both overlapping and non-overlapping documents, are chosen as the population (Table 1). Subsequently, a frequency analysis—ranking—is executed on the descriptor field code, for the sample and the population, respectively. A Chi-square test for homogeneity between sample and population is used to measure the agreement (homogeneity) between the distributions of MeSH® in the sample and in the population.

Table 2. Results of chi-square test of agreement in descriptor distributions between sample and population.

Chi-square tests of homogeneity			
Overlapping sets	Critical a: 0.01	$X^{2 \ (at \ 99 \ df)}$	Conclusion
1989	134.641	26.49	Accept of H_0
1993	133.475	25.29	Accept of H_0
1997	132.308	28.43	Accept of H_0

Table 2 shows the statistical results of the three tests, indicating the agreement in the descriptor distributions of the sample and population. The positive results in all three tests indicate an almost certain statistical assurance that the sample distribution of descriptors is not skewed in regard to the distribution of descriptors in the population. This means that it is valid to continue the bibliometric investigations with these three samples, since there is no evidence pointing to odd distribution of descriptors. They therefore represent a solid sample of documents dealing with a variety of aspects of periodontics in the given time period.

4.2. Step two: bibliometric document clustering

After the creation of three valid overlapping document sets with different time origin, a bibliometric analysis is undertaken. The analysis applied for this study is bibliographic coupling (Kessler, 1963). A coupling unit is a single reference used and shared by two scientific works. The number of coupling units between the two scientific works measures the strength of the coupling. When two citing items have a strong bibliographic coupling, they share and have a great number of bibliographic references in common, and the two citing items are presumably dealing with the same subject matter.

The actual bibliometric analysis is processed by use of the Bibexcel software, which is a tool for offline bibliometric analyses (www.umu.se/inforsk/). The analysis of bibliographic coupling is carried out on the *cited reference* string (CR) in the three downloaded document sets from SCI®. Bibexcel is used to standardise the references to facilitate a higher quality of matching between the individual units. The CR-string is reduced to cited author, cited year and cited volume in order to minimise false pairs.

The bibliographic coupling analysis is a two-step procedure. The first step identifies the frequency of bibliographic coupled pairs in common to the document sets. The second step generates clusters from the bibliographic coupled documents verified in step one, indicating the number of individual coupled units attached to the cluster-representative unit. The clustering algorithm in Bibexcel is Person's Party Clustering. It is a non-hierarchic, single link clustering method, which divides the dataset into a series of subsets, with similar objects in the same cluster being separated from non-similar objects placed in different clusters. The clustering algorithm is described in the help file to the Bibexcel software (www.umu.se/inforsk/).

Table 3 is an extraction of the cluster file generated from the 1989-document set comprising 322 overlapping documents. Altogether 143 clusters were generated from this overlapping document set. Table 3 illustrates the final cluster (i.e., number 143) comprising four bibliographic coupled documents. In other words, Table 3 shows cluster no. 143, with the core document no. 179, the so-called cluster representative unit, with which the documents no. 189, 182, 185, and 187 shares a bibliographic coupling.

Table 3. Example of cluster: cluster representative unit is depicted to the left and its coupled unit to the right.

Cluster	Doc. no.	Left side pair	Doc. No.	Right side pair
143	179	ISHIHARA Y; KATO H; KOGAT T; MAKI E; NISHIHARA T; NOGUCHI T	189	ALCOUEFFE F
143	179	ISHIHARA Y; KATO H; KOGAT T; MAKI E; NISHIHARA T; NOGUCHI T	182	GALGUT PN
143	179	ISHIHARA Y; KATO H; KOGAT T; MAKI E; NISHIHARA T; NOGUCHI T	185	BERGMANN OJ; ELLEGAARD B; ELLEGAARD J
143	179	ISHIHARA Y; KATO H; KOGAT T; MAKI E; NISHIHARA T; NOGUCHI T	187	DEGRAAFF J; VANDERVELDEN U; VANSTEENBERGEN JM; VANWINKELHOFF AJ

Table 4 illustrates the most frequent occurring individual bibliographic coupling units, expressed in number of *in links* to the clusters. The underlying assumption is that clusters with high numbers of in links may reveal candidate terms due to their strong bibliographic couplings, for example cluster no. 8, and the cluster representative unit, document no. 28 with the 71 in links.

Table 4. Most frequent occurring coupling units.

Number of in links	Cluster	Doc. no.	Cluster representative unit (cluster core document)
71	8	28	HAFFAJEE A; LINDHE J; OKAMOTO H; SOCRAMSKY SS; YONEYAMA T
67	7	26	COLLINS AEM; DEASY PB; MACCARTHY DJ; RUSSELL RJ
60	15	22	BIRD PS; GEMMELL E; HARA K; POLAK B; SEYMOUR GJ; YAMAZAKI K
57	6	13	ABBAS F; DEGRAAFF J; DELAAT VHM; DERUYTER C; DEZOETE OJ; HESSE M; VANDERVELDEN U; VANSTEENBERGEN TJM
....	....	......	....
4	143	179	ISHIHARA Y; KATO H; KOGAT T; MAKI E; NISHIHARA T; NOGUCHI T

4.2.1. Clustering results

The analysis, which is based on all three sets of documents overlaps, results in three frequency distributions of coupled pairs (not illustrated in this paper), and three cluster files over a time span of nine years, see Table 5.

Table 5. Number of clusters.

Document sets	1989	1993	1997
Number of clusters in the sets	143	474	612

What follows is a transformation of these clusters by extraction of nouns and noun phrases indicating subjects, as well as to visualise highly coupled clusters in a map in order to indicate possible term relational structures, which is beyond this paper.

5. DISCUSSION AND FUTURE WORK

The purpose of this paper is partly to present the idea of how bibliometric methods may be applied to thesaurus construction—supplementing the intellectual and manual construction and maintenance processes—and hopefully improve IR. And partly to report on the initial experiment of the bibliometric based creation of a text corpus from which potential thesaurus terms can be extracted and relationships uncovered. The initial experiment shows positive and promising results as to the possibility of creating a valid sample of overlapping documents by use of the data set isolation method. The Chi-square tests indicate that the overlapping document sets are valid for further use.

By the use of bibliometric analyses such as bibliographic coupling and cluster analysis, several clusters in the three overlapping document sets are created. Further analyses may verify whether the cluster documents yields a sufficient amount of candidate thesaurus terms (i.e., is the text corpora large enough). The chosen cluster algorithm determines the outcome of the clustering—another algorithm, another result. In addition, a comparison of the results from two or more cluster analyses, done on the same items, may uncover further structures.

The time span runs from 1989 via 1993 to 1997. The four year span will incorporate 2001 in due time, to get the best possible foundation for investigating the aspects of changes and displacements within a domain over time. This will be done by means of semantic maps generated over time. The proposed method ought to be subsequently reflected in the maintenance of an indexing language, making it less conservative.

Establishing an indexing language from a text corpus creates a paradox, since the chosen terms could be outdated. This is another indication of the need for the supplementary combination of manual and automatic thesaurus construction methods.

Future experiments will follow the method by Noyons and Van Raan (1998) much closer, since the created clusters are expected to indicate some subject similarity, and thus will be subjected to extraction of nouns and noun phrases—potential thesaurus terms. MDS-techniques will be used to identify possible links between clusters indicating potential relationships. Similarly, co-citation analysis will be carried out on the same data set. Finally, other search strategies for creating documents sets will be considered.

ACKNOWLEDGEMENTS

The reported research forms part of the TAPIR project, headed by professor Peter Ingwersen, at the Department of Information Studies, Royal School of Library and Information Science, Denmark. The authors thank Peter Ingwersen for being an inexhaustible source of inspiration. The authors also thank doctoral student Birger Larsen for technical help and advice.

REFERENCES

Aitchison, J., A. Gilchrist, and D. Bawden. (2000) *Thesaurus construction and use: A practical manual.* London: Aslib.

Borgman, C. L. (1990) *Scholarly communication and bibliometrics.* London: Sage.

Chen, H., B. Schatz, T. Yim, and D. Fye. (1995) Automatic thesaurus generation for an electronic community system. *Journal of the American Society for Information Science, 46*(3), 175–93.

Crouch, C. J. (1990) An approach to automatic construction of global thesauri. *Information Processing & Management, 26*(5), 629–40.

Egghe, L., and R. Rousseau. (1990) *Introduction to Informetrics.* Amsterdam: Elsevier.

Garfield, E. (1990) KeyWords Plus. *Current Contents, 32,* 3–7.

Garfield, E. (1994) Research Fronts. *Current Contents, 41,* 3–6.

Hjørland, B. (2002a) Domain analysis in information science: Eleven approaches—traditional as well as innovative. *Journal of Documentation,* (July). In press.

Hjørland, B. (2002b) The methodology of constructing classification schemes. *A discussion of the state-of-the-art.* Paper accepted for the ISKO 7 conference 2002 Granada, Spain, July10–13, 2002.

Ingwersen, P. (1992) *Information Retrieval Interaction.* London: Taylor Graham.

Ingwersen, P. (1996) Cognitive perspectives of information retrieval interaction: Elements of a cognitive IR theory. *Journal of Documentation, 52*(1), 3–50.

Ingwersen, P., and F. H. Christensen. (1997) Data set isolation for bibliometric online analyses of research publications: Fundamental Methodological Issues. *Journal of the American Society for Information Science, 48*(3), 205–17.

Jing, Y., and W. B. Croft. (1994) An association thesaurus for information retrieval. In RIAO 94 Conference Proceedings: *Intelligent Multimedia Information Retrieval Systems and Management* (146–60). Paris: C.I.D.-C.A.S.I.S.

Kessler, M. M. (1963) Bibliographic coupling between scientific papers. *American Documentation, 14*, 10–25.

Lancaster, F. W. (1998) *Indexing and abstracting in theory and practice*. London: Library Association Publishing.

Lykke Nielsen, M. (2001) A framework for work task based thesaurus design. *Journal of Documentation, 57*(6), 774–97.

Leydesdorff, L. (1997) Why words and co-words cannot map the development of the sciences. *Journal of the American Society for Information Science, 48*(5), 418–27.

Miller, U. (1997) Thesaurus construction: Problems and their roots. *Information Processing & Management, 33*(4), 481–93.

Noyons, E. C. M., and A. F. J. van Raan. (1998) *Mapping Scientometrics, Informetrics, and Bibliometrics*. Retrieved January 9, 2002, from: http://www.cwts.nl/ed/sib/home.html.

Peat, H. J., and P. Willett. (1991) The limitations of term co-occurrence data for query expansion in document retrieval systems. *Journal of the American Society for Information Science, 42*(5), 378–83.

Rasmussen, E. (1992) Clustering algorithms. In W. B. Frakes, and R. Baeza-Yates (eds.). *Information Retrieval: Data structures & algorithms* (419–42). Upper Saddle River, NJ: Prentice Hall.

Rees-Potter, L. K. (1987) *A bibliometric analysis of terminological and conceptual change in sociology and economics with the application to the design of dynamic thesaural systems.* 2 volumes. Ph.D. dissertation. London, Ontario: University of Western Ontario.

Rees-Potter, L. K. (1989) Dynamic thesaural systems: a Bibliometric study of terminological and conceptual change in sociology and economics with the application to the design of dynamic thesaural systems. *Information Processing & Management, 25*(6), 677–91.

Rees-Potter, L. K. (1991) Dynamic thesauri: The cognitive function. In R. Fugmann (ed.). *Tools for Knowledge organisation and the human interface.* Proceedings of the 1st International ISKO Conference, Darmstadt, 14–17 August 1990. Part 2, 145–50.

Salton, G., and M. J. McGill. (1983) *Introduction to modern information retrieval*. New York: MaGraw-Hill.

Schütze, H., J. O. Pedersen. (1997) A cooccurrence-based thesaurus and two applications to information retrieval. *Information Processing & Management, 33*(3), 307–18.

Srinivasan, P. (1992) Thesaurus construction. In W. B. Frakes, and R. Baeza-Yates (eds.). *Information Retrieval: Data structures & algorithms* (161–218). Upper Saddle River, NJ: Prentice Hall.

Small, H. (1973) Co-citation in the scientific literature: a new measure of the relationship between two documents. *Journal of the American Society for Information Science, 24*(4), 265–69.

Soergel, D. (1974) *Indexing languages and thesauri: construction and maintenance.* Los Angeles, CA: Melville.

Sparck Jones, K. (1971) *Automatic keyword classification for information retrieval.* London: Butterworths.

Styles, H. E. (1961) The association factor in information retrieval. *Journal of the Association of Computer Machinery, 8*(2), 271–79.

Van Rijsbergen, C. J., D. J. Harper, and M. F. Porter. (1981) The selection of good search terms. *Information Processing & Management, 17*(2), 77–91.

White, H. D., and K. W. McCain. (1989) Bibliometrics. In M. E. Williams (ed.). *Annual Review of Information Science and Technology, 24,* 119–86. Amsterdam: Elsevir.

White, H. D., and K. W. McCain. (1998) Visualizing a discipline. An author co-citation analysis of information science, 1972–1995. *Journal of the American Society for Information Science, 49*(4), 327–55.

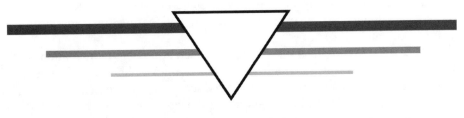

Informetrics and the Use of Bibliographic Data in a Strategic Combination

Irene Wormell
Swedish School of Library and Information Science
Allegatan 1
501 90 Borås, Sweden
Irene.wormell@hb.se

ABSTRACT

Through a sample of research studies the paper presents an approach to knowledge discovery. The novel aspect is the combination of various types of data and quantitative analyses. The reported applications are intended to illustrate the scope and nature of informetric analyses, where advanced information retrieval theories and methodologies are combined with the quantitative study of information flows in a strategic mix. The concept has a close connection to text and data mining techniques, as well as to modern display and visualization techniques. The sample shows how this methodology gathered useful information for business intelligence, trend analysis, and for the evaluation of scientific, political and business developments. It is an appeal to the modern LIS professionals to adapt the use of the classic bibliometric methods in a modern context, and to utilize the databases not only for retrieval of documents or facts, but also as tools for analytical work.

167

1. INTRODUCTION

Our ability to analyse and understand the contents and relationships between massive data sets lags far behind our ability to gather and store data. Competence in the use of advanced retrieval techniques and analytical tools are required to support the extraction of useful knowledge from the rapidly growing volumes of databases.

The creative application of mining techniques in combination with bibliometric analyses in the searching of large bibliographic databases can, to a large extent, facilitate knowledge discovery and the use bibliographic information in a new way. These methodologies are usable for information provision aimed to trace the deeper segments of information and to map those trends and developments in society, science and business which are not directly visible (Raghavan, et al., 1998; Vickery, 1997).

This type of information is, however, visible only to searchers who know how *to read between the lines* of the electronic information, and can apply various types of analytical tools in combination with advanced search and display techniques.

The paper will call attention to the use of methodologies for quantitative analysis/synthesis in searching large bibliographic databases. In this context, *Informetrics* as an emerging sub-field in information science will be presented. A selection of case studies will show how bibliometric methods (quantitative studies of information flows) in combination with statistics, advanced information retrieval, data and text mining techniques can be applied, e.g., to the analyses of subject domains and research fronts, evaluation of portals and electronic libraries, and for gathering useful information for business intelligence and policy making.

Through a sample of research studies the paper aims to show briefly some of the results of this approach: detailed and informative analyses of phenomena, such as, the international impact of the "international" scientific journals; domain analysis of the international/national Welfare research; the critical aspects of the Danish Welfare State; the impact, visibility and connectivity in science, politics and business on the Web; and subject portals and electronic library resources. Most of the studies were conducted at the Centre for Informetric Studies in Copenhagen in the period of time 1997–2000. The objective was to call attention to the relevance of informetric analysis to the work tasks of modern information professionals, and to generate research results in interdisciplinary areas, e.g., trend analysis, issue management, business and social intelligence, research evaluation, innovation studies, etc.

The paper emphasises also the necessity that library and information professionals act as *consolidators of information*: the people who transform raw data into valuable knowledge by identifying patterns and gathering pieces of information, which they interpret in the light of management decisions and other strategically significant circumstances faced by their organisations (Wormell, 1999).

2. INFORMETRICS AS RESEARCH METHOD

Bibliometrics, from which *Informetrics* derives, is traditionally associated with the quantitative measure of documentary materials and it embraces all studies which seek to quantify the process of written communication. Bibliometric methods are used especially in studies, a) analysing the patterns of authorship, publication and literature use, b) mapping the relations within scientific domains and research communities and, c) analysing the structure of specific scientific and research areas.

Bibliometrics refers to a variety of regularities taken from different fields and exhibiting a variety of forms. Although the bibliometric laws and their derivatives are scientific laws with special reference to the field of library and information science, they are, surprisingly, little used today in that discipline. To the majority of LIS professionals today, it sounds like a very traditional and "dusty" part of academic information work. With a few exceptions, it is a neglected area in most current LIS curricula. It is not yet properly understood that advanced online search facilities and information retrieval techniques are relying on Zipf's Law and, at the same time, modern IR techniques have considerably increased the potentialities of bibliometric research methodology. Further, they are opening up new possibilities for tracking down analytic information from large collections of bibliographic data (Garfield, 1998).

Informetrics has a broader scope than Bibliometrics, because it also covers non-scholarly communities in which information is produced, communicated, and used. The classical bibliometric methods are applied not only to the evaluation of science and technology, but also to the analysis of their societal, business and other specific relations. It includes also the analyses of voice and picture records, as well as the World Wide Web, as feasible and reliable tools to evaluate the impact of scientific, political, and business developments (Tague-Sutcliffe, 1992).

Since the beginning of the 1980s, Bibliometrics has evolved into a distinct scientific discipline with several sub-fields and corresponding scientific communication structures. The international journal *Scientometrics*, the first periodical specialising in bibliometric topics, was published in 1979. International conferences of the field started in 1983, and the *International Society for Scientometrics and Informetrics (ISSI)* was founded in 1993.

The individual identities of the sub-fields *bibliometrics, informetrics, scientometrics,* and *technometrics* are unfortunately not very clear, and there is a certain ambiguity in the terminology. At the 1987 international conference some thoughts had been given to changing the name of the discipline to "informetrics" and since the end of the 1980s there is some evidence in favour of the use of this term. The field is becoming a scientific discipline including all the statistical and mathematical analyses related to the study of information flows; evaluation of science and technology; and library, documentation and information problems with strong links to the theoretical aspects of information retrieval. *Webometrics* is still in its experimental stage. Most of the investigations are testing whether the classical bibliometric methods, e.g., for impact analysis applied to the Web, are feasible and reliable means of analysing and comparing web sites (Björneborn, and Ingwersen, 2001).

3. SAMPLE OF RESEARCH STUDIES

3.1. Assessing the international impact of scientific journals

To illustrate the scope and nature of informetric analyses applied to the evaluation of the market for international scientific journals, this sample describes the analysis of the international impact of seven selected scientific journals. It aims to move beyond the simplistic use of the ISI-produced Journal Impact Factor (JIF) and will provide a deeper insight into the "real" impact of the international scientific journals and their market. Regarding the expanding electronic publishing market and the sharp competition between journals, the analysis has great relevance to marketing and publishing strategies, as well as to the development of editorial policies adjusted to the changed market conditions (Wormell, 1998).

The following questions helped to establish how "international" the international scientific journals are in scope and impact:

• Is the journal a national, international, continental, intercontinental product?

• What is the origin of the intellectual input (authors writing in the journal)?

• In which regions are the users concentrated (geographical distribution of citations)?

• Where does the "export of the knowledge" published in the journal go (from which subject areas are the citations coming)?

• Does the distribution of users correspond with the distribution of subscribers?

The sample of selected journals has been designed to include core library and information science journals with the reputation of having an international readership. The list has been defined as follows:

1. Libri	International Journal of Libraries and Information Services
2. Scientometrics	An International Journal for all Quantitative Aspects of the Science of Science, Communication in Science and Science Policy
3. JASIS	Journal of the American Society for Information Science
4. J Doc	Journal of Documentation
5. IPM	Information Management & Processing
6. C&RL	College & Research Libraries
7. Comp J	The International Journal of Computing

The current status, as well as the historical developments of the journals, was measured since 1972, from the beginning of the Social Science Citation Index. The analyses cover two five-year citation windows, 1987–1991 and 1992–1996, with two-year publication windows, 1987–1988 and 1992–1993.

The study was based on subscription data for 1996 (commercially sensitive data), which was provided directly by the publishers. It should be noticed that e-journals, electronic archives, licence agreements etc. have radically changed the use and distribution pattern of journals. Therefore, this part of the analysis has to be extended all the time to cover also alternative types of "use" beside the traditional subscription. The methodology is, however, solid and unique, and it provides robust indicators of quality and impact of the international scientific journals, as well as the relationship between the three main actors of the journal market: authors, users/citations, and subscribers.

Statistical analyses were carried out to test how strong the correlation is between the geographical distribution of authors, citations and subscriptions, as well as to see the significance of differences in their distribution patterns. Considering the small size of the sample, the results of the calculations were interpreted and fine-tuned by regression analysis and also weighted by other possible factors.

The Pearson test examined *first* the correlation between author and citation data in the two periods of the investigation. Influence; cause and effect relationships; and regional effect were measured to verify the homogeneity of the data. *Secondly,* a similar test checked the correlation between the two periods of time. *Finally,* the likelihood ratio chi-square test was run to analyse the significance of the difference in the distribution of authors and subscriptions as well as of citations and subscriptions. These three steps of the analysis were executed for the seven selected journals.

In the following we will present the results of the analysis for one of the selected seven journals, *Libri*. For the full presentation of the analyses one is referred to the article by Wormell (1998).

Libri—International Journal of Libraries and Information Services, is one of the oldest international library journals. It publishes original articles on all aspects of libraries and information services. International visibility, scholarly publishing and good review articles were the main features of the journal. During the 1980s, however, the scholarly level of the journal fell and the share of applied research contributions increased. The severe budget cuts in the Western world libraries caused significant loss both in the European and the U.S. subscriptions.

In 1989, the publisher set up a new editorial team and tried to gear the future developments of the journal in a new direction. The changed publishing and editorial policy, promotion, new design for the cover, etc. resulted in a positive development for the journal. During the period of time 1992–1993, for instance, we can notice an increase in the number of authors coming from North America and a reduction in the number from Africa, see Figure 1.

Figure 1. The international visibility of *Libri*, seen as the geographical distribution of authors writing in *Libri* during the two publication windows.

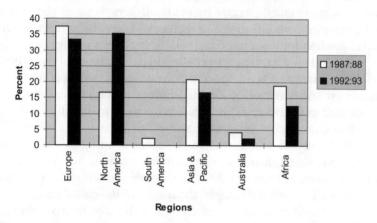

Geographical distribution of authors writing in *Libri*

Figure 2. The international citation impact of *Libri*, seen through the geographical distribution of citations given to the journal.

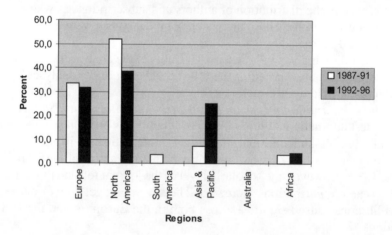

Geographical distribution of citations given to items published in *Libri,* 1987-88 and 1992-93 with five years citation windows

In the case of *Libri,* as regards the intellectual input (authors), as well as the concentration of users (measured as the number of citations given to the journal), Europe and North America are the dominating regions, see Figure 2. Looking at the relation between the concentration of users and subscriptions, however, this dominance is not reflected in the number of subscriptions on the part of North

America, see Figure 3. The available subscription data for 1996 indicates some market opportunities here for the journal: the low 21 percent share of subscriptions in the North America region, compared with the 35 percent share of the authors and the 39 percent share of citation impact, is pointing to the fact that there are potentialities for increasing the number of subscriptions in that region.

The Chi-square test showed low likelihood ratios between authors and subscriptions, and between citations and subscriptions, which normally would be regarded as values of no correlation. However, the calculated values are providing useful indications about the size of differences in these distribution patterns. This calls for the attention of the editors and publishers, and signals special situations in the market position of the journal. For example, compared with the calculated normal distribution of subscriptions, Europe has at present too few authors and citations; in contrast, North America is having both (too) many authors and citations; and Africa is having (too) many authors.

For a small sample like this, the calculated critical values have to be still more carefully analysed and weighted with other possible causes than in the case of large samples.

Figure 3. The 1996 subscription map of *Libri*: percentage of subscription in the six regions.

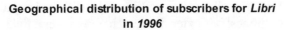

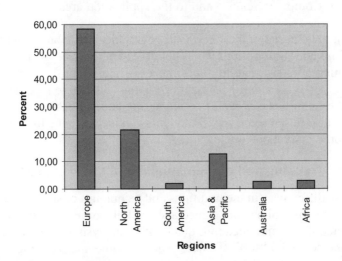

Searching for additional indicators of quality and impact, the study examined also the "knowledge export" of the journals. This indicator measures whether the given journal has the scientific strength and impact to break through the traditional borders of the home field, and whether it can attract authors and citations from neighbouring disciplines. To evaluate how much interdisciplinary impact the journal has in its topical frame, with online citation analysis, we can trace from which journals and subject areas the external citations are coming. The *export of knowledge* from *Libri* had the following distribution patterns during the two periods of the investigation, indicating a very weak interdisciplinary impact:

1987-91

24	92.3%	INFORMATION SCIENCE & LIBRARY SC.
1	03.8%	COMPUTER APPLICATIONS & CYBERN.
1	03.8%	ECONOMICS
1	03.8%	EDUCATION & EDUCATIONAL RESEARCH
1	03.8%	OPERATIONS RESEARCH & MANAGEMENT SCIENCE
1	03.8%	PLANNING & DEVELOPMENT

1992-96

39	100.0%	INFORMATION SCIENCE & LIBRARY SCIENCE
	1 02.6%	COMPUTER SCIENCE, INFORMATION SYSTEMS

Comparing the knowledge export of other journals, it should be mentioned that, e.g., *JASIS* has a smaller concentration to the LIS field and a larger spread to other related disciplines: it is extensive, and having several links outside the LIS field, mainly to Computer Science and to the application areas of Information Science.

Based on the correlation between the geographical distribution pattern of authors, citations and subscriptions it was possible to define a new robust indicator for the "international" visibility and impact of the scientific journals. The analysis of the statistical significance of correlation and differences gave some useful data, the importance of which to marketing and publishing strategies is obvious. They also raised some useful thoughts and ideas among the publishers about unexplored market potentials.

3.2. Issue tracking and domain analysis of the Welfare State

Due to the differences in the traditions and techniques of subject representation between the disciplines of science and the humanities, and the different patterns of scientific communication, quantitative analysis for monitoring the literature in the so-called "soft" sciences requires some alternative techniques and attitudes.

Therefore, the primary aim of the study was to improve the methodology of quantitative analysis in such a wide and complex subject domain as "*Welfare*" within the social sciences.

The aim of the analysis was threefold:

1. to study the past and current developments of the Welfare State as a research phenomenon, and to show what "metric studies" can offer to the exploration of the deeper segments of knowledge production in a broad social science domain.

2. to improve the analytical techniques and methods in handling large bibliographical data sets in the informetric analyses.

3. to test the usability of the *issue tracking* methodology in the monitoring of main issues in the critic of the modern Danish Welfare State, i.e., to analyse the relationship between information flows coming from the research, economic, political and social systems in Denmark, and to track some of the key issues through these sources to analyse how they develop over time.

The first part of the study (domain analysis) used the technique of coordinated online searches in a cluster of international bibliographic databases for mapping the development of topics in the international Welfare research. The quantitative analysis of the number of publications and word frequencies were combined with similarity measures and other statistical methods to produce tables, diagrams, and clusters showing how the topical areas within the research field have developed over the last 25 years, divided in three periods of time. The results of the analyses are quantitative data combined with some "flagged" issues for the consideration of experts and strategic planners (Wormell, 2000a). In the project a panel of domain experts and other specialists contributed advice and the necessary feedback in the evaluation of findings.

Figure 4 illustrates one type of cluster analysis carried out for mapping the subject domain of the international Welfare research in 1990–1997, consisting of the 13 main topics (defined by the expert panel).

The second part of the study focused on Denmark. It aimed to unearth important past, current and future conditions related to the development of the Welfare State concept and monitor how the concept was moving from the theoretical to the empirical problems of the Welfare State. Using the methodology of *issue tracking* as the first step, the analysis followed up the development of selected topics in the research environment. In the next step these topics were tracked through various databases containing information about their implementation in the political, legislative, and social systems of the country. Finally, the reflections they caused in the popular press and media were analysed.

Through the analysis of the information flow between research, media, and the political system, the study was designed to monitor the economic, legitimacy, and functionality aspects of the Welfare State in Denmark, and to trace possible future trends and forecasts (Wormell, 2000b).

Figure 4. Cluster analysis in the form of a dendrogram, showing the similarity between the 13 topical word pairs.

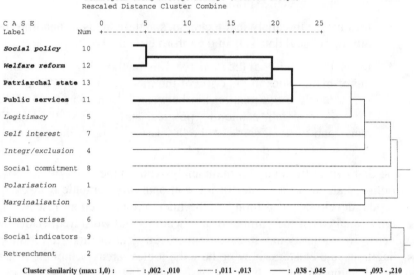

Issue tracking is a useful methodology if one is interested in following how a concept (originating from an innovation or a new idea) is moving through the path of various publication forms, e.g.,

Theoretical research ➔ *applied research* ➔ *techniques and engineering* ➔ *popular press and mass media* ➔ *legislation*

The informetric analysis generated the following types of quantitative data:

- publications originating from publicly funded research
- identification of the funding organisations and executing institutions
- number of books and articles published in the selected topical areas
- publication and term frequency analysis of the popular press and mass media
- welfare related words and expressions (the language of the Welfare)
- legislation work and political activities through some significant types of documents

The Danish national study was based on three main questions in the criticism of the "Welfare State":

Economic aspects	*Can we afford it?*
Legitimacy	*Do the people believe in it*
	and how much do they support it?
Functionality	*How does it work?*

The aim was to improve and develop methodologies to identify trends, current and future conditions related to the concept of Welfare State, and focus them for expert considerations. Generally, the published results are limited in delivering qualitative analysis, but they signal the relevant quantitative data and "flag" the issues which might be candidates for further analysis, e.g., for the production of indicators in the mapping of scientific, social and cultural trends in the development of the modern Welfare State. They are supposed to be used by domain specialists and social policy makers as "raw material" in connection with the further analysis of specific areas, and hopefully they will contribute to a better understanding of the theoretical or empirical aspects of the Welfare State.

In co-operation with the Institute for Future Studies, Denmark, we aim to apply this type of informetric analysis in a planned investigation to show the gap between the politicians and the public opinion about the Welfare State in Denmark. This is an extensive project where the informetric analyses will be (only) one of several other methods used in mapping the opinion of the Danish people vs. the political ambition in the country.

3.3. Study of impact, visibility and connectivity in the Web

The interesting idea of utilising informetric methods on the Web has started to lay the basis for the new emerging area of *Webometrics*. The novel aspect was to regard the Web as a citation network wherein the traditional information entities (scientific articles and citations given *to* and *from* them) are replaced by web pages with external and internal links. In this context these pages are the entities of information on the Web, with hyperlinks from them acting as citations.

The first webometric study tested and described the core of the search options implemented to draw a picture of Denmark's use of the Web compared to Norway and Sweden. The study also reviewed the types of the web pages: by discipline, size and number of links (Almind, and Ingwersen, 1997).

It should be noticed that, although there are other investigations focusing on the Web from quantitative viewpoints, the studies carried out at the Centre for Informetric Studies in Copenhagen (CIS) elaborated on the idea of conducting the same types of informetric analyses on the Web as is possible via citation databases.

Ingwersen demonstrated a workable method to calculate the Web Impact Factor (WIF) for various types of web domains over a series of snapshots taken of the web during a month. For a more detailed description of the data isolation and calculation methods, as well as for the tests discussed, one is referred to the article by Ingwersen (1998).

His definition for the Web Impact Factor takes the logical sum of the number of external and self-link web pages pointing to a given country or web site, divided by the number of pages found in that country or web site—at a given point in time. The numerator thus consists of the number of *link pages*—not the number of links.

Problems and disadvantages in using the informetric analyses on the web are mainly identical to those relating to the citation indexes (restrictive file structures together with flaws in the data validity itself). An additional problem in current research is centred on the flaws in data collection by search engines (Bar-Ilan, 1999). The lack of any enforced conformity of form and content in the web pages, together with the dynamic and real-time nature of the web, creates both advantages and disadvantages in the analytical work, and it is an exciting process to test how the traditional search methods function on this new platform.

Table 1 shows the resulting WIFs in descending order for a selection of smaller and middle-size countries and large, mainly U.S. web sectors. Table 2 displays WIFs for institutions: selected research locations and two well-known scientific journals, *Nature* and *Science*.

The results demonstrate that Web Impact Factors are calculable with high confidence for national and sector domains while institutional WIFs should be approached with caution.

Among the spin-off effects of webometric studies can be mentioned the following: they provide novel insights into the retrieval process on the WWW; the proposed analysis method can be regarded as a tool for measuring the accuracy of web search engine performance and web site organisation, linking, and structuring of pages; and, finally, it is raising awareness about the validity of the matter—in particular because most impact factor analyses are contested. More detailed investigations of the nature of intra-web linkage may uncover the significance and properties of WIFs (Björneborn, and Ingwersen, 2001), as well as provide a better understanding of the complex topology and functionalities of the search engines (Bar-Ilan, 2000).

3.4. Evaluation of subject portals and journal collections

Within the frame of the current digital libraries programme in the Nordic countries, "subject portals" have been set up with the aim of making the libraries' collective information resources of digital and traditional materials available to users over all the five countries. In this integrated information service concept, one of the challenges is to keep balance between the individual libraries and the new co-operative services. Beside the provision of "access," these portals are aimed to facilitate the development of new services and the reallocation of the human resources. These new platforms for information services aimed to support the academic world (dedicated to research and teaching), require an openness for innovative ideas, strategic thinking, new skills and competencies, etc. on the part of the research librarians.

Table 1. Selected National Impact Factors for the WWW: Web-IF - Aug. 20- Sept. 21, 1997.

Countries in rank order	Web Impact Factor	Web-IF Self-link	Web-IF Ext. Link	Deviation % logic A / inv.logic A	Deviation % Simple WIF / Web-IF	Number of Web pages
1. Norway	1,113	0,49	0,62	0,01	-1,2	218.141
Norway	1,127	0,5	0,63	-0,53	-2,37	212.011
2. United Kingdom	0,994	0,46	0,53	-0,17	-2,52	1.046.961
3. France	0,886	0,42	0,46	-0,18	-3,47	454.822
4. Denmark	0,886	0,52	0,37	-0,62	-0,61	144.433
Denmark	0,889	0,52	0,36	0,64	0,06	153.267
5. Sweden	0,866	0,51	0,36	0,66	-0,4	489.905
6. Finland	0,823	0,43	0,39	-0,57	-6,97	317.829
Finland	0,791	0,42	0,37	-1,69	-7,52	313.085
7. Japan	0,404	0,31	0,09	1,11	-1,44	1.826.051
1. Government (.gov)	1,472	0,42	1,05	-1,22	-4,61	646.585
2. Organisations (.org)	1,186	0,4	0,78	-0,59	-4,57	1.677.934
3. Business (.com)	0,942	0,59	0,35	-0,18	1,88	12084719
4. Academic (edu)	0,807	0,47	0,33	-0,57	-2,2	5.390.097
Total: countr.+ sectors	0,899	0,51	0,39	-0,29	-0,68	22497477

Table 2. Selected Institutional Web-IFs - Aug. 20-Sept. 21, 1997.

Countries in rank order	Web Impact Factor	Web-IF Self-link	Web-IF Ext. Link	Deviation % logic A / inv.logic A	Deviation % Simple WIF / Web-IF	Number of Web pages
www.åbo.fi	1,97	0,42	1,55	2,37	0,24	1255
www.db.dk/	2,031	0,68	1,35	1,43	0,82	484
www.dcs.gla.ac.uk/	9,1	0,38	8,72	2,41	10,47	346
Academic(.AC.UK/)	1,194	0,43	0,76	-1,43	-13,56	429.314
Academic(.AC.UK/)	1,068	0,39	0,68	-2,82	-14,14	481.889
meetings.nature.com/	51	0	51	0	0	1
meetings.nature.com/	51	0	51	0	0	1
www.sciencemag.org/	23,762	0,06	23,7	0,835	2,23	86
www.sciencemag.org/	28,846	0,03	28,82	-0,11	3,08	65

At the Swedish School of Library and Information Studies in Borås, two studies have been carried out recently, testing various bibliometric methods in the evaluation of subject portals at the Nordic research libraries. The aim was to gather quantitative data for the following aims:

- to measure how well the information resources of the portal are matching the research profile of the institution

- to explore and visualize the research results of the institution via the portal

- to identify methods for the presentation of current research in a form that is easy to read, easy to understand, and, finally, easy to adapt for the portal users.

The subject portals for social sciences have been chosen as objects for the study. For the analysis of the users' aspects and requirements we have established close co-operation with a group of faculty members at two institutions: *Gothenburg University, Department of Political Sciences* (Sweden), and *Aarhus School of Business, Department of Organization & Management* (Denmark). Librarians and web-managers were the other group with whom we have interacted and discussed the results of our analyses.

The bibliometric analyses were mainly based on the internal information we received from the institutions in electronic form: lists of publications 1999-2000, with various categories of publications listed. Assisted by these lists, we have identified relevant search terms for the main research areas of the department and grouped the authors in thematic groups. The analyses are based on searches in Dialog File 7 (SSCI), File 37 (Sociological Abstracts) and File 88 (Gale Group Business A.R.T.S.).

The study produced various types of *lists and maps* for monitoring the research and publication pattern of the department(s). Their content was mainly designed to provide information about: a) which journals are (the most) relevant for the activities going on at the department, b) useful links to professional institutions, organisations, persons, etc. To facilitate the study of trends and developments in the research history of the department(s), the analyses were carried out for two periods of time, 1974–1992 and 1993–2001. Examples of the presented lists and maps:

> Authors (of the department) publishing in the
> international core journals
> Publishing journals
> Number of publications in the international core
> journals, listed by years
> Cited authors and co-citation networks
>> Map 1. Authors co-cited—see Figure 5
>> Map 2. Journals in the co-cited references
>> Map 3. Intern co-citation pattern
> 10 most cited articles among the publications of the
> department
> Comparative citation analyses in two periods of
> time: 1974-1992 and 1993-2001
> Main research areas and groups (at the Gothenburg
> University, Department of Political Sciences)
>> Group 1: Electoral studies, Political behaviour
>> Group 2: Public policy, Public administration
>> Group 3: Comparative politics, International relations
> Authors grouped in the three main research areas
> The most relevant journals grouped in the three main
> research areas

These lists and maps have been evaluated by the research group(s) as well as by the librarians and portal managers. On the basis of their feedback the report submitted a set of lists, graphs, and maps providing information about subject domains, networks, research results and the most important publications in a way which might satisfy the portal users at the department level (Wormell, 2002).

These forms of presentation and visualisation aim to support the teaching programme of the department, as well as the browsing and navigating activities of the students and young researchers in exploring the domain of their studies or research through the portal.

The metric data of current research will assist librarians to manage their resources in a way which matches the research fronts and strategic important areas of the university. The results gained in the study show that—using some basic bibliometric techniques and presentation tools—librarians can achieve a lot for making the portals, at moderate costs, to viable information platforms. The suggested methods and tools are not yet applied in the library services, but there is a great interest to explore their potentials for meeting the demand of their clients for receiving value-added information service in a form suitable to the current academic working conditions.

Figure 5. Names in capitals indicate departmental staff, size of circles signifies citation amount, and shades of grey indicate research areas.

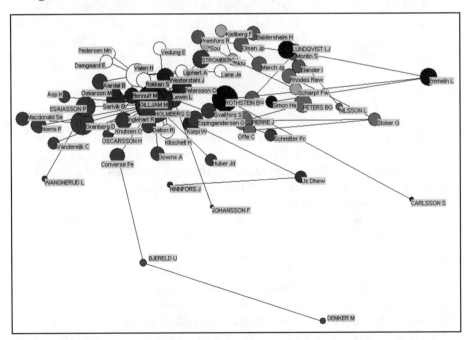

Another study investigated the possible use of bibliometric methods to optimize the journal collection at a smaller college library. The journals pertaining to the subject fields of the Faculty of engineering were sought at the University College in Borås. Both the *local* and *global* perspective of the journal collection were analysed on the basis of inquiries and bibliographic data gathered from publications, citations, reference lists of the MA-thesis, statistics for loans, and copying.

The aim was to create a ranked list of (the most) relevant journals for the Faculty. With reference to earlier research and discussions about the selection principles for ranking of "candidate journals," most of the earlier collection development studies were focused on the global aspect of the collections, in comparison of its standard with some other standard(s). Recent research, however, emphasizes the necessity to use a combination of methods to capture both the local and global aspects of the "use" in collection developments (McCain, 1997; Hughes, 1995).

The present study identified some bibliometric methods and techniques applicable for journal collection development with focus also on the local user groups: publication and citation pattern of the faculty members and MA-students, measuring the size and scope of the external loans and copy service and matching it to their collection and license agreements (Jarneving, 2001).

The outcome showed that the relevance of the technical and scientific journal collection could be enhanced by the use of bibliometric methods combined with local data. The report emphasizes that the role of the librarian as an intermediary and information specialist includes also informing and presenting local as well as global patterns of scientific formal communication. For the efficient management of the portals and library resources, the librarians, in interaction with the user groups, should continuously participate in a repetitive cycle of evaluation for achieving the optimal use of their resources.

4. CONCLUSION

These brief presentations are snapshots of research from the latest five years in the application of Informetrics for the exploration of the deeper segments of information phenomena related to research, business and social intelligence. These studies show how LIS professionals can gather strategic information to support managerial decisions.

The simultaneous analysis of the three categories of actors in the global information market (authors, citations, subscribers) added new dimension to the discussions on the Journal Impact Factor (JIF).

Through the extensive analyses of the Welfare research domain, with the creative combination of analytical tools and techniques, we discovered trends and developments both in the research and the political arena, and "flagged" issues for the consideration of experts and strategic planners.

The presented early study in Webometrics indicates a novel aspect of the bibliometric method: citations are replaced by web pages with external and internal links. It has been suggested that, by calculating the number of web pages pointing to a given site (analogously to the JIF), a Web Impact Factor (WIF) can be calculated as a way of comparing the attractiveness of sites or domains on the WWW.

The latest study is testing the usefulness of the informetric methods in the management and development of the information resources in digital libraries. Searching for methods for the promotion and optimization of the subject portals, we have used a combination of citation analysis and various types of quantitative data for capturing the "local" aspects of the users. We generated a set of information and visualization forms that add several new facets to previous collection development studies. It is also an approach to present the portals as a new and innovative platform to access information or to navigate and explore research and study areas (in an easy way).

The message of this paper is that modern information professionals, by using informetric and other quantitative and qualitative analytical methods in the exploration of databases, have great potential to develop new niches and specialities in their services. Competence in the use of quantitative analysis is also a prerequisite for creating a culture of assessment in libraries and information services, and for bettering their abilities to prove their worth to the users as well as to external funders and decision makers.

REFERENCES

Almind, T., and P. Ingwersen. (1997) Informetric analysis on the World Wide Web: Methodological approaches to "webometrics". *Journal of Documentation, 53*(4), 404–26.

Bar-Ilan, J. (1999) Search engine results over time—A case study on search engine stability. *Cybermetrics, 2/3*(1). Retrieved May 06, 2002, from http://www.cindoc.csic.es/cybermetrics/articles/v2i1p1.html

Bar-Ilan, J. (2000) The Web as information source on informetrics?—A content analysis. *Journal of the American Society for Information Science, 51*(5), 432–43.

Björneborn, L., and P. Ingwersen. (2001) Perspectives of webometrics. *Scientometrics, 50*(1), 65–82.

Garfield, E. (1998) From citation indexes to informetrics: Is the tail now wagging the dog?, *Libri, 48*(2), 67–80.

Hughes, J. (1995) Use of faculty publication lists and ISI citation data to identify a core list of journals with local importance. *Library Acquisitions: Practice & Theory, 19*(4), 403–13.

Ingwersen, P. (1998) The calculation of Web Impact Factors. *Journal of Documentation, 54*(2), 236–43.

Jarneving, B. (2001) Val och anpassning av bibliometriska metoder för utveckling av tidskrifts-bestånd. NORDINFO, Helsingfors, 2001, NORDINFO report 2001:1.

McCain, K. (1997) Bibliometric tools for serials collection management. *Advances in Serials Management, 6*, 105–46.

Raghavan, V. V., J. S. Deogun, and H. Sever. (1998) Knowledge discovery and data mining: introduction. *Journal of the American Society for Information Science, 49*(5), 397–402.

Tague-Sutcliffe, J. (1992) An introduction to informetrics. *Information Processing & Management, 28*(1), 1–3.

Vickery, B. C. (1997) Knowledge discovery from databases: An introductory review. *Journal of Documentation, 53*(2), 107–22.

Wormell, I. (1998) Informetric analysis of the international impact of scientific journals: How 'international' are the international journals? *Journal of Documentation, 54*(5), 584–605.

Wormell, I. (1999) Adding values to the retrieved information. Competitive intelligence from the perspective of today's information professional. *FID Review, 1*(4–5), 83–90.

Wormell, I. (2000a) Critical aspects of the Danish Welfare State—as revealed by issue tracking. *Scientometrics, 43*(2), 237–50.

Wormell, I. (2000b) Bibliometric analysis of the Welfare topic. *Scientometrics, 43*(2), 203–36.

Wormell, I. (2001) Informetrics and webometrics for measuring impact, visibility, and connectivity in science, politics, and business. *Competitive Intelligence Review, 12*(1), 12–23.

Wormell, I. (2002) Informetric analyses for the evaluation of subject portals. NORDINFO, Helsingfors, 2002, NORDINFO report 2002:x. In Press.

Visualizing Library and Information Science Concept Spaces Through Keyword and Citation Based Maps and Clusters

Fredrik Åström
Inforsk, Department of Sociology
Umeå University
901 87 Umeå, Sweden
Fredrik.astrom@soc.umu.se

ABSTRACT

Co-citation analysis has been widely accepted as the foremost method for bibliometric mapping of research fields, whereas analyses based on keywords have been discussed, without gaining any overall acceptance. There are, however, advantages with keywords such as being understandable by others than those immediately connected to the field analyzed. This study aims at testing the relation between keyword and citation based analyses, and showing the significance of journal selection while mapping scientific fields. The preliminary study is based on 1135 *Social Science Citation Index (SSCI)* records from nine library and information science journals with descriptors added from the *Resources Information Center Database (ERIC)* database. Three maps are compared: one based on co-citations, one on keyword co-occurrences, and one merging citations and keywords. The mappings show the same basic structures, and when merged, cited authors and keywords form corresponding relations. In comparison with earlier bibliometric studies, the wider journal selection makes it possible to identify a library science research area within library and information science.

1. INTRODUCTION

The outcome of the bibliometric analysis is dependent on what information within the database is being analyzed. Another aspect with strong implications is the journal selection. Both of these are questions related to types of information being used in the analysis. Citations and keywords are examples of two types of analyzable bibliographic information, but how can they be used in bibliometric analyses? What are the similarities and differences between bibliometric mappings based on keywords or citations, and how does journal selection affect how the field is described? These questions are important in the case of analyzing cognitive structures of a research field. Library and information science (LIS) is an example of a field that has been subject to various attempts at definitions: by bibliometric analyses (e.g., Persson, 1994; White, and Griffith, 1981; White, and McCain, 1998), in essays (e.g., Saracevic, 1999), in research papers taking a theoretical standpoint (e.g., Hjørland, 2000; Ingwersen, 1992; Vakkari, 1994), and in historical studies (e.g., Hahn, and Buckland, 1998). These texts come to different conclusions on the nature of LIS, even on fundamental issues such as basic sub-fields of the discipline and relations between library science and information science.

The most comprehensive bibliometric study of LIS so far was made by White and McCain (1998). The analysis identifies two sub-disciplines—information retrieval (IR) and studies of aspects of literature and communication—and 11 research specialties. This was done by an author co-citation analysis based on the 120 most cited authors in 12 key LIS journals during the years 1972–1995. One issue that requires comment is the selection of journals, where there is a strong emphasis on information science journals, whereas library science journals are few and only cover issues on library automation.

Co-citation techniques were introduced by Small and Griffith (1974), and further developed by Small and Sweeney (1985). A development of co-citation analysis for mapping of research fields is author co-citation, where the relationships between authors and their *oeuvres* are analyzed (McCain, 1986; White, and Griffith, 1981). Methods for co-word analysis have been developed to measure the associative strength of terms representing publications and documents (Callon, Courtial, and Laville, 1991; Courtial, 1994; Courtial, and Law 1989; Law, and Whittaker, 1992; Whittaker, 1989). But word and co-word analyses in bibliometrics have also been criticized due to their instability: words change, both in terms of usage and meaning. This renders the networks representing the cognitive spaces likely to destabilize over time, as opposed to citation analysis, where stability is assured by the use of whole documents (Leydesdorff, 1997).

The use of combinations of different analyses has been tested by, for example, Braam, Moed and Van Raan (1991a; 1991b), who investigated the structural and dynamical aspects of a combined co-citation and word analysis to map scientific structures. They combined a co-author analysis with a frequency analysis of index terms and classification codes, keywords from abstracts and so on. The results indicate a complimentary role of the two analyses. Relations between subject and citation indexing from an information retrieval point of view have been analyzed in a number of studies. McCain (1989) compared descriptor and citation retrieval in 11 search topics and evaluated these for relevance and novelty. Both search strategies gave a good result, even though the recall ratio was larger for the descriptor retrieval, and the overlap between the different strategies was moderate. The complimentary role of citation retrieval has also been confirmed by Pao (1993) and Pao and Worthen (1989). A database was constructed with document representations consisting of both semantic information and information on cited documents. Also here the semantic retrieval led to higher recall, both strategies provided good precision, and the overlap was relatively small.

2. AIM

This paper aims at comparing and analyzing different indexing methods—keywords and citations—to see how they affect bibliometric analyses of LIS. Do the different kinds of indexing bring on major changes in the perception of fields of research, or do they show the same structures when used as a base for mapping of cognitive fields? This will be examined by analyzing one set of records according to three modes of co-occurrence analysis. The first two will provide results that can be compared. The third analysis will merge the two first analyses, to see if there is any level of concordance. A second aim is to test an alternative journal selection for an analysis of LIS, to see what differences can be found in comparison to previous analyses of LIS. The main questions in this paper are: what different kinds of bibliometric analyses can be used for describing the cognitive structures of LIS? What differences or similarities can be found in different bibliometric analyses on one set of records? What are the implications of different journal selections when analyzing LIS?

3. METHOD

This paper compares three different bibliometric analyses on one set of records. Articles from nine LIS journals were selected, based on ranking in *the Institute for Scientific Information (ISI) Journal Citation Reports*. The four highest ranked general information science journals, and the five highest ranked library science journals were selected. Searches for research articles from the years 1998–2000 from the nine journals were made and the result was downloaded from the *Web of Science, Social Science Citation Index* (*SSCI*), and from the *Resources Information Center Database* (*ERIC*) SilverPlatter 1992–2001/03 edition (Table 1). The search criterion for finding research articles were made by using the document type selection, choosing the "articles" alternative, in *Web of Science*. After downloading the results, the files were merged into one, adding the descriptors from the DX-field in the *ERIC* database to the *SSCI* records, except for the cases where a match could not be made.

Table 1. Number of articles downloaded from
SSCI and ERIC 1998–2000.

Journal name	SSCI	ERIC	Analyzed
Journal of Documentation	69	54	
Journal of the American Soc. for Info. Sci.	324	278	
Information Processing & Management	124	127	
Journal of Information Science	101	30	
College & Research Libraries	111	104	
Information Technology and Libraries	87	38	
Library Quarterly	38	36	
Library Trends	136	100	
Journal of Academic Librarianship	145	78	
Total	1135	845	797

One of the aims of the journal selection was to avoid the strong emphasis on information science that can be found in for example the White and McCain (1998) material. The reason for using fewer information science related journals is to level the uneven amount of documents in the respective journals. The use of multiple databases also affected the journal selection, where some top ranked information science journals were not indexed in the *ERIC* database. The use of two databases also led to a decrease in documents to analysis, since there are some discrepancies in the number of documents indexed in the two databases. The analyses are based on the documents where a match could be made between the *SSCI* and *ERIC* records. The reason for combining the two databases is of course that *SSCI/ISI* does not add keywords to all the records in their databases. Problems concerning completeness in coverage in different databases, and the characteristics and use of the index terms in the case of LIS, have been discussed by authors such as Harter, Nisonger and Weng (1993).

The three different bibliometric analyses are co-occurrence of keywords, co-citations and a merged citation and keyword co-occurrence analysis. The short time span of citing journals made the co-citation analysis seem more appropriate—even though author co-citation analyses are usually preferred for scientific mapping—to get a more recognizable set of cited authors. The analysis was made by coupling co-occurring keywords and/or authors. These couples form a matrix that can be visualized by mapping techniques such as multi-dimensional scaling (MDS). By using the *Bibexcel* software, the downloaded data is processed, analyzed according to the different bibliometric analyses, formed into a matrix, and visualized in the form of a map through MDS. The analysis is further clarified by the use of a clustering routine suggested by Persson (1994).

The maps can be qualitatively analyzed by comparing the different structures formed by the different analyses. Comparisons can be made in terms of how authors or research areas relate to each other, and finding different places on the map. The third analysis, the merged map of citation and keywords, is also a way to compare the behavior of the different forms of indexing, seeing if authors and keywords are placed in a way that corresponds with what topics the authors are writing about. These comparisons of the maps can also be amplified by cluster analysis, to make the structures within the maps clearer. This makes it easier to compare the maps, since the clusters enhance the main trends in the maps.

4. RESULTS

For the first part of the analysis, the 52 most cited authors were selected and coupled. These couples formed a matrix that was processed through a MDS routine, resulting in a map containing the authors and their relations to each other (Figure 1).

**Figure 1. Co-citation map of nine LIS journals 1998–2000.
Included are the 52 most cited authors.**

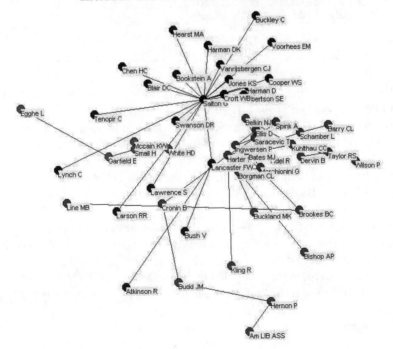

The couples were also clustered, to help form the lines connecting the names on the map, and amplify the structure of the map. Three clusters were formed (Table 2).

Table 2. Clusters formed by the 52 most cited authors in nine LIS journals 1998–2000.

Cluster1: Hard IR	Cluster2: Soft IR	Cluster3: Bibliometrics
SALTON G	HARTER SP	SMALL H
LANCASTER FW	SARACEVIC T	WHITE HD
BLAIR DC	BATES MJ	GARFIELD E
BUCKLEY C	KUHLTHAU CC	EGGHE L
BUSH V	INGWERSEN P	MCCAIN KW
CHEN HC	SCHAMBER L	
COOPER WS	HERNON P	
CROFT WB	BELKIN NJ	
HARMAN D	BUDD JM	
HARMAN DK	CRONIN B	
HEARST MA	DERVIN B	
JONES KS	BROOKES BC	
BOOKSTEIN A	MARCHIONINI G	
LARSON RR	BORGMAN CL	
LAWRENCE S	BARRY CL	
LYNCH C	ELLIS D	
ROBERTSON SE	KLING R	
ATKINSON R	AM LIB ASS	
SWANSON DR	LINE MB	
TENOPIR C	FIDEL R	
VANRIJSBERGEN	BUCKLAND MK	
VOORHEES EM	BISHOP AP	
	SPINK A	
	TAYLOR RS	
	WILSON P	

The structure of the map is essentially the same as in Persson (1994; 2001) and White and McCain (1998). Distinguishable groups are the two sub-fields, information retrieval and bibliometrics, and aspects of literatures and communication. The IR field can be further divided into one "hard" area centered around Salton, dealing with algorithm and system development; and one "soft" area dealing with user-system interaction. Here the center is not as obvious, but key figures are Harter, Bates, Saracevic, Kuhlthau and Ingwersen. These areas are also supported by the clusters.

A closer look at the map also reveals smaller groups not noticeable in the clusters. This raises questions as to whether they actually form their own research areas, or remain within the general structure because of the small amount of representation. One is the group that includes Dervin and Kuhlthau, where the question can be raised if the "information needs and uses" research is really part of the IR research, or an independent research area. Another group, perhaps of stronger importance, is one with for example Hernon and Budd, representing a library science oriented research area. Library science is only connected to the IR area by links, while the location on the map suggests separation from the IR research. That this area does not show in the clustering is probably due to the fact that library science authors are represented by so few names that they cannot form a cluster on their own. A further consideration, in comparison with the White and McCain analysis, is the differences in names of cited authors. Some, such as the inclusion of Peter Ingwersen, are probably due to the different time span. But other names, such as John M Budd, are probably related to the inclusion of library science journals.

The second part of the analysis followed the same basic procedure as the first. Instead of cited authors, the 47 most frequent occurring keywords were selected and coupled, resulting in a map containing the keywords and their relations to each other (Figure 2).

Figure 2. Co-occurrence map of *ERIC* keywords from nine LIS journals 1998–2000. Included are the 47 most frequent occurring keywords.

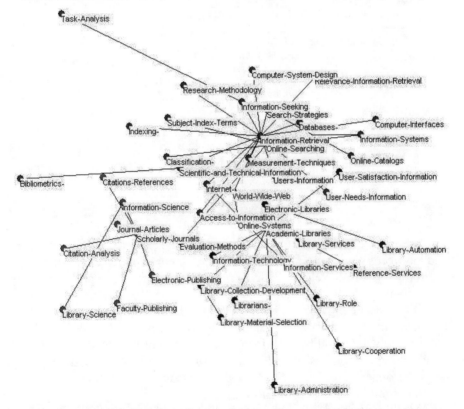

Here, the couples were also clustered (Table 3). In this map, the separation between different areas is not as clearly distinguishable as with the cited authors. But the same structures and areas can still be found, with the same location on the map. What can be noted is the remaining sub-area of "information needs and uses" keywords being somewhat separated from the rest of the IR area, while the IR area in general seems to have become less divided and the library science area is more visible.

Table 3. Clusters formed by the 47 most frequent occurring ERIC keywords in nine LIS journals 1998–2000.

Cluster 1: Library Sci.	Cluster 2. IR	Cluster 3: Bibliometrics
Academic-Libraries	Information-Retrieval	Scholarly-Journals
Electronic-Libraries	Online-Searching	Information-Science
Library-Services	Internet-	Electronic-Publishing
Libr.-Collection-Dev.	Information-Systems	Faculty-Publishing
Library-Administration	Sci.-and-Tech.-Info.	Citation-Analysis
Library-Automation	World-Wide-Web	Journal-Articles
Librarians-	Information-Seeking	Library-Science
Library-Cooperation	Search-Strategies	Citations-References
Libr.-Material-Sel.	Classification-	
Library-Role	Evaluation-Methods	
Info.-Technology	Information-Services	
Reference-Services	Computer-Interfaces	
User-Satisfaction-Info.	Bibliometrics-	
	Measurement-Tech.	
	Online-Catalogs	
	Indexing-	
	Online-Systems	
	Relevance-Info.	
	Res.-Methodology	
	Comp.-System-Design	
	Access-to-Information	
	Subject-Index-Terms	
	Task-Analysis	
	User-Needs-Info.	
	Users-Information	
	Databases-	

The trends of the map are also supported by the clustering, where the IR related keywords have merged into one cluster, and the library science keywords have formed a separate cluster. The merging of the IR field can probably be explained by the indexing. Although the articles deals with different aspects of IR, the similarities are big enough in terms of subject description for them to form one cluster instead of two. More interesting to note is how library science has evolved into what could be described as a sub-field of its own within LIS. Although some reservations should be made for the quality of the indexing (e.g., Harter, Nisonger, and Weng, 1993), the different and wider journal selection has important implications for how LIS is perceived.

In the third part of the analysis the keywords and citations were merged and ranked, and the 53 most frequently occurring keywords and authors were selected, coupled, mapped and clustered (Figure 3). The structure of this map is basically the same as in the former two analyses.

Figure 3. Co-occurrence map of *ERIC* keywords and cited authors from nine LIS journals 1998–2000. Included are the 53 most frequent occurring keywords and authors.

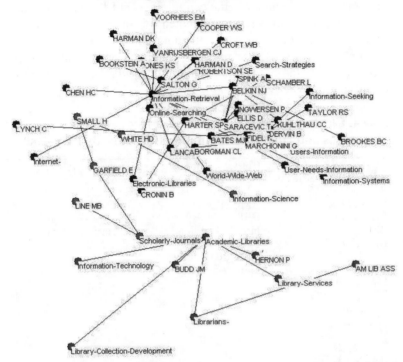

The clustering also gives the same results as the keyword based analysis, with three main areas: library science, IR and bibliometrics (Table 4). On the map, the distinction between "soft" and "hard" IR is still visible, even though the clustering does not show the same trends, and the "information needs and uses" sub-field is also slightly distanced from the main IR area. The main difference is that the library science area is now clearly separated from the IR field, both in location and by links. Another, very interesting, feature is how well the keywords and the authors correspond to each other. The connection between authors and keywords is very close in terms of actual research interests of the authors.

5. DISCUSSION

The starting point of this paper was the general, and perhaps obvious, statement that the outcome of bibliometric analyses are dependent on the presentation of the data, and what kind of data is being analyzed. The first aim of the paper was to compare and analyze different methods of indexing to see how they affect bibliometric analyses of LIS. This aim raised questions about which different types of bibliometric analyses can be used for describing cognitive structures and what differences can be found in different kinds of bibliometric analyses. This was done by first producing separate maps containing either citations or keywords, and then a map with both. The results indicate quite strong relations between citations and keywords. The two separate maps formed the same basic structures, identifying the same central areas in LIS: bibliometrics, information retrieval and a library science oriented sub-field. These tendencies were also supported by the close fit when mapping and clustering combinations of cited authors and keywords. The respective location on the map largely corresponds to what topics the cited authors have addressed in their writings, which is also evident in the clustering.

Table 4. Clusters formed by the 53 most frequent occurring *ERIC* keywords and cited authors in nine LIS journals 1998–2000.

Cluster 1: IR	Cluster 2: Library Sci.	Cluster 3: Bibliometrics
Information-Retrieval	Academic-Libraries	GARFIELD E
SARACEVIC T	Librarians-	SMALL H
KUHLTHAU CC	AM LIB ASS	WHITE HD
BATES MJ	HERNON P	Scholarly-Journals
BELKIN NJ	Info.-Technology	Information-Science
HARTER SP	BUDD JM	LINE MB
SALTON G	Libr.-Coll.-Dev.	
DERVIN B	Library-Services	
MARCHIONINI G		
BROOKES BC		
Electronic-Libraries		
ELLIS D		
CROFT WB		
HARMAN D		
HARMAN DK		
CRONIN B		
BORGMAN CL		
Information-Seeking		
Information-Systems		
INGWERSEN P		
Internet-		
JONES KS		
FIDEL R		
LANCASTER FW		
LYNCH C		
BOOKSTEIN A		
Online-Searching		
ROBERTSON SE		
CHEN HC		
COOPER WS		
SCHAMBER L		
Search-Strategies		
SPINK A		
TAYLOR RS		
User-Needs-Info.		
Users-Information		
VANRIJSBERGEN CJ		
VOORHEES EM		
World-Wide-Web		

The only significant variation detected in the material was in the clustering: the cited author analysis formed three clusters containing "hard" IR, "soft" IR and bibliometrics; whereas the keywords and the keywords plus author analysis formed three clusters containing IR, bibliometrics and library science. This is probably caused by the author selection, where library science authors were under-represented in the citation based ranking. One reason for this might be publication patterns in library science, where a lot of the research is published in books, and also in regional or national journals, channels of communication that are not covered by, for instance, *SSCI*. It should however be noted that in the keyword based map, the different research areas are not as clearly defined as in the citation and citation/keyword maps. And it should be kept in mind that the citation analysis is based on the documents per se, which makes the connection to the research itself closer, while the keywords are created to represent texts and make them searchable. This can to some extent explain the dissappearance of the distinction between "hard" and "soft" IR. While the distinction is visible as research areas, keywords for IR purposes do not need to make the same distinction.

What is interesting with the relation between the author and keyword maps and clusters is of course that they show such a similar structure. This would suggest that keywords are a good starting point for scientific mapping, or that they at least can serve as complimentary to the co-citation maps. That they in some way reflect research is quite obvious, but the results here support the premise for analyzing co-occurrence of keywords, that similar documents are represented by the same keywords or indexing terms (Whittaker, 1989), and thus, that statistical aggregates of keywords also represent cognitive spaces. Another interesting aspect of this is the analyses of the keyword-citation relations in information retrieval situations (e.g., McCain, 1989; Pao, 1993; Pao, and Worthen, 1989), suggesting a complimentary role with a relatively small overlap. The maps in this analysis suggest a closer relation between citations and keywords than seen in those studies.

The second aim of this paper was to investigate if and how a changed journal selection would change the perceived structure of LIS. This was done in comparison with the White and McCain (1998) analysis. The analysis showed some substantial differences in comparison with White and McCain, introducing library science as a sub-field of LIS on the level with IR and bibliometrics. While the White and McCain analysis is based on a journal selection with a strong emphasis on information science, this analysis sets out to make a more balanced selection of information science and library science journals. The findings in the analysis suggest that the journal selection does affect how research fields can be perceived and defined. When changing the journal selection, the analysis shows a different structure of the field. This is important, since studies such as the White and McCain analysis has been used as empirical basis for further discussion on the nature and cognitive structure of LIS (e.g., Saracevic, 1999).

The selection of nine journals and a time span of only three years is obviously not enough to draw any wider conclusions on the cognitive structure of LIS. But it has been useful for making some obsverations on the usefulness of the methodology suggested. The selection of both library science and information science journals shows differences in comparison with earlier mappings of LIS, highlighting journal selection as an important factor when mapping research fields. This can be developed further. For instance, even though there are five library science journals and only four information science journals, the number of articles analyzed still shows a majority of information science research articles. Another issue of methodological interest is differing citation behavior in library and information science, respectively. This has implications for the results of the analyses: when citing a lot of diverse sources the internal links get weaker and it gets harder to identify a distinct set of highly cited authors. A third issue is the relation between citations and keywords, two different concepts with different functions. The differences are visible when comparing the two maps based on either citations or keywords, where the structure of LIS is more clearly defined in the citation based map. While citations represent some sort of cognitive relation between documents, keywords are representations of documents assigned to them for information retrieval purposes. One way of solving this problem, or at least to come closer to the actual documents, is by using keywords derived directly from the text. Despite these problems, when merging the keywords and citations into one map they largely correspond with each other, resulting in a map that is easier to interpret than a map showing only author names, for example.

REFERENCES

Braam, R. R., H. F. Moed, and A. F. J. van Raan. (1991a) Mapping of science by combined co-citation and word analysis: I: Structural aspects. *Journal of the American Society for Information Science, 42*(4), 233–51.

Braam, R. R., H. F. Moed, and A. F. J. van Raan. (1991b) Mapping of science by combined co-citation and word analysis: II: Dynamical aspects. *Journal of the American Society for Information Science, 42*(4), 252–66.

Callon, M., J.-P. Courtial, and F. Laville. (1991) Co-word analysis as a tool for describing the network of interactions between basic and technological research: The case of polymer chemistry. *Scientometrics, 22*(1), 153–203.

Courtial, J.-P. (1994) A co-word analysis of scientometrics. *Scientometrics, 31*(2), 251–60.

Courtial, J.-P., and J. Law. (1989) A co-word study of artificial intelligence. *Social Studies of Science, 19*, 301–11.

Hahn, T. B., and M. K. Buckland, eds. (1998) *Historical studies in Information Science.* Medford, NJ: Information Today.

Harter, S. P., T. E. Nisonger, and A. Weng. (1993) Semantic relationships between cited and citing articles in Library and Information Science journals. *Journal of the American Society for Information Science, 44*(9), 543–52.

Hjørland, B. (2000) Library and Information Science: Practice, theory, and philosophical basis. *Information Processing & Management, 36*, 501–31.

Ingwersen, P. (1992) Information and Information Science in context. *Libri, 42*(2), 99–135.

Law, J., and J. Whittaker. (1992) Mapping acidification research: A test of the co-word method. *Scientometrics, 23*(3), 417–61.

Leydesdorff, L. (1997) Why words and co-words cannot map the development of the sciences. *Journal of the American Society for Information Science, 48*(5), 418–27.

McCain, K. W. (1986) Cocited author mapping as a valid representation of intellectual structure. *Journal of the American Society for Information Science, 37*, 111–22.

McCain, K. W. (1989) Descriptor and citation retrieval in the medical behavioral sciences literature: Retrieval overlaps and novelty distribution. *Journal of the American Society for Information Science, 40*(2), 110–14.

Pao, M. L. (1993) Term and citation retrieval: A field study. *Information Processing and Management, 29*(1), 95–112.

Pao, M. L., and D. B. Worthen. (1989) Retrieval effectiveness by semantic and citation searching. *Journal of the American Society for Information Science, 40*(4), 226–35.

Persson, O. (1994) The intellectual base and research fronts of JASIS 1986–1990. *Journal of the American Society for Information Science, 45*(1), 31–38.

Persson, O. (2001) All author citations versus first author citations. *Scientometrics, 50*(2), 339–44.

Saracevic, T. (1999) Information Science. *Journal of the American Society for Information Science, 50*(12), 1051–63.

Small, H. G., and B. C. Griffith. (1974) The structure of scientific literatures: I: Identifying and graphing specialties. *Science Studies, 4*, 17–40.

Small, H. G., and E. Sweeney. (1985) Clustering the Science Citation Index. *Scientometrics, 7*, 391–409.

Vakkari, P. (1994) Library and Information Science: Its content and scope. In I. P. Godden (ed.). *Advances in librarianship: Volume 18* (pp. 1–55). San Diego, CA: Academic Press.

White, H. D., and B. C. Griffith. (1981) Author cocitation: A literature measure of intellectual structure, *Journal of the American Society for Information Science, 32*, 163–72.

White, H. D., and K. W. McCain. (1998) Visualizing a discipline: An author co-citation analysis of information science, 1972–1995, *Journal of the American Society for Information Science, 49*(4), 327–55.

Whittaker, J. (1989) Creativity and conformity in science: Titles, keywords, and co-word analysis. *Social Studies of Science, 19*, 473–96.

Ranking Expansion Terms with Partial and Ostensive Evidence

Ian Ruthven
Department of Computer and Information Sciences
University of Strathclyde
Glasgow, G1 1XH
Ian.Ruthven@cis.strath.ac.uk

Mounia Lalmas
Department of Computer Science
Queen Mary
University of London
London, E1 4NS
mounia@dcs.qmul.ac.uk

Keith van Rijsbergen
Department of Computing Science
University of Glasgow
Glasgow, G12 8QQ
keith@dcs.gla.ac.uk

ABSTRACT

In this paper we examine the problem of ranking candidate expansion terms for query expansion. We show, by an extension to the traditional F_4 scheme, how partial relevance assessments (*how* relevant a document is) and ostensive evidence (*when* a document was assessed relevant) can be incorporated into a term ranking function. We then investigate this new term ranking function in three user experiments, examining the performance of our function for automatic and interactive query expansion. We show that the new function not only suggests terms that are preferred by searchers but suggests terms that can lead to more use of expansion terms.

1. INTRODUCTION

Information retrieval (IR) systems are intended to retrieve documents that are relevant to a searcher's information need, usually expressed as a query. However selecting good words (or *terms*) to use as a query can be difficult. If a searcher has found some relevant material she can avoid generating more query terms by asking the system to suggest or add terms to her query. This process is generally known as Relevance Feedback (**RF**) (Harman, 1992): the system exploits those documents the searcher considered relevant to create a better representation of the searcher's information need.

RF is generally composed of three stages: the system first selects possible candidate terms[1] to add to the query and ranks these terms according to some measure of how useful the terms might be in a new query (*term ranking*); the system then selects a number of these terms to add to the query (*query expansion*); and finally the system weights the terms before carrying out a new retrieval (*term weighting*).

In this paper we concentrate on the first stage—term ranking—deciding which terms are most likely to be useful in a new query. The reason that this stage is important is that most RF applications will only choose a small proportion of the candidate expansion terms to add to the query. This is not only more computationally efficient than adding all candidate expansion terms (Salton, and Buckley, 1990), but the retrieval effectiveness of a small set of good terms is usually as good as (Salton, and Buckley, 1990), or better than (Harman, 1992), adding all candidate expansion terms. In addition, adding relatively few expansion terms means that the searcher can easily edit the reformulated query manually.

Standard methods of ranking terms, e.g., F_4, Porter's scheme, or *wpq* (surveyed in Efthimiadis, 1995), treat all relevant documents as a uniform set; all documents are treated as being of equal relevance and no attention is paid to *when* in the search the documents were assessed relevant. These techniques, then, do not incorporate important aspects of searching such as the degree to which a document is relevant to a searcher (Spink, et al., 1998), or the temporal nature of relevance (Vakkari, 2000a).

The term ranking function we present in this paper incorporates the nonbinary nature of relevance (through the use of partial relevance assessments) and the temporal nature of information seeking (through the use of ostensive evidence). These are to be discussed, along with the motivation and methodology for incorporating these aspects, in section 2. This is followed by a description of a user study on the term ranking function. In section 3, we give a brief introduction to the overall experimental system used in our experiments, and, in section 4, we present the experimental methodology used. In sections 5–7 we present the experiments we performed. We conclude with a discussion in section 8.

2. TERM RANKING FUNCTION

Our intention is to show that traditional RF techniques can be extended to incorporate more realistic assumptions about searching. Most RF algorithms perform statistical analyses of what searchers assess as relevant: the content of the documents marked relevant by searchers. However, these RF algorithms typically do not consider the complexity behind the process of making relevance assessments. As noted above RF algorithms usually assume binary relevance and assume that a searcher's definition of relevance does not change over the course of a search. However many studies of how searchers assess documents show that relevance assessments can be relative to each other, e.g. (Florance, and Marchionini, 1995; Tiamiyu, and Ajiferuke, 1988), dynamic, e.g. (Vakkari, 2000a; 2000b), and dependent on individual features such as task, and domain knowledge, e.g. (Heuer, 1999). The process of assessing relevance is, therefore, a complex process. However the output of this complex process—the relevant assessments—are compressed into a simple representation for use by RF algorithms— a set of relevant documents.

What motivated us in this study is the belief that advanced search engines are required to take more notice and use of evidence from how searchers are interacting with the system. In particular the evidence provided by searchers whilst interacting should be combined with the retrieval algorithms themselves to provide integrated search systems.

Our term ranking function is one example of this, and is based on the standard F_4 term weighting function (Robertson, and Sparck Jones, 1976). Although this function was specifically designed to weight query terms based on relevance information, it has been heavily investigated as a means of ranking terms for query expansion (Efthimiadis, 1995).

The F4 function, Equation 1, is based on the odds of how likely term t is to appear in a relevant document to how likely term t is to appear in a non-relevant document. The higher the F4 weight for term t the more likely that t appears in one of the relevant documents used to calculate the F4 weight. To order terms for query expansion, all candidate expansion terms are assigned an F4 weight and ranked in decreasing order of their F4 weight.

Equation 1. F_4 term weighting function where   is the number of relevant documents containing term t, R is the number of relevant documents found so far, is the number of documents containing term t and N is the number of documents in the collection.

$$ostensive_t = \left(\sum_{j=1}^{s} j * r_{jt} \right) \bigg/ \max_{ostensive}$$

We propose a new term ranking algorithm, the F4_po algorithm[2], Equation 2, that is composed of two components: one component that measures the information coming from partial relevance assessments, section 2.1; and one component that calculates the ostensive evidence for a term, section 2.2. Although there are other possible methods for combining these two components we have made these two components separate, to allow for a future separate study of the effect of the two components.

Equation 2. F4_po term ranking scheme.

$$F_4\_po_t = partial_t * ostensive_t$$

2.1. Incorporating partial relevance assessments —*partial$_t$* component

The use of partial relevance assessments—allowing searchers to make non-binary assessments on the relevance of retrieved documents has long been seen as important in obtaining more accurate and realistic assessments of a document's relevance to a searcher, e.g. (Borlund, 2000; Spink, et al., 1998).

In the majority of RF interfaces, searchers are asked to make assessments on entire documents as individual entities. This infers that searchers make assessments on the complete document and can identify relevant material. However, often only part of a document may be relevant and the criteria for relevance themselves may be vague, i.e., the searcher may not yet have a well-defined idea of what information is actually required. These two issues point to the partiality of relevance. The latter definition of partial relevance—the vagueness of the searcher's criteria for relevance—has been explored by Spink, et al. (1998) who show a correlation between the number of partial relevance assessments and how well-defined was a searcher's information need. Vakkari (2000b) also showed that a searcher's lack of understanding of their search task correlated with a high number of partial relevance assessments. Incorporating some measure of the *degree* of relevance into the RF process is therefore important in modelling what may be of interest to a searcher.

Our interface (section 3, Figure 2) asks searchers to indicate, using a scroll bar, how relevant is an individual document to their search. Internal to the system this is mapped to a number between 1 and 10, with 0 indicating non-relevant. In our term ranking function we treat these partial relevance assessments as part of a complete relevance assessment, e.g., a document that is assigned a relevance score of 10 by the searcher is treated as a complete relevant document, whereas a document that received a relevance score of 5 is treated as half a relevant document, and so on.

This is integrated into the *partial*, component of our algorithm by replacement of the variables r_t, R, n_t and N in the original F_4 weight in the following manner: r_t is the sum of all relevance scores for relevant documents containing term t, n_t is the sum of all relevance scores for all relevant documents, R and N are replaced by $R*10$, $N*10$, respectively[3]. This means that the higher the relevance scores for documents containing term t the higher the *partial*, score for term t.

2.2. Incorporating ostensive evidence—*ostensive*, component

The previous section was motivated by the argument that partial relevance assessments are necessary to capture degree of relevance of a document to a searcher. However, the relevance of a document is subject to change throughout the course of a search. This may happen as the result of searchers changing their criteria for relevance or, as indicated by Vakkari (2000b), the searcher either developing more knowledge about the task or requiring different types of information at different stages in a search.

Although it is difficult to establish *why* a searcher may have made a particular relevance decision, we can allow for the possible change in relevance criteria by the use of *ostensive* evidence. Campbell and Van Rijsbergen (1996), argued that *when* in a search a document was marked relevant should be treated as important. Therefore the documents most recently marked relevant are more indicative of what the searcher currently finds relevant—provide more ostensive evidence as to relevance. The incorporation of ostensive evidence, then, does not target reasons for relevance but asserts that newly assessed documents are more likely to demonstrate the searcher's current criteria for relevance.

The ostensive evidence for a term is given by Equation 3.

Equation 3. Calculation of *ostensive*, component where s = total number of feedback iterations, r_{jt} = number of relevant documents containing term t in iteration j, $\max_{ostensive}$ = maximum possible ostensive evidence.

$$ostensive_t = \left(\sum_{j=1}^{s} j * r_{jt} \right) \Big/ \max_{ostensive}$$

In Equation 3 the ostensive weight of term t, is based on a proportion of the ostensive evidence for t relative to the maximum ostensive weight that could be assigned to a term, $\max_{ostensive}$. This maximum ostensive weight will be equal to 1, if all relevant documents, at every iteration of feedback, contained the term t. The ostensive evidence for term t is the sum of the relevant documents containing t multiplied by the iteration in which the documents were marked relevant. Therefore the more relevant documents term t appears in, the higher weight it receives and the more recently-viewed relevant documents t appears in the higher weight it receives. What the *ostensive$_t$* component measures then is how indicative of relevance term t is at the current search stage.

An example of this is shown in Figure 1, for two terms—term t and term s, based on the data given in Table 1. In Table 1, we have five iterations of feedback. At each iteration a number of documents are marked relevant (**R** row 5), some of which contain term t, (**r**$_t$ row 3), and some of which contain term s (**r**$_s$ row 4). The maximum ostensive weight for both terms is identical: both terms could have appeared in all relevant documents at each iteration of feedback. What differs between the two terms is when the documents containing the terms were marked relevant: the relevant documents containing term t were assessed as relevant later in the search than the relevant documents containing term s. Hence term t receives a higher ostensive weight than term s.

Table 1. Example ostensive data.

	Iterations of feedback					
	1	2	3	4	5	Total
r$_t$	1	0	0	1	5	7
r$_s$	5	1	0	0	1	7
R	5	2	3	1	10	21

Figure 1. Example ostensive calculation.

$$max_{ostensive} = (5*1) + (2*2) + (3*3) + (1*4) + (10*5) = 72$$
$$t = (1*1) + (1*4) + (5*5) = 30$$
$$s = (5*1) + (1*2) + (1*5) = 12$$
$$ostensive_t = 28/72 = 0.417$$
$$ostensive_s = 12/72 = 0.167$$

3. EXPERIMENTAL SYSTEM

Our experiments used five systems. In this section we briefly outline the components that were common to all systems; in sections 5–7 we describe the specific variations of the experimental systems used in our experiments.

Our basic retrieval algorithm followed the approach given in Ruthven, et al. (2001). This assigns each term in the collection a set of weights. Each weight is calculated by a separate weighting scheme and reflects different aspects of how the term is used within the collection and individual documents. The retrieval score of a document is given by the sum of all the term weights of the query terms contained within the documents. This approach generally gives better results than the more standard *tf*idf* approaches (Ruthven, et al., 2001).

After query expansion, sections 5–7, the RF systems traditionally weight query terms according to some measure of how useful they are in attracting relevant material (section 1). Our systems, instead, select which weighting schemes are best at indicating relevant material for each query term. This was shown to be preferable to assigning each query term a new weight based on relevance information (Ruthven, et al., 2001).

In our system, searchers entered a natural language expression as a query and were shown the titles of the retrieved documents in groups of ten titles. A screen-shot of one of our interfaces is given in Appendix A, Figure A.1. Clicking on the title displayed the full-text of the title with query terms highlighted in bold. The searchers were asked to mark any document that they felt contained useful information using the slider shown in Figure 2. We asked our subjects to assess the usefulness of documents, rather than the relevance, to encourage the subjects to make personal assessments on the relation between the documents and search tasks rather than make topical assessments of the match of the query and documents.

The relevance slider in Figure 2 was initially set to *Not useful* for each retrieved document. Unassessed documents were considered by default to be not useful to the searcher and counted as not relevant for the purposes of RF (see section 5).

Figure 2. Relevance slider.

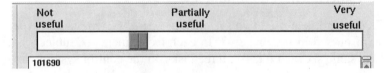

4. EXPERIMENTAL DETAILS

4.1. Document collection

The document collection we used in our experiments consisted of a set of full-length newspaper articles, comprised of the LA Times and Financial Times collections from the TREC[4] initiative (Voorhees, and Harman, 1997). This gave a single collection consisting of over 340,000 documents.

4.2. Search tasks

The search tasks for these experiments were based on the topics used in the interactive track of TREC-6. We modified the topic descriptions, placing them within simulated situations as proposed by Borlund (2000). This technique asserts that searchers should be given search scenarios that reflect and promote a real information-seeking situation. The simulated situations allow a subjective and dynamic interpretation of relevance by the searcher. An example of one of the six simulated situations we used is given in Figure 3, the other five topics are given in Appendix B.

Figure 3. Simulated situation.

> Several valuable paintings and other works of art in a local Glasgow museum have been discovered to be fakes. The museum's spokesman claims that art crime—in particular fraud—is becoming more common. He also claims that it is difficult to distinguish deliberate crime from genuine mistakes made by people selling works of art. You wonder if he is correct or whether these are excuses. You think more information on art crime, and on genuine cases of art fraud, can help you decide if the spokesman is correct.

4.3. Experimental subjects

The subjects in our experiments were university students, five female and 13 male, with an average age of 23, and a variety of academic backgrounds. The subjects had experience with web search engines and library search facilities (average four years) but relatively little experience with any other IR system. No subject reported experience with IR systems that offered RF functionality.

4.4 Experimental methodology

Each experiment used two systems; a *control* system and an *experimental* system, discussed in sections 5–7. In each experiment six subjects each completed the same six search tasks: three tasks on the control system; three on the experimental system. The order of presentation of task and allocation of tasks to the control and experimental systems was randomised across the experimental subjects. No subject could take part in more than one experiment to limit familiarity with the search tasks and learning. In the experiments the subjects were given 15 minutes to search on each of the six search tasks.

The subjects were given a short tutorial on the main features of the system and were walked-through a sample search and then allowed to practice searching on the system. The subjects were instructed to search in any way they felt comfortable using the search systems and were encouraged to make their own assessments as to the utility of the documents found. The only specific task the subjects were given was to mark any useful document found. After each search the subjects were encouraged to discuss the search and the information they found whilst searching.

5. EXPERIMENT ONE: RF WITH F₄-PO AGAINST NO RF

Our first experiment compared the performance of RF incorporating our new term ranking algorithm, F_4_po, against no RF. In this experiment we were interested in how well the terms suggested by the system compared against the terms suggested by the searcher. In this experiment neither the control nor experimental system explicitly offered the subject a RF option; the subject was only offered a new search option. However, on the experimental system each time the subject performed a new search, the system implicitly performed a RF iteration[5]. That is, although the searcher asked for a new search, the system actually ran an iteration of RF instead. In the experimental system any new query terms added by the searcher were also included in the new search; the experimental hypothesis, then, was a comparison of searcher query modification (control system) versus searcher query modification plus RF query modification (experimental system).

The system therefore added terms to the query before retrieving a new set of documents but the changes to the query were hidden from the searcher. The query expansion method we used comes from Ruthven, et al. (2001). For each relevant document found the system adds the first expansion term, from the expansion term ranking, which appears in the document. This method of query expansion adds a variable number of terms to the query and was shown to be generally better than adding a fixed number of expansion terms to each query (Ruthven, et al., 2001).

For the subject there was no observable difference between the two systems at the interface level: both systems appeared to do a new search each time. The only difference between the control and experimental system was the method by which the query was modified and the documents were ranked—the RF method of the experimental system. As we were interested only in the performance of RF against no RF the information regarding the initial search was excluded and the results from Experiment One only refer to the searches carried out after the initial search formulation for each search task. This allows a direct comparison of RF only against no RF.

Table 2. Results of documents relevant per retrieved.
Bold figures indicate higher value.

Condition	Topics					
	1	2	3	4	5	6
Control	**31.67%**	4.07%	6.67%	4.07%	10.00%	13.33%
Experimental	7.78%	**6.00%**	**10.83%**	**11.67%**	**17.33%**	**20.83%**

The subjects carried out twice as many post-initial searches on the control than experimental system (2.28 per search task control, 1.56 experimental). Comparing the precision by measuring the number of documents assessed relevant by the number of documents retrieved, Table 2, it can be seen that the experimental system gives better precision for five of the six search topics.

A second comparison is to compare how many of the documents the subjects viewed were assessed as being relevant, shown in Table 3. Again, for the majority of topics the subjects found a higher proportion of relevant documents with the experimental (feedback) system. This was in spite of viewing the same proportion of retrieved documents on the control and experimental systems (12.94 documents viewed per search task on the control system, 13.67 documents on the experimental system).

Therefore the searchers are, generally, finding a higher percentage of relevant documents with the experimental system per documents retrieved and documents that the subject chooses to view. This shows that the $F_{4-}po$ method of ranking terms does work as a RF component: it does lead to better retrieval than the searcher's choice of query terms alone.

Table 3. Results of documents relevant per viewed.
Bold figures indicate higher value.

Condition	Topics					
	1	2	3	4	5	6
Control	**70.37%**	29.73%	34.78%	22.92%	**55.26%**	54.05%
Experimental	22.95%	**60.00%**	**56.52%**	**41.18%**	32.10%	**78.13%**

6. EXPERIMENT TWO: F_{4-}PO AGAINST F_4 FOR RANKING CANDIDATE EXPANSION TERMS

In Experiment Two we compared the performance of the $F_{4-}po$ method of ranking candidate expansion terms against the original F_4 term ranking technique. The intention is to see whether the $F_{4-}po$ technique gives different results than those given by F_4. The interfaces for the control and experimental systems are identical and both offer an explicit RF option, Appendix A, Figure A.1. The retrieval and RF algorithms underlying the experimental interface for this experiment are the same as for Experiment One; the control RF system is identical to the experimental system except that it uses F_4 instead of $F_{4-}po$.

Details regarding the overall search behaviour of the subjects and the search effectiveness of the two systems are summarised in Table 4. All figures in Table 4 are average values per search task.

Table 4. Overall search behaviour. Bold figures indicate higher figures.

	Control (F4)	Experimental (F4_po)
New search iterations	2.72	**2.89**
RF iterations	**2.00**	1.39
Documents viewed	**23.98**	19.67
Documents retrieved	**101.83**	97.17
Precision (relevant/viewed)	**54%**	49%
Relevant documents	**12.89**	9.56

The values given in Table 4 would appear to indicate a favour for the control system: the subjects performed more RF, viewed more documents and found more relevant documents per search task. However the subjects' perceptions of the terms suggested by the systems were in favour of the experimental (F_{4_po}) system. At the end of each search the subjects were asked how useful the terms added by the system were to their search. This was on a 5-point scale, rated from 1 (*Not at all* [useful]) to 5 (*Extremely* [useful]). The average response when the subjects rated the terms suggested by the control system was 1.67 compared with 2.44 when the subjects used the experimental system. This value was found to be statistically significant ($t = -2.80$)[6]. That is, the subjects found the F4_po terms more useful than the $F_{4\_standard}$ ones.

The subjects also informally, whilst searching, remarked on the more obvious nature of the F_{4_po} term suggestions. An example of the type of terms added by F_4 and F_{4_po} systems is shown in Figure 4. This example is drawn from a real search, chosen at random. The subject submitted the query '*hubble space telescope*' and marked four documents relevant at the first iteration. Figure 4 shows the top ten terms ranked by F_4 and F_{4_po}.

Figure 4. Example candidate expansion terms ranked by F_4 and F_{4_po}.

F_4	F_{4_po}
accrete	astronomer
chaisson	hubble
cullers	telescope
goldreich	universe
sandpile	astronomers
terrile	telescopes
borucki	scientists
machtley	orbit
nebula	nasa
astronomer	earth

The F_4 algorithm selected terms that are less usual in the collection (*accrete*, *chaisson*) whereas the F_4_po algorithm selected variants of existing terms (*telescopes*), and more obvious terms (*orbit, nasa, earth*). The F_4_po algorithm also returned the original query terms higher up than the F_4 algorithm.

A further analysis was used to uncover how the expansion terms were actually treated by the subject: were the expansion terms often retained or removed by the subject? One justification for this kind of analysis is that subjects may be put off using RF because the suggested terms do not appear useful. Consequently they may lose out on the potential benefits from RF. The results of this analysis are summarised in Table 5.

In Table 5 (rows 3 and 4) we show the source of query terms that were added after the initial query: either added by the subjects (row 3) or the system through RF (row 4). We also show how many of the terms the subjects added were removed later by the subjects (row 5) and how many terms added by the system were removed by the subjects (row 6). The figures are averaged over search tasks.

Table 5. Summary of query term addition and removal per search task. Bold figures indicate higher value.

	F_4	F_4_po
Source of added terms		
subject	2.00	**2.33**
system	**3.33**	1.11
Source of removed terms		
subject	0.72	**1.17**
system	**2.28**	0.67

Comparing the two systems, Table 5 shows that the subjects added more of their own terms per task with the experimental system and RF added more terms when using the F_4 than the F_4_po algorithm per feedback iteration The main reason for the latter finding is that the F_4_po function in the experimental system prioritises the original query terms more than the F_4 algorithm, and is likely to add fewer expansion terms to the query. This also, perhaps, relates to the fewer RF iterations performed on the experimental system. A different query expansion algorithm should be tested here to elicit any relation between the number of terms added and the number of RF iterations performed as it may be the case that the subjects were performing less RF as RF was making fewer query term changes in the experimental system.

The difference between the number of the subjects' own terms removed was not significant ($t = -1.16$). However the difference between the number of *system* suggested terms removed was significant ($t = 2.54$). This latter finding suggests that the terms suggested by the F_4_po system were felt to be better search terms by the subject. Although the F_4_po system did not improve more queries or give better overall results it was seen by the subjects as a better term suggestion technique. The next experiment tests the effectiveness of the two term ranking schemes when the subject is selecting new query terms—Interactive Query Expansion.

7. EXPERIMENT THREE: F4_PO AGAINST F4 FOR INTERACTIVE QUERY EXPANSION

The third experiment compared the effectiveness of the F_4 and F_4_po term ranking schemes in suggesting new expansion terms for selection by the subjects. In this experiment the control system used the F_4 algorithm to suggest 20 possible expansion terms and the experimental system used the F_4_po algorithm to suggest expansion terms. Both control and experimental systems used the same interface, the only difference between the two systems was the underlying term suggestion technique. The interface is shown in Appendix A, Figure A.2.

In this experiment we are primarily interested in how the subjects used the suggested expansion terms compared with how they used their own terms. In Table 6 we present details on how the subjects added or removed query terms based on the source of the query term.

From Table 6, there were differences in how the subjects added new query terms. For example, in the control system the subjects were more likely to add their own terms to their query than ones suggested by the system (8.83 own terms added vs 1.61 system suggested expansion terms). On the experimental system, however, this was reversed: the subjects were more likely to add terms suggested by the system (6.67 own terms added vs 8.17 system suggested expansion terms).

The difference between the number of their *own* terms the subjects added was not significant ($t = 0.69$) however the difference in the number of the *system*-suggested terms added was significant ($t = -3.16$). That is, subjects were more likely to use the system-suggested terms when the system used the F_4_po term algorithm to suggest terms.

**Table 6. Statistics on query terms in Experiment Three.
Bold figures indicate higher value.**

	Topics						
Control	1	2	3	4	5	6	Averages
Own terms added	26	8	**26**	20	64	15	**8.83**
System suggested term added	4	2	9	4	4	6	1.61
Own terms removed	16	**6**	29	18	63	0	7.33
System suggested term removed	1	2	9	**1**	2	0	**0.83**
Experimental	1	2	3	4	5	6	Averages
Own terms added	**31**	**14**	**26**	16	11	**22**	6.67
System suggested term added	**36**	12	2	29	33	35	**8.17**
Own terms removed	**20**	4	23	2	10	**10**	3.83
System suggested term removed	**2**	0	2	0	**6**	0	0.56

Next, we investigate whether the increase in term use led to an increase in retrieval effectiveness. In Table 7 we present the number of unique relevant documents found on average per topic and the average relevance score given by the subjects to the documents they assessed as relevant. From Table 7, it can be seen that on all topics, with the exception of topic 3, the subjects found at least as many relevant documents on average and the average relevance score given to the documents found was higher. The difference between numbers of documents found was not significant ($t = -0.69$). However the difference between the average score given to a relevant document was significant ($t = -5.29$). These results indicate that, although the F_4_po suggested terms did not help find significantly more relevant documents, the F_4_po terms helped find *better* relevant documents[7].

**Table 7. Comparison of relevant documents found and average relevance score. Bold figures indicate higher value.
Exptl = experimental system, Avg = average.**

		Topics						
		1	2	3	4	5	6	Averages
Control	Relevant documents	10.00	**8.00**	**12.33**	7.33	9.67	8.00	9.22
Exptl	Relevant documents	**11.00**	**8.00**	7.00	**9.33**	**21.67**	**9.33**	**11.06**
Control	Average relevance score	3.78	5.37	5.14	5.05	4.49	4.31	4.69
Exptl	Average relevance score	**6.91**	**6.82**	**6.01**	**7.33**	**7.08**	**5.48**	**6.61**

This also accords with the subjects' perceptions of the suggested expansion terms. As in Experiment Two we asked the subjects, after each search, how useful they thought were the terms suggested by the systems. As seen in Table 8 where the average response per topic for this question is shown, the subjects reported the terms suggested by the experimental, F_4_po, system as being more useful than the control, F_4, suggested terms. This difference held across the search tasks and the difference is statistically significant ($t = -3.73$).

Table 8. Comparison of subject responses in Experiment Two regarding term utility. Bold figures indicate higher value.

	Topics					
Utility of terms	1	2	3	4	5	6
Control	1.33	2.33	1.33	1.67	2.00	2.00
Experimental	**3.33**	**2.67**	**1.67**	**3.67**	**4.50**	**5.00**

This experiment showed that the terms suggested by the F_4_po weighting scheme could give better term suggestions: those that were preferred by the subjects and which led to the retrieval of better relevant documents.

8. DISCUSSION AND CONCLUSIONS

The previous experiment showed the subjects used more expansion terms that were suggested by the F_4_po function. However, as noted throughout the experiments the use of the F_4_po function did not necessarily increase the retrieval of more relevant documents over the $F_4\_standard$ function. That is, whether used interactively or automatically the terms chosen by the two functions perform in a similar fashion. This is the case even though the terms ranked highly by the two algorithms are often very different.

To demonstrate this we took, for each of the subjects' searches, all the documents marked relevant by the subject and used these documents to create two lists of expansion terms; one list ranked by $F_4\_standard$ and one ranked by F_4_po. We then compared the top 20 terms in each list—the ones presented in interactive query expansion—and compared the overlap between the two lists, i.e., how many terms appeared in both lists. The results, Table 9, are averaged over all searches on a topic and show that, for an individual search, the two term ranking algorithms will only share around three terms (column 8). This means that the terms at the top of the expansion term ranking—the ones most likely to be used in query expansion—are different. Therefore even though different terms are being added to the query, similar retrieval results are being obtained. This is an issue that requires further investigation. In particular we should consider the searchers' intention behind selecting individual terms and the effect the searcher intends on the kind of documents being retrieved.

**Table 9. Overlap between top 20 terms suggested
by $F_4\_standard$ and F_4_po functions.**

	Topics						
	1	**2**	**3**	**4**	**5**	**6**	**All topics**
%age overlap	19.83%	14.33%	11.17%	17.17%	16.83%	6.67%	14.33%
Shared terms	3.97	2.87	2.23	3.43	3.37	1.33	2.87

Table 9 demonstrates that the terms suggested by the two term ranking algorithms are different. The subjects' perceptions of the two term ranking techniques, section 7, show that the subjects also perceive a difference regarding the terms' utility. However, the subjects' perceptions regarding a term's utility for searching do not necessarily match their judgements on the relevance of documents containing the terms, and neither does the subjects' perceptions on the search effectiveness of the systems used. In Experiments Two and Three we asked the subjects to assess their satisfaction on their search[8]. The results for the systems that used $F_4\_standard$ were both lower than for those systems that used F_4_po (Experiment Two 3.05 $F_4\_standard$ vs 3.44 F_4_po, Experiment Three 2.72 $F_4\_standard$ vs 3.83 F_4_po). Therefore the main strength of the F_4_po function is that the terms it suggests are preferred by searchers.

The main contribution in this paper was a new method of ranking candidate expansion terms based on relevance information that incorporates partial relevance assessments and ostensive information. There are limitations to our experiments. In particular we used a small number of searchers, and a limited set of search tasks. These both limit the conclusions we can draw from these experiments. In addition we only used one set of interfaces. The presentation of documents, the method by which searchers assess documents and how expansion terms are presented to the searcher are obviously important factors in the *use* of RF and query expansion techniques. The presentation of interactive query expansion, for example, has been shown to be an important variable in the success and uptake of query expansion in Koenemann and Belkin (1996) and Beaulieu (1997).

Finally, we only attempted to incorporate behavioural information into one term ranking algorithm. We cannot guarantee that similar results will be obtained from other algorithms without further investigation. These sets of experiments are intended to be viewed as a proof-of-concept investigation to investigate the general principle of incorporating user search information into the term ranking principle.

Our experiments indicate that our term ranking function performs well in RF, selects terms that are preferred by the searcher in automatic query expansion, and suggests better terms for interactive query expansion. This shows that incorporating information on the user's search activity *can* improve RF algorithms but we do require much more investigation to provide robust methods of connecting the search to the system. We hope that this initial investigation will promote interest in this area.

NOTES

1. Usually all the terms which appear in at least one relevant document.

2. F_4_p(artial)o(stensive)

3. The maximum relevance score that can be assigned to a document is 10. Therefore R becomes the maximum total relevance score that can be assigned to the set of documents assessed relevant by the user.

4. The interactive TREC track is an initiative intended to investigate search systems with a highly interactive nature. More information is available at http://trec.nist.gov/

5. Not including the initial search.

6. Measured using a *t*-test for related samples, $p < 0.05$

7. These figures and the ones regarding term utility in Table 8 are only for searches in which the subject used the term suggestion option. Out of the 18 searches on each system, 3 searches on the control system and 2 searches on the experimental system did not include use of the term suggestion option. All subjects used this option in the majority of their searches.

8. The assessment was a score from 1–5 with 5 reflecting the highest satisfaction with the search.

ACKNOWLEDGEMENTS

We would like to thank Mark Dunlop and Pia Borlund for their helpful comments on the experimental design. We are especially grateful for the many useful comments from the anonymous referees which helped improve the content of this paper. This work was completed as part of the Library and Information Commission project Retrieval Through Explanation http://www.dcs.gla.ac.uk/ir/explanation, whilst the first author was at the University of Glasgow.

REFERENCES

Beaulieu, M. (1997) Experiments with interfaces to support query expansion. *Journal of Documentation, 53*, 8–19.

Borlund, P. (2000) Experimental components for the evaluation of interactive information retrieval systems. *Journal of Documentation, 56*, 1.

Campbell, I., and C. van Rijsbergen. (1996) The ostensive model for developing information needs. In *Proceedings of CoLIS 2, Second International Conference on Conceptions of Library and Information Science: Integration in Perspective* (pp. 251–68). The Royal School of Librarianship, Copenhagen.

Efthimiadis, E. N. (1995) User choices: A new yardstick for the evaluation of ranking algorithms for interactive query expansion. *Information Processing and Management, 31,* 605–20.

Florance, V., and G. Marchionini. (1995) Information processing in the context of medical care. In *Proceedings of the 18th Annual International ACM SIGIR Conference on Research and Development in Information Retrieval* (pp. 158–63). Seattle.

Harman, D. (1992) Relevance feedback revisited. In *Proceedings of the 15th Annual International ACM SIGIR Conference on Research and Development in Information Retrieval* (pp. 1–10). Copenhagen.

Heuer, R. (1999) *Psychology of intelligence analysis.* Center for the Study of Intelligence. Central Intelligence Agency.

Koenemann, J., and N. Belkin. (1996) A case for interaction: a study of interactive information retrieval behavior and effectiveness. In *Proceedings of the Human Factors in Computing Systems Conference (CHI'96)* (pp. 205–12). Zurich.

Robertson, S., and K. Sparck Jones. (1976) Relevance weighting of search terms. *Journal of the American Society for Information Science, 27*, 129–46.

Ruthven, I., M. Lalmas, and C. van Rijsbergen. (2001) Empirical investigations on query modification using abductive explanations. In *Proceedings of the 24th ACM SIGIR Conference on Research and Development in Information Retrieval.* New Orleans.

Salton, G., and C. Buckley. (1990) Improving retrieval performance by relevance feedback. *Journal of the American Society for Information Science, 41,* 288–97.

Spink, A., H. Greisdorf, and J. Bateman. (1998) From highly relevant to not relevant: examining different regions of relevance. *Information Processing and Management, 34,* 599–621.

Tiamiyu, M., and I. Ajiferuke. (1988) A total relevance and document interaction effects model for the evaluation of information retrieval processes. *Information Processing and Management, 24,* 391–404.

Vakkari, P. (2000a) Cognition and changes of search terms and tactics during task performance: a longitudinal study. In *Proceedings of the RIAO '2000 Conference* (pp. 894–907). Paris.

Vakkari, P. (2000b) Relevance and contributing information types of searched documents in task performance. In *Proceedings of the twenty-third annual international ACM SIGIR Conference on Research and development in information retrieval* (pp. 2–9). Athens.

Voorhees, E., and D. Harman. (1997) *Proceedings of the sixth Text REtrieval Conference (TREC-6).* National Institute of Standards and Technology (NIST), Special Publication 500–240.

APPENDIX A

Figure A.1. Interface for Experiment Two.

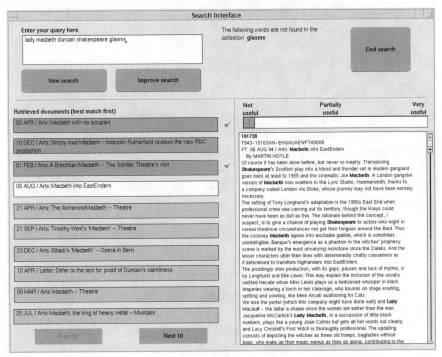

Figure A.2. Interface for Experiment Three.

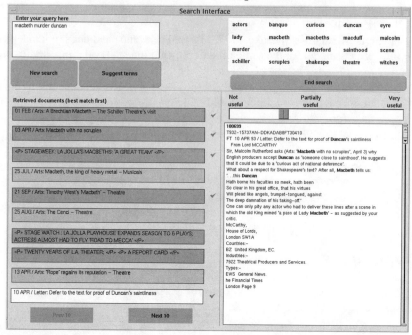

APPENDIX B

Topic one

At a recent party you overhear a discussion about whether science funding gives value for money. One person claimed that many expensive projects, such as the Hubble Telescope, do not produce significant positive advances. You are not sure how true this statement is, and would like to find more information on the positive achievements of the Hubble Telescope since it was launched in 1991.

Topic two

The new Scottish Parliament is considering planning permission for a series of large hydroelectric projects. These projects will use water power to produce electricity for a large area of Scotland. Supporters of the projects claim that they will give cheaper electricity and reduce global-warming, opponents argue that the projects may cause environmental damage and harm tourism. The Parliament has decided to hold a vote for all Scottish residents to decide if these projects should go ahead. You have little independent information upon which to base your decision, and would like information on similar projects.

Topic three

It is likely that a British General Election will be held in May this year. In the last General Election, one of the main issues was the relatively low number of female members of parliament. This prompted one party to introduce special measures to increase the number of female candidates in the election. Other politicians argue that poor representation of women in parliament is not a specific feature of British politics. As the poor representation is likely to be a major issue in the forthcoming election, you would like to be more informed about the representation of women in politics.

Topic five

You and a friend are trying to choose a holiday for later this summer. One possible holiday destination will mean taking several ferry trips but you have heard rumours that ferries in this area have a poor safety record. You need to book your holiday soon but need more information on the dangers of ferry travel.

Topic six

Your best friend is an active member of a major wildlife preservation group. She is working on a project to build an electronic database of wildlife species that are in danger of extinction and the steps that different countries have taken to protect these species. She has asked you for help in providing information on international attempts to save native species, and the causes of wildlife extinction.

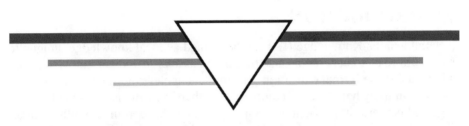

Information Access in Indigenous Languages: A Case Study in Zulu

Erica Cosijn
Department of Information Science
University of Pretoria
Pretoria 0002, South Africa
ecosijn@postino.up.ac.za

Ari Pirkola
Department of Information Studies
University of Tampere
P O Box 607
33101 Tampere, Finland
pirkola@tukki.cc.jyu.fi

Theo Bothma
Department of Information Science
University of Pretoria
Pretoria 0002, South Africa
tbothma@postino.up.ac.za

Kalervo Järvelin
Department of Information Studies
University of Tampere
P O Box 607
33101 Tampere, Finland
likaja@uta.fi

ABSTRACT

This study focuses on the intellectual accessibility of information in indigenous languages, using Zulu, one of the main indigenous languages in South Africa, as a test case. Both Cross-Lingual Information Retrieval (CLIR) and metadata are discussed as possible means of facilitating access and a bilateral approach combining these two methods is proposed. Popular CLIR approaches and their resource requirements are analysed and the dictionary-based approach combined with approximate string-matching for query translation from Zulu to

221

English are discussed in detail. Metadata formats for knowledge representation from the Indigenous Knowledge (IK) viewpoint are discussed, in particular the advantages and limitations of the Dublin Core (DC) metadata format.

1. INTRODUCTION

Indigenous Knowledge (IK) can be termed as local knowledge, unique to every culture or society. It can also be defined as a large body of knowledge and skills outside the formal education system that enables communities to survive, and is commonly held by communities rather than individuals. IK is tacit knowledge and is therefore difficult to codify, as it is embedded in community practices, relationships and rituals. Recently, there have been several efforts to collect IK in order to analyse it and to prevent it from being lost to posterity. IK has thus been collected into large paper archives and more recently into electronic databases.

Using databases for the representation of IK may offer several advantages. Most importantly, access from a retrieval point of view is much easier in electronic database format than in paper or linear electronic text formats. Secondly, IK can be stored and delivered in multiple copies for those that need it. Furthermore, in database format, it is possible to annotate IK in various ways from multiple viewpoints to facilitate its analysis. However, in order to realise these advantages, IK in databases must be made accessible.

In this study we focus on the problem of intellectual accessibility of IK, as opposed to the problems of database technology (e.g., file structures and their access methods) or availability of equipment. We will analyse and discuss Cross-Lingual Information Retrieval (CLIR) as means of access to such databases. Various problems were experienced, viz. the standard problems associated with CLIR, the lack of suitable electronic resources and the characteristics of Zulu as language. We therefore suggest that one should also consider the use of metadata to describe the content. Regarding CLIR, we analyse popular CLIR approaches and their resource requirements, and discuss in detail the dictionary-based approach for query translation for accessing IK. We also develop means for circumventing the problems caused by insufficient linguistic resources for query translation. Regarding metadata, we analyse metadata formats for knowledge representation from the IK viewpoint and discuss, in particular, the advantages and limitations of the Dublin Core (DC) metadata format.

The paper is organised as follows. In Section 2 we present and analyse basic CLIR approaches and techniques for IK access, and indicate why some of the approaches are not suitable. Section 3 is a discussion of the viability and advantages of using CLIR as access to IK databases in South African indigenous languages (specifically Zulu). In Section 4 we discuss the applicability of metadata to facilitate access to IK databases. Section 5 contains some concluding remarks in which we indicate that retrieval through a combination of CLIR techniques and metadata will enhance precision.

2. THE APPLICABILITY OF CLIR FOR IK DATABASES IN A SOUTH AFRICAN CONTEXT

IK is normally stored in databases in textual form, based on transcribed speech in some indigenous language. Any large IK database is likely to contain IK in several indigenous languages. The analysts and other users of IK may well be capable of reading IK texts directly in several indigenous languages. However, they may have difficulties in expressing their interests properly in these languages, which is the requirement for successful direct content access.

The basic idea of Cross Language Information Retrieval (CLIR) (Hull, and Greffenstette, 1996; Oard, and Diekema, 1998) is to provide access in one language (the source language) to documents written in another language (the target language). South Africa has a very complex language situation due to the fact that there are eleven official languages, *viz*. English, Afrikaans and nine African languages, including Zulu and Xhosa. In the case of IK, the source language would often be English or Afrikaans, but could also be an African language. The target language(s) would typically be the indigenous African language(s).

The basic approaches in CLIR involve *query translation* from source language to target language(s) and/or *document translation* from target language(s) to source language. Document translation requires good machine translation systems for the languages in which the IK documents are written, but such systems will not be available any time soon. Query translation requires fewer resources, but there is the additional requirement that the users should be able to read the IK documents in the languages in which they were written. It is often the case that the user is able to read a foreign language, but is not fluent enough to construct an appropriate query in that language. However, even if the user cannot read the retrieved documents, the user has at least a relevant set of retrieved documents that may be translated manually.

In CLIR, the main strategies for query translation are based on parallel corpora, machine translation and (bilingual) translation dictionaries (Oard, and Diekema, 1998). We review below the three methods briefly and then show how the third can be supplemented with approximate string matching.

2.1. Corpus-based

In corpus-based technologies, the source language query is translated in a parallel text corpus to a target language query to be run in the target language database (Figure 1). A parallel corpus consists of document pairs such that one document is in the source language of the user query and the other in the target language. Moreover, the document pairs are translations of each other. In some approaches the documents are not exact translations of each other but nevertheless about the same topic (comparable document collections).

Figure 1. Parallel corpora in CLIR.

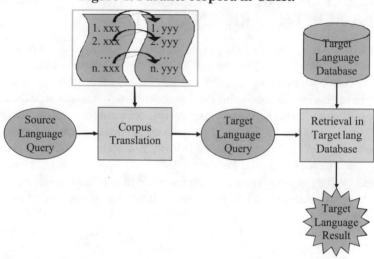

When a source language query is entered into the system, it is run against the source language documents of the parallel corpus. Best-matching documents are identified and then their target language pairs are retrieved. Statistical criteria and possible sentence-by-sentence alignment are used to identify best topic words to be used in the target language query. The target language query is a bag-of-words query, which then is run against the target language collection.

The corpus-based approach requires a parallel collection in the domain of the queries and the target collection. It can be much smaller than the target collection but needs to contain pertinent vocabulary for the query topics. There is no word-by-word correspondence between the source and target language queries. In fact, the latter contains words that are statistically associated with the source language query words in the parallel corpus.

Because electronic parallel corpora are not readily available in the different languages, this CLIR approach is not a practical option in the South African context.

2.2. Machine translation

In this approach, a machine translation system is employed for query translation. Such systems aim at correct target language translation of source language texts. Translation is based on translation dictionaries, other linguistic resources and syntax analysis to arrive at an unambiguous and high-quality target language text (Figure 2). The source language query in CLIR applications must be a grammatically correct sentence (or a longer text) for the translation to be successful.

A major problem for this approach is the availability of good machine translation systems. For many language pairs no systems exist, and for many others, the quality of the systems is rather poor and/or their topical scope limited.

In the South African context, there is a machine translation system between English, Afrikaans and several African languages (http://lexica.epiuse.co.za) but its quality for CLIR applications is inadequate.

Figure 2. CLIR based on machine translation.

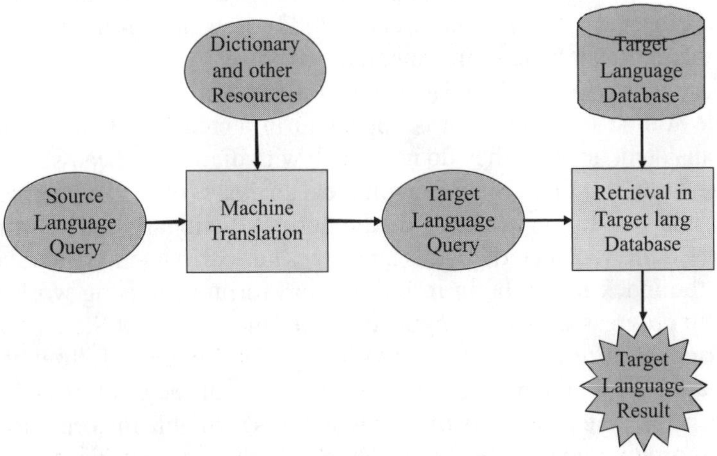

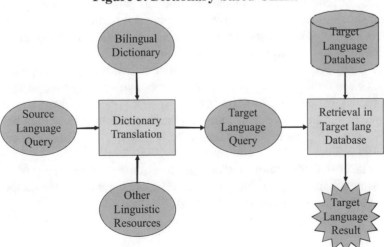

2.3. Dictionary-based techniques

When the linguistic resources for a language pair are limited, dictionaries are the most likely to be available in machine-readable form. Therefore one may say that the dictionary-based approach is viable when linguistic resources are scarce.

The dictionary-based approaches use bilingual dictionaries for query translation (Figure 3). A very basic strategy for query translation is to process it word-by-word and, for each source language word, look up its target language equivalents and put them into the target language query.

Figure 3. Dictionary-based CLIR.

No translation dictionary available for CLIR is as extensive as the lexicon of the language listing all its words. This is because natural languages are productive systems that continuously generate new words. The most important categories of untranslatable query keys generally not found in general dictionaries are new compound words, proper names and other spelling variants, and special terms (Pirkola, et al., 2001). Pirkola, et al. (2002) show how n-grams can be used to match the untranslatable source language words with similar words in the target database index. We will consider this in more detail in the next subsection.

If the source language words appear in inflected forms, they cannot be readily translated, because they do not match with dictionary headwords (which are in base forms). If there is a morphological analyser (parser) available, words can be normalised to the lemma, i.e., the normal dictionary entry form. In the case of the South African indigenous languages no such parsers are available and therefore the index has to be in inflected word form. Promising work on such parsers is in progress for some languages at the Universities of Stellenbosch and South Africa (http://www.ast.sun.ac.za). The possibility that a full set of parsers will be available for all languages in South Africa in the near future is, however, slight. Therefore, the possibility of having indexes available in normalised form, based on morphological parsers, is not likely. In the South African context the retrieval techniques therefore have to work on an index containing words in their inflected form from multiple target languages and matching can be achieved through approximate string matching.

2.4. Approximate string matching in IR

A common method to handle untranslatable words, e.g., many proper names, in dictionary-based CLIR, is to pass them as such to the target language query. However, in the case of spelling variants or inflectional forms, a source language form does not match the variant form in the target database index, causing loss of retrieval effectiveness. To find target language spelling variants for untranslatable source language words, some *approximate string matching* technique, such as *n-gram based matching*, *edit distance* or *LCS* (longest common subsequence) technique has to be applied.

In *n-gram matching* query keys and index entries are decomposed into n-grams, i.e., into the sub-strings of length n, which usually consist of the adjacent characters of strings. *Digrams* contain two and *trigrams* three characters. The degree of similarity between query keys and index entries can then be computed by comparing their n-gram sets (Pfeifer, et al., 1996; Robertson, and Willett, 1998; Salton, 1989; Zobel, and Dart, 1995).

Pirkola, et al. (2002) showed that n-gram matching is effective in searching for cross-lingual spelling variants. It can also be used an alternative method for stemming algorithms (Xu, and Croft, 1998).

N-gram matching is a *non-metric* approximate matching technique. A *metric* similarity measure *distance* is a similarity function, which satisfies the following conditions (Berghel, 1987):

1. *distance*(s, s') >= 0
2. *distance*(s, s') = 0 <—> s=s'
3. *distance*(s, s') = *distance*(s', s)
4. *distance*(s, s') + *distance*(s', s'') >= *distance*(s, s'')

for arbitrary character strings s, s', s''.

Metric similarity measures involve *edit distance* and *LCS*. Edit distance is defined as the minimum cost required to convert one string into another. Conversion includes character insertions, deletions and substitutions. For example, the minimum number of steps required to change the string *industry* into *interest* is six (Kruskal, 1983). For two words, their LCS is the longest character sequence of the sequences that occur in both words. For example, for the words

r e t r i e v a l and *r e v i v a l* LCS is *r e i v a l*.

When using approximate matching in IR, the query key is matched against database index entries and the best matching entries can be added to the query. These will then be treated as a synonym list. The number of entries added may be limited, either through a threshold value (the calculated value of the similarity must exceed a set limit value for the index entry to be accepted), or by adding only the *k* best-matching index entries to the query, or by both criteria.

3. THE VIABILITY OF USING CLIR TO ACCESS ZULU LANGUAGE DATABASES

3.1. The Zulu language

Zulu is spoken by more than 8.8 million people in South and Southern Africa. Of all the languages (including Afrikaans and English) spoken in South Africa, Zulu has the largest number of speakers. Zulu is an agglutinative language, which means that grammatical information is conveyed by attaching prefixes and suffixes to roots and stems. All Bantu languages are divided into classes or sets, called grammatical genders. Each gender has two distinct prefixes, one for singular and one for plural nouns. The classes far exceed the familiar European classifications of masculine, feminine and neuter, and are roughly associated with semantic characteristics relating to, for instance, human beings, kinship terms, animals, plants, artifacts, abstract concepts and so on. *Umlimi* and *abalimi* are, for example, the singular and plural forms of the noun meaning *farmer*, and most words denoting human beings are in the *umu-*, *aba-* class (Class 1) of nouns. Verbal nouns, on the other hand, belong to the Class 8 group of nouns, of which the prefix is *uku-*, for example *ukugula*, which is the Zulu word for either *death* or the infinitive *to die*.

Verbs are complex: a system of affixes marks the different grammatical relations, such as subject, object, tense, aspect and mood. For example, suffixes on verbs are used to derive passive, active, causative, reciprocal and prepositional verb forms. There is a system of concordial agreement in which subject nouns, object nouns and other words must agree with the verb of the sentence in class and number. Adjectives, possessive nouns and demonstratives also agree with the noun that they modify in class and number.

The phonology of Zulu is characterized by a simple noun inventory and a highly marked consonantal system with ejectives, implosives and click-sounds. It also is a tone language with inherent low and high tones (Doke, 1990; "UCLA," 2002).

3.2. Methodology

In order for an English-speaking person (source language) to access an IK database in Zulu (target language), the process may be described as follows (see Figure 4):

Figure 4. English to Zulu CLIR Process.

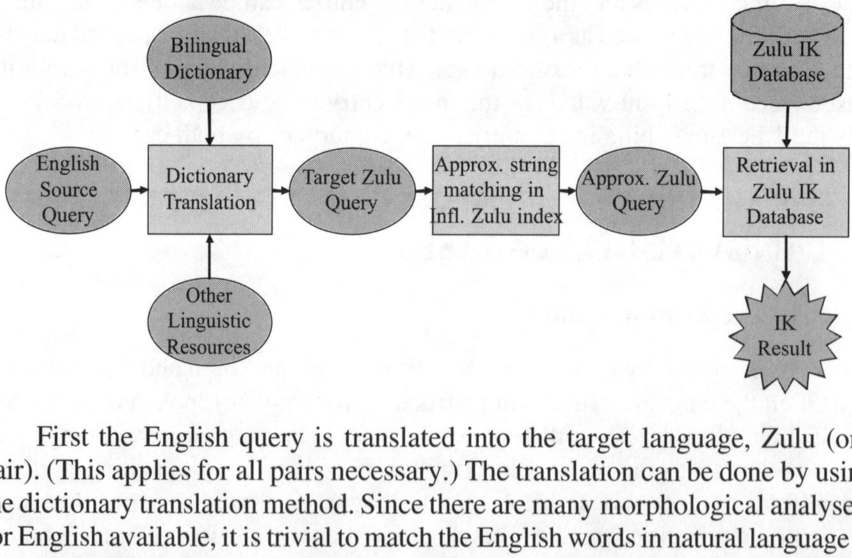

First the English query is translated into the target language, Zulu (one pair). (This applies for all pairs necessary.) The translation can be done by using the dictionary translation method. Since there are many morphological analysers for English available, it is trivial to match the English words in natural language to the translation dictionary entries. For each English word we then get a number of Zulu translations, some of which are correct and some of which are incorrect for the query context (due to the ambiguity of natural language). All these words are then matched against the inverted index of the Zulu database. The inverted index is not normalized because there are no suitable Zulu morphological analyzers available. Therefore, approximate matching between the query words and indexed words are necessary. For each Zulu word (base form), a number of best matches in the index are identified. These are treated as synonym sets and query structure (Pirkola, et al., 2001) is utilized to reduce ambiguity.

Some parts of this process have been tested empirically on a corpus, and this will be described below, including some of the problems experienced so far. Due to the fact that there are no large-scale Zulu language databases available, the reverse of the process is being tested, that is, Zulu queries put to an English language database (Figure 5).

Figure 5. The reverse process tested.

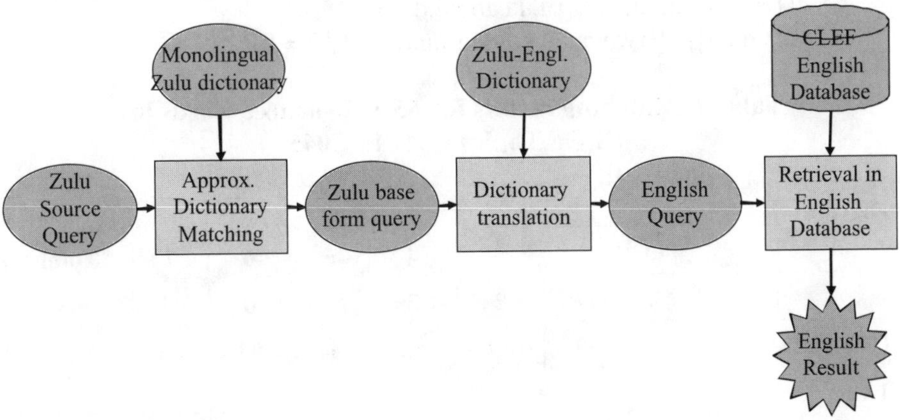

The corpus used was the CLEF English document collection with 50 topics (CLEF 2001). The title and description fields were translated from English into Zulu by independent translators. As there were no Zulu-English bilingual trans- lation dictionaries available in electronic format, part of a printed dictionary had to be retyped manually in a word-processing program. Due to various restraints and restrictions, it was decided to only create a monolingual word list (Zulu en- tries only) in electronic format. The dictionary used was the 1990 edition of the Zulu dictionary by Doke, et al., where singular forms, plural forms as well as stems for nouns are listed. Using this particular dictionary should thus alleviate ambiguity problems for nouns. Verbs, however, are listed only as stems.

We tested the following approximate matching techniques to match the in- dividual Zulu words in the topics with Zulu dictionary entries: (1) conventional digrams and (2) conventional trigrams, i.e., digrams and trigrams combined of adjacent letters of words, (3) classified s-grams, (4) edit distance, and (5) LCS.

The classified s-gram matching technique (where *s* refers to the term *skip*) refers to a novel n-gram matching technique described in detail in Pirkola, et al. (2002). In the technique, digrams are combined both of adjacent and non-adjacent characters of words. Digrams are classified into categories on the basis of the num- ber of skipped characters. Digrams belonging to the same category are compared with one another, but not with digrams belonging to a different category.

In the case of n-grams (the cases 1–3 above) similarity values were computed using the following string similarity scheme (Pfeifer, et al., 1996):

$$SIM(N_1, N_2) = |N1 \cap N2| / |N1 \cup N2|,$$

where N1 and N2 are n-gram sets of two words. $|N1 \cap N2|$ denotes the number of intersecting (similar) n-grams, and $|N1 \cup N2|$ the number of unique n-grams in the union of N1 and N2. For example, the degree of similarity for the words *rwanda* and *ruanda* is calculated as follows (for conventional digrams):

SIM({rw,wa,an,nd,da},{ru,ua,an,nd,da})
= |{an,nd,da}| / |{rw,wa,an,nd,da,ru,ua}| = 3 / 7 = 0.429.

Table 1. Matching results for 65 Zulu source words in CLEF Topics C041 to C045.

Digram

	1	2	3	4	5	6	7	Total
	36	11	2	3	2	0	11	65
Cumulative		47	49	52	54	54	65	

LCS

	1	2	3	4	5	6	7	Total
	38	6	4	3	0	0	14	65
Cumulative		44	44	51	51	51	65	

Edit

	1	2	3	4	5	6	7	Total
	33	4	2	5	4	1	16	65
Cumulative		37	39	44	48	49	65	

Tigram

	1	2	3	4	5	6	7	Total
	37	7	4	1	3	0	13	65
Cumulative		44	48	49	52	52	65	

Skipgram

	1	2	3	4	5	6	7	Total
	38	10	3	2	1	1	10	65
Cumulative		48	51	53	54	55	65	

Five of the CLEF 2001 topics were used as a trial to establish which of the procedures described above would give the best results. For topics C041 to C045 there were 75 Zulu source words. Ten of these were proper nouns, which were not matched, and therefore not used in the calculations. The results were thus based on 65 source words. For each procedure the six approximate best matches were listed for each of these source words. It was then manually established which one of these six words was the correct match for the source word. If the first word was the correct match, a value of 1 was allocated, a value of 2 if the second word was the correct match, and so on, and if there was no match, a value of 7 was given. The results are given in the table above.

Based on the five trial topics, skipgrams yielded the best results. For skipgrams, the signal to noise ratio for n=3 is calculated as follows:

$$51 \text{ hits} / (3*65-51) \text{ nonhits} = 35\%$$

The signal to noise ratio results for all six matches are as follows:

n=1: 141% (more signal than noise), n=2: 59%, n=3: 35%, n=4: 26%, n=5: 20%, n=6: 16%.

It was thus found that the signal to noise ratio drops rapidly as n grows.

It was calculated that the stem identification rate would be 78% if n=3 and 82 percent if n=4. Saturation occurs around n=3. This means that the correct Zulu word should be identified within a set of three words about 80 percent of the time.

Translations from the Zulu **source** words into English were again done manually, following strict mechanical rules (all senses collected). The first type of problem experienced in this phase related to long English descriptions needed to paraphrase single Zulu words, and these had to be marked-up as phrases. Examples of these are the Zulu nouns *idlingozi* which is paraphrased as *an outburst of intense interest* and *isinyabulala* which is paraphrased as *a person weak from age*. This problem is also a result of the disparate vocabularies between "Western" and indigenous languages described below. The second problem was related to homonyms, where one word has various meanings, for example the **source** noun entry—*zwe isizwe izizwe* can mean either *tribe* or *a rapidly spreading brain disease*.

The retrieval results of the translated Zulu queries in the English collection are reported in a later paper.

3.3. Problems regarding resources

3.3.1. No electronic dictionary

At present there are no (comprehensive) electronic dictionaries for any of the African languages of South Africa. Various projects of the different dictionary units are in the process of being established; however, nothing that can be used for research is available at this stage. We therefore used a retyped monolingual dictionary with manual translations from Zulu to English, as explained above.

3.3.2. Test database—CLEF suitability

The aim of the research is to test whether English search strings could be run against a Zulu database, and to see which technologies are possibly viable in this regard. Since no Zulu database was available, we had to reverse the process, i.e., to run Zulu queries, translated into English, against an English database. We used the CLEF 2001 database, as explained above. We therefore tested whether inflected Zulu words can be matched with a dictionary entry through approximate matching. This proved to be fairly successful, as indicated in Table 1. The reverse process, i.e., to match dictionary entries to inverted indexes that contain non-normalized, inflected text, should therefore also be possible. However, the process indicated another interesting problem that should be investigated in its own right, *viz.* the impact of the lack of technical terminology in Zulu CLIR. The CLEF database and queries are very Euro-centric, and many of the search terms could not be translated directly into Zulu.

The problems in such matching are classified and discussed below.

3.4. Problems experienced with matching

Zulu does not have single word translation equivalents for many technical and scientific terms. This problem is solved either by paraphrasing to explain concepts or by borrowing words from other languages.

3.4.1. Paraphrasing

Paraphrasing is very commonly used to describe words or phrases in technical or scientific terminology. Two examples will suffice:

CLEF 2001 topic C041 contains the word *pesticides*. The Zulu translation of this reads *amakhemikheli abulala zonke izifo enzinengozi* which translated directly back to English means *chemicals that kill all illnesses which are dangerous*.

CLEF 2001 C046 topic contains the phrase *embargo*, which is translated into Zulu as *ukuvimbela kohwebo*, which literally means *to prevent trade*.

Mechanically, n-grams match most of the individual words quite well to the dictionary entries. On a conceptual level however, the result is not always very good.

3.4.2. Borrowed words

Zulu has borrowed extensively from Khoisan (the languages of the southern African aboriginal hunter-gatherer populations) and in modern times from English and Afrikaans. These borrowed words may take one of two forms—the word is either kept as in the original language, but prefixed as if it is a Zulu noun, or assimilated into the Zulu language. Examples of the latter are the English nouns *bicycle* which becomes *ibhayisekili* in Zulu, *post office* becomes *iposihovisi* and *tea* becomes *itiye*. Even though the spelling is vastly different from the English, the pronunciation is similar to the original. Some of these borrowed words are of acceptable use and are included in the dictionaries. However, some are new additions, and the modern concepts are very often not entered in dictionaries (which are not updated very often). An example in the CLEF topic set is *amakhemikheli* (consisting of the prefix *ama-* indicating that it is an artifact and—*khemikheli* which is borrowed from the English word *chemicals*) which was not found in the dictionary.

Some of the words are not assimilated into the language, but stay in the original language from which they were borrowed, with Zulu class-prefixes added. Examples which occurred in the translated CLEF topic set are, *inter alia*, *ama*"computer viruses," *ama*"computer mouse," *i*"film festival," *i*"green power," *i*"mad cow disease," *i*"German property speculator" and *iTurqoise*.

In the first six examples above, the prefix is not added to a single word, but to an entire phrase and the whole phrase is put in inverted commas, which may compound the problem of identifying phrases in CLIR.

3.4.3. Inflected word forms

If the source language words appear in inflected forms, they cannot be readily matched, because they do not match the dictionary base forms. As stemming is not an option in Zulu due to the lack of morphological parsers, approximate matches have to be made by n-gramming or similar string-matching techniques.

Below are two examples of approximate matching ? the first of a noun and the second of a verb:

The Zulu monolingual dictionary entries for nouns are of the format:
stem, singular (prefix + stem), plural (prefix + stem)
The entry for *danger* thus is:
-ngozi ingozi izingozi
In one of the translated CLEF topics the inflected form is *ezinengozi*. This inflected form was matched as follows by the five different matching techniques:

Trigram: n=3, LCS: n=1, Edit: n=7 (no match), Skipgram: n=4 and Digram: n=2

In the case of verbs the stem only is listed, e.g., *bulala* for *to kill*. In the running text of a topic it appears as *abulala* (in concord with the noun *amakhemikheli*). This was matched as follows:

Trigram: n=2, LCS: n=2, Edit: n=2=3, Skipgram: n=2 and Digram: n=3

Although these two examples were arbitrarily chosen, they do show that inflected word forms have a significant influence on accuracy of retrieval, due to the increased possibility of noise.

Even though the CLIR techniques discussed above provide significant results there are a number of problems due to *inter alia* noise, untranslatability, paraphrasing, conceptual mismatching, problems inherent to the Zulu language, etc. The refinement of CLIR techniques may result in improved recall and precision in future. However, in practice, such as IK databases, precision could be insufficient, and we would suggest that further techniques be employed to improve it. A practical solution would be to employ metadata. It is therefore also necessary to look at metadata as a mechanism to improve precision in conjunction with CLIR.

4. METADATA AS A FILTERING MECHANISM

The content of a knowledge source may be described though metadata. The purpose of metadata is thus to describe the structure of the data, and more importantly, to capture any additional properties that may characterize it.

The *de facto* standard for metadata, especially on the Web, is Dublin Core. The elements and definitions of Dublin Core as listed in Table 2, columns 1 and 2 are based on the official standard for the element set of DC (ANSI/NISO Z39.85-2001). The elements can be seen as describing three different dimensions of metadata, viz describing the content or *data*, describing the *source*, and describing the *collection process* to collect the content, as given in column 4 of Table 2. This subdivision is very relevant for IK—and may be relevant in other cases as well—since it describes the aboutness, isness and processing of the information objects.

Dublin Core is a general set of metadata elements and is very often enriched by application domain dependent additions, such as the NDLTD (Networked Digital Library of Theses and Dissertations http://www.ndltd.org) and the LOM (Learning Object Metadata http://ltsc.ieee.org/wg12/). It would therefore be natural to extend the metadata set for the description of IK objects, and we propose the additions as listed in column 3 of Table 2. The detail of these additions are described elsewhere (Cosijn, et al., 2002). These additions are the minimum that are required, and more can be proposed.

Table 2. Description of DC with proposed added subdivisions.

Name of element	Definition	Proposed added sub-divisions	Dimension of description
Title	Name given to the resource		Data
Creator	Entity primarily responsible for making the content of the resource	creator.status	Source
Subject	Topic of the content of the resource	subject.keyword subject.domain	Data
Description	Account of the content of the resource		Data
Publisher	Entity responsible for making the resource available		Collection process
Contributor	Entity responsible for making contributions to the content of the resource	contributor.recorder contributor.editor	Collection process
Date	Date associated with an event in the lifecycle of the resource	date.recorded date.published date.added	Collection process
Type	Nature or genre of the content of the resource		Source
Format	Physical or digital manifestation of the resource		Source
Identifier	Unambiguous reference to the resource within a given context		Source
Source	Reference to a resource from which the present resource is derived		Source
Language	Language of the intellectual content of the resource		Source
Relation	Reference to a related resource		Source
Coverage	Extent or scope of the content of the resource	coverage.location coverage.timespan coverage.tribe	Source / Data
Rights	Information about rights held in and over the resource		Source
Proposed addition		funding.agency	Collection process

Source: Based on http://dublincore.org.

The proposed metadata structure provides a multi-viewpoint access to the content. However, it is limited and constrained by all the limitations of bibliographic databases and controlled vocabulary access, such as incomplete indexing, incorrect and inconsistent keywords, uninformative abstracts, missing data, lack of thesauri and controlled vocabulary lists, etc.

The needs that the users may have are unpredictable and therefore one cannot outline any finite element set that would cover the needs. It might be possible to develop and populate such a set, but this becomes economically unfeasible. This is a complex area, and needs further investigation.

We may use the following example to illustrate the value of using both metadata and full-text access to increase precision in retrieval of IK: a user is looking for information on herbs, specifically on the use of herbs for curing fever. By specifying, for instance, the proposed DC field subject.domain in the above example as *medicine,* items dealing with *agriculture* will not be retrieved. The effect of this is that results will be limited to the domain of medicine only, and therefore potentially ambiguous results outside the field of medicine will not be included in the search results.

5. CONCLUSION

The contributions of the present paper are:

- An outline for an approach for information retrieval in IK databases based on CLIR and metadata techniques.

- An outline of the CLIR process, involving approximate string matching, when the target (or the source) language is an indigenous language lacking linguistic resources and exhibiting strong inflectional morphology.

- An analysis of approximate string matching success in identifying inflected Zulu word forms based on their base forms (dictionary forms).

- An analysis of the translation problems between an indigenous language and a western language.

- An outline for the application of the Dublin Core metadata format for IK databases.

We have shown that there are many limitations inherent to querying the full text of IK databases if we rely solely on CLIR techniques, such as ambiguity, incorrect stemming, paraphrasing in translations, untranslatability, conceptual mismatching, etc., which may have a negative impact on the quality of retrieval. On the other hand, there are a variety of limitations impacting on the quality of search results when querying an IK database using metadata only, for example, low precision due to broad keywords, lack of synonyms in the query, etc. It may, however, be possible to improve both precision and recall, as required, by querying content in combination with metadata searching, and we therefore recommend that a bilateral approach is followed to enhance accessibility of IK databases.

Regarding CLIR techniques, we outlined the process translating queries from English to Zulu. The translation of English words into Zulu base form words is for a large part manageable while it sometimes presents difficult problems of conceptual incompatibility between the languages. However, matching the Zulu base forms to the Zulu inflected form index, due to the lack of morphological analyzers, was a novel challenge. We outlined a process based on monolingual approximate string matching in Zulu to identify the inflected forms of query words in the database index. However, it was not possible to test the process directly because there are no large-scale Zulu databases available. We therefore tested the opposite, and focused on the translation problems of Zulu topic words into English queries. The first step of identifying correct base forms for Zulu was already problematic. While approximate string matching gave relatively good results, they were far from perfect (not all words were translated, the correct base forms were not always top-ranked, etc.). This introduced ambiguity into the translation process. Typical matching problems at this stage were unmatched proper nouns, inflected word forms, borrowed words and paraphrased translations.

Translation of the identified Zulu base forms (several for each topic word) was done manually but simulating a mechanical process based on a translation dictionary. In this process, a number of problems between the languages turned up. Problems encountered at this stage were mainly related to the paraphrasing of the Zulu to English translations, and the translations had to be marked-up as English phrases. Similar problems are encountered in the opposite direction of translation.

Present research in CLIR concentrates on languages with comparable vocabularies in terms of, for instance, technical and scientific terminology. This research has shown that a set of new problems will be encountered if the language pairs used contain disparate vocabularies and this increases the complexity of CLIR. The complexity is increased when one of the languages dealt with lacks resources for word form analysis. These problems need further investigation, and techniques will have to be found to deal with this. This may present unique opportunities for research in CLIR.

REFERENCES

Berghel, H. L. (1987) A logical framework for the correction of spelling errors in electronic documents. *Information Processing and Management, 23*, 477–94.

Cosijn, E., K. Järvelin, T. Bothma, J. G. Nel, and J. Theophanous. (2002) Facilitating access to knowledge databases in indigenous languages. In *Proceedings of the 15th Standing Conference of Eastern, Central and Southern African Library and Information Associations. SCECSAL 2002* (to appear).

Doke, C. M., D. M. Malcolm, J. M. A. Sikakana, and B. W. Vilakazi, comp. (1990) *English—Zulu Zulu—English Dictionary.* Johannesburg: Witwatersrand University Press.

Hull, D., and G. Grefenstette. (1996) Querying across languages: a dictionary-based approach to multilingual information retrieval. In *Proceedings of the 19th Annual International ACM SIGIR Conference on Research and Development in Information Retrieval* (pp. 49–57). Zürich, Switzerland.

Kruskal, J. B. (1983) An overview of sequence comparison. In D. Sankoff, and J. B. Kruskal, eds. *Time warps, string edits, and macromolecules: The theory and practice of sequence comparison.* Reading, MA: Addison-Wesley.

Oard, D., and A. Diekema. (1998) Cross Language Information Retrieval. *Annual Review of Information Science and Technology, 33,* 223–56.

Pfeifer, U., T. Poersch, and N. Fuhr. (1996) Retrieval effectiveness of proper name search methods. *Information Processing & Management, 32(6),* 667–79.

Pirkola, A., T. Hedlund, H. Keskustalo, and K. Järvelin. (2001) Dictionary-based cross-language information retrieval: problems, methods and research findings. *Information Retrieval 4,* 209–30.

Pirkola, A., H. Keskustalo, E. Leppänen, H. Känsälä, and K. Järvelin. (2002) Targeted s-gram matching: a novel n-gram matching technique for cross-and monolingual word form variants. *Information Research* (to appear).

Robertson, A. M., and P. Willett. (1998) Applications of n-grams in textual information systems. *Journal of Documentation, 54,* 48–69.

Salton, G. (1989) *Automatic text processing: the transformation analysis and retrieval of information by computer.* Reading, MA: Addison-Wesley.

UCLA Language Materials Project. (2002) *Zulu Profile.* Retrieved January, 9, 2002 from: http://www.lmp.ucla.edu/profiles/profz01.htm

Xu, J., and W. B. Croft. (1998) Corpus-based stemming using co-occurrence of word variants. *ACM Transactions on Information Systems, 16,* 61–81.

Zobel, J., and P. Dart. (1995) Finding approximate matches in large lexicons. *Software—practice and experience, 25,* 331–45.

Work Tasks As Units for Analysis in Information Seeking and Retrieval Studies

Katriina Byström
The Swedish School of Library and Information Studies
University College of Borås
50190 Borås, Sweden
katriina.bystrom@hb.se

Preben Hansen
SICS—Swedish Institute of Computer Science
Box 1263
SE-164 28 Kista, Sweden
preben@sics.se

ABSTRACT

In this article, we analyze the concept of work task in information intensive environments. In these environments information seeking (IS) and information retrieval (IR) are never performed in isolation. First, we discuss some general aspects of task-based information studies. Second, tasks are defined in three levels that are relevant for information studies. These levels are work tasks, information-seeking tasks and information-retrieval tasks. We argue that information intensive work tasks contain one or more information-seeking tasks as sub-tasks to

239

the work tasks, and that information-seeking tasks contain one or more information-retrieval tasks. Finally, we conclude that work task performance provides a common ground for both information seeking and retrieval studies and that this approach is useful for bridging the gap between IS and IR research.

1. INTRODUCTION

In information seeking (IS) and information retrieval (IR) studies *tasks* are coming to play a central role. Besides the mainstream studies that explore information seeking on the basis of different occupations or individual characteristics and information retrieval on the basis of manipulated queries, the concept of task is gaining increasing attention in both of these fields. Tasks are diligently used in information seeking contexts (e.g., Feinman, et al., 1976; Mick, et al., 1980; Kuhlthau, 1993; Kuhlthau, and Tama, 2001; Rasmussen, et al., 1994; Byström, and Järvelin, 1995; Sonnenwald, and Lievrouw, 1997; Solomon, 1997; Byström, 1999, 2002; Herzum, and Pejtersen, 2000) as well as in information retrieval contexts (e.g., Belkin, et al., 1982; Ingwersen, 1996; Marchionini, 1995; Wang, 1997; Hansen, 1999; Hansen, and Järvelin, 2000; Borlund, 2000; Vakkari, 2001). Thus, the scope of this paper to consider the concept of task in the context of information studies is highly relevant.

In this paper, we focus on information intensive work tasks in professional settings and their information related sub-tasks. We have chosen to base our analysis on work tasks simply because it is a common context for many information seeking activities. The analysis is naturally relevant for other related kinds of tasks, such as educational assignments.

An information intensive work task involves inherently or explicitly information related activities and the work task might initiate these activities due to a lack of information (e.g., Belkin, et al., 1982; Wilson, 1981). We believe that the concept of task is essential in understanding why people need information, how they choose to acquire it and what use they make of it.

- The *concept of task* provides a frame to analyse and develop information access in general and to design information retrieval systems in particular.

- The *context of tasks* is vague and not well understood and therefore several findings from obviously related information studies are sometimes difficult to compare with each other.

The present article provides a definitional foundation for task-based information studies. First, tasks are generally discussed by introducing some central aspects of them. Second, tasks are defined in three levels that are relevant for information studies. These levels are work tasks, information-seeking tasks and information-retrieval tasks. The article concludes with a discussion of the implications of the analysis for information studies.

2. GENERAL ASPECTS OF A TASK

In research that utilises the concept of task, task may be viewed either as an abstract construction or as a concrete set of sequences. The first view, *task description*, focuses on defining a particular item of work. This description settles the requirements and the goal of a task. It may also include a description of methods linked to the goal and/or requirements. The second view, *task performance*, focuses on doing a particular item of work. In other words, a task is manifested through its performance. A task is seen as a series of (physical and/or cognitive) actions in pursuit of a certain aim. This view emphasises the process, development and change, whereas viewing tasks descriptively is based on stability and one moment in time.

A task focuses on *a particular item of work*. This implies that a task has, when performed, a recognisable beginning and end. It also indicates that a task has a goal and it normally has a meaningful purpose. For instance, the goal of a construction task may be to strengthen a riverbank whereas the purpose of the task is to protect the landscape around. Furthermore, every task has *requirements* for its performance. Some of them are unconditional and must be fulfilled. Others may be conditional and alter the quality of the result.

A task, especially a larger one, may consist of specifiable smaller sub-tasks that each has individual requirements and goals. However, these sub-tasks need to be taken together in order to build a meaningful whole. Examples of such sub-tasks are information seeking processes and information retrieval processes.

Especially tasks considered as descriptions may be defined from a *subjective or an objective* point of view. Objective tasks are understood to be external to the performer and imposed on her/him. They have a specific existence that is independent of their performers. Subjective tasks are seen internal to the performer and defined by her/him. They are subordinate to the comprehension of the task performers. However, as the tasks are attended to and performed, even objective tasks will be adjusted by their performers (Hackman, 1969). Thus, one objective task may be the origin of several perceived (that is, subjective) tasks which all can be distinguished from each other (Newell, and Simon, 1972).

Tasks may also be divided into real life tasks and simulated tasks. Real life tasks are authentic to their performers with the existing situational factors and have tangible consequences. Thus, they are a part of a highly complex context that is impossible to control in detail. Simulated tasks are similar in varying degrees to real life tasks, but are, as well as their contexts, possible to manipulate and control. Some of them have no or few consequences for their performers (for example, a layperson performing a simulated management task) whereas others may clearly affect the performer's life (such as a pilot performing a simulated flight in a licence control). Tasks with actual consequences are likely to result in an authentic engagement in the task performance.

3. TASKS IN TASKS

Task performance is commonly divided into three parts, which may be further specified into smaller parts. One main part focuses on *task construction* on a conceptual level. This part consists of comprehending the preconditions and goals for performance and completion in relation to a given assignment and/or to "free" situation-based judgements. Depending, among other things, on how unfamiliar or difficult the task is perceived by the task performer this may be more or less problematic phase (e.g., Byström, 1999; 2002). This part is active throughout the whole task performance although it is most in focus at the beginning of the process (e.g., Marchionini, 1995). Task construction plays a major role for the other parts of the task but is impossible to observe directly and difficult even to fully communicate (at an interview).

Another main part of tasks focuses on *actual performance*. It consists of the practical and conceptual actions taken in order to achieve the goals (e.g., Hackman, 1969). It is the practical actions of task performance that we are able to observe directly and even conceptual actions are often communicable. The third main part of a task focuses on *task completion*. The separate results of actions taken are brought together and eventually the task performer completes the task performance. For some tasks this is self-evident: the task performer arrives at a satisfactory result. In other tasks a satisfactory result remains unattained, but the task performer considers further effort futile (e.g., Feinman, et al., 1976). The reasoning leading to the decision of task completion is not directly observable, but often possible to communicate.

When studying tasks, we may acknowledge both contextual and situational aspects (Hackos, 1998). In professional work, a context may be defined as the environment or domain in which task performance takes place (Taylor, 1991) and within them different information seeking and retrieval activities may be embedded.

- *Contextual attributes* are stable over longer periods of time. Examples of these are types of tasks, domains, processes, actors and organisational factors such as constraints.

- *Situational attributes* are more readily adjusted. Examples of these are knowledge levels, types of information needs, information sources, types of media, information seeking strategies, IR techniques, level of success, time, information use (e.g., Ingwersen, 1992; Preece, et al., 1994).

These attributes will be discussed in the following sections.

3.1. Work task

Work tasks are separable parts of a person's duties towards his/her employer. This means that although the work tasks may not be explicitly defined, both they and their performance are always to some degree outlined by the work organization. This occurs for example in established routines, available resources and expectations that seldom are even reflected upon by the task performer or the employer (e.g., March, and Simon, 1969). This being said, the task performer may at any moment reflect upon the preconceptions and act differently (e.g., Giddens, 1979).

The extent to which a work task has a recognisable beginning end, goal and a meaningful purpose, may vary. Additionally, work tasks often consist of sub-tasks and may themselves be considered as sub-tasks to a larger project. In this paper, we see work tasks as a meaningful whole for one task performer. Thus, projects where several people are usually working together are not focussed on here. Similarly, a work task may be divided into sub-tasks that need to be accomplished and brought together in order to reach a meaningful result that is related to the task performer's duties. For instance, samples of relevant information may constitute a meaningful result of a work task to an information specialist but not to a manager who needs it for making a decision. Thus, information-seeking activities are sub-tasks that are not independent, nor perhaps even interesting without a connection to the primary purposes or goals of a work task (e.g., Rouse, and Rouse, 1984).

Some of the related factors at this level are:

- *Work-tasks' characteristics.* An important factor in the study of the task performance process is the characteristics of tasks. Tasks may include the following characteristics: simple or complex tasks (Byström, and Järvelin, 1995); structured or unstructured tasks (O'Day, and Jeffries, 1993); active or passive tasks; routine or specific tasks (Hill, et al., 1993); single or multiple tasks (Preece, et al., 1994; Hill, et al., 1993; Belkin, et al., 1993; Smith, et al., 1997); task continuity or discontinuity (O'Day, and Jeffries, 1993); defined or muddled work tasks (Ingwersen, 1996); and external vs. internal initiated tasks (Reid, 1999). The task can be initiated by the task performer or imposed by the organisation or be a result of the existence of that organisation. All these aspects of the task may each individually affect the task performance process and are vital for understanding, as well as for the analysis and evaluation of the task performance process. Finally, they also provide indications for system design requirements.

- *Task performer's prior knowledge and experience of the domain and task.* We can distinguish between task performer's know-what and know-how. Know-what means task performer's conceptual knowledge (Preece, et al., 1994) or semantic knowledge (Shneiderman, 1992) on what the task involves. Know-how, in Preece, et al.'s (1994) terms physical knowledge, or syntactic knowledge by Shneiderman (1992), focus on how to accomplish a task at hand (for example, device-dependent details). Knowledge of how to plan, structure and perform the task is based on task performer's a) knowledge of procedural criteria (how the task is supposed to be performed in the actual context) and b) individual experience (based on the prior performance of similar tasks). These might be affected by, for instance, a shift in subject domain and a shift in the introduction of a new technology.

- *Identification of a lack of knowledge.* From a situational perspective, the task performer may perceive a lack of knowledge ("gap") in the task performance process. This lack of knowledge or need for information leads to the formulation of an information need, which in turn is the starting point for information seeking and information retrieval activities. Usually, this lack of knowledge is something that is perceived by the task performer, but it could also be explicitly stated, as a task requirement and the task performer then has to identify what the gap concerns.

3.2. Information seeking as a sub-task to a work task

Information seeking is a central part of information intensive work tasks. It may also be seen as a "task" that includes task construction, task performance, and task completion. Task construction consists of the analysis of the information needed. Task performance is comparable with actual information seeking, that is, the actions taken to gather the needed information. Task completion for information seeking tasks may be described as the evaluation of the results of information seeking. As a part of the work task, information-seeking tasks are also outlined by the work organization. This means that information-seeking tasks depend on the work task being attended to but the range of information needs and the resources required to satisfy them are limited (occasionally) for no apparent reason (e.g., Salancik, and Pfeffer, 1978).

Information seeking is initiated by a recognised information need and a decision to try to satisfy this need. Both of these actions relate to the task performer's perception of the task requirements, first, in deciding what information will be relevant in order to fulfil the requirements and, second, in deciding whether to seek all this information. Similarly the results of information seeking are considered with regard to the task requirements: their relevance and sufficiency is defined. Information seeking is successfully completed when enough relevant information for meeting the perceived task requirements is collected. In some cases the task requirements and result of information seeking does not correspond to the adequate degree, and further information seeking is considered to require unreasonable effort. This may lead to reconstruction of the task or in leaving the task performance uncompleted.

An essential part in a work task context is *information use*. As a result of information seeking, certain information is retrieved and may be used in different ways (for example, for clarifying task requirements, for problem solutions or for verification). Retrieved information may be used as a whole, in part or in combination with other information, and it is used in order to contribute to the accomplishment of the task. In information intensive tasks, it is likely that information is constantly used during performance.

Between the information need analysis and result evaluation information seeking involves practical actions such as identification of possible information channels and sources[1] (documentary or human), decisions on which alternative(s) to utilise, and implementing the channel and/or source use. Channels and sources that are judged in advance as being likely to provide the sought information are selected. It ought to be kept in mind that there are several other factors connected to this decision, such as, the accessibility, timescale, cost, skill requirements and timeliness (e.g., O'Reilly, 1982; Hardy, 1982).

Some of the factors involved at the information seeking level are:

- *Task performer knowledge and experience.* When the need for information is recognized the task performer structures how he will proceed with the task. The task performer now activates prior knowledge concerning different channels and sources such as personal networks and other formal and informal information channels.

- *Information seeking strategies.* Strategies are the dynamic processes for acquiring the information needed. The strategies are plans and actions for retrieving information (human-based, paper-based and IR-based) that are formalized and operationalized. An IR system may provide good support for an information seeking strategy in solving specific information need and work task, but provide poor support for other strategies and tasks. This means that we need to take into account different information seeking strategies (e.g., Kuhlthau, 1993; Marchionini, 1995). Bates (1990) defines a strategy as "a plan, which may contain moves, tactics and/or stratagems, for the entire information search" (p. 578). She also relates the different levels of information seeking to different task situations.

- *Source selection.* When identified, the recognized need for information leads to the adoption of an information seeking strategy in which different information sources are considered and interacted with. These sources may be human-based, paper-based or computer-based (IR systems). In some tasks, or within some sub-task of the overall work-task, it would be enough to ask an expert in order to complete the task. In other cases this is not enough. Whatever information source the task performer decides to use, this decision may lead to the next sub-task level in a work-task embedded information seeking and retrieval framework.

3.3. Information retrieval as a sub-task to information seeking

Often, although not always, the information needs of a work task require consulting several information sources. We argue that information retrieval is a sub-task of an information seeking-task (e.g., Wilson, 1999). Whereas information-seeking tasks focus on the satisfaction of an entire information need through the consultation of several sources, information-retrieval tasks focus on the satisfaction of a separable fraction of an information need through the consultation of a single source. Thus, one information-seeking task may include several information-retrieval tasks or in cases where the whole information need is satisfied by using a single source, an information seeking-task becomes equal to an information-retrieval task (Figure 1).

Figure 1. Information seeking and retrieval embedded in a work task environment.

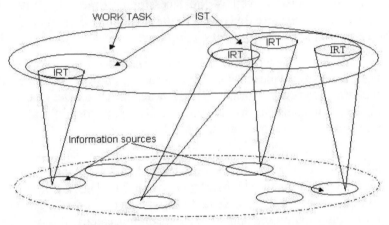

Legend: IST = Information seeking task; IRT = Information retrieval task

In this light, information-retrieval tasks gain a broader meaning than they are traditionally understood to have. In the traditional sense, information retrieval focuses on searching for and extracting information from an electronic set of information objects. We argue that several aspects of information retrieval are present when consulting other type of sources. For instance, consulting a person or a network of persons requires that we articulate a request based on our information need in a manner that the person(s) we are addressing can understand it, a process comparable to querying a database. We may consider and decide upon a suitable strategy for the consultation (starting with a specific question or with a general theme). We evaluate the information delivered from the source. We may consider whether to return to consult the same source. Finally, we select for use all or parts of the gathered information. Thus, models for information retrieval may, with some adjustments, also be relevant for studying other types of information source use as well as information retrieval becomes an integrated part of information seeking in general.

At the information retrieval level, the following factors are involved:

- *Source selection.* In this context, source selection entails the decision to approach an information source (such as electronic or human). This also implies that the task performer is familiar with the source and its content and has some prior knowledge on how to operate it.

- *Search approach or strategy*. From an IR perspective, the analytic search strategy is generally referred to at this stage. This strategy is based on the matching between the query and document representation. Usually, there is no possibility for the system to have situational or contextual information about the overall task to be performed, and hence the system cannot help the task performer in that respect. However, Bates (1990) gives some examples of different stratagems for the performance of different tasks. As to the knowledge of the authors, this is the only exception to the mainstream IR research.

- *IR techniques*. Generally, IR systems provide different exact-match or best-match techniques to be used (Ingwersen, and Willett, 1995). Furthermore, the user may be able to navigate and browse through the content space. However, other techniques have lately been suggested in combination with content-based techniques, for example, filtering techniques. Some of these techniques give the task performer other traits to be evaluated, such as opinions.

- *IR interaction*: Information retrieval interaction involves interactive actions between the task performer and the IR system. The information retrieval task is traditionally mainly concerned with the following sub-tasks or activities: a) *query formulation*. This activity involves formulating the information need to the information source. The formulation is a result of the perceived information need and requires different knowledge levels such as domain and subject knowledge as well as knowledge and experience of interacting with IR systems; b) *query re-formulation*. In the interactive process of retrieving information the task performer may need to reformulate the query due, for example, to inappropriate term selection, too narrow/broad term selection; c) *relevance feedback*. Usually the relevance feedback is the task performer reply to the information processing of the system. If there is a gap between the original query and the retrieved set of documents, the task performer reacts in some way by ordering the system to re-assess task performer input. We might say that both query re-formulation and relevance assessment/judgement is a part of relevance feedback and *relevance judgement*. Generally, relevance is judged according to the query representation of the information need and is measured according to well-known statistical measurement of precision/recall. However, if we view relevance judgements from a work-task perspective, it should take into account both relevance within a single IR session as well as in combination with other information seeking and IR sessions. In this way the IR task is connected back to the information seeking level. Furthermore, relevance judgement should also be related to the overall work task and thus we can speak of task-relevance (Reid, 1999). The outcome of the IR session will have implications for the successful accomplishment of a task. Finally, to take the issue one step further, relevance judgement should be measured according to information use. Although a set of documents may be considered relevant, only a smaller set or parts of a smaller set may actually be used in order to accomplish the task.

Traditionally, the whole process of IR interaction is based on query input and the systems response though matching algorithms to that request. However, from a task-based approach this interaction process needs to take into account the work-task process. The IR interaction process must be related to the information seeking level as well as to the work-task level.

4. DISCUSSION

In this article, we have analysed the concept of task for information studies and arrive at the conclusion that work task performance provides a common ground for both information seeking and retrieval studies. Information seeking and retrieval are usually an integrated part of task performance in real life work settings. We suggest that information intensive work tasks contain one or several information-seeking tasks as sub-tasks, and that information-seeking tasks contain one or more information-retrieval tasks. Information-retrieval tasks are seen in a broad meaning, where a consultation of any type of information channel or source (for example, electronic or manual document or a set of documents as well as people) is considered as an information retrieval task. We have also proposed a preliminary set of critical factors for each type of tasks that we believe to be of importance for information activities. All these factors will implicitly or explicitly affect the task performance process and its outcome. This also applies to developing analysis and evaluation methods. Support that takes the factors described above into account must be developed. However, we acknowledge that the concept of task does not cover all information activities (for example, continual information updating). Also, the affects of social and cultural contexts on the information activities remain unexplored. Research in these areas is relevant to understanding the development of contextual preconceptions for task performance processes, and, using the concept of task in this way, it becomes feasible to naturally combine information seeking and information retrieval studies.

One of the greatest advantages of anchoring information seeking and information retrieval studies to the concept of task is the creation of a common context. We believe that these kinds of studies will become a central area of information studies. Byström and Järvelin (1995) used the concept of task as proposed here in their empirical studies. Wang (1997) has adopted a similar perspective. Hansen (1999), Borlund (2000), Hansen, and Järvelin (2000), and Vakkari and colleagues (2001, in an educational setting) have all developed these ideas in their work. However, there are very few, if any, completed studies that fully make use of the context of work task with integrated information seeking and information retrieval tasks in a real life professional setting. Bennett

(1972) concludes that the challenge is to transform theories into engineering by developing an "agreement on ways for characterizing user tasks, for allocating interface resources to meet task requirements and for evaluating user effectiveness in task performance" (p. 189).

NOTES

1. Information channels are used to become aware of and locate appropriate information sources that contain, or are expected to contain, the actual information sought for.

REFERENCES

Bates, M. (1990) Where Should the Person Stop and Information Interface Start? *Information Processing & Management 26*(5), 575–91.

Belkin, N., R. Oddy, and H. Brooks. (1982) ASK for information retrieval: part 1: background and theory. *Journal of Documentation, 38*(2), 61–71.

Belkin, N. J., P. G. Marchetti, and C. Cool. (1993) BRAQUE: Design of an interface to support user interaction in Information Retrieval. *Information Processing & Management 29*(3), 325–44.

Bennett, J. L. (1972) The user interface in interactive systems. *ARIST, 7,* 159–96.

Borlund, P. (2000) *Evaluation of Interactive Information Retrieval Systems. Doctoral dissertation.* Åbo, Finland: Åbo Academi.

Byström, K. (2002) Information and information sources in tasks of varying complexity. *Journal of the American Society for Information Science and Technology, 53*(7), 581–91.

Byström, K. (1999) *Task complexity, information types and information sources: examination of relationships.* Doctoral dissertation. Acta Universitatis Tamperensis ser. A Vol.688. Tampere: University of Tampere.

Byström, K., and K. Järvelin. (1995) Task complexity affects information seeking and use. *Information Processing & Management, 31*(2), 191–213.

Feinman, S., C. Mick, J. Saalberg, and C. Thompson. (1976) A conceptual framework for information flow studies. In Martin (ed.). *Information politics: proceedings of the 38th annual meeting of the American Society for Information Science 13*(1), 106–16. Washington.

Giddens, A. (1979) *Central Problems in Social Theory: Action, Structure and Contradiction in Social Analysis.* Berkeley, CA: University of California Press.

Hackman, J. R. (1969) Towards understanding the role of tasks in behavioral research. *Acta Psychologica, 31,* 97–128.

Hackos, J., and J. Redish. (1998) *User and Task Analysis for Interface Design.* New York: Wiley.

Hansen, P. (1999) *User Interface design for IR Interaction. A Task-oriented approach.* COLIS 3, Dubrovnik.

Hansen, P., and K. Järvelin. (2000) The Information Seeking and Retrieval process at the Swedish Patent- and Registration Office. Moving from Lab-based to real life work-task environment. *Proceedings of the ACM-SIGIR 2000 Workshop on Patent Retrieval*, Athens, Greece, July 28, 2000, 43–53.

Hardy, A. P. (1982) The selection of channels when seeking information: cost/benefit vs least-effort. *Information Processing & Management, 18*(6), 289–93.

Herzum, M., and A. M. Pejtersen. (2000) The information-seeking practices of engineers: searching for documents as well as for people. *Information Processing & Management, 36*(5), 761–78.

Hill, B., J. Long, A. Smith, and A. Whitefield. (1993) Planning for Multiple Task Work—an Analysis of a Medical Reception Worksystem. In S. Ahslund, et al. (eds.). *INTERCHI'93* Conference on Human Factors in Computing Systems. Bridges Between Worlds. Amsterdam, The Netherlands, 24–29 April 1993, 314–20.

Ingwersen, P. (1992) *Information Retrieval Interaction*. London, UK: Taylor Graham.

Ingwersen, P. (1996) Cognitive perspectives of information retrieval interaction: elements of a cognitive IR theory. *Journal of Documentation, 52*(1), 3–50.

Ingwersen, P., and P. Willett. (1997) Algorithmic and Cognitive approaches to information retrieval. An introduction. A tutorial for SIGIR '97, *the 20th Annual International ACM SIGIR Conference on Research and Development in Information Retrieval (SIGIR'97)*, Philadelphia, PA, July 27–31, 1997.

Kuhlthau, C. C. (1993) A principle of uncertainty for information seeking. *Journal of Documentation, 49*(4), 339–55.

Kuhlthau, C. C., and S. L. Tama. (2001) Information search process of lawyers: a call for "just for me" information services. *Journal of Documentation, 57*(1), 25–43.

March, J., and H. Simon. (1967) *Organizations*. 2d ed. New York: Wiley.

Marchionini, G. (1995) *Information Seeking in Electronic Environments*. Cambridge Series on Human Computer Interaction 9. Cambridge: University Press.

Mick, C., G. Lindsey, and D. Callahan. (1980) Toward usable user studies. *Journal of the American Society for Information Science, 31*(5), 347–56.

Newell, A., and H. Simon. (1972) *Human Problem Solving*. Englewood Cliffs, NJ: Prentice-Hall.

O'Day, V., and R. Jeffries. (1993) Orienteering in an Information Landscape. How Information Seekers Get From Here to There. In S. Ahslund, et al. (eds.). *INTERCHI'93* Conference on Human Factors in Computing Systems. Bridges Between Worlds. Amsterdam, The Netherlands, 24–29 April 1993, 438–45.

O'Reilly, C. A. (1982) Variations in decision makers' use of information sources: the impact of quality and accessibility of information. *Academy of Management Journal, 25*(4), 756–71.

Preece, J., Y. Rogers, H. Sharp, D. Benyon, S. Holland, and T. Carey. (1994) *Human-Computer Interaction*. Wokingham, England: Addison Wesley.

Reid, J. (1999) A new, task-oriented paradigm for information retrieval: implications for evaluation of information retrieval systems. In T. Aparac, T. Saracevic, P. Ingwersen, and P. Vakkari, eds. *Proceedings of the Third International Conference on Conceptions of Library and Information Science.* Dubrovnik, Croatia, 1999 (pp. 97–108).

Rouse, W., and S. Rouse. (1984) Human information seeking and design of information system. *Information Processing & Management, 20*(1–2), 129–38.

Rasmussen, J., A. M. Pejtersen, and L. P. Goodstein. (1994) *Cognitive Systems Engineering.* New York: Wiley.

Salancik, G., and J. Pfeffer. (1978) A social information processing approach to job attitudes and task design. *Administrative Science Quarterly, 23,* 224–53.

Shneiderman, B. (1992) *Designing the User Interface: Strategies for Effective Human-Computer-Interaction.* 2d ed. Boston: Addison-Wesley.

Smith, W., B. Hill, J. Long, and A. Whitefield. (1997) A design-oriented framework for modelling the planning and control of multiple task work in secretarial office administration. *Behaviour & information technology, 16*(3), 161–83.

Solomon, P. (1997) Discovering information behavior in sense making. II. The social. *Journal of the American Society for Information Science, 48*(12), 1109–26.

Sonnenwald, D., and L. Lievrouw. (1997) Collaboration during the design process: a case study of communication, information behavior, and project performance. In P. Vakkari, R. Savolainen, and B. Dervin, eds. *Information Seeking in Context* (pp. 279–304). London: Taylor Graham.

Taylor, R. (1991) Information use environments. In B. Dervin, and M. J. Voigt, eds. *Progress in Communication Sciences.* Norwood, NJ: Ablex, 217–55.

Vakkari, P. (2001) The theory of the task-based information retrieval process: a summary and generalisation of a longitudinal study. *Journal of Documentation, 57*(1), 44–60.

Wang, P. (1997) User's information needs at different stage of a research project: a cognitive view. In P. Vakkari, R. Savolainen, and B. Dervin, eds. *Information Seeking in Context* (pp. 307–18). London: Taylor Graham.

Wilson, T. D. (1999) Models in information behaviour research. *Journal of Documentation, 55*(3), 249–70.

Wilson, T. D. (1981) On user studies and information needs. *Journal of Documentation, 37*(1), 3–15.

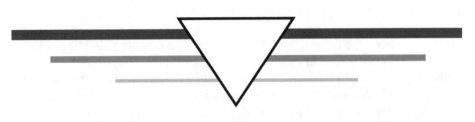

Evaluating Information Retrieval Systems Under the Challenges of Interaction and Multidimensional Dynamic Relevance

Jaana Kekäläinen and Kalervo Järvelin
Department of Information Studies
University of Tampere
33014 University of Tampere, Finland
jaana.kekalainen@uta.fi; kalervo.jarvelin@uta.fi

ABSTRACT

The Laboratory Model of information retrieval (IR) evaluation has been challenged by progress in research related to relevance and information seeking as well as by the growing need for accounting for interaction in evaluation. Real human users introduce non-binary, subjective and dynamic relevance judgments into IR processes and affect these processes. Therefore the traditional evaluation based on the Laboratory Model is challenged for its (lack of) realism. This paper examines the rationale of evaluating the IR algorithms, the status of the traditional evaluation, and the applicability of the proposed novel evaluation methods and measures. It further points out research problems requiring attention for further advances in the area. The Laboratory Model is found limited but still useful for the specific tasks it fulfills in the development of IR algorithms.

253

1. INTRODUCTION

The Laboratory Model of information retrieval (IR) evaluation has its origins in the Cranfield II project (Cleverdon, 1967). It is the paradigm of the Computer Science oriented IR research, seeking to develop ever better IR algorithms and systems. In recent years, the TREC conferences (Voorhees, and Harman, 2001) have been the major forum for research based on the Laboratory Model. An essential component in evaluation based on the Model is a test collection consisting of a document database, a set of fairly well defined requests, and a set of (typically binary) relevance assessments identifying the documents that are topically relevant to each request. IR algorithms are evaluated for their ability of finding the relevant documents. The test results are typically expressed in terms of recall and precision.

The Laboratory Model has been challenged by progress in research related to relevance and information seeking as well as by the growing need for accounting for interaction in evaluation. Work in analyzing the concept of relevance has resulted in identifying higher-order relevances, such as cognitive relevance and situational relevance, in addition to algorithmic and topical relevance (Borlund, 2000; Cosijn, and Ingwersen, 2000; Saracevic, 1996, 1997; Schamber, Eisenberg, and Nilan, 1990). Real human users of IR systems introduce non-binary, subjective and dynamic relevance judgments into IR processes, which affect the processes directly. In this sense relevance is multidimensional and cannot be derived from any single relevance criterion (Cuadra, and Katter, 1967; Barry, 1994; Saracevic, 1975, 1997; Schamber, 1994). By *higher-order relevance* we refer to this subjective whole which besides topicality includes, *among others,* situational, cognitive, and affective relevance.

Theoretical and empirical work in information seeking and retrieval (Belkin, 1993; Byström, and Järvelin, 1995; Ellis, and Haugan, 1997; Ingwersen, 1996; Kuhlthau, 1993; Schamber, 1994; Vakkari, 2001; Wilson, 1999) suggests that IR is but one means of information seeking which takes place in a context determined by, e.g., a person's task, its phase, and situation. IR tactics and relevance assessments are affected by the stages of task performance. Also some user-oriented research in IR, e.g., by Bates (1989; 1990) points out the variety of strategies users might use in accessing information, topical retrieval being only one.

Because of these empirical findings and theoretical arguments, the traditional Laboratory Model of IR evaluation is challenged for its (lack of) realism. Harter and Hert (1997) give a detailed analysis of the evaluation of IR systems and the criticism towards traditional IR experiments. There are proposals (Borlund, 2000; Hersh, and Over, 2000) concerning how IR evaluation should be done realistically and at the same time retaining as much control as possible. There also is empirical work (e.g., Vakkari, 2001) tracing interactive information seeking and IR processes providing models and methods for IR evaluation.

Developers of IR algorithms should therefore consider how the algorithms are to be evaluated in a valid way from now on.

This paper examines the status of the traditional methods and measures, and the rationale of evaluating IR algorithms in an interactive system environment. It proposes research problems requiring attention for both objectors and defenders of the Laboratory Model. It further seeks to combine the traditional experimenting with users and interaction. The main focus of the discussion is textual IR.

2. EVALUATING THE ALGORITHMIC COMPONENTS

The Laboratory Model is depicted in Figure 1. In this view the IR system consists of a database, algorithms, requests, and stored relevance assessments. The system components are represented in the middle and the evaluation components on top, left, and bottom in the lightly shaded area. The main thrust of the research has been on document and request representation and the matching methods of these representations. Only recently, in the Interactive Track of TREC (see Over, 1997), have users been involved (the darkly shaded area). Even so, the systems still have been evaluated on the basis of how the users are able to find documents deemed relevant in the test collection.

Figure 1. The Laboratory Model schematized.

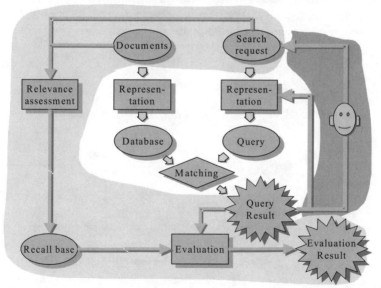

In this view, real users and tasks are not seen as necessary. Test requests typically are quite well-defined requests with verbose descriptions that give the algorithms much more data to work with for query construction than typical real life IR situations do. Relevance is taken as topical, but factual features (based on structural data items, like author names and other bibliographic features) could be included. Relevance is static, between a request and a document as seen by an assessor. The assessments are independent of each other (e.g., no learning effects, no inferences across documents) and there are no saturation effects (i.e., in principle the assessors do not get tired of, or mind, repetition). The assessors do not know in which order the documents would be retrieved so they cannot do otherwise or properly model user saturation.

The rationale of evaluating the algorithmic components consists of the goals, scope, and justifications of the evaluation approach. The *goal* of research is to develop algorithms to identify and rank a number of topically relevant documents for presentation, given a topical request. Research is based on constructing novel algorithms and on comparing their performance with each other, seeking ways of improving them. On the theoretical side, the goals include the analysis of basic problems of IR (e.g., the vocabulary problem, document and query representation and matching) and the development of theories and methods for attacking them.

The *scope* of experiments is characterized in terms of types of experiments, test collections and requests as well as performance measures. The experiments mainly are batch-mode experiments. Therefore each algorithm is evaluated by running a test set of queries, measuring its performance for individual queries and averaging over the query set. Some recent efforts seek to focus on interactive retrieval with a human subject, the TREC interactive track being predominant. The major modern test collections are news document collections. The major performance measures are recall and precision.

Figure 2. Justification of the Laboratory Model.

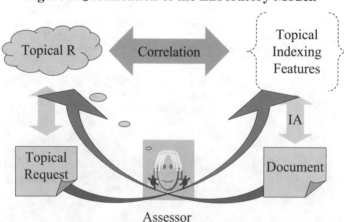

Assessor

The *justifications* of the Model may be discussed in terms of Figure 2. The main strength is that words and other character strings from texts, when distilled as indexing features by an indexing algorithm (IA), correlate, with fair probability, to the topical content of the documents they represent and to the queries which they match (save for problems of homography). When a test user (or algorithm) processes a topical request, it is possible to predict, with fair probability, which indexing features should be considered (save for problems of synonymy, paraphrases). Because the topical request also suggests the topical relevance criteria, there is a fair correlation (clearly better than random) between the indexing features of matching documents and a positive relevance judgment. Indexing features correlate to meaning in the topical sense.

3. THE STATUS OF TRADITIONAL EVALUATION APPROACHES: OBJECTIONS AND RESPONSES

Objection 1. Lack of users and tasks.

There is no real user or task or situation involved; the Model is essentially based on "objective" assessors. Real IR is a subtask in task-based information seeking, and is thus affected by the latter (Kuhlthau, 1993; Vakkari, 2001; Wilson, 1999).

Response: True, but users and tasks are not needed for testing the algorithms for the limited goal they are intended for: retrieval and ranking of topical documents or their parts.

Objection 2. Lack of interaction and dynamic requests.

There is no real interaction and dynamics; it is essentially a batch mode evaluation. Real interaction involves user learning, problem redefinition and changing relevance criteria (Beaulieu, Robertson, and Rasmussen, 1996; Borlund, 2000; Vakkari, 2001). Test requests in interactive experiments are too rigid for the test users, and all documents that the users consider relevant are not deemed as relevant by the assessors, nor do the users accept all documents deemed relevant by the assessors.

Response: True, but not needed because all system activities in the interaction may be seen as individual retrieval tasks to be served well as such. Complex dynamic interaction is a sequence of simple topical interactions and thus good one-shot performance by an algorithm should be rewarded in evaluation. Changes in the user's understanding of his information need and relevance should affect the consequent request and query. Although a user is likely to modify his/her request and relevance criteria in subsequent interactions, it has not been shown that this should affect the design of the retrieval algorithm.

Objection 3. Lack of tactical variability.

The only tactic of interest is a batch mode topical (or question-answering) request while people in real life approach information in many different ways, including, e.g., bibliographic and other structured attributes or links (Bates, 1989).

Response: True, tactics deserve more attention, but the model is no hindrance for this.

Objection 4. Lack of ambiguity.

The requests are only well-defined requests, which do not correctly reflect all kinds of real-life requests; they are too well-specified and wordy for that (Ingwersen, and Willett, 1995; Sparck Jones, 1995). They do not reflect the users' tasks or situations (Borlund, 2000).

Response: True, typical test requests are too well specified. This should be looked at and can be done within the model. For example, the different parts of TREC topics allow to investigate the effects of different query lengths (Voorhees, and Harman, 2001). Otherwise some IR models developed within the Laboratory Model explicitly tackle uncertainty (van Rijsbergen, and Lalmas, 1996).

Objection 5. Lack of user-oriented relevance.

The tests are based on algorithmic and topical relevance, which are unable to take into account the user's situation, tasks, or state of knowledge. Relevance assessments also are stable—far from real-life (Beaulieu, et al., 1996; Borlund, 2000; Cosijn, and Ingwersen, 2000).

Response: True, but not needed for testing the algorithms for the limited task they are intended for. Higher-order relevance is out of scope of the framework unless explicated as request and document features to be processed—the algorithms do not read the users' minds. The heart of IR is matching explicit representations of documents and requests. The machine cannot do better if not designed to do so, which would require explication of higher-order relevance features both theoretically and in practice.

Objection 6. Lack of variety in collections.

The test collections, albeit nowadays large, are structurally simple (mainly unstructured text) and topically narrow (mainly news domain). The test documents mostly lack interesting internal structure that some real-life collections do have (e.g., field structure, XML, citations).

Response: True and should be looked at, the model is no hindrance. There is recent work in this direction (e.g., TREC Web Track, Hawking, et al., 2000).

Objection 7. Document independence and overlap.

There are unrealistic assumptions regarding document independence (some may be relevant only if juxtaposed) and user saturation (repeated reproduction of very similar "relevant" information results in irrelevance) (Robertson, 1977).

Response: True, but the assumptions are a necessity since the relevance assessment stage is not informed about the possible combinations of documents retrieved by a query. No one has been able to formalize the process of arguing across documents, such a task remains entirely in the user's domain.

Objection 8. Insufficiency of recall and precision.

Recall and precision are insufficient as evaluation measures, the former being system-oriented and often irrelevant to the user. They do not handle non-binary relevance (Borlund, 2000). They do not describe users' success in information problem explication.

Response: Recall and precision are major effectiveness measures for the limited retrieval goal. They reflect the kind of relevance that was used in the assessments be it topical or higher. Recall and precision may also be generalized to handle non-binary relevance assessments, as shown by Kekäläinen and Järvelin (2002). In the TREC interactive track, *instance precision and recall* break document level in relevance judgments. The user-system pairs are rewarded for retrieving distinct instances of answers rather than multiple overlapping documents (Hersh, and Over, 2000).

Objection 9. Heavy averaging.

Many experiments are based on heavy averaging over sets of query results, perhaps never looking at the performance differences at the individual query level (Hull, 1996), or individual documents / requests.

Response: Often true, but not a limitation of the model. It may be a limitation of the IR evaluation culture.

Objection 10. Just document retrieval.

IR is just document retrieval with little, if any, attention to document/information presentation for use.

Response: True, but document retrieval is a genuine task in information access and deserves attention. Clearly, other stages of information access and use should be examined as well. There is recent relevant work in Question Answering, e.g., in TREC (Voorhees, 2001b), and Information Extraction, e.g., in the Message Understanding Conferences (Gaizauskas, and Wilks, 1998).

Objection 11. IR is tested in isolation.

In the Laboratory Model IR is tested in isolation, not as part of a larger system or as one alternative of information seeking.

Response: True, but if IR systems are embedded in a larger context, the variables of interest may turn out to be uncontrollable, or effects may be unobservable.

A Concession

The Laboratory Model provides a controllable setting, and repeatable and generalizable results. Admittedly this is building and testing retrieval engines in isolation. There is no guarantee of solving any real life problems unless informed by information seeking studies. The approach may have a distorted view on information access problems, and may miss some important ones.

4. TWO BROADER EVALUATION SCENARIOS

We shall first look at recent conceptions of relevance and then assess novel user-oriented measures. We consider for each of these, which problems, if any, of the Laboratory Model they attack and whether they are successful in this. Finally, we look at two IR evaluation scenarios to which the proposals and their assessment lead.

4.1. Higher-order relevance

The concept of relevance has been a difficult problem in Information Science throughout the years. Schamber (1994; Eisenberg, and Nilan, 1990) have argued that relevance is a *multidimensional* and *dynamic* phenomenon. Several recent studies have focused on *factors* affecting relevance judgements, and *dimensions* (or criteria) of relevance (Barry, 1994; Barry, and Schamber, 1998; Bateman, 1998; Borlund, 2000; Cosijn, and Ingwersen, 2000; Vakkari, and Hakala, 2000; Wang, and Soergel, 1998). Others have argued that there are various *kinds* of relevance (algorithmic, topical, cognitive, situational, motivational relevance; Saracevic, 1996). Elements of these typologies can be traced back to, e.g., Cuadra and Katter (1967) and Wilson (1973).

In many studies topicality is seen as the basic criterion for relevance—a necessary but not sufficient condition (Burgin, 1992; Cooper, 1971; Froehlich, 1994). The other criteria used in real users' relevance assessments are tied either to the state of knowledge or situation of the user. By higher-order relevance we refer to relevance which is not solely based on topicality but *also the other criteria*.

One of the main problems of the Laboratory Model was seen to be its lack of user-oriented relevance, thus sacrificing realism to control. Below, we consider situational relevance as an example of higher-order relevance. Cosijn and Ingwersen (2000) define situational relevance as a relation between the perceived situation, work-task or problem at hand and the information objects under assessment. Incorporation of higher-order relevance into evaluation also brings interaction, dynamic requests/needs and tasks into evaluation thereby improving the realism of evaluation.

Some of the problems of using higher-order relevance in IR systems, or their design, may be discussed in terms of Figure 3. A real user, being thrown into a situation, may well be able to recognize a relevant document once presented (therefore the exclamation mark). However, he may have difficulty in discussing the relevance criteria of the task and situation. Further, he certainly has difficulty in expressing a request and formulating a query to the IR system, at least anything other than topical *as long as text is concerned* (but save for bibliographic fields etc., if available, as discussed below), because current systems do not provide for anything else. The system designer probably never had the slightest idea of other than explicit topical indexing features, because there is no known pattern of situational indexing features that are explicit in text—the computer does not handle implicit features—and useful to users (see Cooper, 1971). Therefore the available indexing features may not correlate to the situational relevance criteria, which the user did not express, save for one thing: topical relevance heavily correlates to situational as shown by Burgin (1992), and Vakkari and Hakala (2000).

Figure 3. Situational relevance in retrieval.

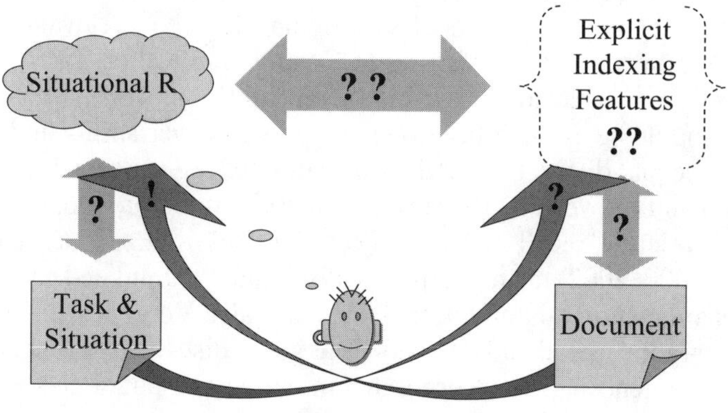

Situational R   ? ?   Explicit Indexing Features ??

? !   ? ?

Task & Situation   Document

Real User

As soon as one moves away from collections consisting of plain text toward structured documents, the possibilities of applying situational relevance become better. For example, bibliographic data of a document (e.g., author, journal, year), its references and citations received may be useful a clues for situational relevance—and people actually use such criteria in relevance assessments (Barry, 1994; Schamber, 1994; Barry, and Schamber, 1998). It is possible to compile lists of author names, institution names, journal and conference names in ranked order to signal relevance from a work-task or personal point-of-view. Also documents citing, or cited by, known situationally relevant documents might be ranked higher than documents lacking these explicit features. However, the person-to-person and task-to-task variation in such criteria may cause management problems—even if the criteria are explicit, they may be very private.

We therefore conclude that although it is easy to admit the realism of the higher-order relevance criteria, serving them by system features is a challenge because of lack of understanding on the variability of the criteria and on the combination of evidence on the criteria. There neither is much sense in evaluating the current algorithms' performance on criteria, which they completely ignore (save for correlation of topical and higher-order relevance).

4.2. Novel performance measures

Relevance is a *multilevel* phenomenon, i.e., some documents are more relevant than others to an information need of a user. Multiple *degrees* of relevance and their expression have been studied in laboratory settings (Cuadra, and

Katter, 1967; Rees, and Schultz, 1967; Tang, Shaw, and Vevea, 1999) as well as in field studies of information seeking and retrieval (Vakkari, and Hakala, 2000). The former groups experimented with multiple point rating scales (from two to eleven). Tang, Shaw, and Vevea found that a seven-point scale for relevance assessments is optimal in terms of the assessors' confidence in their assessments.

However, until 2000 in the practise of IR evaluation, the binary scale has been the norm. This is unfortunate since it does not allow testing whether some IR methods are better than others at a particular degree of relevance. Borlund (2000) and Schamber (1994; referring to Cuadra, and Katter, 1967; Rees, and Schultz, 1967) note that measures like recall and precision based on binary judgements should be avoided because they ignore the variability and complexity of relevance and distort the continuous nature of relevance judgements.

Borlund and Ingwersen (1998; Borlund, 2000) therefore propose the novel measures of relative recall (RR), ranked half-life (RHL), and Järvelin and Kekäläinen (2000; 2002) the measures of (discounted) cumulated gain ([D]CG), as measures augmenting the traditional ones (see also Voorhees, 2001a). An alternative to avoiding recall and precision is to generalise them so that continuous relevance judgements can be incorporated into their computation—as proposed by Kekäläinen and Järvelin (2002).

The proposed measures indeed allow for subjective non-binary multidimensional relevance assessments and may therefore augment recall and precision in evaluation. The new measures, however, like recall and precision, are just measuring devices based on any kind of relevance assessments they are supplied with. They are all immune to the way of assessing relevance (whether binary, dynamic and subjective or not). For example, Borlund (2000) states that the RHL and RR measures may well be used in non-interactive experiments within the Laboratory Model. Järvelin and Kekäläinen's (2000; 2002) measures are directly used within the Laboratory Model.

Borlund (2000) notes that there is a need for a measure bridging between the subjective assessments and objective system performance. She also correctly states that the RR measure does this (save for identified problems with differing scales of evaluation in some cases). However, traditional PR-curves already do this between any chosen kinds of subjective assessments and the objective system performance, indicated by retrieval scores of documents and their ranking (or algorithmic relevance).

As the new measures are well defined, they are usable in the evaluation of IR algorithms but they do not directly affect the design of IR algorithms.

4.3. Two Evaluation Scenarios

We shall now present two evaluation scenarios. The first one has a broader approach to IR than the Laboratory Model, paying attention to various IR strategies and tactics, and interfaces supporting them. We call it the IR Interfaces Scenario. The second is still broader, allowing for real users engaged in various types of tasks in various types of situations. We call it the Task IR Scenario. The components of the scenarios are illustrated in Figure 4.

Figure 4. IR evaluation frameworks.

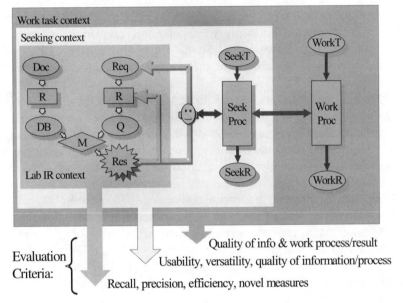

A System Developer's View—the IR Interfaces Scenario

In this scenario, the system consists of the database(s), algorithms, requests, and users (two inner frameworks in Figure 4). Stored relevance assessments are not banned but are not the key of evaluation, either. The users are real users experienced with the kind of real or simulated tasks giving rise to search tasks. Only topical relevance is used for retrieval, unless theory and representations are developed for higher-order relevance. The scenario deliberately allows for fuzzy requests. The goal is to develop IR algorithms to (1) support the exploration of information spaces (documents, concepts) to aid request formulation, (2) identify and rank a number of relevant documents for sequences of varying requests, and (3) present such documents so as to support their judgment in terms of higher-order relevance. The success measures include criteria for usability and versatility, as well as precision and recall and the novel measures discussed in the preceding section. The plain retrieval component may be evaluated through recall and precision, but the whole algorithmic component needs broader measures. Simulated work tasks may be used as proposed by Borlund (2000).

The rationale of the framework is as follows: After all, the heart of IR is aiding the user to formulate requests, acquiring for the algorithms as much evidence as possible on relevance features, and then matching explicit request and document representations. Formally matching features suggest topical relevance, which predicts higher-order relevance (Gluck, 1996). The framework focuses on interfaces that help query formulation or allow alternative approaches. Complex dynamic interaction is a sequence of topical interactions. Recall and precision describe the filtering capability of the IR system at any stage in the process but play a lesser role (especially the former). Usability and versatility criteria should be explicated for classes of users/tasks. This is, in effect, building and testing whole systems for real users with real search tasks, and simulated work tasks. There is no guarantee however of solving any real life IR problems of user groups unless informed by studies on information seeking and retrieval of such groups.

There is empirical work (e.g., Ellis, 1989; Ellis, and Haugan, 1997) suggesting that various tactics would be desirable for some user communities. On the theoretical side, e.g., Bates (1989; 1990), points out possibilities as calls for work in the area. Some of the issues may seem, from the engineering point of view, simple and thus uninteresting to computer scientists (e.g., providing for tactics like author or journal name search, or citation linking), not touching the "tough issues" of representation and matching.

The framework accounts for part of the criticism leveled against the Laboratory Model. It involves users and tasks, at least simulated tasks. A basic feature of the framework is the active user learning and assessing relevance. Recall and precision are used for the algorithmic component in isolation, other measures are looked for assessing usability and versatility.

Developing IR, not just algorithms—the Task IR Framework

In this scenario, the system consists of the database(s), algorithms, requests, users, tasks, and task processes (see Figure 4, all the frameworks). Stored relevance assessments are not banned but the focus is at higher-order relevance. The users are real users experienced with real or simulated tasks giving rise to search tasks. Only topical relevance is used for retrieval, unless theory and representations are developed. The scenario deliberately allows for fuzzy requests. The goal is to support task process, improve the quality of task outcomes through improved IR algorithms. The success measures are case-based, usability and versatility criteria included. Recall and precision are not irrelevant but not primary, either. The plain retrieval component may be evaluated through recall and precision, but the whole algorithmic component needs broader measures. Simulated work tasks may be used as proposed by Borlund (2000).

The rationale is that, after all, IR is a support activity. By studying the information interaction of people engaged in real life tasks it is possible to learn, which aspects of interaction are amenable to IR type of processing. Database contents, representations, matching and interfaces all are tailored to the task setting. Working practices of actors are adapted to the system setting (through learning by doing or training). The algorithmic retrieval components perform as much (or as little) as can explicitly be specified and the intelligent human actors do the rest. IR may happen without explicit activation. IR becomes one function in a composite systems environment. Documents found may still be only topically relevant, if better explicit representations cannot be specified in the environment. This is, in effect, building and testing whole systems for real users with real tasks. There is a guarantee of solving typical real life problems of the user group, if anything.

It is clear that the criticisms leveled at the Laboratory Model are all accounted for. There are new ones, e.g., the findings may not be generalizable to other circumstances.

5. DISCUSSION

Higher-Order Relevance in the Evaluation of IR Algorithms?

Higher-order relevance concepts clearly play a role in IR interaction. Therefore they should be accounted for in IR evaluation. However, using them for the evaluation of IR algorithms presents difficulties, at least for the moment.

If we try to find out, whether IR algorithm A is better than algorithm B, based on situational relevance, we face some difficulties. Best-match IR systems have been designed on the basis of topical relevance solely—while some more traditional Boolean systems allow the use of bibliographic data which may relate to higher-order relevance criteria. However, there is no established theoretical connection between higher-order relevance criteria and explicit document features. This is not to say that such connections cannot exist. People use explicit situational criteria based on bibliographic attributes and citation links in relevance assessments. Yet serving these criteria by system features is a challenge because of lack of understanding on the variability of the criteria and on the combination of evidence on the criteria. There neither is much sense in evaluating the current algorithms' performance on criteria, which they completely ignore (save for correlation of topical and higher-order relevance).

If the proposals to use higher-order relevance, based on textual features, for evaluating IR algorithms were successful to show differences (after normalizing for topical relevance), it would be a real breakthrough. However, this would require that IR software should be able to recognize indications of higher-order relevance in document texts. Because software deals with explicit text (representations) at the level of character strings, the software should be equipped with the capability to recognize character strings in text that indicate higher-order relevance. As early as 1971 Cooper stated: "Logical relevance is almost the only factor in utility which the [system] designer does know how to deal with effectively at present. This suggestion, if true, would help to explain why topical relevance, and not utility, has received the most attention in the literature." Nothing has changed in thirty years?

Even if there were in document representations explicit features that indicate higher-order relevance, or they could be added to them, this might have just minor effects on present-day IR algorithms. The current representation and matching approaches might serve these features well. If the bibliographic and citation attributes of documents cannot be used as relevance indicators generally, the system *interfaces* might be developed to allow easy situational relevance input by the user on such attributes. The algorithms would be affected by the need to combine relevance evidence based on textual features and bibliographic and citation attributes for fair ranking. Evidence based on textual features is computed in current IR practice from textual feature occurrence statistics. Evidence based on bibliographic and citation attributes is of different nature (e.g., weighted preference lists) and has different statistical properties (citation statistics).

Interaction—Sequences of Batch Searches?

Interaction with dynamic needs can be seen as a sequence of retrieval actions where for each step there is a short-term request that can be learned. The IR algorithm should perform, as well as possible, to serve that request, taken topically, as long as features predicting anything of higher-order are beyond reach. And then serve the next, perhaps highly modified, request. Although a user is likely to modify his/her request and relevance criteria in subsequent interactions, it has not been shown that this should affect the design of the retrieval algorithms.

Proper Systems, Proper Measures

We considered above the Laboratory Model and two evaluation scenarios, which see the system to be evaluated differently. Care should be taken in deciding which system to evaluate and how. In the Laboratory Model, focusing on representation and matching, recall and precision seem suitable and sufficient measures (Robertson, 2000). However, if there is interaction involved, the system contains the user, and recall and precision lose their dominance. Measures for usability and learning are needed. If tasks/situations are involved, evaluation needs a broader scope to reveal its support to task performance. Within the two scenarios we need to work toward establishing relevant evaluation criteria above the representation/matching level. Where should IR stop and Sociology start? It's a question of how far the IR community wants to go. We should not discontinue developing IR algorithms along the Laboratory Model. Other things we should consider as well are suggested in Figure 4.

Some Research Problems Requiring Attention

We finally consider research problems requiring attention, if further advances are required in realistic user/task-oriented IR evaluation, especially if this is to affect the design of the algorithmic components:

- *Relevance and representation.* We should investigate the relationship of topical relevance to the higher-order relevance. What remains unexplained by topical relevance? How could it be (effectively and efficiently) accounted for, if at all?

- *IR interfaces.* Interface capabilities that allow users to express conditions on non-topical attributes as evidence for higher-order relevance need to be developed. Such interface capabilities should also handle the great variability of representation of, e.g., person names or citations.

- *Role of IR, goals for IR systems in various situations.* How could users be supported in learning and expressing their needs/requests, or better performing their tasks through IR methods? What kinds of interface components are required? How are the retrieval results used? How to embed IR into the users' systems environment?

- *Evaluation measures.* Above the traditional and proposed evaluation measures, how do we evaluate system effectiveness in supporting users in learning, exploring and expressing their needs/requests, or their contribution to task performance?

6. CONCLUSION

We propose as a conclusion, that the Laboratory Model is, while clearly limited in scope, not as notorious as criticized when used as a model for developing and evaluating IR algorithms for Interactive IR systems. The critics of the model are right in their claims but this rather suggests additional, broader evaluation scenarios than discarding the old one. Also the innovations may touch other areas than text matching between topical requests and document texts: other strategies may be relevant (or rehabilitated), system interfaces may need novel (or rehabilitated) components. Broader evaluation scenarios and further novel evaluation measures are needed. In particular, topical relevance judgment seems well founded for developing IR algorithms for representation and matching. In order to apply the higher-order relevance within the IR algorithms, advances regarding the explicit document/request features or attributes (suggesting such relevance) and their representation are required.

REFERENCES

Barry, C. L. (1994) User-defined relevance criteria: An exploratory study. *Journal of the American Society for Information Science, 45*(3), 149–59.

Barry, C. L., and L. Schamber. (1998) Users' criteria for relevance evaluation: a cross-situational comparison. *Information Processing & Management, 34*(2/3), 219–36.

Bateman, J. (1998) Changes in Relevance Criteria: A Longitudinal Study. In *Proceedings of the 61st American Society for Information Science Annual Meeting 35* (pp. 23–32).

Bates, M. (1989) The design of browsing and berrypicking techniques for the online search interface. *Online Review, 13*, 407–24.

Bates, M. (1990) Where should the person stop and the information search interface start? *Information Processing and Management, 26*(5), 575–91.

Beaulieu, M., S. Robertson, and E. Rasmussen. (1996) Evaluating interactive systems in TREC. *Journal of the American Society for Information Science, 47*(1), 85–94.

Belkin, N. (1993) Interaction with texts: Information retrieval as information seeking behavior. In *Information Retrieval '93*. Konstanz: Universitetsverlag Konstanz.

Borlund, P. (2000) Experimental components for the evaluation of interactive information retrieval systems. *Journal of Documentation, 56*(1), 71–90.

Borlund, P., and P. Ingwersen. (1998) Measures of relative relevance and ranked half-life: Performance indicators for interactive IR. In *Proceedings of the 21st Annual International ACM SIGIR Conference on Research and Development in Information Retrieval* (pp. 324–31). New York: ACM.

Burgin, R. (1992) Variations in relevance judgements and the evaluation of retrieval performance. *Information Processing & Management, 28*(5), 619–27.

Byström, K., and K. Järvelin. (1995) Task Complexity Affects Information Seeking and Use. *Information Processing & Management, 31*(2), 191–213.

Cleverdon, C. W. (1967) The Cranfield tests on index language devices. *Aslib Proceedings, 19*, 173–94.

Cosijn, E., and P. Ingwersen. (2000) Dimensions of relevance. *Information Processing & Management, 36*, 533–50.

Cuadra, C. A., and R. V. Katter. (1967) *Experimental studies of relevance judgments: Final report. Vol. I: Project summary*. Santa Monica, CA: System Development Corporation.

Ellis, D. (1989) A behavioural approach to information retrieval design. *Journal of Documentation, 45*(3), 171–212.

Ellis, D., and M. Haugan. (1997) Modeling the information seeking patterns of engineers and research scientists in an industrial environment. *Journal of Documentation, 53*(4), 384–403.

Froehlich, T. J. (1994) Relevance reconsidered—towards an agenda for the 21st century: Introduction to special topic issue on relevance research. *Journal of the American Society for Information Science, 45*(3), 124–34.

Gaizauskas, R., and Y. Wilks. (1998) Information extraction: Beyond Document Retrieval. *Journal of Documentation, 54*(1), 70–105.

Gluck, M. (1996) Exploring the relationship between user satisfaction and relevance in information systems. *Information Processing & Management, 32*(1), 89–104.

Harter, S. P., and C. A. Hert. (1997) Evaluation of information retrieval systems: Approachs, issues, and methods. In *Annual Review of Information Science and Technology*, vol. 32 (pp. 3–94).

Hawking, D., E. Voorhees, N. Craswell, and P. Bailey. (2000) Overview of TREC-8 Web Track. In *Proceedings of the eight Text REtrieval Conference*. NIST Special Publication 500–246 (pp. 131–50).

Hersh, W., and P. Over. (2000) SIGIR workshop on interactive retrieval at TREC and beyond. *SIGIR Forum 34* (1). Retrieved April 25, 2002, from: http://www.acm.org/sigir/forum/S2000/Interactive_report.pdf

Hull, D. (1996) Stemming Algorithms: a case study for detailed evaluation. *Journal of the American Society for Information Science, 47,* 70–84.

Ingwersen, P. (1996) Cognitive Perspectives of IR Interaction: Elements of a Cognitive IR Theory. *Journal of Documentation, 51*(1), 3–50.

Ingwersen, P., and P. Willett. (1995) An introduction to algorithmic and cognitive approaches for information retrieval. *Libri, 45,* 160–77.

Järvelin, K., and J. Kekäläinen. (2000) IR evaluation methods for highly relevant documents. In *Proceedings of the 23rd Annual International ACM SIGIR Conference on Research and Development in Information Retrieval* (pp. 41–48). New York: ACM.

Järvelin, K., and J. Kekäläinen. (2002) Cumulated gain-based evaluation of IR techniques. Submitted to *ACM Transactions on Information Systems.*

Kekäläinen, J., and K. Järvelin. (2002) Using graded relevance assessments in IR evaluation. To appear in *Journal of the American Society for Information Science and Technology.*

Kuhlthau, C. (1993) *Seeking Meaning.* Norwood, NJ: Ablex.

Over, P. (1997) TREC-5 Interactive Track Report. In *Proceedings of the Fifth Text REtrieval Conference.* NIST Special Publication 500–238 (pp. 29–56).

Rees, A. M., and D. G. Schultz. (1967) *A field experimental approach to the study of relevance assessments in relation to document searching.* Cleveland: Case Western Reserve University.

Robertson, S. E. (1977) The probability ranking principle in IR. *Journal of Documentation, 33*(4), 294–304.

Robertson, S. E. (2000) Salton Award Lecture: On theoretical argument in information retrieval. *SIGIR Forum, 34* (1). Retrieved January 29, 2001, from: http://www.acm.org/sigir/forum/F2000-TOC.html.

Saracevic, T. (1975) Relevance: A review of and framework for the thinking on the notion in information science. *Journal of the American Society for Information Science 26*(6), 321–43.

Saracevic, T. (1996) Relevance reconsidered '96. In *Proceedings of the Second International Conference on Conceptions of Library and Information Science: Integration in Perspective* (pp. 201–18). Copenhagen: The Royal School of Librarianship.

Saracevic, T. (1997) The stratified model of information retrieval interaction: Extension and applications. In *ASIS '97: Proceedings of the 60th ASIS annual meeting* (pp. 313–27). Medford, NJ: Information Today.

Schamber, L. (1994) Relevance and information behavior. In *Annual Review of Information Science and Technology,* vol. 29 (pp. 3-48). Medford, NJ: Information Today.

Schamber, L., M. B. Eisenberg, and M. S. Nilan. (1990) A re-examination of relevance: toward a dynamic, situational definition. *Information Processing & Management, 26*(6), 755–76.

Sparck Jones, K. (1995) Reflection on TREC. *Information Processing & Management, 31*(3), 291–314.

Tang, R., W. M. Shaw, and J. L. Vevea. (1999) Towards the identification of the optimal number of relevance categories. *Journal of the American Society for Information Science, 50*(3), 254–64.

Vakkari, P., and N. Hakala. (2000) Changes in Relevance Criteria and Problem Stages in Task Performance. *Journal of Documentation, 56*(5), 540–62.

Vakkari, P. (2001) A theory of the task-based information retrieval process: a summary and generalization of a longitudinal study. *Journal of Documentation, 57*(1), 44–60.

van Rijsbergen, C. J., and M. Lalmas. (1996) Information calculus for information retrieval. *Journal of the American Society for Information Science, 47,* 385–98.

Voorhees, E. (2001a) Evaluation by highly relevant documents. In *Proceedings of the 24th Annual International ACM SIGIR Conference on Research and Development in Information Retrieval* (pp. 74–82). New York: ACM.

Voorhees, E. (2001b) Overview of the TREC 2001 question answering track. In *The Tenth Text REtrieval Conference (TREC 2001).* Retrieved April 25, 2002, from: http://trec.nist.gov/pubs/trec10/papers/qa10.pdf.

Voorhees, E., and D. Harman. (2001) Overview of TREC 2001. In *The Tenth Text REtrieval Conference (TREC 2001).* Retrieved April 25, 2002, from: http://trec.nist.gov/pubs/trec10/papers/overview_10.pdf.

Wang, P., and D. Soergel. (1998) A Cognitive Model of Document Use during a Research Project. Study I. Document Selection. *Journal of the American Society for Information Science, 49*(2), 115–33.

Wilson, P. (1973) Situational Relevance. *Information Storage and Retrieval, 9*(8), 457–71.

Wilson, T. (1999) Models in information behaviour research. *Journal of Documentation, 55*(3), 249–70.

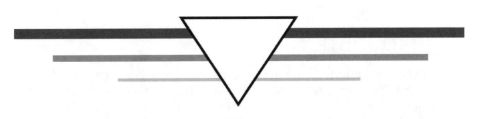

Discourse, Cognition, and Reality: Toward a Social Constructionist Metatheory for Library and Information Science

Kimmo Tuominen
Arts Faculty Library
PO Box 4 (Yliopistonkatu 3)
00014 University of Helsinki
Finland
kimmo.tuominen@helsinki.fi

Sanna Talja and Reijo Savolainen
Department of Information Studies
University of Tampere
33014 Tampere, Finland
sanna.talja@uta.fi; reijo.savolainen@uta.f

ABSTRACT

The paper discusses ontological and epistemological commitments in library and information science (LIS) research. Three different metatheories—the information transfer model, constructivism, and social constructionism—are identified and their assumptions about the relationships between discourse, cognition, and reality are described. Social constructionist ideas about the formation of knowledge provide the reflexive standpoint towards the metatheories that currently seem to orient much of the research within the field and the development of information infrastructures. The authors describe how social constructionist ideas about the conversational production of knowledge in discourses would reorient LIS research.

1. INTRODUCTION

Library and information science (LIS) has grown to a complex field of research, and there are various and even contrasting perspectives to information processes inside the field. This paper seeks to clarify the basic premises of existing research approaches by identifying and analyzing three broad-scale metatheories: the information transfer model, constructivism, and social constructionism. The importance of metatheoretical reflection has been emphasized, for example, by Hjørland (2000, p. 513) who argues that LIS as a field tends to focus too much on providing solutions to practical problems without first analyzing how the adoption of various epistemological standpoints affects the definitions of the problems to be solved. As a consequence, problems that are essentially theoretical in nature are too easily treated as practical tasks.

The term 'metatheory' refers to the often unarticulated premises upon which empirical research and theorization is based. Metatheories, for example, constructivism, are broader and less specific than theories: they are orientation strategies to the world (Vakkari, 1997). They bring into researchers' view a specific research object, and a specific way of conceptualizing, thinking about, and studying this object. Different metatheories build different, even contrasting, research objects and research programs. In short: a metatheory enables researchers to determine what kinds of entities, for example, information, knowledge, users, and information systems, are.

Previously, Ellis (1996) has termed the most important metatheories in LIS as the physical paradigm and the cognitive paradigm. Hjørland (1998a), in turn, names the metatheories within LIS as empiricism, rationalism, and historicism. From our social constructionist (in short: constructionist) perspective that emphasizes the central role of language in the production of knowledge, we classify the central metatheories in LIS as the information transfer model, constructivism, and constructionism. The distinction between constructivism and constructionism follows Gergen's (1999, pp. 59–60) terminological choice. What we call the information transfer model closely corresponds to Ellis' physical paradigm and Hjørland's empiricism. Hjørland (1998a) points out that empiricism—applied research that does not build on specific theories but rests on more or less unconscious metatheoretical assumptions—has been typical for information retrieval research. Rationalistic assumptions in the information-processing paradigm and information seeking research have been thoroughly analyzed in Capurro (1992), Dervin (1994), and Cornelius (1996). Hjørland's (1998a, p. 608) suggestion for a new metatheoretical perspective in LIS, historicism, is a sociocognitive metatheory emphasizing that perception and thinking are always influenced by language and culture.

As a language-based metatheory, constructionism does not operate with conceptualizations such as cognitive space, cognitive functions, mental models, or individual knowledge structures. The above mentioned conceptualizations are based on the distinction between mind and language, on the subject-object dichotomy characterizing modern thinking (cf. Capurro, 1992; Tuominen, 1997). Constructionism speaks about discourses, articulations, and vocabularies, and replaces the concept of cognition with *conversations*. Constructionism differs from sociocognitive and constructivist theories in that it is a dialogic theory about the conversational constitution of knowledge, as opposed to monologic theories that place the formation of knowledge inside individual minds (Tuominen, 2000; 2001). As discussed in more detail below, both sociocognitive and constructivist theories argue that the mind constructs reality in its relationship to the world, although this mental process is seen as being significantly informed by influences from history and social relationships. The primary emphasis of constructionism is not on mental but on linguistic processes. In constructionism, language is seen as constitutive for the construction of selves, and formation of meanings, not merely something that influences thinking. The primary emphasis is on discourse as the vehicle through which the self and the world are articulated, and on the way different discourses enable different versions of selves and reality to be built.

In the present paper, we first explore how the relationships between *discourse, cognition,* and *reality* are understood within the information transfer model, constructivism, and constructionism. Second, we ask what kind of implications do the definitions of the above concepts have for LIS as a discipline studying information and information processes. Our suggestion is that constructionism is as suitable for a general theory for information science as the two other metatheories, because in information studies, and information retrieval research, especially, the researchers are always concerned with language and linguistic products. Documents consist of language, and search terms are words. Therefore, LIS would benefit from including an explicit theory of language into its metatheoretical repertoire. Buckland (1999) has made a similar argument by stressing that "vocabulary" should be a central concept in LIS.

In recent years, constructionist ideas have gained more attention within LIS, manifesting itself in the use of terms such as "discourse" and "discourse community." Constructionism has also become the mainstream paradigm in many social scientific fields, for example, sociology, communication, cultural studies, and the social study of science. However, there are not many detailed suggestions as to how to incorporate constructionist ideas into LIS research (for exceptions, cf. Talja, 1999; Talja, et al., 1997, 1998; Tuominen, and Savolainen, 1997; Tuominen, 2001; Tuominen, Talja, and Savolainen, 2001).

Our main argument in this paper is that defining the subject matter of LIS as discourses and conversations—rather than information or cognition—would lead to promising research programs and approaches. The information transfer model has an *information orientation*, constructivism a *cognition orientation*, and constructionism a *knowledge formation* orientation.

2. THE INFORMATION TRANSFER MODEL

The information transfer model has its roots in Shannon's and Weaver's mathematical information theory. Ronald E. Day (2000, 2001) demonstrates how the transfer model has constructed the metalanguage of information science and how pervasively it has affected both the self-understanding and research programs of LIS. Drawing on the Shannonian ideas, the transfer model provided a new vocabulary for library and information professionals, enabling them to construct convincing narratives of the practices of information seeking and retrieval (Tuominen, 2001; cf. Brier, 1996; Cornelius, 1996). The transfer model appeared as natural and inevitable because it closely corresponded with the mundane understanding of information as the direct communication of messages between senders and receivers (Mokros, 1993, p. 62). As much LIS research has from the beginning been practice-oriented, the transfer model has often remained in the background of applied research as an undiscussed idea of information as a "granular, uniform, and self-sufficient kind of entity, a nugget of informing content that can be mined from texts and classified with great precision for retrieval" (Frohmann, 2001).

In the transfer model, information is an abstract, disembodied entity originally existing in the mind of the sender of the message. The sender is usually understood as an expert who forms knowledge by making empirical observations of the world. The sender, the knower, is believed to be able to transmit his message intact from his own mind to the mind of the receiver through the mechanism of language (Reddy, 1979).

Considering the basic concepts of our study, the transfer model sees *discourse* mostly as a technology by means of which one can represent *reality* isomorphically: language is seen as a mere vehicle for transporting ideas put on the "containers" of words. Thus, language is a slave obeying the wishes of its user. The message is converted into signals by which it is represented, and the message is a disembodied entity hiding behind the signals. *Cognition* is seen important in two senses. First, the sender should observe reality correctly so that his or her perceptions can be put reliably in linguistic form. Second, the user or the receiver should try to understand the message in the way in which the sender originally intended it to be understood. Only in that way can the message, typically understood as an information brick (Dervin, 1994), be transmitted from the sender's mind to the mind of the user.

The information transfer model expresses a belief in the possibility to capture reality, "the truth out there," objectively in "information" (Dervin, 1994). It is implicitly based on trust in science and scientific methods (cf. Enmark, 1998): by using the means and methods of science the observer's subjectivity can be neutralized and the objective truth concerning a particular topic or state of things be captured. Information is seen as reducing uncertainty (Dervin, 1994): when something has been investigated, it is known, and the truth can be transmitted to everyone in the form of information. As the transfer model is characterized by the faith in the authority of scientific and other experts (Day, 2000, p. 809), it limits the role of information user to that of a passive recipient (Dervin, 1994). The transfer model basically relies on a narrative in which immaterial contents (usually accorded with unquestioned truth-value) flow from person to person, and time-space to time-space without much interrogation and interpretation (ibid.).

3. CONSTRUCTIVISM

Nowadays constructivist research approaches are more common in LIS, at least in information seeking research. During the past thirty years, researchers like Nicholas Belkin, Peter Ingwersen, Tom D. Wilson, Brenda Dervin, and Carol C. Kuhlthau pointed out the flaws and shortcomings of the information transfer model, the way that the model emphasized the authoritative role of the sender, and the way it constructed information as an entity-like, objective, and neutral informing brick. Constructivism undermines the sender-based viewpoint by emphasizing that the information user is—and has to be—an active and imaginative processor of information. Users not only receive messages but actively invent a meaning for them.

Although the information transfer model and constructivism are in many ways opposite standpoints, they also have much in common. The following description of the basic assumptions of constructivism should not be read as a critique of the work done by Belkin or any other researcher mentioned above. These researchers' work crystallizes the way prominent theorists generally work: they never stay in one place but follow the general movements in philosophy, human, social, and natural sciences, bringing the most advanced and fruitful ideas into the LIS context, which results in new conceptualizations, definitions, and research programs. In essence, the way we describe constructivism corresponds with how cognitive theories are generally viewed in constructionism (cf. Edwards, 1997; Potter, 1996).

Constructivist theories in LIS basically are theories about the Information Man, about the individual as a processor and seeker of information (Talja, 1997). These approaches describe information and information processes not from the viewpoint of the social construction of knowledge and meanings, but by describing how individuals interact with knowledge resources to construct meanings. Constructivism tends to approach information processes by describing how information needs, seeking, and relevance criteria of individuals are affected by their current situations, tasks, and social contexts.

Of course, there are major differences in the ways that various theories of information seeking or information processing conceptualize and take into account social and cultural factors. In the past, general theories of information seeking usually defined these factors as sets of variables which directly or indirectly affected the individual user (Talja, Keso, and Pietiläinen, 1999). Thus, the general theories developed in information studies suggested that information behavior is affected by group memberships, social and cultural norms, personal styles and preferences, situational, organizational, and domain factors. Still, the emphasis on individuals in situations and contexts results in that broader societal aspects of information use, and the cultural creation of representations, meanings, and interpretations, are discussed only in a peripheral sense.

Constructivism sees individuals as the true originators of knowledge and meanings. Individuals' cognitive structures are influenced by language, history, and social and cultural factors such as domain and cultural environment but, essentially, the creation of knowledge and interpretations is assumed to take place in individual minds.

Constructivism mentalizes language and information in assuming that by means of linguistic manifestations produced by informants, one may directly observe or measure their mental models (see, for example, Todd [1999, p. 12], who is fully aware of the centrality of this assumption for the reliability of empirical studies conducted from a constructivist viewpoint). Constructivism sees discourse as a window to the minds of the informants. When data elicited by interviewing or asking the informants to think aloud is set under the analytic microscope, the researcher is believed to be able to differentiate the linguistic expression from the underlying cognitive or mental model (or from knowledge structures). These models are conceived as sets of highly abstract rules which control and causally antecede all human action, such as the production of linguistic representations.

The separation of language use and mental models is based on the distinction between surface and essence: by systematically analyzing surface structures (language) we gain access to the Platonic conceptual structures orienting one's talk. Both in the transfer model and constructivism, language is essentially a neutral instrument for reporting observations.

Constructivist user studies and studies that measure the performance and efficiency of information systems mathematically without any reference to users' relevance criteria are, of course, very different research programs. However, both the information transfer model and constructivism are based on monologic assumptions about knowledge formation. Representations and interpretations of reality are seen as entities residing inside rather than between individuals. When the social and cultural context of information processes is objectified as variables affecting individuals, representations and interpretations are separated from the concrete situations in which they are formed as parts of our ongoing conversations.

4. CONSTRUCTIONISM

In itself, the criticism of the approaches above is not new. As early as in the 1940s, C. Wright Mills discussed the need to go beyond the mechanistic differentiation between language and mind. Mills (1940) pointed out that the motives that individuals associate with their (or other people's) acts should not be seen as parts of their psychic machinery. One cannot reliably demonstrate the existence of a one-to-one relationship between these constructions and the occurrences taking place inside individuals' minds'. Mills refutes the assumption that the actual function of talking about motives is to directly describe the speaker's or writer's mental states. According to Mills, motives are primarily linguistic constructions. Indicating a motive is a way to give linguistic reasons for one's action when somebody else demands an account. Hence, motives are not something that exist prior to their linguistic expression, they are context-dependent discursive constructions. By motive attributions, people make their own and others' acts understandable. Speakers producing motives draw on vocabularies of motive that have developed historically. The motive is an achievement of practical interaction rather than an entity determining one's action beforehand. Mills' arguments are similar with the ideas presented by Ludwig Wittgenstein (1953).

According to Mills and Wittgenstein, language is social, both in regard to its origin and ways of use. There are no private languages capable of expressing mental states or models. Even if such a language existed, no one except the speaker him- or herself would be able to understand it. When we produce linguistic representations of thoughts and emotions, we engage in historically shaped ways of language use; we step into existing discourses and participate in ongoing conversations. Therefore, we have to approach language as designed "for discourse, for public performances, rather than having public actions as a kind of lucky consequence of people representing things mentally" (Edwards, 1997, p. 259).

Constructionism stresses the dialogic and contextual nature of knowledge production and the dialogic and contextual nature of users, information needs and relevance criteria. The information user makes the same pieces of knowledge or document mean different things depending on what kind of social action he or she is performing with the help of language in a specific interactional and conversational context (Tuominen, and Savolainen, 1997; Tuominen, 2001). The dialogic and contextual nature of information needs and relevance criteria are evident, for instance, in situations in which a speaker or writer has to move knowledge from one conversational context to another. The writer has to invest a lot of energy in legitimizing and modifying the knowledge to the new context. The writer has to enter into a dialogue with the ideas previously expressed in that context. This shows that individual conversation participants are truly "inter-subjects"; they are engaged in language games attracting multiple players with different interpretations of the world (Crossley, 1996, p. 173).

Constructionism understands *discourse, cognition,* and *reality* in the following manner: we produce and organize social reality together by using language. Communicating is always a two-way process, taking place between two or more human beings sharing the same conversation space. Knowledge (about reality) is a linguistic and social product created between people, in conversation and communication, not in the hidden recesses of individual minds. Conversation is the *condition sine qua non* for the constitution of the social world, knowledge, and identities (Rorty, 1979, pp. 389–90). If we accept the argument that "knowing is made and remade, reified and maintained, challenged and destroyed in communication: in dialogue, contest and negotiation" (Dervin, 1994, p. 377), reality cannot be mirrored by "information." Rather, this "information" *consists of social arguments that take part in ongoing conversations about the meaning of an issue or a phenomenon.* Information is all about building credible models or versions of reality that can be defended against potential or actual criticism.

The things we hold as facts are materially, rhetorically, and discursively crafted in institutionalized social practices, and there is no secure ground on which we can stand being sure that our versions of reality will be accepted tomorrow. There are no outside criteria or a God's-eye view that we could utilize to assess the truth value of different knowledge claims, because the criteria and standards we use are also constructed in the conversation (Rorty, 1979, p. 389). This statement does not imply relativism or postmodernism, because the methodological principles and rules that guide knowledge formation inside scientific communities are essential and important, and because the potential merits of different knowledge claims can be analyzed. Nevertheless, our truths can only be well-founded in a certain conversational context.

The basic assumption of constructionism is that knowledge is always positioned: we do not know about reality, we know in reality (Tuominen, 2001). We are not dealing with a pure reflection of a single position but rather with dynamic tensions among multiple positions (Bowker, and Star, 1999). In contrast to the information transfer model, constructionism is based on the assumption that discontinuities, conflicting worldviews, and competing viewpoints lie at the heart of science, research, and knowledge production. Fundamental discontinuities in knowledge production and perspective shifts occur when large numbers of people working together develop new ways of formulating and investigating interesting problems. The term "discourse" refers expressly to perspectives. Different discourses approach the same topics from different angles and conceptualize these topics differently (Foucault, 1972).

Adopting constructionism as a metatheory shifts the focus of research from understanding the needs, situations, and contexts of individual users to the production of knowledge in discourses, that is, within distinct conversational traditions and communities of practice (Brown, 1989, p. 8). When constructionist ideas are applied in, for instance, digital library design, the aim is to develop an information architecture that maps the diversity in viewpoints, in epistemological, political, and ethical positions in a systematic manner (Tuominen, Talja, and Savolainen, 2001). It is the existence of different discourses or conversations concerning a particular topic or scientific issue we want to capture by using suitable methods and information architectural solutions (about the identification of discourses, cf. Talja, 1999, 2001). A constructionist digital library (DL) puts different versions of the same issue or state of things into a dialogical relationship with one another, thus weaving the social, political, and organizational context of knowledge production to representations of knowledge in DLs.

5. CONCLUSIONS

As a metatheory, constructionism has a different orientation when compared with the information transfer model and constructivism. It moves the research focus from, for instance, users' sensemaking and knowledge structures to the production of knowledge in discourses and discourse communities, and reorients research strategies for mapping and visualizing conversations, literatures, and debates (Tuominen, Talja, and Savolainen, 2001). Constructionism as a metatheory does not refute the findings of LIS studies representing different metatheoretical assumptions; rather, it calls for their recontextualization. When we analyze information needs, users' sensemaking, relevance criteria, or keywords, we are always concerned with practices of language use that are "overt, public, disciplined, and institutionalized" (Frohmann, 2001). Recently, Hjørland (2002) has similarly stressed that all information seeking takes place within the boundaries of specific discourses, discourse communities, paradigms, ontologic, and epistemic positions.

It is not possible here to go into a more detailed discussion about how the research questions, methods, and programs in LIS would change with the adoption of the constructionist metatheory, but we will concentrate to this issue in future publications. This paper described the metatheoretical landscape and options in LIS. An analysis of the essential differences between metatheories may enable researchers to choose more consciously between different options.

Historically, the three different metatheories—the information transfer model, constructivism, and constructionism—form a continuum. Novel metatheories are developed as corrections to prior metatheories, and, therefore, new metatheories in many ways depend on the formulations created in theories that preceded them. New metatheories would not have been possible without the preceding metatheories. They do not entirely refute or replace older metatheories: they are only in some aspects different. We have explained these differences by contrasting monologic and dialogic approaches to information processes, and by explaining how the relationships between the concepts *discourse*, *cognition* and *reality* are understood within the three different metatheories. These differences are summarized in Table 1.

Table 1. Metatheoretical approaches to reality, cognition, and discourse.

	Transfer Model	Constructivism	Constructionism
Reality	Source of obser-vations ("out there") to be captured in information	Things "out there" to be rep-resented in men-tal models	Social practices pro-duced in interaction, in cultural, eco-nomic and material contexts of action
Cognition	Receiving / sending messages	Creating (more or less) subjec-tive mental mod-els representing observed or ex-perienced or dreamed things	Not relevant as a the-oretical concept, due to discursive view of communication
Discourse	Not relevant as a theoretical concept, due to asynchronous and decontextualize d view of communication	Exchange of messages be-tween individual minds (mono-logic approach)	Production of meanings, forma-tion of knowledge in conversations (dialogic approach)

LIS as a discipline is concerned with finding the theoretically most well-founded and for the system providers most helpful rules for the design of information systems and for collecting, organizing, classifying, indexing, stor-ing, and retrieving documents. Saracevic (1999, p. 1057) notes that the user-ori-ented research tradition has not had direct connections to systems design thus far. Due to this, and to the fact that information transfer model in the past domi-nated the way the computer industry looked at the problems of building document mediating electronic systems (Brier, 1996), there is clearly a need for a metatheory that could knit the user- and system-oriented camps together under a unified re-search program and provide a fruitful way of conceptualizing the problems of docu-ment retrieval. Ingwersen (1999, p. 32) stresses that our potential for understanding problems of document retrieval is greatly reduced if document-mediating sys-tems, knowledge resources (documents), actors/users, domains, and social con-texts of interaction, are fragmented into separate research areas.

We invite the LIS community to examine if constructionism could be a uni-fying metatheory in LIS in the same way as the cognitive viewpoint. The central assumption of constructionism is that the boundaries of social knowledge are set by discourses that describe and categorize the world for us and bring phenomena into our sight. According to this view, information, information systems, and information needs can all be analyzed as linguistic and conversational constructions, as entities that are produced within existing discourses.

As documents and search terms consist of words, the development of information systems necessarily needs to be based on well-founded and explicit theories of language, knowledge, meaning, and representation. As long as information systems are not designed to systematically model and visualize the fundamental differences in the ways that scientists and other users conceptualize the topics or phenomena that interest them, these systems fail to optimize access to recorded information (cf. Bates, 1998, p. 1200; Hjørland, 1998b).

Constructionism provides a critical standpoint towards the view that language describes inner processes and external reality in a referential and representationalist way. It emphasizes that knowledge is produced from limited viewpoints as parts of our ongoing conversations. Thus, constructionism reorients research strategies towards mapping the structure of existing discourses.

REFERENCES

Bates, M. J. (1998) Indexing and access for digital libraries and the Internet: Human, database, and domain factors. *Journal of the American Society for Information Science 49*(13), 1185–1205.

Bowker, G. C., and S. L. Star. (1999) *Sorting things out: Classification and its consequences*. Cambridge: MIT Press.

Brier, S. (1996) Cybersemiotics: A new interdisciplinary development applied to the problems of knowledge organization and document retrieval in information science. *Journal of Documentation, 52*(3), 296–344.

Brown, R. H. (1989) A poetic for sociology: Towards a logic of discovery for the human sciences. Chicago: University of Chicago Press.

Buckland, M. (1999) Vocabulary as a central concept in library and information science. In T. Aparec, T. Saracevic, P. Ingwersen, and P. Vakkari, eds. *Digital libraries: interdisciplinary concepts, challenges and opportunities* (pp. 3–12). Zagreb: Zavod za informacijske studije Ofsjeka za informacijske znanosti, Filozofski fakultet.

Capurro, R. (1992) What is information science for? A philosophical reflection. In P. Vakkari, and B. Cronin, eds. *Conceptions of library and information science: Historical, empirical and theoretical perspectives* (pp. 82–96). London: Taylor Graham.

Cornelius, I. (1996) *Meaning and method in information studies*. Norwood, NJ: Ablex.

Crossley, N. (1996) Intersubjectivity: The fabric of social becoming. London: Sage.

Day, R. E. (2000) The "conduit metaphor" and the nature and politics of information studies. *Journal of the American Society for Information Science, 51*(9), 805–11.

Day, R. E. (2001) *The modern invention of information: Discourse, history, and power*. Carbondale and Edwardsville: Southern Illinois University Press.

Dervin, B. (1994) Information<—>democracy: An examination of underlying assumptions. *Journal of the American Society for Information Science, 45*(6), 369–85.

Edwards, D. (1997) *Discourse and cognition*. London: Sage.

Ellis, D. (1996) *Progress and problems in information retrieval*. London: Library Association Publishing.

Enmark, R. (1998) The non-existent point: On the subject of defining library and information science and the concept of information. Paper presented at the *64th IFLA Council and General Conference*, Amsterdam, The Netherlands. Retrieved January 13, 2002, from http://www.ifla.org/IV/ifla64/029-94e.htm

Foucault, M. (1972) *The archaeology of knowledge*. London: Routledge.

Frohmann, B. (2001) Discourse and documentation: Some implications for pedagogy and research. *Journal of Library and Information Science Education, 42*(1), 13–28.

Gergen, K. J. (1999) *An invitation to social construction*. London: Sage.

Hjørland, B. (1998a) Theory and metatheory of information science: A new interpretation. *Journal of Documentation, 54*(5), 606–21.

Hjørland, B. (1998b) Information retrieval, text composition, and semantics. *Knowledge Organization, 25*(1/2), 16–31.

Hjørland, B. (2000) Library and information science: Practice, theory and philosophical basis. *Information Processing & Management, 36*(3), 501–31.

Hjørland, B. (2002) Epistemology and the socio-cognitive perspective in information science. *Journal of the American Society for Information Science and Technology 53*(4), 257–70.

Ingwersen, P. (1999) Cognitive information retrieval. Martha E. Williams, ed. *Annual Review of Information Science and Technology 34* (pp. 3–49). Medford, NJ: Information Today.

Mills, C. W. (1940) Situated actions and vocabularies of motive. *American Sociological Review 5*(6), 904–13.

Mokros, H. B. (1993) The impact of a native theory of information on two privileged accounts of personhood. In J. R. Schement, and B. D. Ruben, eds. *Between communication and information* (pp. 57–79). New Brunswick, NJ: Transaction Publishers.

Potter, J. (1996) Representing reality: Discourse, rhetoric and social construction. London: Sage.

Reddy, M. J. (1979) The conduit metaphor: A case of frame conflict in our language about language. In A. Ortony, ed. *Metaphor and thought* (pp. 284–324). Cambridge: Cambridge University Press.

Rorty, R. (1979) *Philosophy and the mirror of nature*. Princeton: Princeton University Press.

Talja, S. (1997) Constituting "information" and "user" as research objects: A theory of knowledge formations as an alternative to the information man theory. In P. Vakkari, R. Savolainen, and B. Dervin, eds. *Information seeking in context* (pp. 81–96). London: Taylor Graham.

Talja, S. (1999) Analyzing qualitative interview data: The discourse analytic method. *Library & Information Science Research, 21,* 459–77.

Talja, S. (2001) Music, culture, and the library: An analysis of discourses. Lanham, MD: Scarecrow Press.

Talja, S., R. Heinisuo, K. Pispa, S. Luukkainen, and K. Järvelin. (1997) Discourse analysis in the development of a regional information service. In M. Beaulieu, E. Davenport, and N. O. Pors, eds. *Library and information studies: Research and professional practice* (pp. 109–28). London: Taylor Graham.

Talja, S., R. Heinisuo, E.-L. Kasesniemi, H. Kemppainen, S. Luukkainen, K. Pispa, and K. Järvelin. (1998) Discourse analysis of user requests. *Communications of the ACM, 41*(4), 93–94.

Talja, S., H. Keso, T. Pietiläinen. (1999) The production of context in information seeking research: A metatheoretical view. *Information Processing & Management, 35*(6), 751–63.

Todd, R. J. (1999) Utilization of heroin information by adolescent girls in Australia: A cognitive analysis. *Journal of the American Society for Information Science, 50*(1), 10–23.

Tuominen, K. (1997) User-centered discourse: An analysis of the subject positions of the user and the librarian. *The Library Quarterly, 67*(4), 350–71.

Tuominen, K. (2000) Monologue or dialogue in the web environment: The role of networked library and information services in the future. Paper presented at the 66th IFLA Council and General Conference, Jerusalem, Israel. Retrieved January 13, 2002, from http://www.ifla.org/IV/ifla66/papers/004-131e.htm

Tuominen, K. (2001) *Tiedon muodostus ja virtuaalikirjaston rakentaminen: konstruktionistinen analyysi* [Knowledge formation and digital library design: A constructionist analysis]. Academic Dissertation. Espoo, Finland: CSC—Tieteellinen laskenta Oy.

Tuominen, K., and R. Savolainen. (1997) Social constructionist approach to the study of information use as discursive action. In P. Vakkari, R. Savolainen, and B. Dervin, eds. *Information seeking in context* (pp. 81–96). London: Taylor Graham.

Tuominen, K., S. Talja, and R. Savolainen. (2001) Multiperspective digital libraries: The implications of constructionism for the development of digital libraries. Paper presented at *the Nordic and International Colloquium on Social and Cultural Awareness and Responsibility in Library, Information and Documentation Studies (SCARLID)*, 13–14 December 2001, Oulu, Finland.

Vakkari, P. (1997) Information seeking in context: A challenging metatheory. In P. Vakkari, R. Savolainen, and B. Dervin, eds. *Information seeking in context* (pp. 451–64). London: Taylor Graham.

Wittgenstein, L. (1953) *Philosophical investigations.* New York: Macmillan.

Cognitive Perspectives of
Document Representation

Peter Ingwersen
Department of Information studies
Royal School of Library and Information Science
Birketinget 6, DK 2300 Copenhagen S, Denmark
pi@db.dk

ABSTRACT

The paper reviews and analyses the cognitive conception of polyrepresentation or multi-evidence applied to information retrieval. Three types of aboutness are discussed, i.e., author, indexer, and user aboutness, as well as isness of information objects, that is, other forms of metadata, also serving as document features. The assumption that highly relevant objects are found in the retrieval overlaps of cognitively and functionally different origin is analysed with reference to performed empirical tests, and the utility of clustering of objects by complex representations for navigation or visualisation purposes is briefly analysed.

1. INTRODUCTION

Knowledge organisation, information retrieval and informetrics are interwoven sub-disciplines of information science. Obviously, information retrieval (IR) is necessary for informetric, bibliometric or scientometric analyses for data collection purposes (Christensen, and Ingwersen, 1996). IR relies in many ways on informetric laws, such as Zipf's Law on term frequency in text corpora. Both

285

IR and informetrics have shared clustering models, such as the Vector Space Model, and the use of similarity measures (Salton, and McGill, 1983; Willett, 1984). Map visualization is vital in both areas as a means of presentation. For both areas knowledge or document representation is crucial for success. The aim of this paper is to point to the *cognitive variety* of interpretations of information objects. They may take the form of cognitively different representations, named polyrepresentation (Ingwersen, 1992), that are useful for retrieval purposes in digital environments of full-text (or image, sound, etc.) by improving the intellectual access to knowledge sources. Representation implies subject access in various forms concerned with contents of documents (Hjørland, 1992; 1997). However, representation *in addition* implies access possibilities to document contents *beyond subject matter*—e.g., by form, structural elements, reference or outlink structures, citations or inlinks, or a variety of metadata elements like author, employer or journal (carrier) name.

The paper is structured as follows. The next section explores the idea, assumptions and theory of polyrepresentation. This is followed by a discussion of types of aboutness leading to the variety of cognitively different types of representations concerned with subject matter as well as other access points of information objects, illustrated by representation samples from scientific communication. This is followed by a discussion of the association between the variation of representation and relevance conceptions as well as a brief illustration of alternative or additional ways of representing and visualising information objects, and concluding remarks.

2. POLYREPRESENTATION OF SCIENTIFIC INFORMATION OBJECTS

Initially Ingwersen (1992) put forward the idea of polyrepresentation as a tool for high precision retrieval. The idea derives from the experimental results gained in mainstream IR research on best match principles, as represented by Salton and McGill (1983) and Belkin and Croft (1987): the various best match IR techniques retrieve different but overlapping results, and the more alike the retrieval algorithms, the larger the overlap. The I3R prototype (Croft, and Thomson, 1987) was based on this experience, featuring two different search engines. Intersected they should provide high precision results and, applied in union, high recall. The idea also draws upon the theories of uncertainty logic proposed by van Rijsbergen (1986).

Polyrepresentation goes beyond the simplistic well-known method of intersection of topical facets as applied, for instance, to traditional online searching of bibliographic databases. Ingwersen (1996) extended the idea into a theory of IR and discusses, as a spin-off, in detail how to deal with the logical implementation of polyrepresentation in Boolean IR systems. The core of the theory is, however, to explore the potential value of matching the multidimensional *cognitive variety* of representations inherently existing, extracted, or interpreted from information objects *and* from the cognitive space of a user in *a best match* retrieval environment.

Polyrepresentation is defined as a variety of different presuppositions and interpretations of situations made by the different cognitive agents that take part in the processes of information generation and transfer. In information retrieval such agents are predominantly authors, indexers, algorithmic or computational designers, thesaurus constructors, interface designers, journal and database editors or publishers, and users. Each actor, situated in a social context, contributes his or her cognitive interpretation of the available information objects (or documents) or adds to its presentation. Hence, the representations are of different cognitive origin, also over *time*. They may derive from the same origin but being of different functional nature, for instance, author-generated text, diagram captions, and references or out-links. The representations can be made in different presentation *styles* according to conventions in the domain and media. The theory proposes that indexing algorithms geared to one domain probably should be applied differently in another domain, exactly due to differences in presentation style. In some media and domains, for instance, in scientific full-text documents, many different agents participate. In other media, as for image objects, fewer different actors manifest automatically their cognitive and emotional imprint on the objects, leading to a smaller number of cognitively different kinds of representation. In addition, the representations are often poor and hence semantically open. In total, objects from such media types present quite difficult retrieval.

Following the cognitive theory of information science and retrieval, the processes of information transfer are seen as processes of cognition in which the variety of representations acts as supplementary contexts to one another. A second notion becomes thus important, i.e., that of *cognitive retrieval overlaps* of different representations. Traditional simplistic triangulation does not operate with intersections (overlaps) made by different kinds of observations or measurements. However, the use of several different data collection methods in the same investigation is a well-known methodological procedure in the social sciences, as, e.g., pointed out in connection to studies of users' information behaviour by Ingwersen and Pejtersen (1986). The paper seeks to extend the model of such overlaps, originating from Ingwersen (1996), by including a variety of metadata seen as cognitive manifestations.

The presented research form part of the TAPIR project that is aimed at the exploration of cognitive retrieval overlaps in scientific full-text environments. TAPIR stands for Text Access Potentials for interactive IR. Very few empirical attempts have been made to explore cognitive intersections between documents retrieved by, for instance, citations (citing author interpretations) and topical features (original author cognition). Pao (1993; 1994) carried out experiments in bibliographic databases, i.e., in surrogate (metadata) databases with no abstracts. In scientific full-text environments little has been done, except in relation to the web by Citeseer/ResearchIndex.com. See section 3.3 below.

Cognitive overlaps produced during processes of information retrieval imply that representations of different cognitive origin or different functional nature point to the same information objects: The more different in cognitive origin the higher the probability that such objects are *relevant*. This assumption is based on very few experiments carried out in the citation analysis research environment, for instance, by McCain (1989) and Pao (1993; 1994). In Pao's detailed investigation (1994) sets of bibliographic records were retrieved by intersecting index and title terms with sets retrieved by citation analysis based on an initial pertinent seed document. The intersection, i.e., in a cognitive sense the document overlap made of different cognitive origin from authors, indexers, and citing authors, was then evaluated by domain experts for topical relevance—but without the experts knowing from which sets the documents derived. Pao found that the density of relevant documents in the overlap was more then six times higher than in the original separate sets. Basically, McCain's studies showed similar patterns. However, no theory building was made based on the results, although already Garfield (1979) had advocated the use of citation indexing as an alternative means to IR.

Quite recently as a part of the TAPIR project, Nielsen has blind-tested two different pharmaceutical thesaurus constructions against one another with domain expert users. One thesaurus was a traditional design by an academic expert. The other was created by means of term associations by pharmaceutical researchers (2001). As expected from the cognitive theory, both thesauri supplement each other during interactive retrieval, although individually displaying similar performance results. Also Ruthven, Lalmas, and van Rijsbergen (2002) base their automatic relevance feedback experiments on ideas similar to polyrepresentation. In their case various combinations of different weighting and indexing algorithms were tested experimentally with end-user participation. Each algorithm is regarded a particular representation of a cognitive structure and interpretation of a designer. The TAPIR group is currently performing experiments to explore further the application of cognitive retrieval overlaps in scientific full-text environments. Preliminary studies by Larsen and Ingwersen (2001; 2002) attempts to extend Pao's approach by applying functionally different author-generated features, like text and title terms, as well as descriptors, combined with the use of the reference network back in time, and the cognitively different citation networks forward in time. How far back can be determined by citing and cited half-life measurements in the collection. This so-called boomerang effect obtains high precision results by retrieving a high density of relevant documents in the central cognitive overlaps, as compared to the retrieval of each feature alone, as assessed by domain experts (2001). In Larsen and Ingwersen (2002) the polyrepresentation model is extended with a ranking algorithm based on weights of references and terms. An alternative approach of polyrepresentation is directly to combine and fuse the contents features and other access points simultaneously, within a short time window and based on their cognitive difference.

In a cognitive theory for information retrieval, central elements are the representations of the *user's* information need and his or her current cognitive and emotional state, and interpretations of the work tasks or interest situation in context, underlying the information need. In the cognitive space of the user, the request formulation is *but one* representation of the user's current cognitive and emotional state concerned with an information need. Similarly, obtainable problem statements and work task or interest descriptions are representations of intrinsic cognitive and affective structures in context framing the user's information seeking. From the cognitive perspective, information retrieval sessions are frequently uncertain and exploratory throughout initial phases (Bates, 1989; Kuhlthau, 1993). Structures of knowledge representations, and most probably also a visual presentation of such structures, are hence of central importance for the cognitive support of the user during retrieval. Many other access points, modes of searching and representation, in addition to the document structure and subject matter, are often available, and may form part of the user's conceptual and search task knowledge and need for information. The search task is regarded the means to fulfilling a perceived work task. However, the remainder of the paper will concentrate on the phenomena of representations of information space, and not pursue further the cognitive space of the user.

3. TYPES OF ABOUTNESS AND ISNESS

In Ingwersen (1992), a tri-partite typology of aboutness is proposed which associates to the original meaning of aboutness put forward by Hutchins (1978). The typology operates with the following categories, to which a fourth is added:

1. Author aboutness, i.e., the *contents as is*;

2. Indexer aboutness, i.e., the *interpretation of contents* (subject matter) with a purpose;

3. Request aboutness, i.e., the user or intermediary interpretation or *understanding of the information need* as represented by the request;

4. User aboutness, i.e., *user interpretation* of objects, e.g., as *relevance feedback* during interactive IR or the use of information and giving credit in the form of references.

In this paper only author, indexer and user aboutness are analysed.

3.1. Author aboutness

Author aboutness signifies the contents of the information objects in the form of signs, i.e., the transformations of the interpretations, ideas, and cognitive structures of the author(s) with respect to their goals and intentionality. If we consider scientific communication by means of articles or monographs, the contents (and signs) are text structures, commonly organised in specific ways according to convention, e.g., introduction, theory, or methodological sections, results, discussion, and/or conclusions. Like presentation style, the *structural organisation* is domain and media-dependent and very useful as a supplement to subject matter. For instance, the passage retrieval approach (Salton, 1989) illustrates how structural entities, like full article sections, sub-sections, paragraphs, etc., can replace the complete document as semantic retrieval entities. The passage approach extends previous alternative ways of representing documents in the form of their structure via table of contents (Wormell, 1981) and to a degree moves into a semantic approach to interactive IR (Smeaton, 1992). For instance, contents features like terms found in section titles or in selected paragraphs or sentences from scientific articles may be expected to better signify the subject matter of scientific information objects. Such features ought hence to obtain higher weighting scores in automatic indexing than, e.g., terms from other document elements. One would then expect improved IR performance. Previous results from computer linguistics have, albeit, not been convincing (Smeaton, 1992). Yet, Lahtinen has recently empirically investigated this linguistic aspect of algorithmic representation of textual information objects. He compared human indexing at conceptual level with syntactic parsing of selected spots in the same objects (2000). The results look very promising from linguistic and cognitive perspectives of interactive IR.

Aside from author-generated subject matter and structure of information objects, we may have references (in scholarly communication) or outlinks to related work that has been interpreted in some way by the author(s). Like diagrams or figures, and their captions, references or outlinks signify functionally different ways of representing an object. The application of references given to other related work is an *alternative form* of knowledge representation, which can be used for automated retrieval purposes, as was originally the idea by Garfield in the 60s in connection with his citation indexing approach (1979; 1998). Note, that what is counted operationally when performing citation analysis is not references but *citations* received over time by a scholarly entity, like an author, an article, an institution, a journal or a country. We may thus talk of two different but intermingled networks of references and citations. Their cognitive and functional nature in representation is quite different from one another and from that of the text itself. The context around the reference or quotation (or outlink) in the citing object as well as the context of the cited (or inlinked) object or passage are indeed cognitively supplementary document representations.

Author aboutness consequently provides the full text, image, video, etc., the document structure, the chapter and section titles, the captions, and the references and outlinks as means for automated indexing. In modern (topical) information retrieval the words from the text corpus are weighted according to a scheme (van Rijsbergen, 1979). However, as stated above, weighting of the references has *not* been attempted due to the online citation database structures and their lack of full-text. All references weight the same. Nevertheless, cited authors or journals, for instance, could easily be weighted by means of the citation indexes—also in co-citation analyses. But again, such analyses are commonly kept on the citing document (i.e., item) level, not at the cited entity (i.e., postings) level (Christensen, and Ingwersen, 1996).

Author aboutness provides many commonly well known but functionally different access points to information objects. The vocabulary is that of the domain as interpreted by the author(s). Supposedly, the vocabulary corresponds to that of the future users within a *timeline* of the average lifetime of documents in the domain(s). However, this is no guarantee that the *semantic* contents correspond to the users' information needs. During retrieval, all the original intentionality of the author(s) as well as the meaning of the text is fundamentally *lost* (Smeaton, 1992; Ingwersen, 1996; 1999). It can only be recovered by the interpretation of users, and if not perceived the object conveys potential information only (Ingwersen, 1992).

In order to ease meaningful access to the information objects alternative or supplementary human representations have been introduced in the form of classification and indexing, i.e., human indexer aboutness. A recent article looks specifically into the nature of indexing both from a human perspective and in an automatic sense (Anderson, and Pérez-Carballo, 2001). Also Hjørland and Nielsen (2001) review forms of indexing in electronic environments.

3.2. Indexer aboutness

Indexer aboutness is based on human interpretation of information objects, different from that of authors. Aside from topically classifying objects, indexers may add new perspectives to the contents of such objects and ease the access to meaning. Cognitively speaking—and in practice—human indexing is directed towards the entire document. This is logical when categorising the document type or information mode. However, the actual number of indexing terms or phrases added to the contents description of the information object is commonly very limited. This leads to *reductionism*, in particular when only the major themes and aspects are represented by the indexer. Another drawback is the difficulty of applying weighting schemes to indexing structures. Too few term occurrences exist for adequate weighting purposes. Inter-indexer-inconsistency— also over time—is also an issue (Lancaster, 1998). However, in a cognitive sense, inconsistency is preferable to consistency due to a wider range of available access possibilities (Ingwersen, 1996). The conceptual web becomes fine-meshed. Human indexing may also be supportive during retrieval by cleaning up the name form mess increasingly experienced in databases and knowledge resources.

Indexer aboutness can be directed towards the subject matter and meaning of the information object or towards its future potential intellectual use or user grouping(s). The former purpose is the common issue of indexing while the latter calls for tremendous predictive power of the domain expert indexer. Some information researchers regard the socio-scientific domain as the determining force during the indexing process (Hjørland, 1997; Jacob, and Shaw, 1998). From a cognitive perspective this is *not* so. The indexer interprets the information object situated in the domain(s) and is *influenced* by the social and scientific (present and historical) context. However, the indexer determines the interpretation—not the social scientific construct surrounding the object and indexer at a given point in time. A recent interesting analysis by Jacob discusses two approaches to classification in situated context (2001). Classification and similar knowledge organisational structures are seen as functionally different from the process of indexing—and again cognitively different from authoring.

Designing classification systems or generating thesaurus structures are processes that are cognitively different from the processes of classifying and indexing, for instance, by using a structured controlled vocabulary from a domain thesaurus. Such structures are socio-cognitive by nature, as they are negotiated at a certain point in time by a team of domain experts. As such, both an academic or associative domain thesaurus displays *cognitive authority*—at least for a while and targeted to different client groups and work tasks (Nielsen, 2001). In an authoritative way, thesauri and domain specific author or journal co-citation maps are similar. Both derive from interpretations of the domain(s) in question, but author or journal co-citations are dynamic and the document clusters and relations are changing over time. Many other forms of representations might also be applied to clustering of a domain. For example, Figure 2, below, displays a map that clusters documents according to national *research profiles*, each consisting of the publication distributions from nine different sub-disciplines of the social sciences.

3.3. User aboutness: relevance feedback and information use over time

The fourth notion of aboutness, that of *user aboutness*, is associated with relevance feedback during IR interaction or use of information over time. As mentioned, Citeseer/ResearchIndex.com experiments with this type of aboutness when ranking *already* retrieved scientific documents, i.e., by means of the amount of articles citing such objects over time. Citations are representations of a *use* of the documents by some (scientific) agent. However, in full-text it becomes possible to weight references, cited authors or journals, not taken from the list of references alone as in the present citation indexes, but taken from the original text body itself. Weighting of incoming citations (or inlinks) is thus also possible over time. The reference and citation weights can then be fused with traditional term weights in the cognitive retrieval overlaps.

Like Citeseer, the Google search engine applies the amount of inlinks as a ranking instrument when traditional topical retrieval has been performed. These attempts to apply representations somewhat different from topical representations of documents are related to a socio-cognitive type of relevance, discussed further in section 5. However, the mentioned web information providers are not following the theory of polyrepresentation. There exists no attempt to make use of the cognitive variety of representation and to construct cognitive retrieval overlaps. Traditional Boolean overlaps by intersection can be seen—but the common logic applied in web engines is that of union of search terms. The additional means of representations are simply applied, as always, in a pragmatic and non-theoretical way.

The association to relevance feedback (behaviour) during interactive IR seems a more promising track of research on *integrated* information seeking and retrieval processes as well as user aboutness. Campbell (2000) has applied users' relevance feedback in an image retrieval system in which the probabilistic retrieval model becomes adjusted to the most *recent* statements of relevance by down-weighting relevance scores from earlier feedback. Ruthven (2001) has investigated in a detailed manner a range of different kinds of interactive user behaviour to be used as tools for guiding the system's relevance feedback and query modification algorithms. Since logging of the behaviour is possible during interactive IR, we may observe possible patterns of access and use of documents in relation to real or simulated information situations in context (Borlund, 2000). Such knowledge may indeed enhance the possibility of dynamically adjusting retrieval and ranking algorithms, including polyrepresentative configurations of interactive IR. The findings of Kuhlthau (1993) on uncertainty levels and later Vakkari (2001) on relevance assessment, based on Kuhlthau's research framework, paired with Spink, Greisdorf, and Bateman's tri-partite relevance regions (1998), suggest that algorithmic IR may indeed profit from knowledge of information (seeking) behaviour.

4. ISNESS IN COGNITIVE RETRIEVAL OVERLAPS

Figure 1 demonstrates the variety of cognitive aboutness structures, dealing with aspects of contents and subject matter, *and* structures of different interpretative nature (user aboutness). In addition, the model, Figure 1, contains structures that are *selective* and different from those of indexers and users. Instead of aboutness, such structures reflect *isness* by making available non-topical features connected to information objects—depending on media, domain, and presentation style. Most of the common bibliographic data or metadata thus belong to representations of isness. They are results of selection or assessment processes performed by various actors on information objects and their authors over time. In scientific communication articles, books or conference papers are commonly submitted for peer reviewing to be accepted or rejected by a journal, publisher or conference. The reviewing process is socio-cognitive by nature, taking into account the book or paper and its scientific contribution, the journal or conference reputation and scope, in context of the domain(s) treated by the journal or conference. If selected by the journal *editors* or conference committee for publishing, the paper receives a portion of the cognitive authority of the *journal name* and itself contributes to that authority. How and when it is published, e.g., categorised together with other selected papers, is determined by the same editors of the journal or the programme committee or chairs of the conference.

Also the author affiliation (and country) belongs to the isness features, together with database names later to index and incorporate the journal or conference as part of their structures. It is not uncommon that a particular topic is covered by hundreds of databases and that single articles can be found in several different systems due to the inclusion of the journal in the files.

Figure 1. Polyrepresentative overlaps of cognitively and functionally different representations of information objects. Retrieved sets generated by one search engine and associated with one searcher statement. Extension of Ingwersen, 1996, p. 28.

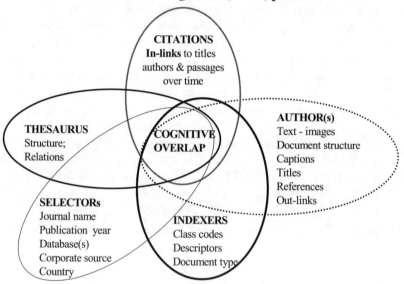

Aside from illustrating the different representations (or access points) associated with scholarly papers and described above, the model, Figure 1 points to the central cognitive as well as some of the many possible overlaps between the sets of information objects retrieved. The central cognitive overlap is defined by one retrieval engine that acts on one user statement, for instance, concerned with describing the work task situation underlying the information need. In principle, two or more retrieval engines can be fused, creating even more central overlaps. In addition, user statements causally associated with one another, e.g., the work task description and information need request formulation, may form new logically related overlaps. The model extends the original version from Ingwersen (1996) by incorporating the additional features of isness related to the objects, that is, selectors such as journal name and publication date. Further, the logical separation of references (and out-links) from citations (and in-links) as features of user aboutness is shown in the model.

5. POLYREPRESENTATION AND RELEVANCE PERSPECTIVES

From a cognitive stand, the objects found in the central cognitive overlap should be ranked *prior* to other objects since they are assumed most relevant. With data fusion we encounter the issue of scaling: which of the fused ranking scales to apply. This issue calls for further investigations, for instance, if we assume that the best fusion is obtained by giving the probabilistic ranking scheme priority over number of inlinks or citations; or perhaps the opposite order or aggregation of scores might lead to improvement of interactive retrieval performance (Smeaton, 1998).

We observe that the model takes into consideration that users in practice prefer to access retrieval systems partly by means of topical representations, partly via non-topical access points, like document structure, country, or journal name. That depends on the actual search task. Since the central overlaps are considered highly relevant in accordance with Pao's investigations (1993; 1994) the notions of relevance come into play (Schamber, Eisenberg, and Nilan, 1990; Saracevic, 1996; Cosijn, and Ingwersen, 2000). Obviously, traditional topical relevance assessments may take place in relation to the representative structures adhering to author and indexer aboutness (Hjørland, 2001). However, judgments of *pertinence* are also possible. Pertinence signifies the relation between the information objects and the user perception of the information need (Saracevic, 1996), for instance, in the form of novelty or cognitive authority of author, affiliation or journal. *Situational* relevance defined as the relation between the work task situation as perceived by the user and the retrieved objects, i.e., their usefulness, is conceivable due to full-text availability, including diagrams and figures. Indeed, references or out-links in context may signal an understanding of the object relevant to the user.

Lastly, *socio-cognitive* relevance assessments, originating from epistemological relevance (Hjørland, 1997) and contextual relevance (Ørom, 2000) are tangible, e.g., by means of the citations (or in-links) given to the objects. The citations by scholarly colleagues imply commonly a certain degree of recognition, acceptance and use, and cognitive authority. While topicality, pertinence, and socio-cognitive relevance, per definition, signify the use of tangible features of the objects, situational relevance assessments imply a specific *combination of features* determined at individual user level during IR interaction. References or outlinks are objective features, at least situational to the author at publishing time, and probably also situational to users in their context. Monitoring the relevance feedback behaviour of the user may probably indicate something about the features in question (Spink, Greisdorf, and Bateman, 1998; Ruthven, 2001). It might, for example, be a figure or a methodological description or results that trigger the situational usefulness of the passage or information object.

6. MAPPING AND VISUALISATION BY MEANS OF REPRESENTATION

All information objects can be represented by all their features, added or inherent, depending on media, domain and style; and, in addition, the features may in turn be represented by the objects. This is useful for the purpose of mapping and visualisation by means of multi-dimensional scaling (MDS) techniques. Domain maps serve as authoritative visualisation tools for relevance feedback or navigation in retrieval systems.

Figure 2. Publication profile map 1994–1998 of 17 OECD countries covering nine social science disciplines, representing each country. Source: NSI, ISI, 1999. Circle size signifies amount of journal articles. From Ingwersen, Larsen, and Noyons, 2001.

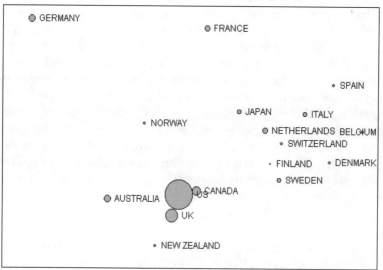

Figure 2 demonstrates a map visualisation of the social sciences, 1994–1998, by clustering 17 selected OECD countries according to their publication profiles similarity (Ingwersen, Larsen, and Noyons, 2001). The profiles consist of nine fields, including economics, sociology, political science, management research, social work, and library and information science. The common practice in informetrics is to apply author co-citation, term co-occurrence, or even journal co-citedness to construct domain maps. The current MDS map is made from the journal articles classified into nine social science sub-fields *and* affiliated to their author countries. The cosine similarity measure is applied to a matrix of 17x17 vector representations. It is not recommended to apply the Pearson correlation measure for similarity calculations (White, and McCain, 1998) for several reasons, one being that the more empty cells found in the similarity matrix the more similar the objects (Ahlgren, Jarnevig, and Rousseau, 2002).

The map illustrates the expected dominance of the Anglo-American articles in the social science domain, as indexed by ISI, but also that some clusters of smaller EU countries begin to form East of the core cluster. The map may serve as entry into the social science research space at an instance during retrieval. An alternative map might show clusters of documents co-authored from groups of countries.

7. CONCLUDING REMARKS

We have demonstrated that information retrieval and informetrics are closely connected by means of the variety of knowledge representations that are available as features associated with information objects. The analysis isolated the representations according to cognitive origin, i.e., to the type of interpretation associated with an information object. The cognitive *variety* of origin is media, domain and presentation style dependent. For each cognitive agent we may observe differences in the functionality of representations, like the difference between references and text terms in scientific documents. It is assumed useful to explore this cognitive variety for the purposes of retrieval and intellectual access to documents by means of the conception of cognitive retrieval overlaps. The more different in origin of the representations and their interpretation, the higher the probability that objects found in the overlap are relevant. The conceived model of cognitive overlaps points to additional features of information objects, only lately associated with subject matter and topical best match retrieval. Such features concern, for instance, the document structure, references and citations, links, journal names or affiliations. Some features are commonly seen as kinds of bibliographic entry points or metadata. The analysis reveals that such features can be seen as determined by cognitive interpretations and assessments often remote in time and place, for instance, by reviewing processes or (re-)use.

Finally the paper demonstrates that a fruitful connection exists between modern relevance and conceptions *and* knowledge representation, seen in a cognitive and socio-cognitive perspective. It seems useful further to explore that connection, in particular concerning the relevance feedback and query modification issues associated with user aboutness.

ACKNOWLEDGEMENTS

This work is sponsored by research grants from the Research Council of the Danish Cultural Ministry as well as from NordInfo, and forms part of the TAPIR Research Project (Text Access Potentials for interactive Information Retrieval).

REFERENCES

Ahlgren, P., B. Jarnevig, and R. Rousseau. (2002) Why Pearson's correlation coefficient should not be used in author co-citation analysis. *Journal of the American Society for Information Science and Technology.* (In press).

Anderson, J. D., and J. Pérez-Carballo. (2001) The Nature of indexing: how humans and machines analyze messages and texts for retrieval: Part 1: Research and the nature of human indexing; Part 2: machine indexing and the allocation of human versus machine effort. *Information Processing & Management, 37*(2), 231–77.

Bates, M. (1989) The design of browsing and berry-picking techniques for the online interface. *Online Review* (now Online & CD-ROM Review), *13*(5), 407–24.

Belkin, N. J., and W. B. Croft. (1987) Retrieval techniques. *Annual review of Information Science and technology, 22,* 109–45.

Borlund, P. (2000) *Evaluation of Interactive Information Retrieval Systems.* Åbo, Finland: Åbo Akademi University.

Campbell, I. (2000) Interactive evaluation of the ostensive model using a new test collection of images with multiple relevance assessments. *Information Retrieval, 2*(1), 87–114.

Christensen, F. H., and P. Ingwersen. (1996) Online citation analysis: A methodological approach. *Scientometrics, 37*(1), 39–62.

Cosijn, E., and P. Ingwersen. (2000) Dimensions of relevance. *Information Processing & Management, 36,* 533–50.

Croft, W. B., and R. H. Thomson. (1987) I3R: A new approach to the design of document retrieval systems. *Journal of the American Society for Information Science and Technology, 38*(6), 389–404.

Garfield, E. (1979) *Citation Indexing: Its Theory and Application in Science.* New York: Wiley.

Garfield, E. (1998) From citation indexes to informetrics: Is the tail wagging the dog? *Libri, 48,* 67–80.

Hjørland, B. (1992) The concept of 'subject' in information science. *Journal of Documentation, 48*(2), 172–200.

Hjørland, B. (1997) *Information seeking and subject representation: An activity-theoretical approach to information science.* Westport, CT: Greenwood Press.

Hjørland, B. (2001) Towards a theory of aboutness, subject, topicality, theme, domain, field, content ... and relevance. *Journal of the American Society for Information Science and Technology, 52*(9), 774–78.

Hjørland, B., and L. K. Nielsen. (2001) Subject access points in electronic retrieval. In M. E. Williams, ed. *Annual Review of Information Science and Technology, 31,* 249–98.

Hutchins, W. J. (1978) The subject of 'boutness' in subject searching. *Aslib Proceedings, 30*(5), 172–81.

Ingwersen, P. (1992) *Information Retrieval Interaction.* London: Taylor Graham.

Ingwersen, P. (1996) Cognitive perspectives of information retrieval interaction: Elements of a cognitive IR theory. *Journal of Documentation, 52*(1), 3–50.

Ingwersen, P. (2001) Cognitive information retrieval. In M. Williams, ed. *Annual Review of Information Science and Technology, 34* (1999), 3–51.

Ingwersen, P., B. Larsen, and E. Noyons. (2001) Mapping national research profiles in social science disciplines. *Journal of Documentation, 57*(6), 715–40.

Ingwersen, P., and A. M. Pejtersen. (1986) User requirements: Empirical research and information systems design. In P. Ingwersen, L. Kajberg, and A. M. Pejtersen, eds. *Information Technology and Information Use* (pp. 111–24). London: Taylor Graham.

Jacob, E. K. (2001) The everyday world of work: putting classification in context. *Journal of Documentation, 57*(1), 76–99.

Jacob, E. K., and D. Shaw. (1998) Sociocognitive perspectives of representation. In M. E. Williams, ed. *Annual Review of Information Science and Technology, 33,* 131–85.

Kuhlthau, C. C. (1993) *Seeking Meaning.* New York: Ablex.

Lahtinen, T. (2000) *Automatic Indexing: An Approach Using an Index Term Corpus and Combining Linguistic and Statistical Methods.* Helsinki: University of Helsinki, Department of General Linguistics. (Publications: 34).

Lancaster, F. W. (1998) *Indexing and Abstracting in Theory and Practice.* London: UK, Library Association Publishing.

Larsen, B. (2002) Exploiting citation overlaps for information retrieval: generating a boomerang effect from the network of scientific papers. *Scientometrics, 54*(2), 131–54.

Larsen, B., and P. Ingwersen. (2001) Synchronous and diachronous citation analysis for information retrieval: Generating a Boomerang effect from the network of scientific papers. In M. Davis, and C. S. Wilson, eds. *Proceedings of the 8th International Conference on Scientometrics & Informetrics, ISSI2001, Sydney, July 16–20, 2001,* (Vol. 1, pp. 355–68). Sydney: The University of New South Wales.

Larsen, B., and P. Ingwersen. (2002) The boomerang effect: Retrieving scientific documents through the network of references and citations. In *Proceedings from the 25th Annual Conference on Research and Development in Information Retrieval: ACM-SIGIR 2002.* New York: ACM Press. (In press).

McCain, K. W. (1989) Descriptor and citation retrieval in the medicine behavioral sciences literature: Retrieval overlaps and novelty distribution. *Journal of the American Society for Information Science and Technology, 40,* 110–14.

Nielsen, M. L. (2001) A framework for work task based thesaurus design. *Journal of Documentation, 57*(6), 774–97.

Pao, M. (1993) Term and citation searching: A field of study. *Information Processing & Management, 29*(1), 95–112.

Pao, M. (1994) Relevance odds of retrieval overlaps from seven search fields. *Information Processing & Management, 30*(3), 305–14.

Ruthven, I. (2001) *Abduction, Explanation and Relevance Feedback.* Glasgow, UK: Department of Computing Science, University of Glasgow.

Ruthven, I., M. Lalmas, and C. J. van Rijsbergen. (2002) Combining and selecting characteristics of information use. *Journal of the American Society for Information Science, 53*(5), 378–96.

Salton, G. (1989) *Automatic Text Processing: The Transformation, Analysis And Retrieval of Information by Computer.* Reading, MA: Addison-Wesley.

Salton, G., and J. M. McGill. (1983) *Introduction to Modern Information Retrieval.* New York: McGraw-Hill.

Saracevic, T. (1996) Relevance reconsidered '96. In P. Ingwersen, and N. O. Pors, eds. *Information Science: Integration in* Perspective (pp. 201–18). Copenhagen, Denmark: Royal School of Librarianship.

Schamber, L., M. Eisenberg, and M. Nilan. (1990) A re-examination of relevance: Toward a dynamic, situational definition. *Information Processing & Management, 26*(6), 755–76.

Smeaton, A. (1992) Progress in the application of natural language processing to information retrieval tasks. *Computer Journal, 35,* 268–78.

Smeaton, A. (1998) Independence of contributing retrieval strategies in data fusion for effective information retrieval. In *Proceedings of the 20th BCS_IRSG Colloquium.* Grenoble, 1998. Bonn: Springer-Verlag, Electronic Workshops in Computing.

Spink, A., H. Greisdorf, and J. Bateman. (1998) From highly relevant to not relevant: Examining different regions of relevance. *Information Processing and Management, 34*(5), 599–621.

Vakkari, P. (2001) A theory of the task-based information retrieval process: A summary and generalisation of a longitudinal study. *Journal of Documentation, 7*(1), 44–60.

van Rijsbergen, C. J. (1979) *Information retrieval.* 2d ed. London, Butterworth. (Available from: http://www.dcs.gla.ac.uk/)

van Rijsbergen, C. J. (1986) A new theoretical framework for information retrieval. In F. Rabitti, ed. *ACM-SIGIR Proceedings of Research and Development of Information Retrieval* (pp. 194–200). Pisa: IEI.

White, H., and K. McCain. (1998) Visualizing a discipline: An author co-citation analysis of information science, 1972–1995. *Journal of the American Society for Information Science, 49*(4), 327–55.

Willett, P. (1984) A note on the use of nearest neighbors for implementing single linkage document classification. *Journal of the American Society for Information Science, 35*(3), 149–52.

Wormell, I. (1981) SAP—A new way to produce subject descriptions of books. *Journal of Information Science: Principles and Practice, 3,* 39–43.

Where Does Reading Fit in Citation Theory and Information Seeking? Operationalisation of Reading—The "Black Box" of Information Use

Mari Davis
Bibliometric and Informetric Research Group
University of New South Wales
UNSW SYDNEY NSW 2052
Sydney, Australia
M.Davis@unsw.au.edu;

Cristina Scott
School of Information Systems, Technology and Management
University of New South Wales
UNSW SYDNEY NSW 2052
Sydney, Australia

The generative act in scientific discovery is a creative act of mind—a process as mysterious and unpredictable in a scientific context as it is in any other exercise of creativity (Medawar, 1959, p. 80).

1. INTRODUCTION

Reading is not adequately taken into account in its own right as a legitimate step in information seeking (IS) models in information science. Most models simply assume absorption of ideas or learning occurs as a result of reading but do not deal with it as a separate and essential component of IS and use models. Using the flight recorder "Black Box" metaphor highlights the hidden or uninvestigated nature of this essential activity in IS and scholarly communication. Certainly, the empirical investigation of the role of reading, its characteristics, and processes would usefully inform in a number of domains by providing new insights on practice, process and theory.

Reading constitutes a blind spot in a number of important discussions in the sociology of science, scientometrics, social studies of science, library and information studies, and scholarly communication. Reading is a complex interaction requiring skills such as spelling and word recognition, and uses experience including personal understandings about the world and specific bodies of knowledge. The strategies that readers employ are idiosyncratic and shown to be used often without conscious awareness (Sloboda, 1986).

The poster outlines a need for research into the role of reading in information seeking, the learning processes of students and research activities. Reading comprises a range of purposeful or focused activities, some of which hinge on, and are closely related to, information seeking behaviour. Reading behaviour and processes go beyond current models of IS to include:

- Scanning, browsing or reading "informative" material
- Note-taking and absorbing of content
- Remembering and storing of information
- Informative content use in research (e.g., design, methods, writing, etc.)
- Referencing materials read in work to support knowledge claims.

Traditional library use studies have mainly used survey methods and circulation records to gather data on what their readers use from items among collections. Such studies do not focus on the role or meaning of reading within information seeking contexts; the use type of questions relate mainly to allocation of time, and utilization of types and amount of sources and resources. The question left unaddressed by these studies is: where does reading—as activity or process—fit within current models of information seeking behaviour?

2. CURRENT IS MODELS OMIT READING

A number of models have been put forward to illustrate and explain information seeking and behaviour associated with the search for information. The seeking process (information discovery) depends in a major way on reading for its success, that is, to gain the desired outcomes of learning, understanding, absorbing ideas and factual or evidential material in order to generate new ideas, to write reports, papers and so on. Reading is central to both the discovery process and the processing and use stages in IS models.

Figure 1: Potential reading variables.

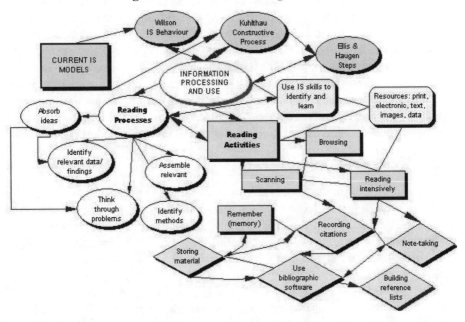

Kuhlthau's model of information seeking (1993) outlines six stages—Initiation, Selection, Exploration, Formulation, Collection, and Presentation. Reading is an assumed function in the model, mentioned specifically in the "Exploration" stage as a strategy (reading to learn about the topic), and note taking under "Formulation" and "Collection." However, no firm place is given to reading as process in Kuhlthau's model. Following "Search Closure," the strategy is to keep " . . . books until completion of writing." The logical link between reading and information seeking is clear; the activities and process of reading appear to constitute a further stage (not modeled) that follows once adequate resources have been identified and collected. The same situation is apparent with IS steps outlined by Ellis and Haugen (1997): surveying; chaining; monitoring; browsing; distinguishing; filtering; extracting; and ending, in which reading is assumed as taking place, but again is not given sufficient amplification. Wilson's (1999) revised model of information behaviour incorporates the node "information processing and use" within which reading is central but left hidden or unexplained. This poster suggests that this node might be treated as a "Black Box" of reading as activity and process, ripe for deconstruction or micro-sociological investigation in a Latourian manner (viz "*Laboratory Life*," Latour, and Woolgar, 1986).

3. THE ROLE OF READING IN IS CONTEXTS—A RESEARCH IMPERATIVE

In order to examine reading as one of the variables affecting scholarly communication and research behaviour, there is a need to operationalise reading to assist in empirical research work on this critical activity. Escarpit (1991) offers guidelines on for researchers working with theoretical and methodical issues related to this particular "Black Box." The operationalisation of reading as a variable would allow attempts to build theoretical explanations for development and testing of hypotheses. The communicative activity of reading is not explained as a sociological variable because of its embeddedness in models of research as a whole. Thus reading is analysed as an integral but never as a separate variable or process in the scholarly communication cycle. Our current research involves operationalisation of the variables (activities and processes) associated with reading in order to augment current IS models.

4. CONCLUSION

Given the comment that heads this poster that the processes of science are mysterious and unpredictable, perhaps it is not unexpected that few have investigated this crucial component in IS models. That empirical examination may be difficult is no reason why attempts should not be made to unravel this "Black Box" in the heart of information science, scientometrics and scholarly communication. The novelist, Jonathan Franzen, author of *The Corrections* stated that: "When you hold a book in your hand, nothing will happen unless you work to make it happen." We in Information Science fields might do well to follow this idea by including investigations of reading in our research agendas and by observing and recording what "happens" when students and scholars read.

REFERENCES

Ellis, D., and M. Haugan. (1997) Modelling, *Journal of Documentation 53*, 384–403.

Escarpit, R. (1991) Methods in reading research. In P. Kaegbin, et al., eds. *Studies on Research in Reading and Libraries: Approaches and Results from Several Countries*, (pp. 1–16). Munich: K. G. Saur.

Kuhlthau, C. (1993) *Seeking meaning: a process approach to library and information services*. Norwood, NJ: Ablex.

Latour, B., and S. Woolgar. (1979/1986) *Laboratory life: the construction of Scientific facts*. 2d ed. Princeton, NJ: Princeton University Press.

Medawar, P. (1959) My life in science. In D. Pyke, ed. *The threat and the glory: reflections on science and scientists*. New York: HarperCollins.

Sloboda, J. (1986) Reading: a case study of cognitive skills. In A. Gellatly, ed. *The skilful mind: an introduction to cognitive psychology* (pp. 39–49). Milton Keynes, UK: Open University Press.

Wilson, T. (1999) Models in information behaviour research, *Journal of Documentation, 55*(3), 249–70.

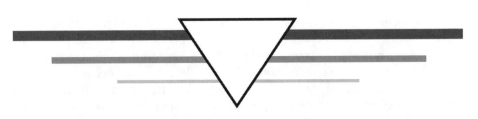

Re-envisioning the Information Concept: Systematic Definitions

Ronald D. Houston and E. Glynn Harmon
GSLIS, University of Texas at Austin
SZB 564, D7000, Austin TX 78712-1276, USA
sofdh@juno.com; gharmon@gslis.utexas.edu

1. INTRODUCTION

This paper suggests a framework and systematic definitions for six words commonly used in the field of information science: data, information, knowledge, wisdom, inspiration, and intelligence. We intend these definitions to lead to a quantification of information science, a quantification that will enable their measurement, manipulation, and prediction.

2. DEFINITIONS

2.1. Data

A datum (d) is one phenomenon: a photon of light, a change in valance of a sodium molecule at a nerve cell receptor site, or a blow to the head. The datum's defining characteristic lies in its INDEPENDENCE FROM TIME, regardless of its duration. In other words, a datum might occupy a nanosecond or an hour, but that nanosecond or hour can exist at ANY point in time. Data (D), by this definition, equal more than one datum. Time dependence/independence will become clearer in the context of information, to follow.

2.2. Information

To become information, data must stand in dynamic interaction with a receiver and thus be time dependent. For example, photons must strike a retina at a given time to become information. The sodium molecule must change valance at a given time to become information. A blow to the head must occur at some specific time to become information—or even to exist. Borrowing from mathematics, let us express information (I), as the organization or summation over time (Σ) of data (D): $I = \Sigma D$. Psychologists call such information "stimulus," and communications authors use "signal," and neither can occur independently of a time context to be meaningful.

2.3. Knowledge

Continuing with this mathematical model, we define knowledge (K) as a second summation with respect to time of data: $K = \Sigma I = \Sigma\Sigma D$. Why?

Information may provoke a response (R). Indeed, according to physicists from Newton (Third Law of Motion) to Heisenberg (Principle of Indeterminacy), everything MUST provoke a response. Why, then, does some information not constitute knowledge? We postulate that the signal must exceed some situation-dependent threshold, usually by REPETITION. One nerve cell firing may provoke a response if sufficiently strong, whereas prolonged sets of firings evoke a BEHAVIOR (B), or pattern of responses over time. Noting that a response without reference to time constitutes data (D), we can express these concepts in a structure parallel to knowledge: Behavior = $B = \Sigma R = \Sigma\Sigma D$. The repetition of information OVER TIME creates summations of information that we call knowledge, and these summations evoke behaviors. This agrees with Bayesian decision theory, which codifies successive information inputs over time into something like a revised knowledge base of an organism. As did Heisenberg, we may measure effects (behavior) to infer magnitudes of causes (knowledge) when we cannot measure causes directly. Unfortunately, common usage blurs the distinction between behaviors and knowledge, e.g., "The rat now KNOWS which button to push." This paper, however, distinguishes causes (knowledge) from effects (behavior) and encourages the reader to do likewise.

2.4. Wisdom

If we define wisdom as an organization of knowledge over time that maximizes success (more on success, later), the mathematical model continues to apply. Wisdom becomes a third summation of data over time: $W = \Sigma K = \Sigma\Sigma I = \Sigma\Sigma\Sigma D$. Treating wisdom as more highly organized knowledge, we can define and perhaps manipulate it.

2.5. Inspiration

This paper proposes a definition of inspiration as wisdom viewed in the absence of evidence of its preceding knowledge. E.g.: When Newton "discovered" gravitation, he added information (the alleged falling apple) to his previous information (observations about gravitation) to produce what some people call inspiration. Our inability, however, to identify his precedent gravitational information does not make his inspiration more organized than wisdom. Thus, this paper treats inspiration as a form of wisdom. Inspiration strikes rapidly, or it might strike slowly, as if the brain must match large sets of information, knowledge, and wisdom, in the process of seeking connections. Thus, we might define inspiration as a further summation of wisdom over time (a fourth summation of data), but wisdom itself functions similarly, coming as flashes of insight or perhaps slowly, after cogitation. Again, inspiration resembles wisdom. To those who would treat wisdom and inspiration as spirituality, please remember that spirituality is an attribute that we assign to people based on their behavior. Therefore, this paper treats spirituality as an effect, rather than a cause.

2.6. Intelligence

Intelligence (N) falls outside the hierarchy of "causes" (information, knowledge, or wisdom), because intelligence is an observed behavior (an "effect") and not a stimulus (a "cause"). Following the mathematical model, we might define intelligence as: $N = \Sigma B = \Sigma\Sigma R = \Sigma\Sigma\Sigma D$.

3. CONUNDRUMS REDUCED

3.1. Locus

Can information (or knowledge) exist outside of a receiver? By this framework, data can (and do), but the others: I, K, W, R, B, and N, cannot. Do books contain information (or knowledge or wisdom)? No. Books (and their contents and their libraries) contain data until they strike a recipient at some point in time. Does DNA contain information (or knowledge or intelligence)? No. DNA contains data until it affects the synthesis of proteins at some point in time.

3.2. Signals and success

The planet between Mars and Jupiter did not coalesce, and we label it unsuccessful. Its pieces, the Asteroids, successfully exist as pieces. Many dinosaurs became extinct, and we brand them as unsuccessful. Cockroaches do exist, and we tend to say that they have been highly successful. "Success," for this paper, is no more and no less than continued existence. With one caveat (explained below), organisms that exist today exist because a significant number of their antecedents formed wisdom through the summation of knowledge born of information acceptance. Organisms extinct today did not. Therefore, signals (information, knowledge, and wisdom) can be measured indirectly by the continued existence of their receivers.

The caveat? "Spontaneous" change, as in species mutation, occurs from unknown causes. Once, humans explained lightning as Zeus speaking. In 1752, Ben Franklin demonstrated the electrical nature of lightning. Once, humans viewed mutation as an act of the gods. Now, some postulate causes such as cosmic radiation altering DNA. Such mutations create the exception mentioned above: organisms that exist today might exist also because they have not existed long enough to become extinct! The point, however, is this: everything in the universe (such as lightning and mutation) appears to be explainable, now or later, as our wisdom grows. Thus, inspiration (wisdom in the absence of preceding knowledge, or as a higher summation of wisdom) might emerge in a third manner: from a currently undetectable cosmic ray knocking aside a sodium electron to form inexplicable information that leads to wisdom.

4. SIGNIFICANCE

This paper attempts to augment contributions that reduce the vagueness of information science to units that we can measure, predict, and manipulate. First, physics postulates four basic dimensions to the universe: mass, distance, time, and electrical charge. Using the above framework, we can now define data in units of mass, distance, or electrical charge, and information, knowledge, and wisdom as summations of those data over time. Second, we can now define information in terms of the success of its receivers. They do or do not exist, and their relative numbers and longevity might be used to measure indirectly the information they and their ancestors received. One day, perhaps, someone with an aptitude for math will determine which, if either, of these methods best serves information science. Here, we have merely tried to show a possibly useful framework and systematic definitions for six common words.

Figure 1.

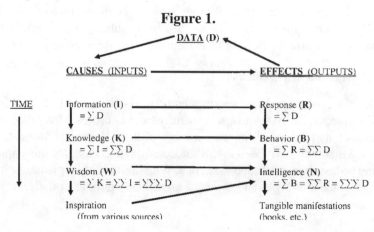

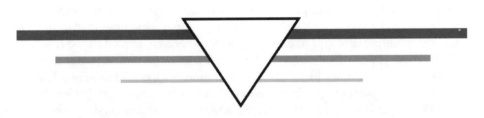

WebTAPIR—Scientific Information Retrieval on the World Wide Web

Erik Thorlund Jepsen, Piet Seiden, Lennart Björneborn,
Haakon Lund, and Peter Ingwersen
Royal School of Library and Information Science
Birketinget 6
2300 Copenhagen, Denmark
etj@db.dk; ps@db.dk; lb@db.dk; hl@db.dk; pi@db.dk

1. INTRODUCTION

The Internet and in particular the World Wide Web has had a significant impact on the dissemination of the results of scientific research (Cronin, and McKim, 1996). Freely accessible scientific material can be found scattered across the Web in a wide variety of document types, such as preprints, conference proceedings, technical reports, e-journals, as well as tutorials and presentations. Although such sources only account for a small fraction of all scientific publication activity, the information is becoming increasingly difficult to control, i.e., to find, identify, access and evaluate. The lack of control has also led to a perception of web based sources as low-quality information that, in many cases, leads to the exclusion of references to Web based scientific information.

In a study from 1999 (Lawrence, and Giles, 1999) it was estimated that only 6 and of randomly selected web sites contained scientific or educational content, here defined as hosted on university, college and research lab servers but excluding sites in other domains. It is an open question whether content of scientific nature should solely be sought in the domains directly associated with research institutions and higher education, as the Web endows the individual with a potential to become her or his own publisher, as commented on by Björneborn and Ingwersen (2001). The ease of producing publications, combined with the absence of centralized quality control, potentially leads to a very low precision, as a topic may be discussed in a great number of contexts often not relevant for a particular query. Furthermore, there is a greater potential for obtaining inaccurate or misleading information on scientific subject matter as indicated by the results of Allen, et al. (1999). In their study based on a sample of web pages retrieved through simple searches using the search engine Northern Light, the reliability of information on three popular biological subjects, "Evolution," "Genetically modified organism," and "Endangered species," was estimated by expert reviewers. They found that only 12–46 percent of sites were considered informative and among these 10–34 percent were judged "inaccurate" (containing factually incorrect information), 20–35 percent were judged "misleading" (misinterpreting science or blatantly omitting facts supporting an opposing position), and more than 48 percent sites for each category were unreferenced (without any peer reviewed references). This distribution illustrates the problem faced by students and scientists, as well as the general user, wishing to obtain qualified scientific information through the Web.

One way to alleviate this problem could be through the development of filters or similar tools to aid in the discrimination process. WebTAPIR (Web based Text Access Potentials for interactive Information Retrieval) is a project aimed at developing filtering and ranking methods in order to enable users to discriminate between web resources containing scientifically relevant content versus other content that fails to live up to the quality criteria employed in the discrimination process. In the development and testing of filtering, ranking and linking algorithms special attention will be given to the utilization of poly-representations and "cognitive retrieval overlaps" (Ingwersen, 1992; 1996). Web sources themselves contain representations of different types (e.g., title, metadata, references, out-links as well as the text, e.g., paragraphs, images, graphs and bulleted lists). Further representations can be obtained from other sources—with different cognitive authority, origin and contexts, e.g., databases, search engines and servers as well as sources producing in-links or citations to the item at hand. The idea of poly-representation or multi-evidence is that the more cognitively or typologically different the representations (evidence) that point to an information object, the higher the probability that the object is relevant to the topic, the information need, the work task/interest situation at hand, or the socio-cognitive environment—as perceived by the information seeker (Ingwersen, 1996).

To bootstrap the filter development process, a set of criteria that fits the purpose of the filtering process must be established. To this aim we have performed a partial survey of a scientific domain, Plant Biology, where domain expertise was readily at hand for evaluating the located resources (web pages). Within the domain, three different topics were chosen in order to retrieve pages ranging from a popular topic expected to occur in many types of publications (photosynthesis), a controversial subject often debated in the news media (herbicide resistance), and a highly specialized topic expected to occur mainly in scientific publications (plant hormones). From these topics, a rough estimate of the variability in the content could be established, thereby providing necessary information for the establishment of a design goal for the filter development process reported in the poster. To achieve this, three popular search engines (Altavista, Alltheweb, and Google) were queried. The accessible URLs from the search outcome were analysed according to attributes such as language, search engine overlap, file formats and search engine indexing level. In the spring of 2002 a panel of domain experts (plant biologists) will perform a structured quality analysis of a sample of the retrieved sites. The resulting quality ratings will be compared to the indices examined and to the presence of isolable attributes like citations, references in context, structured metadata, links and statements of responsibility, and incorporated in the poster results. A further development for 2002 is to construct a web test collection to be used in filter development and studies of interactive information retrieval.

2. RESULTS

For each of the three topics a domain expert (plant biologist) and various subject lists and vocabularies, English as well as Nordic (Danish, Swedish and Norwegian), were consulted, in order to broaden the search statements with relevant synonyms, quasi synonyms and spelling variations. The searches were performed in the period November 14–December 19, 2001 as simple searches. Precision could probably have been improved in each of the three search engines, but in order to compare the results and to retrieve as many pages as possible, the more advanced search facilities like spelling control mechanisms, language matching as well as exact match and truncation facilities offered by each host (see Sullivan [2001] for a thorough list) were not used. The search engine cut-offs of accessible URLs (Altavista = 200, Alltheweb = 4100, Google < 1000), prompted us to search for each term individually (including synonyms and spelling variations). Possible problems arising from default control of spelling variations or stemming were neglected, since a later removal of duplicates eliminated this problem.

In the light of the limited outcome of the Nordic searches, the strategy appears to be well chosen. The search results showed that the Nordic (lingual) dimension seems to be negligible, as the popular subject "photosynthesis" only yielded 2.3–3.8 percent hits in the Nordic searches, as compared to the yields from the English searches, depending on the employed search engine. "Herbicide resistance" showed even fewer Nordic hits, 0.5–0.9 percent, and "plant hormones," not surprisingly, was 0.1 percent in two of the search engines, but had a Nordic score of 2.0 percent in Alltheweb.

Search engines rank and prioritize web resources according to proprietary algorithms. As we only have access to the highest ranked pages, with many pages inaccessible due to the cut-off mentioned above, a sample gathered in this manner can only be considered representative of the users' experience of the Internet, as search engines inarguably are one of the primary access roads to the Web. However, an analysis of the overlap between the accessible URLs returned by the three different search engines showed a high degree of complementarity, as the search engine yielding the lowest number of unique URLs, Altavista, still yielded 42 percent unique URLs in the worst case. In order to gauge whether the search engines used different harvesting strategies, the indexing depth was analyzed, but found to be similar across engines.

To gain a perspective on the prevalent document types within the domain, the results returned by Google, which indexes all major document types found on the net, were analyzed. Even though HTML was the most important format by far, PDF should not be ignored as it constituted 7.7 percent of the retrievable URLs in the English searches and 18.6 percent in the Nordic searches. Other document types were not found to be of significant occurrence. There was no discernible difference between the three topics on this matter, leading to the tentative conclusion that this could be expected for the domain as a whole.

3. CONCLUSION

These preliminary investigations have provided a starting point for the development of filtering methods. The search engines utilized only returned the highest ranking fraction of the found URLs and could thus only be used as tools for generating a skewed sample of the documents expected to reside on web servers. But by analyzing a subset of the retrieved URLs, a basis for preparing filtering methods has been established, which then can be further tested to improve relevance in information retrieval of scientific information on the World Wide Web.

REFERENCES

Allen, E., J. Burke, M. Welch, and L. Rieseberg. (1999) How reliable is science information on the Web? *Nature, 402,* 722.

Björneborn, L., and P. Ingwersen. (2001) Perspectives of webometrics. *Scientometrics, 50*(1), 65–82.

Cronin, B., and G. McKim. (1996) Science and scholarship on the World Wide Web: A North American perspective. *Journal of Documentation, 52,* 163–72.

Ingwersen, P. (1992) *Information retrieval interaction.* London: Taylor Graham.

Ingwersen, P. (1996) Cognitive perspectives of information retrieval interaction: elements of a cognitive IR theory. *Journal of Documentation, 52,* 3–50.

Lawrence, S., and C. Giles. (1999) Accessibility and distribution of information on the Web. *Nature, 400,* 107–10.

Sullivan, D., ed. (2001) Search Engine Features for Searchers. Retrieved October 26, 2001 from *http://searchenginewatch.com/facts/ataglance.html*

Information Behavior of the Informal Sector Entrepreneurs: A Ugandan Context

Dennis N. Ocholla
Department of Library and Information Science
University of Zululand
KwaDlangezwa 3886, South Africa
docholla@pan.uzulu.ac.za

Robert Ikoja-Odongo
East African School of Library and Information Science
Makarere University
P.O.Box 7062
Kampala, Uganda
robert_ikoja@yahoo.com

1. INTRODUCTION

The purpose of this study was to determine the information needs and uses of the informal sector in Uganda (Ikoja-Odongo, 2001; 2002). The theoretical framework is based on related international studies concerning literature and theory in the field of information behavior-seeking, retrieval and provision (e.g., Belkin, et al., 1982; Dervin, 1995, 1999; Dervin, and Nilan, 1986; Ingwersen, 1986, 1992, 2000; Marchionini, 1992; Wilson, 1981, 1994, 1997, 1999; Xie,

2000). Similar studies were completed in other parts of Africa as well (e.g., Kaniki, 1991, 1995; Mchombu, 1982; Mchombu, 2000; Ocholla, 1998, 1999; etc.).

2. METHODOLOGY

The qualitative design (see Neuman, 2000) of the study was generally based on the historical, survey—utilizing critical incident interviews (see Flanagan, 1954; Fisher, and Oulton, 1999; Allen in Hewins, 1990) and unobtrusive observation methods and techniques. The survey population representing the national population sample involving purposive or judgmental sampling techniques as well as proportionate and disproportionate stratified sampling were drawn from six Ugandan districts and consisted of 602 entrepreneurs, 23 organization representatives, and 35 informants in the informal sector. Basically, three instruments were used, namely interview schedules, observation where incidences were recorded in a self- observation guide consisting of five sections on characteristics of informal businesses, management system in the informal enterprises, relationship between the informal sector and the society, communication methods in the work environment and finally problems in the workplace (utilizing voice recording and photography) as well as analysis and review of recorded sources. The data collected were analyzed by using largely qualitative methods.

3. RESULTS

The findings show that the informal sector in Uganda, which has ancient economic roots, is served by diversified information systems and services comprising both an informal, indigenous Afrocentric component as well as a modern, Eurocentric formal element. The system employs both adults and children who, generally, earn low wages from the business activities. While entrepreneurs largely have only a basic education, well-educated people such as the university graduates also serve the system. Working hours are flexible and depend on the type of activity. Involvement in the sector is basically motivated by personal survival, possibilities for obtaining training, availability of markets for products and services and the acquisition of specific skills. The sector offers over 800,000 jobs and employs 1.5 million people in rural as well as urban areas—yet there is little division of labour and organisation of production. While most of the businesses are unregistered, record keeping is prevalent. Personal capital is mostly relied on for starting up businesses. Products tend to be inferior and there is limited evidence to suggest that cultural beliefs have any influence on the sector's activities or performance.

Information needs within the sector are determined contextually and pragmatically. Information is generally required with regard to training and skills, markets and marketing techniques, cheaper sources of raw materials/supplies, finance, tools and equipment, business management and development, knowledge of production processes, advocacy and lobbying skills, new areas of investment, record keeping, quality improvement and recognition by government. Inquiries concerning the establishment of an information center indicated the need for more comprehensive, permanent sources of information. Information-seeking is largely an informal activity, while instances of reading and the use of libraries for accessing information are almost non existent due to illiteracy, very few or no libraries, irrelevant content, inaccessibility due to form of information presentation, lack of infrastructure and a poor reading culture among this community. There is no evidence that radio, considered to be popular among the entrepreneurs, is maximised for information accessibility. This is partly due to poor timing of broadcasts, the high costs of maintenance, traditions dictating who should access broadcasts and irrelevant content for entrepreneurs.

Information is used in marketing, locating raw materials/supplies, pricing of products and services, improvement of skills, decision-making, enlightening oneself, promoting self-reliance, familiarizing oneself with current affairs (including government regulations), and dealing with and relating to other people. The impact of information usage is judged by business improvement, co-ordination of workers and activities, upgrading of skills, improved opportunities and living standards, and increased sales and profits, among other things.

Factors that negatively impact accessibility of information from an entrepreneur's point of view include: the inability to obtain the required information, lack of a specific location where information can be obtained, cost of information, the length of time taken to acquire the required information, lack of marketing and promotion of information products and services to the entrepreneur, apathy to information, language barriers and illiteracy. While the few available public libraries are irrelevant to this market segment, the existing information services provided by the government and non-governmental organizations and associations are underutilized. This is largely due to poor infrastructure, including the telephone system throughout the country, poor timing of broadcasting programs on radio, low priority given to information in budgets, the publication of newspapers in only a few local languages and poor marketing of information services.

4. CONCLUSION

It is observed that information could be supplied more effectively to the informal sector if illiteracy could be reduced significantly or if it could be eliminated entirely. This could be achieved through increased basic and adult education activities and programs by means of re- packaging information. Creating and supporting special units within and outside the governmental domain to tackle the task could facilitate such a goal. Radio broadcasts could be reviewed for effectiveness, while the role of the public library in society could be re-defined. This, in turn, would call for increased research by the various trades into the specific types of information needed by the entrepreneurs and by wide dissemination of the results. Government should be urged to establish an information center and to provide an effective service for entrepreneurs. Suggestions on how this can be achieved at both the policy level and the system and services level could be based on a theoretical model. For example, it is suggested that by intensifying the publication of information in other local languages, channels of information dissemination could be increased. In addition, it is suggested that Government should work hand in hand with the private sector and NGOs to build capacity for provision of information services to the informal sector. The popularity of oral-based information services that are also easily available and accessible to the entrepreneur is not unique to this information consumer category alone. Modern push-and-pull technology increasingly favors and exploits close proximity in the environment for the delivery of audio-visual information products and services. This trend also needs to be exploited to the advantage of the informal sector entrepreneur. It is furthermore suggested that it would perhaps be worthwhile to explore the role that indigenous knowledge systems could play in order to enhance information diffusion among the informal sector entrepreneurs. The main paper consists of 9,000 words and several tables, charts and photographs.

REFERENCES

Belkin, N., R. Oddy, and H. Brooks. (1982) ASK for information retrieval: Pt1: Background theory. *Journal of Documentation, 38*, 61–71.

Dervin, B., and M. Nilan. (1986) Information needs and users. *Annual Review of Information Science and Technology, 21*, 3–33.

Dervin, B. (1995) Chaos, order, and sense making: A proposed theory for information design. Retrieved April 24, 2002 from http:edfu.lis.uiuc.edu./allerton/95/s5/dervin.draft.html.

Dervin, B. (1999) Sense-making's theory of dialogue: a brief introduction. Retrieved September 2, 2000 from http://communication.sbs.ohio-state.edu/sense-making/meet/m99Aicadervessay.html

Fisher, S., and T. Oulton. (1999) The critical incident technique in library and information management research. *Education for Information, 17*, 113.

Flanagan, J. (1954) The critical incident technique. *Psychological Bulletin, 51*, 327–58.

Hewins, E. (1990) Information needs and use studies. *ARIST, 25*, 145–72.

Ingwersen, P. (1992) *Information retrieval interaction*. London: Taylor Graham.

Ingwersen, P. (2000) The cognitive information structures in information retrieval. In Irene Wormel, ed. ProLISSA.DIS (pp. 205–19). Pretoria.

Kaniki, A. M. (1991) Information seeking and information providers among Zambian farmers. *Libri, 41*, 147–69.

Kaniki, A. (1995) Exploratory study of information needs in the Kwa-Ngwanase (Natal) and Qumbu (Transkei) communities of South Africa. *South African Journal of Library & Information Science, 63*(1), 9–18.

Marchionini, G. (1992) Interfaces for end-user information seeking. *Journal of American Society of Information Science. JASIS 43*, 156–63.

Mchombu, C. (2000) Information needs of women in small businesses in Botswana *International Information & Library Review, 32*, 39–67.

Mchombu, K. (1982) On the librarianship of poverty. *Libri, 32*, 241–50.

Neuman, L. W. (2000) *Social research methods: qualitative and quantitative approaches.* 4th ed. Boston: Allyn & Bacon.

Ocholla, D. (1998) Information consultancy and brokerage in Botswana. *Journal of Information Science, 24*, 83–95.

Ocholla, D. (1999) Insights into information-seeking and communicating behavior of academics. *International Information & Library Review, 31*, 119–43.

Odongo, I. (2001) A study of the information needs and uses of the informal sector in Uganda. Preliminary Findings. *LIBRES: Library and Information Science Research Electronic Journal, 11*(1). Retrieved April 30, 2001 from http://aztec.lib.utk.edu/libres11n1/Ocholla.htm

Odongo, I. (2002) *A study of the information needs and uses of the informal sector of Uganda.* University of Zululand, South Africa (unpublished Ph.D. thesis)

Wilson, T. (1981) On user studies and information needs. *Journal of Documentation. 37*, 3–15.

Wilson, T. (1994) Information needs and uses fifty years of progress? In V. Vickery, ed. *Fifty years of information progress: Journal of Documentation review.* London: Aslib.

Wilson, T. (1997) Information behavior: An interdisciplinary perspective. *Information Processing & Management, 33*(4), 551–72.

Wilson, T. (1999) Models in information behavior research. *Journal of Documentation, 55*, 249–70.

Xie, H. (2000) Shifts of interactive intentions and information-seeking strategies in interactive information retrieval. *Journal of the American Society for information Science, 51*, 841–57.

Human Information Behavior Research Clearinghouse: Interaction Framework for a New Digital Library

Linda Schamber
School of Library and Information Sciences
University of North Texas
Denton, TX 76203, USA
schamber@unt.edu

1. INTRODUCTION

The Human Information Behavior Research Clearinghouse (HIBRC) is a startup project for a Web-based digital library that will serve academic and professional researchers and learners with interests in information behavior. Its mission is to promote and facilitate research in an open and collaborative environment.

Human information behavior covers processes of seeking, evaluating, and using information that are relevant to all user-centered information resources, services, and systems. Yet information science lacks public resources such as data archives that are common for other social sciences (e.g., sociology, education, psychology, economics) and many government agencies.

HIBRC's goals are geared toward research, education, and communication:

1. To facilitate primary and secondary studies by providing archives of data, instruments, and related literature.

2. To increase knowledge and skills of new researchers by providing bibliographies and texts on research studies and methods.

3. To strengthen and build the research community by providing communication channels for discussion, news, and email.

2. INTERACTIONS

Resources are both deposited and accessed by researchers. Communication channels offer a forum for discussion among researchers and students:

Figure 1. HIBRC.

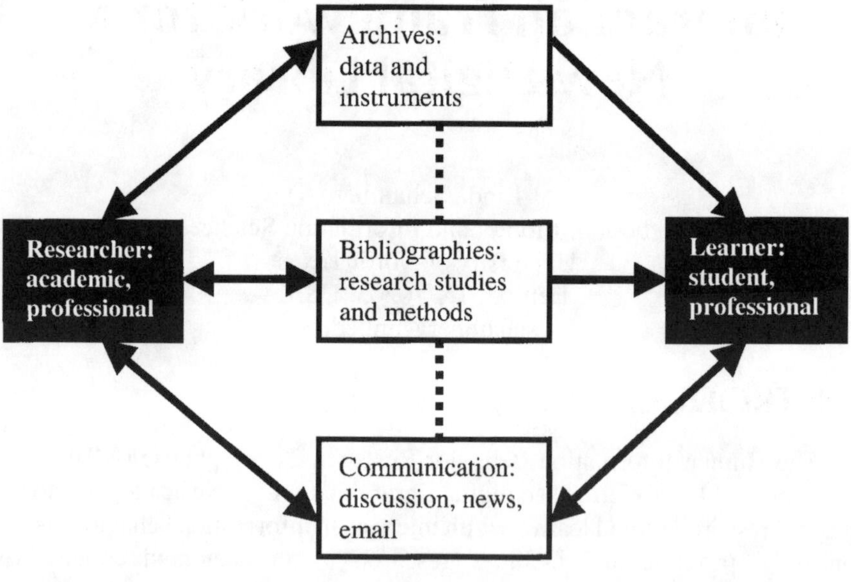

3. RESEARCH

Participants can . . .

• Understand and build on previous research

• Access data for secondary studies and meta-analyses

• Adopt or adapt data-collection instruments

• Find sources for literature reviews

Potential impacts are . . .

- Open environment for data sharing
- More efficient use and reuse of large data sets
- Establishment of baselines for longitudinal and evaluation studies
- Summaries and meta-analyses that help set research agendas
- Adoption of successful instruments
- Standardization of major types of instruments
- Potential increase in quality and comparability of results
- Growing body of literature with associated data sets
- Increased citations and credibility for authors

4. EDUCATION

Participants can . . .

- Learn how to conduct research
- Practice data collection and analysis
- Evaluate data and instrument quality
- Learn how to write proposals and reports
- Find deadlines for scholarships, awards, workshops, jobs
- (Faculty) prepare reading lists, course content, and assignments

Potential impacts are . . .

- Source of material for theses and other projects
- Graduates and professionals with enhanced research knowledge and skills
- Recruitment of students to information behavior research
- Exposure for students and grads who win awards and contribute content

5. COMMUNICATION

Participants can . . .

- Get general research news: recent projects, grants, awards
- Find deadlines for RFPs, CFPs, awards
- Link to scholarly and professional associations

- Exchange ideas, ask questions, and debate issues
- Send feedback and suggestions for HIBRC development

Potential impacts are . . .

- Stronger community of researchers across institutions and disciplines
- Growing community that attracts and supports new researchers
- Visibility and expansion of research area with hot topics and research ideas
- Participation of scholarly and professional associations

6. HOW CAN YOU PARTICIPATE?

Visit our demonstration site at www.hibrc.org.
Subscribe to our discussion list.
Tell us . . .

- What kinds of studies and data you would like to access or contribute
- What topics and issues you would like to discuss (e.g., methodology, metadata, interoperability)

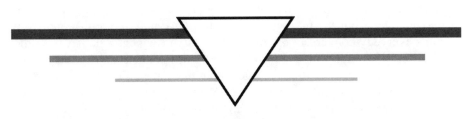

A Communication Perspective on Meta-Search Engine Query Structure: A Pilot Study

Edward V. Springer III and Rong Tang
School of Information Science and Policy
University at Albany, SUNY
Albany, NY 12222, USA
rus.springer@att.net; tangr@albany.edu

1. INTRODUCTION

The rapidly increasing quantity of documents on the World Wide Web often leaves a searcher in a quandary between a fear of missing some valuable sites and the tediousness of submitting queries to multiple search engines. This quandary has led to the development of meta-search engine technologies that allow the user to easily submit a single query to multiple individual search engines simultaneously. Query formulation is a key to successful use of the technology.

1.1. Search engine query log studies

Two research projects analyzing large corpuses of data from the query logs of Excite (Jansen, et al., 2000b; Jansen, et al., 2000a) and AltaVista (Silverstein, et al., 1999) showed special characteristics for the language structure used in queries. In general, users showed a strong preference to ignore system language conventions in favor of simple natural language queries. Most often the queries submitted to both systems consisted of only one word or a brief phrase and frequently these queries failed to conform to English syntax. As a result, Jansen, et al. (2000a) concluded that users are "abandoning the way they think and communicate in English in order to communicate with the computer" (p. 174). That may be true if one's expectation for the way people communicate is a formal, written document but the divergence from formal syntax is no different from people's everyday conversational messages, which frequently depart from the expectations of formal language use. If we look for alternative principles of query composition beyond the syntactical grammars that guide the construction of words into sentences in formal documents, we may find additional principles of query formulation that allow wider explanations of query structures.

1.2. A communication perspective

Communication involves more than the selection of a sentence structure from among choices of syntactic categories. Language is a resource that people use strategically in communication and the meanings of messages are to be found in the strategies by which messages are structured in order to achieve desired ends. In that light, Jacobs (1985) elaborated how discourse analysts are turning from a "normative code" view of language use to an "inferential/strategic" or rational model. Within a rational model, it is the connections between communicative plans, message structures and contextual background knowledge that give utterances meaning and coherence, rather than the rigid application of a normative code of language grammar. Thus, deviations from syntactic language conventions could still be meaningful and coherent if they are seen as rational means towards speaker goals. Extending a rational model of communication to query formulation, a query is strategic action as a part of information seeking. Could it be that World Wide Web search engine queries, like conversational utterances, often deviate from standard conventions of an information retrieval (IR) system or from a formal natural language because they are not organized solely by normative codes of the language's syntax? Our task, in attempting to better understand queries as communication, was to consider the communicative goals and strategies that query structures serve. Beyond syntax, we addressed the pragmatics of query formulation.

2. METHODOLOGY

In order to inductively develop a coding scheme grounded in the observed characteristics of the data, a pilot study was conducted to address the following research questions:

1. Do queries of users of meta-search engines reflect broad characteristics similar to the queries of individual search engine users?

2. Viewing queries as examples of human discourse, what are the basic structural components and recognizable patterns of organization that make up a query?

3. As a form of communication, what are the communicative functions resulting from structurally relating components in a query?

Out of a sample of 2,000 queries submitted to the meta-search engine Search.com, pilot data of 500 queries were analyzed in order to derive a category scheme that described the structure of the queries, both reflecting the lexical structure as identified by Jansen, et al. (2000a) and keeping in mind the pragmatic functions that the structures may serve.

3. RESULTS

The overall results of the data coding are shown in the following table:

Table 1.

Type of Query		Frequency (N=500)	Proportion of Language Type	Proportion of Total
System Convention	Exact Wording	55	78.57 %	11.00 %
	Boolean Operators	8	11.43 %	1.60 %
	Enforced Terms	5	7.14 %	1.00 %
	Combination of Conventions	2	2.86 %	0.40 %
Natural Language	Basic Structural Unit	158	36.83 %	31.60 %
	Single Modified Structural Unit	130	30.30 %	26.00 %
	Multiple Modified Structural Unit	133	31.00 %	26.60 %
	Complex Structural Unit – dependent clause	2	0.47 %	0.40 %
	Complex Structural Unit – independent sentence	6	1.40 %	1.20 %
	Indecipherable	1	N/A	0.20

Queries were first differentiated by language conventions. For those queries using the system conventions, the main distinctions were among the specific convention used. On the surface, the natural language queries showed general structural characteristics of a single term, multiple terms in phrase structure, and multiple terms in clause structure. Closer inspection of the natural language queries revealed a functional relationship between elements of the linguistic structure: single term queries consisted of a single core term by itself and multiple term queries consisted of the core term with added modifiers arranged syntactically into phrase or clause structures. Any queries with an unrecognizable structure were coded as indecipherable.

Much like users of individual search engines, meta-search engine users preferred using single term (31.6%) or short phrase (52.6%), natural language queries. The general pattern of structural organization revealed that the overwhelming majority of queries (84.2%) were formulated in a natural language as either single core terms by themselves or a core term extended by adding one or more modifier terms. This suggests that users most often combine functionally interrelated terms into an unelaborated or elaborated whole around the core term; they are not merely organizing terms as proper syntactical phrases or as strings of individual terms best connected with Boolean operators.

4. DISCUSSION

As part of information seeking on the World Wide Web, the use of natural language queries transforms the situation into something more similar to human-human conversations that are made meaningful and coherent based partially on informal conventions of strategic language use. The most frequently recurring pattern of query structure observed (that is, single or modified core terms using natural language conventions) makes for the most efficient means of specifying a request for relevant documents. Natural language provides users with a familiar and easy mode of expression and structuring queries by adding modifiers to a core term enables them to specify greater precision without having to resort to the cumbersome conventions of the system. In order for such a strategy to be most effective, the system needs to be able to make inferences about meanings from variations in the structure of the query, inferences that any other language user would routinely make from variations in utterance structure in person-to-person conversations. The degree to which IR system designers are successful in facilitating the pragmatics of users' language preferences in query formulation will help determine how useful and accessible the World Wide Web will be as an effective information retrieval system.

REFERENCES

Jacobs, S. (1985) Language. In M. L. Knapp, and G. R. Miller, eds. *Handbook of interpersonal communication*, (pp. 313–43). Beverly Hills, CA: Sage.

Jansen, B. J., A. Spink, and M. A. Pfaff. (2000a) Linguistic aspects of web queries. *Proceedings of the 63rd Annual Meeting the American Society for Information Science and Technology*, 37, 169–76.

Jansen, B. J., A. Spink, and T. Saracevic. (2000b) Real life, real users, and real needs: study and analysis of user queries on the Web. *Information Processing and Management, 36*, 207–77.

Silverstein, C. M., M. Henzinger, H. Marais, and M. Moricz. (1999) Analysis of a very large web search engine query log. *ACM SIGIR Forum*, 33(1), 6–12.

Bibliometric Analysis of Indexing and Abstracting Literature, 1977–2000

Ming-yueh Tsay and Hui-min Yu
Department of Information and Library Science
Tamkang University
Tamsui, Taiwan, 251 R.O.C.
tsay@mail.tku.edu.tw

1. INTRODUCTION

Indexing and abstracting have become popular topics during recent decades, especially the focus on automatic and computer-aided indexing and abstracting. The early literature of indexing and abstracting through 1976 was well analyzed in a study based on the first volume of Wellisch's bibliography (ABC-Clio, 1980) and published in *Indexer* by Tsay (1989). Modern information retrieval systems depend heavily on various indexing and abstracting methods. Thus it may be anticipated that literature dealing with this subject will be very abundant and that interesting phenomena can be observed through a bibliometric study. This motivates the present study, which explores some bibliometric phenomena of the literature of indexing and abstracting from 1977 to 2000. Using the computer as a tool and employing the bibliometric techniques, the present study intends to accomplish the following objectives: 1. to explore the growth pattern of indexing and abstracting literature; 2. to determine a nucleus of primary journals that contains a substantial proportion of the totality of journal literature in indexing and abstracting and to investigate the features of these core journals; 3. to find the productivity distribution of authors in indexing and abstracting and to identify the most productive authors and their characteristics. It is expected that this information will provide useful insights into the nature and scope of the field of indexing and abstracting in 1977–2000.

2. METHODOLOGY

In this study, Library and Information Science Abstracts (LISA), produced by Cambridge Scientific Abstracts from British Library Association, was used to retrieve data from 1977 to 2000. The search terms, include indexing, abstracting, index language, concordance, thesauri or thesaurus, were limited to the descriptor field by truncation search. The descriptor field utilizes controlled vocabulary from the thesaurus or subject headings that are produced by the database producer. Therefore, the search indexing?. de or abstracting?. de would retrieve items with indexing or abstracting as their synonyms, near synonyms, homographs and related terms, such as indexing evaluation, index types, subject indexing, computerized subject indexing, etc. LISA tends to include broad descriptive terms in its indexing; hence the strategy used in this study would be expected to retrieve most of the papers on indexing and abstracting, excluding names of indexing and abstracting services, such as Chemical Abstracts or Biological and Agricultural Index. Each relevant record that was retrieved from LISA was then downloaded to compact disk, analyzed and processed by Access database software, Excel and Perl scripting language. Some careful verification and editing of data were executed.

3. RESULTS AND DISCUSSION

3.1. Literature Growth

The present study retrieved 15,842 items on indexing and abstracting from 1977 to October 2000 from LISA. The growth of indexing and abstracting literature is shown in Figure 1 with three fitting curves, namely, linear, exponential and logistic fitting. The literature grew rapidly from 1977 to 1990 and approached the asymptotic value after 1990. Obviously, the linear regression does not fit the literature growth well except for the years immediately after 1977. The exponential fitting cannot account for the literature growth in indexing and abstracting at all. This shows that the literature growth in indexing and abstracting cannot sustain a constant growth rate. On the other hand, the logistic fitting can explain the literature growth in indexing and abstracting very well. The logistic fitting curve is $P=16000/\{1+18.534\exp[-0.3319(t-1977)]\}$. The point of inflection of the logistic curve is $\ln(18.534)/0.3319$, i.e., 8.8 years after 1977. This suggests that the literature in indexing and abstracting grew exponentially until approximately 1986 and the growth rate slowed down after 1986. Indeed, the data suggests that the literature in indexing and abstracting leveled off and approached the asymptotic value after 1991. A dramatic drop occurred between 1991 and 1993. It could be that LISA changed its use of descriptors at that time. However, further study is needed.

Figure 1. Literature growth and linear, exponential and logistic fitting.

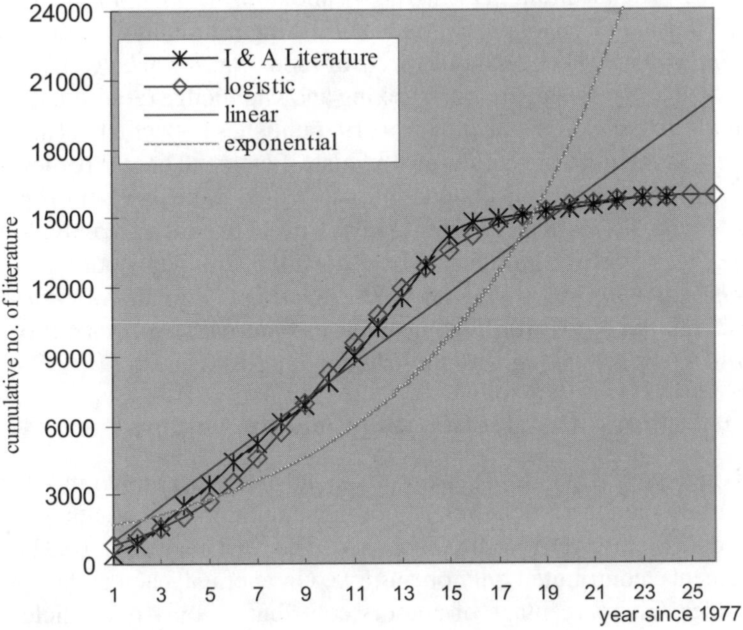

3.2. Bradford-Zipf's Plot and Core Journals

The journal distribution of the indexing and abstracting literature was fit to the Bradford's law by plotting the cumulative number of papers for each journal versus the logarithm of its rank. The plot obtained in this study is closer to the typical Bradford plot that has a characteristic smooth S-shaped curve, with the final droop portion lying below the linear portion of the curve. The curve rises gradually and nonlinearly for the first top twenty journals but then goes through a linear portion. These top 20 journals may be considered as the core journals in indexing and abstracting literature. The core (top 20 journals) contained 5,043 papers (40 percent of the journal articles). The subject scope of the 20 core journals has been drawn from *Magazines for Libraries, 2000, Ulrich's International Periodical Directory, 2001* and Web page of the journal. Sixteen out of twenty core journals were published in the USA or UK in 1977–2000. Most of them emphasize the coverage of the subject of indexing and abstracting in the area of information retrieval, information processing, organization of knowledge, information systems and services, information management and bibliographic control. *Online* (no.2), *Econtent* (no.3) and *Online Information Review* (no.7) are selected by McCarthy (2000) as the most important journals of electronic and online resources in libraries. In addition to *Online* and *Econtent*, two more journals that emphasize the subject of online databases, electronic information products, CDROM, electronic content and multimedia systems and services are *CDROM Professional* (no.9) and *Multimedia World* (no.10). As indicated by McCarthy, three major information science journals are *JASIST* (no.5), *Information Processing and Management* (no.4) and *Journal of Information Science* (no.13). They are all scholarly journals publishing information science research papers. *Indexer* (no.8) covers all aspects of indexing. *Knowledge Organization* (no.12), devoted to classification, indexing and knowledge representation. *Cataloging and Classification Quarterly* (no.19) publishes both practical and theoretical papers in the field of cataloging and classification. These three journals are devoted entirely to the subject. One journal related to medical information services is *Medical Reference Services Quarterly* (no.16). Significantly, four of the core are non-English journals. They are: the Russian journal, *Nauchno Tekhnicheskaya Informatsiya,* (no.1); the German journal, *Nfd Information: Wissenschaft und Praxis* (no.11); the Japanese journal *Joho Kanri* (no.17); and *Informatika* (no.20), which was published in Yugoslavia.

3.3. Authors' Distribution and Leading Authors

Giving every author of a paper one credit to measure author productivity, a total of 13,864 authors, including senior personal authors, co-authors, and corporate bodies, were retrieved from LISA. The vast majority, 10,311 authors (74.5 percent), contributed only one article. On average, each author published 1.65 articles. The percentage of authors contributing only one article is much larger than that of the original Lotka's data of 60 percent. This indicates that authors contributing to the subject are dispersed widely. Willett, the first leading author in the field of indexing and abstracting, published 70 items in 15 years (from 1977 to 1994). Tenopir, the second leading author, contributed 60 items in 21 years. O'jala, the third most productive author, produced 56 articles in ten years; among them 55 were journal papers which he published by himself. Hawkins, the most active author, kept working on indexing and abstracting, from 1977 to 2000, and his total number of publications came to 54. Snow began his research very late in 1984 and stopped in 1992. He became very active and contributed 46 articles within a short time interval, i.e., 9 years. VanCamp and Desmarais published their articles, 35 and 31 respectively, all in the form of journal papers. Williams was the most active author engaged in presenting works at conferences, especially the National Online Meetings. The articles published in proceedings constitute about 70 percent (27 out of 40) of her all publications. Robertson is the author who published 10 books, pamphlets or book chapters. Most of these leading authors were either the single author or the leading author, except Willett and Lynch. Most of their works are co-authored. By examining the descriptor field of each record of LISA, it can be found that information storage and retrieval, information work, subject indexing, computerized information storage and retrieval, computerized subject indexing, searching, technical services, online information retrieval, databases, information services, full-text and natural language information retrieval, evaluation and specialized subject search and information services are key concepts presented by the most productive authors.

** This study was supported by the National Science Council of Taiwan, Republic of China.

REFERENCES

McCarthy, C. (2000) Journals of the century in library and information science. *The Serial Librarian*, *39*(2), 131–32.

Tsay, M. Y. (1989) A bibliometric study of indexing and abstracting, 1876–1976. *Indexer*, *16*(4), 234–39.

Aspects of Learning in the Business Information Culture: A Qualitative Study of Finnish Insurance Businesses

Gunilla Widén-Wulff
Department of Information Studies
Åbo Akademi
Domkyrkotorget 3
20500 Åbo Finland

1. INTRODUCTION

This poster paper is based on my doctoral dissertation and focuses on the learning aspects in the business information culture (Widén-Wulff, 2001). The dissertation is a study of the information culture and how information is used throughout the organisation. Questions of interest are how does information become a resource in the organisation, and how is the knowledge base built up? The information culture is a hidden resource and can be highlighted from different angles. In this study the learning ability is considered as an important base for effective information and knowledge use in a company.

2. MATERIAL AND METHODS

The material for the study was gathered during the spring of 1998 and consists of 40 in-depth interviews in fifteen Finnish insurance businesses. The overall aim was to study the information culture in these companies. The information culture is seen as a phenomenon that is studied in a business organisational context. The insurance business was selected because the insurance companies are information intensive in their activities, and knowledge management is very important. In order to make the big qualitative material manageable the companies were divided into groups according to their internal environments. The dimension open vs. closed organisation milieu was chosen as the starting point in the analysis, because the information aspects are best seen in this dimension of organisation study (e.g., Correia, and Wilson, 1997; Dewhirst, 1971; Hofstede, 1991; Muchinsky, 1977; Samuels, and McClure, 1983). The internal environments were measured through aspects on network thinking and ability to change which resulted in three groups of internal environments: closed internal environments (3); open internal environments (4); and one group with elements of both open and closed environments (8). In this presentation the companies with open environments will be described because the learning aspects are best developed in these organisations.

3. THE PERSPECTIVE OF THE LEARNING ORGANISATION

The learning organisation consists of factors that build up a system in which the individual learning, in order to become effective, is anchored in the whole organisational activity. The learning organisation is constructed from the human and the intellectual capital in the organisations. The commitment to innovation, creativity, motivation, and learning are measures of the human capital and the intellectual capital is described by the core competencies, co-operation, and knowledge creation in the organisations. These activities need support from many levels in the organisation. The support by the management is especially important, but the creation of common strategies, values and getting the personnel's interest for these processes are also underlined in the theoretical framework (Andreau, and Ciborra, 1996; Nicholson, 1990). It is important that these components create the common base for the organisation. This is considered the starting point for effective information and knowledge use in a business company (Koenig, 1998; Nonaka, and Takeuchi, 1995).

3.1. The human capital

This study shows that those companies with a strong emphasis on human capital have created a good platform for active information communication. The role of the information is best communicated through teamwork, where the processes are systematically implemented. Creativity is a very strong component and there are official channels for creativity. Besides that these companies underline even more the creative atmosphere in the company. The processes of learning and innovation support the personnel on an individual level, not only the activities of the company. This also means that the personnel develop an interest for these processes, and the units and the management also support the processes.

3.2. The intellectual capital

The intellectual capital is a measure of how well the human capital is incorporated in the activities and how well the companies use the knowledge and the core competencies as resources for the human capital. In the open companies the versatility of the knowledge is underlined as well as its content and communication in the company. The core competencies are well defined and so are the measures for evaluating and developing them. Continuity, technology and the ability to change are the most central factors in this process. The development of the core competencies is a natural activity in the open companies and does not demand separate attention or special actions. The companies have clear aims with knowledge creation but also with the development of the tools that are needed for the knowledge creation (information technology, networks). Open companies assume that their core competencies should be maintained by the corporate strategies, where creating the circumstances for change also creates co-operation between the different processes in the learning organisation

3.3. Information culture and learning

It is established here that those organisations where the learning aspect is underlined, also build an understanding of the information culture as a whole. Organisational learning becomes visible and more important in companies with open and change intensive internal environments. The knowledge is embedded in social networks and to reach this knowledge it seems to be important to emphasise the human and intellectual capital. It is a way in which to achieve an awareness of the role of the knowledge base in the company and, further, to reach integrated processes of a learning organisation. Studies of the companies in the middle group, those who are developing towards an open internal environment, show that they place a strong emphasis on intellectual capital, mostly on the evaluation of the core competence and on the development of it. This development process strives to underline the core competencies and knowledge in the units and also to communicate them in as many ways as possible. Through this process, the core competencies are integrated in the business as a whole and become visible also in the activities on the individual level. This means that through the concrete work with the intellectual capital, the human capital must be also focused, and the perspective of the learning organisation becomes more integrated in the business processes.

4. CONCLUSIONS

Development is transferred through organisational learning and it is interesting to ask if those companies with an active approach to learning also have a more stable financial activity. This question is naturally affected by several factors, but in this study it was clear that the most open companies, where the learning aspects were actively supported, had a very stable economy. In the more closed companies, where the human and intellectual capital lack in the overall picture, the financial success is not as obvious. The learning aspects seem to be very important in the business world and the human capital could be even more underlined and emphasised. Knowledge in the social networks needs to be more visible in the business activities (Cross, et al., 2001). This is a very difficult task and requires new thinking on the part of the business organisation. Defining the internal environment and mapping the role of the knowledge in the company are some concrete actions that can contribute to this development. The specialised business world of today needs an information culture in which it is possible to keep together the knowledge base and the social capital. The integrated thought—involving everyone—is important, leading to good results.

REFERENCES

Andreau, R., and C. Ciborra. (1996) Organisational learning and core capabilities development: the role of IT. *Journal of strategic information systems, 5*, 111–27.

Correia, Z., and T. D. Wilson. (1997) Scanning the business environment for information: a grounded theory approach. *Information research: an international electronic journal, 2(4)*. Retrieved September 10, 2001, from: http://InformationR.net/ir/2-4/paper21.html

Cross, R., A. Parker, L. Prusak, and S. P. Borgatti. (2001) Supporting knowledge creation and sharing in social networks. *Organizational dynamics, 30*(2), 100–120.

Dewhirst, H. D. (1971) Influence of perceived information-sharing norms on communication channel utilization. *Academy of management journal, 14,* 305–15.

Hofstede, G. (1991) *Kulturer og organisatione.* København: Schultz.

Koenig, M. (1998) *Information driven management concepts and themes.* München: Saur. (IFLA Publications; 86).

Muchinsky, P. M. (1977) Organizational communication: relationships to organizational climate and job satisfaction. *Academy of management journal, 20,* 592–607.

Nicholson, N., A. Rees, and A. Brooks-Rooney. (1990) Strategy, innovation, and performance. *Journal of management studies, 27,* 511–34.

Nonaka, I., and H. Takeuchi. (1995) *The knowledge-creating company.* New York: Oxford U.P.

Samuels, A. R., and C. R. McClure. (1983) Utilization of information decision making under varying organizational climate conditions in public libraries. *Journal of library administration, 4*(3), 1–20.

Widén-Wulff, G. (2001) *Informationskulturen som drivkraft i företagsorganisationen.* Åbo: Åbo Akademi University.